W9-BCG-992

THE JEW IN AMERICAN SOCIETY

Library of Jewish Studies

THE JEW IN AMERICAN SOCIETY

Edited, with introductions and notes, by

MARSHALL SKLARE

BEHRMAN HOUSE, INC. | PUBLISHERS | NEW YORK

ACKNOWLEDGMENTS

The author and publisher thank the following for permission to reprint:

American Jewish Archives for Henry Cohen, "Jewish Life and Thought in an Academic Community." ©1962 by *American Jewish Archives.*

The American Jewish Committee for Sidney Goldstein, "American Jewry, 1970: A Demographic Profile"; Seymour Martin Lipset and Everett Carll Ladd, Jr., "Jewish Academics in the United States"; and Arnold Schwartz, "Intermarriage in the United States." © 1970, 1971 by the American Jewish Committee and the Jewish Publication Society of America.

Conservative Judaism for Lucy S. Dawidowicz, "From Past to Past: Jewish East Europe to Jewish East Side." ©1968 by the Rabbinical Assembly.

The Jewish Journal of Sociology and William E. Mitchell for William E. Mitchell, "Descent Groups Among New York City Jews." © 1961 by the World Jewish Congress.

The Jewish Publication Society of America for selections from Charles S. Liebman, *The Ambivalent American Jew.* © 1973 by the Jewish Publication Society of America.

Prentice-Hall, Inc., for selections from Sidney Goldstein and Calvin Goldscheider, *Jewish Americans: Three Generations in a Jewish Community.* © 1968 by Prentice-Hall, Inc.

Schocken Books Inc., for Lloyd P. Gartner, "Immigration and the Formation of American Jewry, 1840–1925," in H. H. Ben-Sasson and S. Ettinger, ed., *Jewish Society through the Ages.* © 1969 by UNESCO.

The Theodor Herzl Foundation for selections from Ben Halpern, *The American Jew* and for Zena Smith Blau, "In Defense of the Jewish Mother." © 1956, 1967 by the Theodor Herzl Foundation.

Wayne State University Press for selections from C. Bezalel Sherman, *The Jew Within American Society.* © 1960 by Wayne State University Press.

Calvin Goldscheider, "American Aliya: Sociological and Demographic Perspectives," original for this volume.

Library of Congress Cataloging in Publication Data

Sklare, Marshall. comp.
The Jew in American society.

(Library of Jewish studies)
CONTENTS: Gartner, L. P. Immigration and the formation of American Jewry, 1840–1925.—Sherman, C. B. Immigration and emigration: the Jewish case.—Dawidowicz, L. S. From past to past: Jewish East Europe to Jewish east side. [etc.]
1. Jews in the United States—Political and social conditions—Addresses, essays, lectures. 2. Judaism—United States—Addresses, essays, lectures. I. Title.
E184.J5S5475 301.45'19'24073 74-3051
ISBN 0-87441-203-X

Published by Behrman House, Inc., 1261 Broadway, New York, N.Y. 10001
Manufactured in the United States of America

CONTENTS

PREFACE

THERE IS NO shortage of new books on the American Jew: the subject matter is accessible and interest is widespread. However, as all who have taught the sociology of American Jewry know, the greater part of this literature is unusable. In most cases it is written to entertain; it seeks to exploit the insatiable curiosity of Jews about themselves and of Gentiles about Jews. Such works, moreover, frequently reveal more about the convictions of their authors than about American Jewry.

My own teaching in the field of contemporary Jewish studies has highlighted the need for source books which will make available the best writing of social scientists who have studied the American Jew. Such books are particularly crucial at a time not only when there is a renewed interest in classical Jewish sources as well as in Jewish history, but when students are turning in increasing numbers to the study of contemporary Jewish life. Attraction to the contemporary can be altogether wholesome, particularly if it represents a belief in the worthiness of Jewish life and a sense of confidence in its possibilities. Only those who consider the Jewish future hopeless are moved to deny the validity of contemporary Jewish studies and to find their sole satisfaction in the study of the Jewish past.

The need for new source books became particularly evident to me in the course of writing *America's Jews*, a concise sociological treatment of American Jewry. The selections contained in the present volume and its companion (devoted to the American Jewish community) cover all the major topics touched on in that book. I should mention too that most of the articles here are of recent vintage; they do not appear in an earlier reader (*The Jews: Social Patterns of an American Group*) which I edited and which was published in 1958. Of course the present volumes also reflect the times in other ways as well: the stress is on issues of current concern and on the historical background necessary for understanding them.

In order to assist the student each article is preceded by an introduction. These introductions are more elaborate than those found in most social-science readers. My purpose in preparing them is to provide guideposts in a field which is still comparatively young. The same purpose animates the preparation of the introductory chapter in which I endeavor to describe the development, special character, hazards, and rewards of contemporary Jewish studies.

One of the risks of the field, discussed at length in the introductory chapter, is the possibility of the intrusion of bias into the analysis and evaluation of contemporary American Jewry. In the pages that follow I attempt to guard against such bias by giving preference to researchers who take American Jewry seriously; who avoid invidious comparisons with other contemporary communities of Jews or with the Jews of the past; who are aware of the corrosive effect of self-hatred and of the need to preserve the integrity of their work against it; and who keep their ethnocentrism under strict control, particularly when it exists in combination with alienation. Finally, I give preference to researchers who are interested in the study of the ordinary as opposed to the merely exotic.

In attempting to cope adequately with the problem of bias, and in attempting at the same time to choose the very best contributors available, I have followed both an overt and a hidden agenda. My overt agenda has been to assist the student who seeks to extend his knowledge of the sociology of the American Jew by presenting him with the finest examples of analytic writing on the subject—examples which the student will find valuable in developing his own mastery of the field. My hidden agenda has been more ambitious: to interest the dedicated student as well as the established social scientist in making his own contribution to the field of contemporary Jewish studies. If the effort proves successful the gap that now separates contemporary Jewish studies from other branches of Jewish studies and from other academic disciplines in general will, to that extent, be narrowed. New research will then appear, the present effort will become outdated, and new anthologies on the sociology of the American Jew will be required. May they appear speedily and in our time.

Part of the attraction of participating in the Library of Jewish Studies lies in working with its editor, Neal Kozodoy. He is the best of his profession, combining a particularly keen intelligence with empathy and objectivity toward those he assists.

I am also grateful to the authors and publishers who have

permitted their works to be utilized in this collection. Joshua Rothenberg and Daniel Lourie of the Goldfarb Library of Brandeis University, and Nathan Kaganoff and his staff at the library of the American Jewish Historical Society, assisted me whenever I required their help. Lucy Steinitz and Arden J. Geldman ably served as my research assistants and Doris Lelchook was of considerable help in coping with the heavy burden of secretarial labor. Mrs. Gerry Gould of the Behrman House staff skillfully oversaw the preparation of the manuscript for publication. The assistance of the Lucius N. Littauer Foundation and the interest of Harry Starr, its president, are gratefully acknowledged.

The last are always the dearest. I am fortunate that my wife Rose is not only an inspiration,. but also an experienced editor who cheerfully assists me with my manuscripts despite the long day which she spends with the manuscripts of other authors. I rely heavily on her expert editorial eye for makeup and design and for assistance with the numerous details which go into the making of a book.

Marshall Sklare
Waltham, Massachusetts

INTRODUCTION
THE SOCIOLOGY OF CONTEMPORARY JEWISH STUDIES

THIS book is a reader in the sociology of the American Jew. A second volume is devoted to the sociology of the American Jewish community. Both volumes fall within a field of scholarship known as "contemporary Jewish studies," a specialty which utilizes the perspectives of social science to gain an understanding of the Jews of today and their immediate forebears.

I

Information about contemporary Jewry, and especially information about contemporary American Jewry, is abundant—in sharp contrast to the situation for earlier eras of Jewish history. Because of the insecurity of Jewish life during the Middle Ages, for example, basic documents and archival records concerning medieval Jewry are scant, and historians must frequently rely on documents preserved in church or governmental archives rather than on Jewish sources. Yet such records have decided limitations; chiefly, that they reveal little of the inner life of the Jew. For this the historian must turn to the *responsa* literature—the questions submitted to rabbinical authorities on various matters of Jewish law together with their answers to these questions.

The difference between the study of the Jews of yesterday and the study of the Jews of today is encountered in its most extreme form when it comes to a subject like Marranism. By definition the Marrano was obliged to cover his tracks; secrecy was his only weapon against the Inquisition. Somewhat the same situation characterizes the Jews of the Soviet Union today; the display and promotion of Jewish identity can have grave consequences for an individual's occupational prospects and even for his physical security. As a result scholars confront formidable difficulties in writing about Soviet Jewry; they must rely on indirect indicators and must painfully assemble facts by way of fugitive documents or interviews with those who have managed to leave the country.

If Marranism in medieval times and the situation of Soviet Jewry in the present are located at one end of a spectrum, the study of American Jewry seems to be at the other: the researcher of contemporary American Jewry is inundated with information. He need only consult his daily newspaper for coverage of the multifaceted activities of Jewish organizations, or for feature articles on individual Jews who have distinguished themselves in one or another area. In an election year political pundits discuss at length the voting preferences of city and suburban Jews. And to supplement the information found in the daily newspaper the researcher can consult the *American Jewish Year Book,* which has appeared annually for over seventy years and presents a wealth of authoritative information on American and world Jewry.[1]

The daily press, the Jewish weeklies, the Jewish and general magazines, the yearbooks and commemorative volumes, and the many hundreds—if not thousands—of reports made available annually by national and local Jewish agencies add up to an almost inexhaustible storehouse of facts, and they lend force to Salo Baron's suggestive characterization of the American Jew as an

[1]In recent years the *American Jewish Year Book* has assumed new importance as a source of material for contemporary Jewish studies. In addition to reporting facts and figures about Jewish life, each volume of the *Year Book* contains one or more feature articles dealing with some of the most significant problems of American Jewry. For the most part the *Year Book* relies on data made available by private rather than by official sources. Recently the *Year Book* has published a series of reviews by Daniel J. Elazar of the literature on various aspects of contemporary Jewish studies. See his "The Pursuit of Community: Selections from the Literature of Jewish Public Affairs, 1965–66," *American Jewish Year Book 1967* (Vol. 68), pp. 178–221; "The Rediscovered Polity: Selections from the Literature of Jewish Public Affairs, 1967–68," *American Jewish Year Book 1969* (Vol. 70), pp. 172–237; "Confrontation and Reconstitution: Selections from the Literature of Jewish Public Affairs, 1969–71," *American Jewish Year Book 1972* (Vol. 73), pp. 301–383.

"inverted Marrano," the very opposite of his medieval Iberian predecessor.[2] It is quite apparent, however, that the very large body of information that has accumulated about contemporary American Jewry has on the whole remained just that: information. Very little systematic scholarly work has been done to assemble and analyze this information, draw conclusions from it, and thereby transform it into real knowledge. Indeed, despite the fact that in our age self-confession is a way of life, the display of Jewishness a common occurrence, and information so accessible as to make historians envious, the field of contemporary Jewish studies has yet to attain the stage of scholarly development which has been achieved in other branches of Jewish studies.

In the 1940's Louis Finkelstein (then president of the Jewish Theological Seminary of America), seeking to recruit experts in all branches of Jewish studies to contribute to a two-volume comprehensive survey of Jewish culture, was surprised to discover how few specialists there were in contemporary Jewish studies. Despite the obvious abundance of information about contemporary Jewry, he found that what was actually known on the subject was far inferior to what was known about ancient and medieval Jewry:

> There are probably a hundred people, and more, whose profession it is to discover all that can be known about the Jews in Jerusalem in the first century; there does not seem to be one who has the same duty for the Jews of New York in the twentieth century.[3]

Since the 1940's knowledge of contemporary Jewry has increased considerably. Nevertheless, the intriguing problem raised by Dr. Finkelstein persists. To address it adequately we must consider the field of contemporary Jewish studies in relation to the

[2]In addition to such data there is the additional resource provided by the vast amount of fictional literature produced during the recent "vogue" of American-Jewish writing. While many of these writers—the most familiar names are Bernard Malamud, Saul Bellow, Philip Roth, Herbert Gold, Bruce Jay Friedman—do not seek to create specifically "Jewish" novels, their books do feature Jewish characters and are often intended to reveal one or another facet of American Jewish life. It is difficult to estimate how long this vogue will continue. Calvin Trillin, in a spoof of the New York literary scene, has suggested that the Jewish period is drawing to a close. See his story "Lester Drentluss, a Jewish Boy from Baltimore, Attempts to Make it through the Summer of 1967," *The Atlantic*, November 1968, pp. 71–73.

[3]Louis Finkelstein in *Proceedings of the Rabbinical Assembly of America*, Vol. XIII (1949), p. 121.

development of Jewish studies generally as a discipline over the past century, as well as the academic development of the social sciences, and specifically of sociology.[4]

II

The field of Jewish studies as an intellectual discipline emerged in Germany in the first half of the nineteenth century, where it became known as *Wissenschaft des Judentums*—the science of Judaism. In the United States the field is even more recent, having developed in the twentieth rather than the nineteenth century. *Wissenschaft des Judentums* traced its intellectual origins to the classical tradition of Jewish learning, with its concern for *halakha* (Jewish law) and its emphasis on the mastery of Talmudic texts. But while resembling traditional Jewish learning in that it studied the past, *Wissenschaft des Judentums* viewed the past from quite a different perspective. It not only expanded the content of Jewish learning by going far beyond the study of halakha, it also radically shifted the methodology and ideological superstructure of Jewish learning. The net effect was to change the study of Judaism from an exercise in religious piety to an academic and intellectual pursuit. As one historian noted, in speaking of the very first document produced by the movement, it

> . . . clearly displays the feature that was to differentiate [the movement] from previous Jewish learning: the assumption of a stand outside of . . . the tradition instead of within it, approaching it with the discerning but cold eye of the scientist.[5]

[4]The section which follows is based in part on a paper presented at a colloquium on the teaching of Jewish studies in American universities held at Brandeis University in the fall of 1969. See Marshall Sklare, "The Problem of Contemporary Jewish Studies," *Midstream*, Vol. 16, No. 4 (April 1970), pp. 27–35. The paper was also published in the proceedings of the colloquium: *The Teaching of Judaica in American Universities*, ed. by Leon A. Jick (New York: Ktav Publishing House, 1970), pp. 57–70.

[5]Michael A. Meyer, *The Origins of the Modern Jew* (Detroit: Wayne State University Press, 1967), p. 162. On the ideology of *Wissenschaft des Judentums* see also Nahum N. Glatzer, "The Beginnings of Modern Jewish Studies," in *Studies in Nineteenth Century Jewish Intellectual History*, ed. by Alexander Altmann (Cambridge, Mass.: Harvard University Press, 1964), pp. 27–45; Gershom Scholem, *The Messianic Idea in Judaism and other Essays on Jewish Spirituality* (New York: Schocken Books, 1971), pp. 304–313; and Max Wiener, "The Ideology of the Founders of Jewish Scientific Research" in *YIVO Annual of Jewish Social Science*, Vol. V (1950), pp. 184–196.

However it is a matter of record that at one time Leopold Zunz stressed the

To be sure there was never a complete break in the link between religious piety and scientific study of Jewish culture. Whatever the public image of Jewish studies in the modern world, some of its adherents continued to conceive of their work in the traditional framework of religious obligation and spiritual exercise. But whether motivated by religious strivings or by a spirit of academic curiosity all modern Jewish scholars were obliged to subscribe to a basic assumption of *Wissenschaft des Judentums* —that priority should be given to scientific evidence in the event that it conflicted with religious dogma. The scholar was of course free to minimize such conflict by concentrating in fields like Jewish history or medieval Hebrew poetry where science and dogma were not on a collision course. He was also free to avoid those fields of study—the most obvious being Bible—where confrontation was inevitable.

Despite their modernism, the founders of *Wissenschaft des Judentums* did not expand the scope of Jewish studies to include research on contemporary Jewry, even though they conceived of their discipline as offering something of great value to the Jews of the time. Indeed they were deeply concerned with contemporary issues, particularly with the relationship of Jewry to the general society. They ardently supported the Jewish struggle for equal rights and wished to assist in this struggle as well as to help combat all forms of anti-Jewish prejudice. Not that they all held a single attitude toward the Jews and the Judaism of their time. Some, believing in the possibility of Jewish survival, sought to utilize the past in order to reconstruct the present. Others harbored doubts over the prospects for Jewish survival. The most pessimistic viewed themselves as morticians charged with giving to the Jewish past the decent, but no less final, burial that had been denied it by prejudiced Gentile theologians and historians. Yet whatever attitude the *Wissenschaft* scholar took toward the importance and likelihood of Jewish survival, he saw his research as centering on the study of the Jews of the past, rather than on those of the present.

The proponents of *Wissenschaft des Judentums* prided themselves on the "scientific" spirit with which they approached the history and culture of Jewry. But they were in fact not attracted as a

importance of statistical research on Jewish life. His memorandum on the subject was published in *Zeitschrift fur die Wissenschaft des Judentums*, Vol. I (1823), pp. 523–532. I am grateful to Prof. Nahum Glatzer for guiding me to this source.

group to the concerns or to the analytical methods of social science, a discipline then in its infancy. They were, first and foremost, humanists, and so may have felt a natural aversion to the social sciences. Then too, Jewish scholars tended to believe that the social sciences involved a denigration of the intrinsic nobility of Jewish culture. Social science seemed to be critical both of traditional Jewish learning, with its belief in Judaism as a unique historical and religious relationship between God and the Jewish people (which it was the duty of the individual Jew both to strengthen and maintain), and of modern Jewish scholarship, with its stress on the broad universal significance of Jewish culture. By highlighting economic relationships, or the significance of social stratification, or the importance of power, social science seemed to imply that the Jews were similar to other groups—though to be sure conceding that the history of the Jews diverged from that of most other ethnic or religious groups. Certainly social science gave no hint that it conceived of the Jews as a kingdom of priests and as a holy people.

The negative attitude of the early Jewish humanists to the social-scientific approach may be seen in its extreme form in an incident which occurred in 1909 at the Academy of Jewish Studies in St. Petersburg. The academy had been established by the preeminent leader of Russian Jewry, Baron David Günzberg, a man of great wealth and of considerable learning, who wished to introduce *Wissenschaft des Judentums* to the Jews of Eastern Europe. The young Zalman Shazar, later to become president of Israel, was at that time a student of the academy; in his autobiography he recounts how he and some other students were dissatisfied with the academy's approach to Jewish history. Led by Shazar, the students confronted the Baron with their complaint:

> One of the disciplines which we students felt to be lacking and necessary was historical study of the social and economic life of Jews in the lands of the Diaspora. It was not easy to find a specialist in this field, and when [the Russian-Jewish historian Simon] Dubnow, whom we had impressed with our desire for such study, came at last to tell us that there was a fine young scholar available, Dr. M. L. Wischnitzer of Vienna, he added with restrained sadness that he feared the Baron would not agree to open the doors of the Academy to a course stressing the "new-fangled" social and economic approach.
>
> We decided to try to appeal to Baron Günzberg directly. . . . He agreed to receive a delegation. There were three of us, and to this day I remember with absolute clarity the talk between us and the fatherly

> Baron. I had been charged with opening our case. There in the Baron's study, facing the picture of Maimonides, I spoke of the need for this new discipline and of the young scholar who was available. Excitedly, the Baron rose from his chair, leaned against the doorpost opening onto his great library . . . and said . . . : "Dear ones, I am deeply grieved by this request of yours. I am certain that you have no intention . . . of causing me unhappiness, and it is very difficult for me to say no to you. But how can I hide my concern from you? You have come here to study the nature and destiny of the Jewish people—and now I hear you asking to be taught what occupations Jews were compelled to engage in. . . . It is as if a scholar had been asked to lecture to you on Kant, and then, instead of teaching you the *Critique of Pure Reason,* spent his time describing the restaurant Kant frequented and the kind of cutlets his wife gave him. And it is not Kant you are studying, but that sublime people God chose for His own! Do you really think it is so important to know exactly when the Gentiles permitted us to engage in trade and when those malicious people forced us to be moneylenders? What good will the information do you? And wouldn't it be a pity to spend your precious time on this when there are still so many rooms in the mansion of Jewish scholarship that are closed to you and so many great books waiting for you?" As he spoke, he pointed to the tens of rooms filled with bookshelves from floor to ceiling, [an] endless, infinite treasure of books. . . .
>
> Walking excitedly across the room between the desk and the books [he] suddenly stood still and went on even more bitingly: "If you do research on horses—there is such a science, too—it is obviously very important to investigate what fodder should be put in the horses' crib: oats or barley. But when the subject of your study is the wisdom of the chosen people, do you think that their fodder . . . should concern you?"[6]

Today, when the utility of the social sciences for the study of the Jewish past is generally conceded, it is almost impossible to imagine a contemporary version of the confrontation between Shazar and Baron Günzberg. While an earlier generation of Jewish humanists could avoid the social sciences, present-day professors of

[6]Zalman Shazar, *Morning Stars* (Philadelphia: Jewish Publication Society of America, 1967), pp. 188–190. Surprisingly enough Shazar and his fellow students achieved their objective despite the fact that the Baron's hold over the students was absolute. (Not only did he underwrite the budget of the academy but bribed the police to arrange residence permits in St. Petersburg for students who lacked them.) Soon after this confrontation the Baron invited Wischnitzer to offer a course on "The Economic History of the Jews." A true aristocrat, Baron Günzberg apparently felt, that despite his power, he had no right to deprive students of knowledge which they sought to acquire.

Jewish studies hold posts at universities where the social sciences are firmly established, and the same can be said even of those who teach at the rabbinical seminaries. Yet as recently as the 1930's, when Salo Baron's *A Social and Religious History of the Jews* appeared, the social-scientific emphasis it embodied still seemed daring. By the 1950's and 1960's, of course, when the revised edition began to appear, this approach to the Jewish past had become commonplace.

The current debate concerns instead the status which should be accorded to the social-scientific study of *contemporary* Jewry. Despite his own modernity the Jewish humanist may feel deeply alienated from the contemporary world; he may feel that the study of the present is unworthy, that the present age is debased and brutish in comparison with the past, that its Jewish culture is inferior. The often ambiguous relation of today's humanist to the culture in which he lives cannot be understood without reference to developments in the social sciences—especially to the role of Jewish intellectuals and academicians in that most contemporary of disciplines, sociology.

III

At virtually no time has there been a lack of Jewish representation in the sociological fraternity. In Europe such preeminent early figures as Emile Durkheim and Georg Simmel were Jewish; in the United States Jews became active in sociology as soon as the field severed its connection with the social-melioration emphasis of liberal Protestantism and established its academic respectability. At present, Jews are strongly represented in American sociology, both as leaders of "establishment" sociology and as active proponents of "new" or "radical" sociology.

Despite their numbers and influence, however, only a handful of Jewish sociologists have been interested in the sociology of the Jews. Until very recently Jewish sociologists hesitated to introduce contemporary Jewish studies into the social-science curriculum. And even those Jewish sociologists who specialized in the study of ethnic groups shied away from the sociology of the Jews. This reluctance to become involved in contemporary Jewish studies has its origin in what sociology as a discipline has traditionally represented to the Jewish academician. More than a profession, sociology has been a calling. For many Jewish academicians it has signified a break with the ethnic and religious parochialism of their past, a way of replacing membership in the Jewish ethnic community with the "universal" community of the academy.

Appropriately, it was a Jewish sociologist, Milton Gordon, who developed the hypothesis that " . . . intellectuals in the United States interact in such patterned ways as to form at least the elementary structure of a subsociety of their own."[7] Furthermore, Gordon developed a rationale for the legitimacy of this intellectual subsociety, pleading for the individual's right to leave behind the narrow confines of the ethnic community for the wider world of academe. Gordon was not alone in his views; Gentile sociologists like Robert M. MacIver and S. C. Dodd had also been critical of Jewish particularism, and an earlier generation of Gentile sociologists—notably Edward A. Ross and Henry Pratt Fairchild—had emphasized the necessity, indeed the obligation, of immigrants to adapt themselves to what is now called Wasp culture. For Gordon, on the other hand, assimilation was a *right*, not a duty. He also wanted the "birthright ethnic group," as he termed it, to desist from criticizing its assimilationist academics and intellectuals:

> . . . the individual, as he matures and reaches the age where rational decision is feasible, should be allowed to choose freely whether to remain within the boundaries of communality created by his birthright ethnic group, to branch out into multiple interethnic contacts, or even to change affiliation to that of another ethnic group should he wish to do so as a result of religious conversion, intermarriage, or simply private wish. If, to the contrary, the ethnic group places such heavy pressures on its birthright members to stay confined to ethnic communality that the individual who consciously wishes to "branch out" or "move away" feels intimidated or subject to major feelings of personal guilt and therefore remains ethnically enclosed, or moves but at considerable psychological cost, then we have, in effect, cultural democracy for groups but not for individuals.[8]

Whatever the position of individual Jewish sociologists toward the question of whether Jews should seek group survival or should pursue the goal of assimilation, for most Jewish sociologists a commitment to intellectuality generally and to sociology specifically precluded involvement with contemporary Jewish studies. As

[7]Milton Gordon, *Assimilation in American Life* (New York: Oxford University Press, 1964), p. 224.

[8]*Ibid.*, p. 263. Cf. Marshall Sklare, "Assimilation and the Sociologists," *Commentary*, May 1965, pp. 63–67.

Seymour Martin Lipset, a concerned Jew as well as a renowned sociologist, has noted:

> The failure of Jewish social scientists to engage in research on the Jews reflects their desire to be perceived as American rather than Jewish intellectuals. To write in depth about the Jewish community would seemingly expose them to being identified as "Jewish Jews," as individuals who are too preoccupied with an ethnic identity, and who lack the universalistic orientation prized by social scientists and American intellectuals generally.[9]

The tendency to avoid contemporary Jewish studies was reinforced by the fact that Jews did not constitute a "problem" for American society. As a consequence neither governmental bodies nor large foundations saw a need to encourage the sociological study of contemporary Jewry. On the contrary, those individuals who were interested in such research found it difficult to locate sources of support. While Jewish organizations occasionally subsidized research, their interest was on the whole sporadic.[10]

The single subject which did excite the imagination of Jewish investigators was the Israeli *kibbutz*. The kibbutz has been written about endlessly; there may already be more books and articles on the kibbutz than there are actual kibbutzim. But the kibbutz is the exception which proves the rule. Most analysts have shown little interest in the kibbutz as an institution in a Jewish society; rather, they have been interested in the kibbutz as an experiment in collective living. Hence the Jewish sociologist, psychologist, or

[9]Seymour Martin Lipset, "The Study of Jewish Communities in a Comparative Context," *The Jewish Journal of Sociology,* Vol. V, No. 2 (December 1963), p. 163. Interestingly enough, the attraction to a universalistic orientation is observable among Jewish social scientists in Israel as well as in the United States. While Israeli social scientists do study Israeli society, they tend to emphasize its universal aspects rather than its particular ones. Accordingly, they have neglected the study of Jewish identity. The problem is briefly analyzed in my review of Simon Herman's *Israelis and Jews,* which appeared in *Commentary,* January 1972, pp. 84–86.

[10]See Marshall Sklare, "The Development and Utilization of Sociological Research: The Case of the American Jewish Community," *Jewish Journal of Sociology,* Vol. V, No. 2 (December 1963), pp. 167–186. There are agencies like the Conference on Jewish Social Studies (formerly the Conference on Jewish Relations) whose main objective is that of stimulating and subventing research on topics related to contemporary Jewish studies. However the Conference has not been able to achieve its objective; in recent years it has been forced to confine itself to the publication of a journal.

anthropologist who has written about the kibbutz has often continued to perceive himself as an American (or European) intellectual rather than as a specifically Jewish intellectual.

IV

Contemporary Jewish studies, then, emerged neither out of the interest of the proponents of *Wissenschaft des Judentums* nor out of the concern of Jewish social scientists teaching at European or American universities. The origins of the discipline lie elsewhere, and the movement led by Zalman Shazar at the Academy of Jewish Studies in St. Petersburg to which we have duly alluded—a movement aided and abetted by a "radical" faculty member, Simon Dubnow—provides the clue to these origins.

It was Jewish nationalism, and Zionism in particular, which caused dissatisfaction with the curriculum of *Wissenschaft des Judentums*, a curriculum that had at first dazzled and intoxicated those who—like Shazar—had been steeped in traditional Jewish learning.[11] Students at the academy came to believe that the approach to Jewish history of the scholars whose books they studied did not speak to their situation. They had need of someone who saw Jewish history differently from an Isaac Marcus Jost or a Heinrich Graetz; even so advanced a thinker as Dubnow was not fully satisfactory. Before Shazar came to St. Petersburg he had carried out missions for the Poale Zion, and he had translated some of Ber Borochov's writings into Yiddish. Other students had been similarly involved in the Jewish social movements of the time. The result was dissatisfaction with a curriculum that called for the scientific study of Jewish culture but placed the emphasis on intellectual history and paid little attention to the economic life of the Jews and their position in society.

Jewish nationalism saw the Jews as constituting a social "problem," and it maintained that the solution of the problem lay in the direction of group survival rather than individual assimilation, a course which was neither desirable nor, some held, possible. Jewish

[11]As the work of the YIVO Institute for Jewish Research demonstrates, Diaspora nationalism and Zionism both gave impetus to the study of contemporary Jewry.

On the tension between Zionism and *Wissenschaft des Judentums* see Alexander Altmann, *Jewish Studies: Their Scope and Meaning Today* (London: Hillel Foundation, 1958), pp. 9–11.

nationalism insisted that the Jewish condition was an abnormality which had to be corrected, and to that end it advocated the establishment of a national home.

In addition to its political program, Jewish nationalism stressed the need for a proper understanding and evaluation of the Jewish condition, a task which called in turn for accumulating meaningful social and economic data and analyzing such data in a conceptual framework. This emphasis on understanding and evaluation, combined with nationalism's survivalist thrust, laid the groundwork for the discipline of contemporary Jewish studies.

Arthur Ruppin (1876–1943), who served as an important official of various Zionist agencies during much of the time that he was also active on the scholarly scene, may be regarded as the father of the discipline. Ruppin's sociological work was infused with a Zionist perspective, even as his efforts to establish settlements in Palestine were filtered through the prism of his sociological understanding.[12] His methodology called for comparing Jews of one country with those of another, and he gathered his data not only from library research and official statistics but also from his contacts and travels as an official of the Zionist movement. Although he conceived of Jews as a worldwide people, like many of his contemporaries Ruppin focused almost exclusively on the Jews of Western and Eastern Europe, as well as upon Jews who had emigrated to Palestine from European countries.[13]

In 1926 Ruppin began teaching the sociology of the Jews at the Hebrew University. His lectures subsequently appeared (in 1930–31) in a two-volume German edition, *Die Soziologie der Juden.* A Hebrew translation followed almost immediately, as did a con-

[12]For biographical details see *Arthur Ruppin: Memoirs, Diaries, Letters,* ed. by Alex Bein (New York: Herzl Press, 1971). Ruppin's work grew out of the German-Jewish milieu; that of another leading scholar, Jacob Lestschinsky (1876–1966), was a product of the East European scene. Ruppin's books seem to have had the greater impact, perhaps because they were less specialized than Lestschinsky's, because they integrated data from a large number of countries, because they were strongly interpretative as well as statistical, and because they were related to German scholarship. Unlike the works of Lestschinsky most of Ruppin's books were translated into several languages, and thus his contributions became accessible to a wide audience. See A. Tartakower, "Jacob Lestschinsky," *Jewish Frontier,* November 1958, pp. 15–17.

[13]Isaac Ben-Zvi, who settled in Palestine in 1907 and served as president of Israel from 1952 until his death in 1963, was one of the few Zionist leaders to become preoccupied with the situation of the Jews of North Africa and the Middle East. The research institute in Jerusalem devoted to the study of these communities is named after him.

densed version in English. This, however, was not Ruppin's first scholarly publication in the field, for his book *Die Juden der Gegenwart* had appeared in 1904. *Die Juden der Gegenwart* became well-known if only because it was a novelty. As Ruppin wrote in his memoirs:

> *Die Juden der Gegenwart* was a new departure in the literature on the Jewish question. People were used to books pleading for or against the Jews, but they did not know what to do with a book which did not take sides but confined itself to marshaling the facts as objectively as possible. The book was given a mixed reception in the Jewish press: the assimilationists tended to disapprove of it, the Zionists to approve.[14]

Two years before the publication of *Die Soziologie der Juden* a significant book in the field of contemporary Jewish studies appeared in the United States: *The Ghetto,* by Louis Wirth (1897–1952).[15] *The Ghetto* had been inspired by Wirth's mentor, Robert E. Park, who was one of the founders of American sociology and was a member of the faculty of the University of Chicago. Park was intensely interested in the sociology of minority groups, and especially in such phenomena as the marginal man and the clash between the ancestral culture of an immigrant group and the new culture with which it came in contact. He persuaded Wirth—then a

[14]See *Arthur Ruppin: Memoirs, Diaries, Letters, op. cit.*, p. 74. Although *Die Juden der Gegenwart* was written before Ruppin committed himself to Zionism, the direction of his thinking was clear enough. Ruppin's first Zionist article was published in 1905 and two years later he became an official of the movement.

[15]Louis Wirth, *The Ghetto* (Chicago: University of Chicago Press, 1928). *The Ghetto* had been preceded by an earlier work by an American author: Maurice Fishberg, *The Jews: A Study of Race and Environment* (New York: Charles Scribner's Sons, 1911). As the title indicates Fishberg's perspective was heavily anthropological. Fishberg was convinced that anti-Semitism would soon be eradicated, and he reasoned that Jews would respond to the new era by intermarrying. His assumptions make interesting reading today: " . . . the differences between Jews and Christians are not everywhere racial, due to anatomical or physiological peculiarities, but are solely the result of the social and political environment. [This] explains our optimism as regards the ultimate obliteration of all distinctions between Jews and Christians in Europe and America. This optimism is confirmed by conditions in Italy, Scandinavia, and Australia, where anti-Semitism is practically unknown. When intermarriage between Jews and Christians will reach the same proportions in other countries, and the facts presented in [this volume] clearly show that the time is not distant, anti-Semitism will everywhere meet with the same fate as in Italy, Scandinavia, and Australia. Both Jews and Christians have been contributing to this end, the former by discarding their separative ritualism, and thus displaying willingness to bridge the gulf which separated them from others, and the latter by legalizing civil marriage." (*Ibid.*, pp. vii-viii.)

graduate student at the university—to select a Jewish topic for his Ph.D. dissertation. The resulting volume became one of the most popular items in the series of sociological monographs published by the University of Chicago Press and established itself as a standard source in its field.

The contrast between Arthur Ruppin and Louis Wirth is instructive. One, the founder of contemporary Jewish studies, was a Zionist whose pioneering work is being continued today at the Institute of Contemporary Jewry of the Hebrew University. The other, a non-Zionist if not an anti-Zionist, became the most influential Jew of his time in American sociology and prefigured the present prominence of Jews in American social science. Wirth served as president of what is now the American Sociological Association, and was the first president of the International Sociological Association. As a leading authority on urban sociology and minority groups (as well as in other areas such as the sociology of knowledge), Wirth was a consultant to many official bodies and private agencies. However, he made no effort to establish contemporary Jewish studies as a distinctive field of scholarly inquiry.

Ruppin's work is limited in that his approach to the sociology of the Jews remained the same throughout his life. And since he carried on his scholarly work at the same time that he was engaged in Zionist activity he was not able to realize many of his plans. Nevertheless, his interest and productivity in the field of contemporary Jewish studies extended over more than three decades. He saw the Jewish people as a living organism, constantly growing and ever changing; Jews were an object of continual fascination to him. Wirth, on the other hand, made no substantial contribution to contemporary Jewish studies after completing his dissertation. In his person and in his career he exemplified the very process he described in *The Ghetto*—the transformation undergone by the individual who leaves the traditionalistic world of the European village and starts a new life in the maelstrom of the American city (Wirth came from the Rhineland and arrived in Omaha, Nebraska, at the age of fourteen). According to his daughter, Wirth was

> . . . the first member of his family to marry a non-Jew . . . [his] assimilationist inclinations and principles, like those of his wife, partly derived from their common reaction against dogmatism and provincial ethnocentrism. Their two daughters were to be encouraged in

agnosticism with audible atheistic overtones, at the same time that they were to acquire a "generalized minority" ethnic identification.[16]

The closing pages of *The Ghetto* make clear Wirth's belief that the Jewish community was an anachronism whose life had been artificially prolonged by Gentile prejudice,[17] and he came to look upon the Jews as a dead—rather than a living—people. He directed his attention to the need for social planning, for better cities, and for improved understanding among racial groups. Nevertheless, his interest in fighting discrimination and his desire to combat Nazism had the effect of keeping him in touch with Jewish organizations, and during World War II he wrote once again on a Jewish topic. In 1943 Wirth published an article in the *American Journal of Sociology* which in effect paid homage to Jewish tenacity in the face of persecution.[18]

V

With the single exception of a noted social psychologist, for several decades no outstanding personalities in American social science displayed a commitment to contemporary Jewish studies. Despite the lack of leadership, however, by the 1940's and 1950's social-science research on the American Jew did begin to accumulate. Occasional studies, subvented by Jewish communal bodies in order to provide a basis for decision-making, were often sufficiently wide in scope to constitute more than service research. Other studies were initiated outside of the Jewish community, generally on topics where Jews might serve as a kind of control group, as in research on alcoholism. There were also investigations by political scientists into voting behavior, another area where Jews deviated from the middle-class norm, and there were community studies in places where Jews happened to constitute a significant segment of the population (Park Forest, Illinois, for example, was intensively studied by social scientists from the University of Chicago). Finally, there were dissertations by graduate students as

[16]Elizabeth Wirth Marvick, "Louis Wirth: A Biographical Memorandum," in *Louis Wirth: On Cities and Social Life*, ed. by Albert J. Reiss, Jr. (Chicago: University of Chicago Press, 1964), p. 337.

[17]See Louis Wirth, *op. cit.*, esp. pp. 263–281.

[18]See Louis Wirth, "Education for Survival: The Jews," *American Journal of Sociology*, Vol. XLVIII, No. 6 (May 1943), pp. 682–691.

well as investigations resulting from the independent initiative of social scientists who had an interest in the study of contemporary Jewry. By the late 1950's it was possible for the present author to compile a book of social-science readings on the contemporary American Jew.[19]

What was responsible for the rise of interest in Jewish research? Part of the answer lies in the strengthened sense of Jewish identity held by Jewish social scientists in the wake of both the Nazi Holocaust and the establishment of the State of Israel. Even more significant was the increase by the 1950's in the number of Jews who were social scientists. To put this development another way, the social sciences had begun to attract a much larger number of Jews than before, and those entering the profession constituted a more representative cross-section of the Jewish community than had been true of their predecessors.

Not all of those who entered sociology with Jewish interests succeeded in maintaining them. Furthermore, some proceeded to compartmentalize their concerns—they pursued their Jewishness privately and their sociology publicly. Yet there were others who saw themselves as belonging simultaneously to the Jewish community and to the academic community, and who sought to integrate the two aspects of their lives. The most highly committed not only felt that social science could be utilized to clarify questions of Jewish communal policy, but also believed that it was essential to furthering Jewish self-understanding.

The emergence of an affirmative sense of Jewishness among some social scientists was signaled by the settlement in Israel of a number of rising Jewish academicians, perhaps the most prominent of whom was Louis Guttman. Born in 1916, Guttman, at

[19]See *The Jews: Social Patterns of an American Group,* ed. by Marshall Sklare (Glencoe, Ill.: The Free Press, 1958). For a detailed analysis of the book see Joshua A. Fishman "American Jewry as a Field of Social Science Research," in *YIVO Annual of Jewish Social Science,* Vol. XII (1958–59), pp. 70–102.

More than a decade before *The Jews: Social Patterns of an American Group* was published a volume appeared which contained articles on American Jewry written by some of the nation's leading social scientists. See *Jews in a Gentile World,* ed. by Isacque Graeber and Steuart Henderson Britt (New York: Macmillan, 1942). Despite the fact that this volume contained some significant data and suggestive interpretations it did not play an important role in advancing contemporary Jewish studies. The primary aim of the book was to serve as a corrective to the various anti-Semitic tracts appearing at the time. Graeber and Britt were at pains to point out that their book was not a Jewish effort, and that more than half of their contributors were Gentile. The first article, which set the tone of the volume, was written by a leading political scientist at Harvard—Carl J. Friedrich—and was entitled "Anti-Semitism: Challenge to Christian Culture."

twenty-five, was invited to join the faculty of Cornell University. His development of the Guttman scalogram method brought him widespread recognition. Despite brilliant prospects in the United States, Guttman settled in Israel in 1947 where he established the Israel Institute of Applied Social Research. Other Jewish social scientists, not prepared to go on *aliyah*, were nevertheless interested in making occasional contributions to contemporary Jewish studies. In a sense Jewish research could serve such individuals as a substitute for a more intense commitment to Jewishness, whether of a religious or nationalist kind. To write on a Jewish topic underlined one's Jewish identity to others and, more importantly served to allay any tension one might feel between his Jewishness and his commitment to the academic life.

Several developments in American life generally, and in academia specifically, encouraged these trends. After World War II the idea of cultural pluralism began to achieve widespread acceptance, as did the accompanying notion that minorities could be oppressed as much by conformism as by overt prejudice and discrimination. Furthermore, it began to be felt that the presence of distinctive minority groups contributed a necessary corrective to the cultural blandness of the nation which resulted from the impact of the mass media, the rising influence of the corporation and of bureaucracy generally, and of the growth of the "other-directed" personality.

In the academy there was a notable lessening of discrimination against Jews. After World War II not only were Jews widely accepted as faculty members, but less pressure was placed on them to conform to the ideals of assimilation. Many of the better universities espoused the new ideal of diversity, even if diversity meant a faculty diverse in social origin and intellectual interests rather than in ideological conviction. The trend toward a more cosmopolitan campus meant greater opportunity to assimilate for Jews who wished to do so, but it also made the academy a more comfortable place for those who wished to retain their Jewishness. And the new diversity and cosmopolitanism also made it possible to maintain and promote an interest in Jewish research as a valid area of inquiry, particularly if it were pursued as part of a larger interest in such recognized fields as social psychology, the sociology of religion, or racial and ethnic relations.

Kurt Lewin (1890–1947) did not live to see the results of these changes but he typified the new trend. Lewin was known in the United States even before he arrived as a refugee scholar in 1933, and his reputation as a social psychologist grew rapidly during his American years.[20] Lewin began to write on Jewish topics in 1935; his most influential article, "Self-Hatred among Jews," was published in 1941.[21] In contrast to Wirth, who stressed the negative consequences of ethnic self-segregation, Lewin pointed to the psychological perils that could result when one alienated oneself from the Jewish community, especially the lack of a firm sense of belongingness. His articles emphasized the importance of self-acceptance and of creating a strong Jewish identity in the Jewish child.[22]

Lewin's interest in the study of contemporary Jewry had been stimulated by his personal encounter with Nazism. It came to occupy such a central part of his professional life that he eventually sought to settle in Palestine and made vigorous, though ultimately unsuccessful, efforts to raise funds for a psychological institute which he wished to establish at the Hebrew University. In the United States, Lewin also sought organizational support for his research into problems of Jewish interest. He conceived of his work as "action research," and he maintained that organizational sponsors could play a vital role in suggesting research problems and in implementing proposed solutions. In 1944 the American Jewish Congress responded to the idea and asked Lewin to set up its new research department, the Commission on Community Interrelations.[23]

[20]For biographical details see Alfred J. Marrow, *The Practical Theorist: The Life and Work of Kurt Lewin* (New York: Basic Books, 1969).

[21]See Kurt Lewin, "Self-Hatred Among Jews," *Contemporary Jewish Record,* Vol. 4, No. 3 (June 1941), pp. 219–232.

[22]While Lewin's views were widely cited in the Jewish community they did not receive universal acclamation among his peers. Bruno Bettleheim, for example, rejected Lewin's theory of group belongingness and the need for a sense of positive Jewish identification in the child. See Bettleheim's article "How to Arm Our Children Against Anti-Semitism—A Psychologist's Advice to Jewish Parents," *Commentary,* September 1951, pp. 209–218.

[23]At the time of Lewin's death the CCI was in full operation. Later it was gradually phased out and the researchers whom Lewin had brought together took posts at universities and at other research institutes.

In May 1944, at about the same time the American Jewish Congress was setting up its Commission on Community Interrelations, the American Jewish Committee held a conference on religious and racial prejudice. This conference also eventuated in the establishment of a research department. It was headed by Max Horkheimer, who, like Lewin, had come to the United States from Nazi Germany. Lewin and Horkheimer differed sharply in their approach to social psychology as well as in their attitude to Jewish identification.

VI

The balance between ethnocentrism on the one hand and self-hatred on the other remains a particularly delicate one for the social scientist of today who rejects assimilation and wishes in some way to affirm his Jewishness. Typically, such an individual is uncomfortable with the patterns of religious and communal practice followed by most of his fellow Jews. Furthermore, he may be more strongly affected by the universalistic orientation of the academy than he knows or can acknowledge, and he may be anxious to show that his Jewish interests do not imply any defection from the world of the academy. The social scientist who wishes to belong to, but at the same time feels alienated from, the Jewish community has become a fairly common type on today's campus. He may be called the "critical academic."

It is apparent that today's critical academic differs from his predecessors; few present-day scholars replicate the experience of a Louis Wirth. They have not emerged from the darkness of the European village into the light of the modern world. Brought up in the metropolis, today's academic does not feel compelled to celebrate urbanism as a way of life—he may in fact prefer suburbia or even exurbia. And unlike Wirth who sought to work within the power structure and who never engaged in radical social criticism despite a brief encounter with Marxism, today's critical academic is typically oriented to the left and prides himself on his feeling of alienation from middle-class America.

The increased acceptability of ethnicity in American society has made the critical academic a more common phenomenon, and it has also brought about a more vocal assertion of Jewishness and a celebration of certain aspects of the Jewish experience. Thus, it is characteristic of the critical academic that he tends to idealize the immigrant Jew of the late nineteenth and early twentieth century. Instead of viewing the Lower East Sides of the nation as retrogressive, as had an earlier generation, the critical academic generally admires them for their embodiment of a sense of "community" and human warmth, for their "authenticity."

A little more than three decades after *The Ghetto* was published, there appeared *Children of the Gilded Ghetto* by Judith Kramer and Seymour Leventman.[24] The volume constitutes a kind

[24]Judith R. Kramer and Seymour Leventman, *Children of the Gilded Ghetto* (New Haven: Yale University Press, 1961).

of sequel to Wirth's book, but also stands in sharp contrast to it. *Children of the Gilded Ghetto* is suffused with nostalgia for the immigrant era when Jews lived on the margins of American society and, according to the authors, were rooted in authentic Jewish culture. Although Jewish immigrants were poor and struggling they led a rich and rewarding existence. Then, with the rise of Jews into the middle and upper classes, American Jewry changed course. Wealthy and successful Jews replaced the ghetto with the gilded ghetto, a new, and worse, environment of their own devising.

The inhabitants of the gilded ghetto lead sterile lives. Prosperity has made them vulgar and ostentatious, conspicuous consumers not only when it comes to clothes and cars but even when it comes to their methods of philanthropy. The gilded-ghetto Jews are part of the American establishment or think that they are. In the authors' view, whatever the limitations of yesterday's immigrant ghetto, it was infinitely preferable to today's suburb. Yet according to the authors the gilded ghetto cannot long endure; the changing occupational structure of the Jewish community, including the attractiveness of employment in academia, will provide the impetus for at least some Jews to turn their backs on the gilded ghetto and enter the larger community.

How can such attitudes as those of the authors of the *Children of the Gilded Ghetto* be explained? In an article reprinted in this volume Seymour Martin Lipset and Everett Ladd point out that Jewish academics are much more inclined to identify their politics as left or liberal than are their Gentile colleagues. Moreover, Jewish academics do so despite their class interests, for they are also considerably more prosperous on the average than their Gentile counterparts. Liberal and left-wing Jewish academicians are critical of the middle and upper classes, including their Jewish segments—perhaps especially of their Jewish segments. Not even the spectacular success which Jews have achieved in the academy has served to moderate the negative attitudes of the critical academic toward middle-class life; in fact it can serve to intensify them, perhaps as a way of showing that the individual in question, despite his success, has not compromised his integrity.

The critical academic finds it difficult to relate to that segment of the Jewish community which he is exposed to by virtue of his own high acculturation and striking occupational success. He takes no pride in the Jewish middle and upper classes, or in the desire of Jews to maintain their identity while simultaneously adapting to

American culture. Despite his own participation in the process, the critical academic tends to view acculturation as a compromise unworthy of descendants of the Biblical prophets. In his work he often finds himself highlighting instances of modern-day Jewish vulgarity and ostentation in contrast to the ghetto Jews who, whatever might be said against them, were in his view at least uncorrupted by bourgeois values.[25] But his most biting criticism is often reserved for the politics of today's American Jew, who is assumed to be conservative (despite continuing evidence to the contrary) if not downright reactionary. Indeed, part of the attraction of the immigrant ghetto community for the critical academic lies in the fact that left-wing movements flourished there, unlike the situation in Jewish suburbia today.[26] In suburbia there are no radical orators haranguing crowds, no talk of the "bosses," no mass demonstrations of "solidarity forever."

The sociologist Melvin Tumin exemplifies the tendency of the critical academic to charge American Jewry with conservatism.[27] One of the most successful of the post-Wirth generation, Tumin took his doctorate in 1944 and three years later, at the age of twenty-eight, was offered a professorship at Princeton. At Princeton Tumin continued to espouse the leftism of his radical past. Nor did he lose touch with Jewish life—during the 1950's and 1960's he was in close contact with Jewish organizations, notably the Anti-Defamation League. Yet though his reasons differed, Tumin came to

[25]Allen Mazur, in a study of the attitudes of Jewish social scientists at Brandeis, Harvard, and Boston universities, has found a substantial percentage reporting strong feelings of alienation from Jews who are on the same class level as themselves: "This sort of alienation was reported by a majority of all respondents, but was particularly strong at Brandeis with 70 percent of the subjects giving alienated responses as opposed to only 48 percent and 53 percent at B.U. and Harvard respectively." (Allen Mazur, "The Socialization of Jews into the Academic Subculture," in *The Professors*, ed. by Charles H. Anderson and John D. Murray (Cambridge, Mass.: Schenkman, 1971, p. 277). Mazur quotes one respondent as follows: "Well I suppose I feel most alienated not from the European-born pushcart peddlers in New York City—I don't feel as alienated from them as I do from American-born Jews who have been to college, who live in the suburbs, who are fairly well-to-do, and who are afraid to let go. . . . It's interesting. I never thought of that before, but I feel less alienated from the Yiddish-speaking pushcart peddler than I do from people who are closer to me (*Ibid.*)."

[26]It is notable that Louis Wirth made only casual reference to Jewish radical activity in first- and second-settlement areas. It is difficult to believe that he was unaware of it; rather we may suppose that he preferred not to publish data on Jewish radical activity lest it be misused by prejudiced Gentiles.

[27]See Melvin M. Tumin, "Conservative Trends in American Jewish Life," *Judaism*, Vol. 13, No. 2 (Spring 1964), pp. 131–142.

feel as alienated from the Jewish community as had Louis Wirth at an earlier time. In an address to a Jewish audience Tumin offered his views on what the proper role of the Jewish community should be in American society:

> . . . it would indeed be radical in American politics if there were an identifiable Jewish vote and if that Jewish vote stood for a morally radical position on the political spectrum. And it would be a beautiful challenge to America if the Jewish vote were known as such and worried about as such by all politicians, and known and responded to as such by all non-Jews. Then, you see, the Jews would stand for something, and something vital and alive on the American scene. Then Jewishness would constitute determinate identity. Then to be a Jew would be to be something definite and impressive, however much Jews might be joined in their political position by non-Jews. Short of that, what do Jews stand for in America? For a normal distribution of political opinions along the same spectrum and in the same proportions as non-Jews. However normal, self-protecting and expectable this may be, in effect it is a phenomenon essentially preservative of the status quo. However much this may, in the long run, be the best strategy for self-preservation, it ducks—as it must—the essential question of what is the self that is being preserved. And however much finally—in view of their history—Jews have a right to find their way to life and safety by whatever means they discover or contrive—they ought not to confuse this right and this technique for self-preservation with either a determinate identity or with anything culturally valuable today.[28]

Failing a truly radical position, Tumin saw little that was "culturally valuable" in American Jewish life. He was particularly embittered because not only had the average Jew sold out to an American establishment but Jewish intellectuals—of whom more might have been expected—had done so as well:

> The most distressing aspect of this move into the sphere of all-rightness is the ways in which it is manifested among Jewish intellectuals. In apparent total forgetfulness of the role which radical criticism of American society played in the first half of this century in helping make America less execrable than it might otherwise have been, Jewish intellectuals have increasingly come to play the role of gentlemen of the Establishment. Beguiled by the chance to become influential—in government, education, industry, the mass media

[28] *Ibid.*, p. 138.

—many Jews have rushed in to take advantage of this opportunity to become insiders.[29]

VII

The negative stance adopted by the critical academic vis-à-vis contemporary American Jewry has as its corollary, as we have noted, an infatuation with the immigrant Jews of the ghetto generation. But these are not the only Jews to whom the present generation has been invidiously compared: the Jews of the East European *shtetl,* the Jews of the Soviet Union, and the Jews of Israel have at various times and in various hands been singled out for such a purpose. The temptation to regard American Jews as inferior to their progenitors as well as to their contemporaries in other lands is a real one, and constitutes a unique problem of bias in contemporary Jewish studies.

Admiration for the *shtetl* Jew was prefigured in the enthusiastic reaction of many writers and intellectuals to the publication in 1952 of *Life Is With People* by Mark Zborowski and Elizabeth Herzog.[30] This book portrayed a world of simple piety in which, despite overwhelming poverty and powerlessness, Jews succeeded in leading a richly human, dignified, and creative existence. The idealized image of the *shtetl* was further refined and elaborated upon some years later in the Broadway musical *Fiddler on the Roof,* which was translated into many languages and performed by innumerable theatrical groups, both amateur and professional, as well as made into a movie. The worldwide success of *Fiddler on the Roof* is a tribute to the appeal of a figure like Tevye, its hero, for people in modern society who feel themselves assailed by rapid change. Whatever Sholom Aleichem may have intended, Tevye has become a prototype of the decent man assailed by forces which would destroy him but who despite all obstacles succeeds, not only in keeping body and soul together but in retaining his dignity and humanity.

[29] *Ibid.,* p. 139. Some of Tumin's assumptions were analyzed in the discussion which followed his paper; see *ibid.,* pp. 143–153. Milton Himmelfarb published a critique of several of Tumin's assumptions, particularly those relating to Jewish conservatism, in "How We Are," *Commentary,* January 1965, pp. 69–72.

[30] Mark Zborowski and Elizabeth Herzog, *Life Is With People* (New York: International Universities Press, 1952). The volume was dedicated to Ruth Benedict and includes a foreword by Margaret Mead.

Judged by the idealized standards of the *shtetl,* the contemporary American Jew may be found wanting. Unless one happens to find social mobility heroic it would be difficult to call American Jews heroes. And among significant numbers of younger Jews there is not even social mobility to admire; born into the middle or upper class, they have little conception of what it means to climb the "greasy pole" of material success. But if the student of contemporary Jewry is to perceive the American Jewish situation in all its dimensions, he must resist the temptation to make invidious comparisons between the American Jew and his *shtetl* forebears, particularly as the latter have been portrayed through the touching affirmations of Zborowski and Herzog, and even of the late Abraham Joshua Heschel.[31] Before he arrives at a judgment he must study the *shtetl* through the eyes of its contemporaries—especially the Hebrew (and Yiddish) writers of the period. These men, themselves the products of the *shtetl* but at the same time exposed to other influences, viewed the *shtetl* as nothing less than an abomination—a place rife with superstition, cursed with a culture that stifled creativity and manliness, and saddled with a class and status system that perpetrated grave injustice. Although it is not incumbent upon the student to render a final judgment on the *shtetl,* he does need to protect himself against uncritical admiration of past generations of Jews, and—a necessary corollary—against unduly harsh evaluations of his own.

If it is possible to devalue the contemporary American Jew by comparing him with his *shtetl* ancestor, it is equally possible to do so by comparing him with the Jew of Israel or of the Soviet Union. Although New Leftists may be critical of Israel, most Jews, including most young Jews, hold the country and its people in the highest possible esteem. In achieving statehood, in successfully defending their nation's sovereignty in the face of concerted attack and continuing acts of terrorism, the Israelis have assumed a truly heroic stature in the minds of the majority of American Jews. Similarly, the courage of a segment of Russian Jewry in asserting its Jewish identity has fired the imagination of many young Jews. But the examples of Israel and of Soviet Jewry may also have the effect of making the American Jew seem drab and uninspiring by comparison.

[31]See Abraham J. Heschel, *The Earth is the Lord's: The Inner World of the Jew in East Europe* (New York: H. Schuman, 1950).

Now, we can take for granted the fact that present-day American Jews enjoy a standard of living which is incomparably higher than that of their forebears. It is also obvious that most American Jews on the one hand enjoy luxuries which are unavailable to their Israeli or Soviet cousins, and on the other hand seem to lead a less "heroic" existence. But the student of the contemporary Jewish scene must go beyond these differences if he hopes to probe successfully the sociological and psychological situation of today's American Jew. For it is clear that American Jewry's distance from the sweatshop, or from the Arab-Israeli conflict, or from the struggle against Soviet repression, has by no means brought about the elimination of all problems. Even if we were to make the bold assumption that American Jewry has no substantial economic worries we could not but realize that new anxieties have taken the place of old struggles. There is, to take only one example, the problem faced by many American Jews who wish but do not know how to create a viable Jewish identity for themselves and their children. The crisis of identity—both in its Jewish and in its "universal" aspect—is a problem which the American Jew confronts more starkly than did his forefather in the *shtetl* or in a first-settlement area in the American city, or for that matter, than does his cousin in Israel. It is no exaggeration to say that with each rise in economic level, each advance in educational level, and each move upward in "brow" level, the difficulty has been compounded.

No discussion of the possible sources of bias in the study of contemporary American Jews would be complete without taking into account that those studying the Jewish group are themselves almost invariably Jewish. While this Jewishness is undoubtedly an asset inasmuch as it gives the student both a competence which the outsider would have laboriously to acquire and a rapport which the non-Jew might find difficult to establish, in some sense it is also a handicap. Scholarly training is not culture-free. In the United States, academic training is strongly oriented to western values as well as to the American milieu, and while exposure to western culture brings enormous benefits, it has its characteristic limitations and dangers which are not always perceived as such, especially by members of minority groups. One such possible danger is that of alienation from one's own group. In its most benign form this alienation may be expressed as cultural relativism, a perspective in which the Jews are viewed as merely one of many ethnic groups and in which emphasis is placed on the similarities rather than on the differences among groups.

But socialization in western culture is capable of producing more than simple alienation in the Jewish researcher. There is the deeper alienation of self-hatred, the phenomenon which came to preoccupy Kurt Lewin and other observers of the Jewish personality, in which the individual unwittingly internalizes the anti-Jewish prejudice endemic to western culture. He comes to view the Jews critically; he identifies with the historical aggressor. In its most serious manifestation self-hatred leads to a view of the Jews as retrogressive and reactionary—as clinging to an outmoded identity. As a consequence Jews come to be seen as being in part responsible for the very prejudice from which they suffer. In the final analysis this view of Jewish life constitutes a secularized version of Christianity's traditional stance with regard to the Jews.

Another possible source of bias arising from the Jewishness of most students of contemporary Jewry is the ethnocentrism which can linger even in those who are seemingly cosmopolitan. Ethnocentrism is of course encountered in many areas of a minority community. Among those who are well integrated into the group, ethnocentrism need not create inner conflict—it is congruous both with the individual's ideology and with his style of life. The alienated, on the other hand, troubled by their enthnocentrism and finding it incompatible with their ideology and their style of life, tend, as we have seen, to become harshly critical of the Jewish group, and to hold Jews to a standard which others would not be expected to achieve. Since the Jews will necessarily fall short of the arbitrary standard set by the analyst, he comes to feel justified in his alienation from the group.

There is a final temptation which may beset the student of contemporary Jewry—the temptation to view the Jewish group from the vantage point of a tourist. The tourist revels in the exotic, the colorful, the different; only the native finds satisfaction in the ordinary. Even analysts who maintain that Jews are like everyone else—only more so—sometimes find themselves irresistibly drawn to picturesque and unusual aspects of Jewish life: to *hasidim,* to Black Jews, to the *havurot.* The exotic, to be sure, has its undeniable attraction, even its value, but unless such phenomena are placed in perspective, the result for the student will be distortion rather than understanding.

Those who would understand American Jewish life must

approach it not in a spirit of tourism, still less in a spirit of preconceived hostility, but seriously, sympathetically, and out of a genuine desire to learn. The challenge of comprehending the twentieth-century Jews of New York, Los Angeles, and even of Oshkosh is still very much before us, as difficult a task as that of comprehending the Jews of first-century Jerusalem, and as inviting.

AMERICAN JEWRY
SOCIAL HISTORY

IMMIGRATION AND THE FORMATION OF AMERICAN JEWRY, 1840–1925

by LLOYD P. GARTNER

INTRODUCTION

JEWISH IMMIGRATION from the colonial period to the 1920's is generally divided into three periods: the Sephardic, the German, and the East European. The division does not always correspond to the actual facts of immigration but rather indicates which group set its cultural stamp upon the Jewish community at a given period.

The understandable tendency of present-day American Jews is to endow their immigrant ancestors with a higher status than they actually attained. The religious piety of these ancestors is also frequently exaggerated. The persistent tendency to change the shape of the past to conform with present needs can be noticed in a variety of different contexts. Thus, individuals who are active in Jewish affairs frequently deplore what they consider a lack of solidarity in the contemporary community. Implicit in their criticism is the belief that at an earlier period in American Jewish history there was strong cohesion within the Jewish community. However, in reality there was a measure of friction between Sephardic and German Jews and at a later period there was serious confrontation and conflict between German and East European Jews. Conflict existed side by side with cohesion—conflict was related to cohesion inasmuch as the established community saw itself as responsible for the newcomers.

In the nineteenth century important groups within the established Jewish community felt that America had reached its absorptive capacity and that prospective Jewish immigrants should be influenced instead to settle in other parts of the globe, or even to remain in Europe. Rather than viewing the newcomers as brothers who would fortify the Jewish community and improve its chances for survival, the established element tended to look upon the immigrants as paupers lacking in the desire to improve themselves, as beggars who would constitute a permanent drain upon the resources of the established group, and as foreigners incapable of understanding American ways or of adapting themselves to the American environment. In reality, the East European immigrants proved exactly the opposite: they eagerly sought self-improvement, they made heroic efforts to be self-sustaining, they were strongly attracted by American culture. The behavior of the established community can only be explained by the fact that despite their patriotism and seeming confidence in the country, they harbored deep doubts about the underlying sentiment of Gentile America toward the Jew. On the one hand, the established element affirmed its confidence in American fair-mindedness but, on the other hand, it was afraid to put the nation to the test.

Lloyd P. Gartner is widely admired for his penetrating writing on American and English-Jewish history. In the present essay, Gartner highlights the way in which American Jewry has been shaped by the traditions of both Western and Eastern European Jews. Furthermore, by stressing the impact of the Kishinev pogrom on the German Jew, as well as the fact that many leading German Jews eventually came to defend the right of free immigration to America, Gartner makes possible a more sophisticated understanding of the complicated relationship between Germans and East Europeans in the Jewish community. Finally, in his treatment of the colonial period, Gartner analyzes the contrast between the position of the Jew in American law and public life and the situation in Europe; the contrast is essential for understanding the character of American Jewish life. The ramifications of this crucial theme are analyzed in the article by Ben Halpern.

M. S.

THE JEWS of the United States form today the largest Jewish group of any country in the world, as they have since the break up of Czarist Russia in 1918. Their number is estimated at 6,060,000 persons.[1] Although they have lived since the mid-seventeenth century in the territories which now compose the United States, only since approximately 1880 has the Jewish population attained great size. Historians generally accept that perhaps 2,000 Jews lived in the Thirteen Colonies at the time of the American Revolution, and fifty years later, about 1825, the number was still no higher than about 6,000. Sharp increase began from then, however, for in 1840 there were about 15,000 Jews, and at the outbreak of the American Civil War in 1861 an estimated 150,000 lived there.[2] When the first rudimentary survey of American Jewry was undertaken in 1877 by the Board of Delegates of American Israelites, the total was put at 280,000.[3] From this point, the Jewish population multiplied with astonishing rapidity, owing almost entirely to mass immigration from Eastern Europe. Contemporaries estimated that 1,000,000 Jews dwelled in the United States in 1900, 3,000,000 in 1915, and 4,500,000 in 1925, when drastic immigration laws took effect.[4] The rate of Jewish population increase between 1840 and 1925 was thus far higher than that for the United States as a whole. While the

[1] *American Jewish Year Book,* 1972, ed. Morris Fine and Milton Himmelfarb (New York and Philadelphia, 1972), pp. 386–87 (abbrev. *AJYB*). The statistics of American Jewish population for all periods are unreliable. For the earliest known head count of an American Jewish community, taken by a Milwaukee rabbi in 1875, see Louis J. Swichkow and Lloyd P. Gartner, *A History of the Jews of Milwaukee* (Philadelphia, 1963), pp. 65–67. There have been, however, numerous quite exact population surveys of local communities during recent decades, based on careful sampling rather than actual count.

[2] Salo W. Baron and Joseph L. Blau, eds., *The Jews of the United States 1790–1840: A Documentary History,* 3 vols. (New York, Philadelphia, London, 1963), I, pp. 85–86, 255 n. 1; Bertram W. Korn, *American Jewry and the Civil War* (Philadelphia, 1951), p. 1.

[3] David Sulzberger, "The Growth of Jewish Population in the United States," *Publication of the American Jewish Historical Society* (abbrev. *PAJHS*), VI (1897), pp. 141–149.

[4] The growth may be seen from the annual estimates in the *AJYB,* "Statistics of Jews" section.

country's 11,000,000 inhabitants multiplied over tenfold to 115,000,000 during this period, the Jews increased more than three hundred times over. Since 1925, however, Jewish population growth has been reversed. With 206,000,000 persons now (November, 1972) living in the United States—an increase of 91,000,000 since 1925—the Jewish increment has been a reatively small 1,560,000. This disproportionately small growth has occurred notwithstanding the fact, that despite immigration laws, American Jewry has received a proportionately greater accession to its numbers since 1925 from foreign immigration than has the general American population.[5]

Between 1825 and 1925, therefore, the increase in American Jewry was owing to immigration from abroad. Since 1925, the relatively small increase seems due to the great decrease in that immigration.

These immigrants became transformed into Americans in culture, language, and loyalties, yet the vast majority also remained distinctly Jewish in consciousness, by desire, and in formal affiliation. It is of great interest, therefore, to examine the sources and character of Jewish immigration, and its adaptation to American life.

Well before substantial Jewish immigration began to flow, the highly favorable terms by which Jews, and others, could enter and accommodate themselves in American life were fixed. Early America was a land of Protestant Christians, whose bugbear in religion was not the near-legendary Jews but recognizable Catholics—a bitter heritage of Reformation struggles. Gradually, however, religion in America was permeated during the eighteenth century with philanthropy and humanitarianism, the belief that the truest Christianity was man's fulfillment of his purpose to do good on earth. These ideas tended to slice through Protestant denominational walls, and very slowly to flatten them. The denigration of the historic dogmas of Christianity opened the chance that the ancient "synagogue of Satan" might be granted rights nearly equal with the church of Christ on American soil. Moreover, the emphasis upon

[5]United States Department of Commerce, Bureau of the Census, *Historical Statistics of the United States: Colonial Times to 1957* (Washington, D.C., 1963), Series A 1–3, p. 7; Series C 88–114, p. 56; Mark Wischnitzer, *To Dwell in Safety: The Story of Jewish Migration since 1800* (Philadelphia, 1948), p. 289; the *AJYB* contains an annual report on Jewish immigration to the United States.

good works was to have very far-reaching consequences for the character of Judaism in America during the nineteenth century.[6]

Thinking about religion during the eighteenth century also helped to produce a change of fundamental character in the relations between Church and State. Most Protestant sects in America stressed the utterly individual nature of human sin and conversion and salvation, and vigorously opposed any coercive ecclesiastical intervention, particularly the Church linked to the State. Members of state churches in Europe, such as Lutherans and Catholics, were generally small, little loved minorities in Colonial America which also became accustomed to maintaining their religious institutions unaided and unhampered.

The power of the Protestant left thus combined with its spiritual opposite, the secular, anti-clerical bias of Enlightenment thinking, to bring about the separation of Church and State. Religious tests and sectarian oaths of office were abolished and prohibited, and the First Amendment to the federal constitution virtually completed the process by forbidding Congress to establish or support any religion. State constitutions made similar provisions.

These momentous developments during the latter half of the eighteenth century were of invaluable importance for the Jews who were destined to come to America. Except for an occasional religious qualification for public office in a few State constitutions, all of which were presently removed, the Jews enjoyed full civil, religious, and political equality with other religions from the time of American independence. This was full emancipation in the European sense, and it was acquired with barely any reference to the Jews as such, but rather as a matter of broad principle.[7] The separation of Church and State also meant that no one was required to profess religious belief or maintain religious affiliation; churches, and religious societies generally, were private associations which

[6]H. Shelton Smith, Robert T. Handy, Lefferts A. Loetscher, *American Christianity: An Historical Interpretation with Representative Documents*, 2 vols. (New York, 1960), pp. 374–414.

[7]Alan Heimert, *Religion and the American Mind from the Great Awakening to the Revolution* (Cambridge, Mass., 1966), pp. 128–129, 136–137, 524–527, 537–539; Anson Phelps Stokes, *Church and State in the United States*, 3 vols. (New York, 1950), I, pp. 133–149, 240–253, 519–552, 731–744, 744–767; for the exceptions to the generalities, see *ibid.*, pp. 428–432 (New Hampshire), 865–878 (Maryland). A useful review is Abram Vossen Goodman, *American Overture: Jewish Rights in Colonial Times* (Philadelphia, 1947).

established rules as they wished. Religious sects and insitutions could be established at will; schismatics enjoyed unlimited freedom alongside orthodox communicants. How deeply Judaism was affected by this pattern may be judged from the fact that most Jewish religious institutions in the United States are synagogues which have deviated more or less from the Jewish canon, and nearly nothing could be done by traditionalists to restrain them. While the constitutional deliberations were in progress, the Jews seem to have remained indifferent to them. They were mainly interested in the abolition of religious tests and oaths,[8] not in the separation of Church and State. But then, these Jews were newcomers, and probably still retained the historic Jewish wariness of intruding into the political affairs of the Gentile world.

Thus, even before European Jewry began its historic struggle for emancipation, which was not consummated until the end of World War I, the entire question was settled quite casually in America. The issue of the enfranchisement of Jews specifically, and the terms of Jewish entry into the general society, never existed here. Jewish immigrants also found that no formal, legally established Jewish community existed here with its traditions, controls, and taxes. They could be or not be Jews, as they pleased, and if they preferred not they did not have to become Christians—an act repugnant to most reluctant Jews. They could occupy the neutral ground of enlightened secular humanism or religious indifferentism. The possibilities of Judaism and Jewish life in America under the regime of free option, state aloofness, and automatic emancipation were to be explored by every generation of Jews who came to America. Such a regime had no precedent in the entire millennial history of the Jews.

The first Jews in America were Sefardim, descendants of Spanish and Portuguese Jews. It has long been known that many of these pioneers were not actually of Spanish culture. By the eighteenth century, formally Sefardi congregations consisted mainly of Ashkenazi (Central and East European) congregants, who accepted the strange liturgy and customs of what was then the single synagogue in the town.[9] In fact, the Philadelphia synagogue,

[8]Stokes, *op. cit.*, pp. 286–290, 528–529; Edwin Wolf 2nd and Maxwell Whiteman, *The History of the Jews of Philadelphia from Colonial Times to the Age of Jackson* (Philadelphia, 1957), pp. 147–149.

[9]David de Sola Pool, *An Old Faith in the New World* (New York, 1955), pp. 437, 461.

founded only a few years after the first recorded appearance of Jews in that city in 1735, had no Sefardi members, yet adopted the Sefardi rite.[10] The continuance of the Sefardi form of worship, despite the minority of Spanish and Portuguese Jews in the little Colonial communities, was assisted by the characteristically Sefardi rule of prohibiting the separate local congregations which proliferated among Ashkenazim, and of centralizing local Jewish affairs in the *Mahamad* (executive) of the single established synagogue.

Colonial Jews who were not Sefardim were mainly recently arrived Central Europeans. The differences between them and the Sefardim lay deeper than in ritual. The latter were for centuries naturalized in Iberian culture, spoke Spanish or Portuguese, and had fused their Judaism with Spanish culture. To that extent they could be called modern Jews. Their Judaism was not learned or passionate, but polite and urbane. The comparative success of this combination of contemporary culture and Jewish tradition, although it was rather superficial, suggests the principal reason why no Sefardi synagogue abandoned Orthodoxy for Reform Judaism during the nineteenth century. On the other hand, the Central European Jewish majority consisted largely of Jews of traditional culture. They were not learned or wealthy stock, nor had they moved in the small circles of German Jews which were reaching out ultimately to create the memorable synthesis of German culture and Judaism. These Bavarian, Posen, or Silesian Jews came to America from the villages and small towns of their native land, generally knew and observed the rudiments of Judaism and little more, and spoke and wrote Yiddish rather than German. In their great majority they were tradesmen, ranging from country peddlers to merchant shippers, and many were independent craftsmen. Apprentices and indentured servants could be found, and rarely a physician, a lawyer, or a leisured gentleman.[11] The main cities were New York City, Philadelphia, and Charleston, South Carolina, with outlying settlements in inland or "fall line" towns like Lancaster, Pennsylvania, Albany, New York, and Richmond, Virginia.

[10]Wolf and Whiteman, *op. cit.*, pp. 7, 32, 41–42, 122, 228; correspondence was conducted in Yiddish (p. 226).

[11]Jacob R. Marcus, *Early American Jewry*, 2 vols. (Philadelphia, 1951–1953), II, pp. 395–428; Wolf and Whiteman, *op. cit.*, pp. 165–186; Leo Hershkowitz, *Wills of Early New York Jews, 1704–1799* (New York, 1967), supplies unique, fresh data.

The 6,000 Jews of 1826 began to increase rapidly from that year. The impulse to emigrate was strongly felt in German Jewry, which by the 1830's and 1840's was more different from its eighteenth-century ancestors than those ancestors had been from sixteenth-century German Jews. Young Jews of the day uniformly received a German education, and even university study was not uncommon. Great political events also had their influence. During the Napoleonic years bright hopes for emancipation and full entry into German society soared, as Prussia and other duchies and cities freed their Jews from venerable restrictions on marriage, settlement, occupation, and from special taxes. But the period of political reaction and economic depression after 1815 brought the deepest disappointments to expectant Jews. Political restrictions were reinstituted, and the restored powers of Christian guilds denied access to some occupations for skilled Jews. The Christian State theories by which these measures were justified were subscribed to by influential politicians and intellectuals, and increased the Jews' sense of deprivation and exclusion. Apostasy was one escape from the predicament, and emigration was another. If the German homeland would not have them as faithful subjects, a new homeland could be found in free America. Land hunger, which drove millions of Germans across the Atlantic, played no role in Jewish emigration.[12]

German Jews had known and idealized America during the eighteenth century. The Constitutional Convention of 1787 received a puzzling but ardent petition from anonymous German Jews about settling in America, and periodic talk of the New World was not rare.[13] To the economic and psychological background of immigration could be added the steady improvement in the safety,

[12]Mack Walker, *Germany and the Emigration 1816–1885* (Cambridge, Mass., 1964), pp. 42–102; Marcus L. Hansen, *The Atlantic Migration 1607–1860* (new ed., New York, 1961), pp. 120–171; Selma Stern-Taeubler, "The Motivation of the German-Jewish Emigration to America in the Post-Mendelssohnian Era," *Essays in American Jewish History* (Cincinnati, 1958), pp. 247–262; Rudolf Glanz, "The Immigration of German Jews up to 1880," *YIVO Annual of Jewish Social Science* (abbrev. *YAJSS*), II/III (1948), pp. 81–99; *idem*, "Source Materials for the History of Jewish Immigration to the United States 1800–1880," *YAJSS*, VI (1951), pp. 73–156 (invaluable gathering of sources, mostly from German-Jewish press).

[13]Baron and Blau, *op. cit.*, III, pp. 891–893; Morris U. Schappes, *A Documentary History of the Jews in the United States 1654–1875* (2nd ed., New York, 1953), pp. 159–160.

speed, and regularity of trans-Atlantic travel. Between the 1820's and 1870's perhaps 150,000 Jews from German lands came to the United States, mainly from Bavarian towns and villages, German Poland, Bohemia, and Hungary.[14] Their geographic diffusion in America was wider than any Jewish immigrant group of earlier or later times. During these mid-nineteenth century decades of newly founded western frontier cities, California gold, and the peak of the southern cotton economy, German Jews scattered throughout the United States. Probably the majority settled in the Northeast, but a large number made their way to newly opened California, centering in San Francisco; a string of Jewish settlements appeared at the ports down the length of the Mississippi River; numerous Jewish communities arose in the cities along the Ohio River and the Great Lakes, centers of commerce and heavy industry; in dozens of small towns in the South, Jewish merchants kept store and traded in the freshly picked cotton.[15]

Jews from German lands took pride in their German culture. They were pillars of American Germandom, contributing and participating heavily in the advancement of German in the United States. They maintained German social and charitable societies, were subscribers to and writers for German newspapers, singers and instrumentalists in German musical societies, impresarios, performers and faithful patrons in the German theaters. It appears also that Jews enjoyed access to the Turnverein athletic societies and German social clubs in many cities. German fraternal orders included many Jewish members. Indeed, Jews were included among the American Germans who articulated the idea that they had the

[14]Rudolf Glanz, "The Immigration of German Jews . . . ," *loc. cit.; idem,* "The 'Bayer' and the 'Pollack' in America," *Jewish Social Studies,* XVII, 1 (January 1955), pp. 27–42; Guido Kisch, *In Search of Freedom: A History of American Jews from Czechoslovakia* (London, 1949), pp. 13–58.

[15]Allan Tarshish, "The Economic Life of the American Jew in the Middle Nineteenth Century," *Essays . . . ,"* pp. 263–293; Rudolf Glanz, *The Jews of California from the Discovery of Gold until 1880* (New York, 1960), pp. 18–91, 106–109; Harris Newmark, *Sixty Years in Southern California 1853–1913* (3rd ed., Boston and New York, 1930); Jacob R. Marcus, *Memoirs of American Jews 1775–1865* (3 vols., Philadelphia, 1955), contains dozens of useful and interesting autobiographical statements, typically by immigrant businessmen of the times; Swichkow and Gartner, *op. cit.*, pp. 12–18, 93–110; W. Gunther Plaut, *The Jews of Minnesota: The First Seventy-Five Years* (New York, 1959), pp. 9–30, 61–68; Stephen Birmingham, "*Our Crowd*": *The Great Jewish Families of New York* (New York, 1967), is a gossipy social chronicle occasionally useful.

mission of diffusing a higher, philosophic culture among the Yankees.[16]

For some German Jews, the German milieu in America was so fully satisfying that they more or less abandoned their ancestral Judaism. One might mention in this connection Abraham Jacobi (1830–1919), the father of American pediatrics, the socialist leader Victor Berger (1860–1929), or Oswald Ottendorfer (1826–1900), who published the leading German newspaper in New York. The great majority, however, remained within Judaism and created a version satisfying to their desire for a religion which harmonized intellectually with contemporary liberalism, rationalism, and historical scholarship. This was Reform Judaism. On the surface, it meant that the old informality and intensity of Jewish worship was replaced by a liturgical model suggestive of Protestantism, housed in a temple which often imitated intentionally the "Golden Age" architecture of Spanish Jewry. All Jewish laws and customs which enforced a social gulf between Jews and Christians were abrogated, with the single, critical exception of Jewish-Christian marriages. The transition from inherited Orthodoxy to new-style Reform took place with astonishing speed. After a false beginning in Charleston during the 1820's, Reform actually began about 1850. By 1890 nearly every synagogue founded by German Jews had overturned the traditions of centuries and taken up the new way. The Orthodox and proto-Conservatives survived as small groups, individual rabbis, and a few congregations.[17]

In any of dozens of American Jewish local communities during the 1880's and 1890's, the typical scene was a representative

[16]Rudolf Glanz, *Jews in Relation to the Cultural Milieu of the Germans in America up to the Eighteen-Eighties* (New York, 1947); Swichkow and Gartner, *op. cit.*, pp. 13–27; John A. Hawgood, *The Tragedy of German-America* (New York and London, 1940), is a penetrating analysis.

[17]David Philipson, *The Reform Movement in Judaism* (new ed., New York, 1967), (originally published in 1907 and somewhat revised in 1931; this rather partisan work is quite antiquated but has not been superseded as a whole); James G. Heller, *Isaac M. Wise: His Life, Work and Thought* (New York, 1965), (a voluminous, compendious biography of the most important leader); Swichkow and Gartner, *op. cit.*, pp. 32–51, 171–192; Morris A. Gutstein, *A Priceless Heritage: The Epic Growth of Nineteenth Century Chicago Jewry* (New York, 1953), pp. 57–92, 139–208 (these studies exemplify local developments); Moshe Davis, *The Emergence of Conservative Judaism: The Historical School in 19th Century America* (Philadelphia, 1963), pp. 149–228 (on the opposition to Reform); the *Dictionary of American Biography* includes Berger, Jacobi, and Ottendorfer, as well as most major nineteenth-century Jewish religious figures.

leadership of prosperous merchants, sometimes bankers and lawyers. By coming to America, they had not left a bitter for a gentler exile, where they would await messianic redemption; the Messiah was the millennium of all mankind, and their own future lay entirely in America. To these Jews, "Jew" meant only to profess the Jewish religion. All that was suggestive of "ghetto" had to be discarded, now that the physical ghetto was a thing of the past and Jews no longer wished to live in segregation. Their Judaism contained nothing mystical or contemplative; it was formulated as an optimistic, reasonable American religion, with happiness and salvation attainable by human effort. The essence of Judaism was only moral and ethical, while the externals of the traditional way of life were classified among changeable outward observances and consequently abandoned. Yet persons who did not practice or believe in any Jewish religious principles were still regarded as Jews. The ethnic basis of Judaism remained alive among the German Jews, but subdued, until vigorously thrust forward by the new arrivals from Eastern Europe.[18]

Germanic Judaism declined in America from the 1880's. The Second Reich founded by Bismarck disappointed the liberal traditions cherished by '48-ers and hastened their American assimilation, while the anti-Semitic trends in Imperial Germany did not encourage Jews.[19] Germanness in the United States was preserved longest not among urban German liberals, but in the conservative, rural, and small-city German Lutheran churches. Yet it was inevitable that children and grandchildren finally ceased to speak and study German and finally forgot it. The close, comfortable association of Germanness with Judaism ended when East European Jewish immigrants inundated the 280,000 Jews of 1880. Although German was still spoken in the privacy of many families, the German age was past at the close of the nineteenth century.

Once again, numbers tell much of the story which began in the 1880's. By 1900, there were 1,000,000 Jews in the United States, and about 3,000,000 in 1915. When free immigration to America ended in 1925, there were probably 4,500,000 Jews; this was the point when

[18]This paraphrases Swichkow and Gartner, *op. cit.*, pp. 169–170.

[19]Glanz, *Jews in Relation to the Cultural Milieu . . .* , pp. 34–37; *Swichkow and Gartner, op. cit.*, pp. 133–136; Carl F. Wittke, *Refugees of Revolution: The German Forty-Eighters in America* (Philadelphia, 1952), pp. 344–373; two small tales recounted in Birmingham, *op. cit.*, pp. 159, 191–192; Hawgood, *op. cit.*

Jews reached their highest proportion in the American population—about four percent. The climactic years of East European immigration came after the pogroms of 1881, again in 1890 and 1891, and above all during the years of war, revolution, and reaction in Russia which began for Jews with the notorious Kishinev pogrom of 1903. From 1904 through 1908, 642,000 Jews entered the United States.[20]

It would be an error to take pogroms as the main cause of emigration. Galicia, with its Jews emancipated from 1867 and without pogroms, showed perhaps the highest proportion of emigration from Eastern Europe. It was the fivefold increase of East European Jewry during the nineteenth century and the failure of the economy to keep pace with this multiplication, which must be considered the most deeply rooted cause. Repressive Russian laws restricted economic opportunities still further, and drove Jews to a feeling of hopelessness about their future in Russia. With railroads and steamships fully developed into instruments of migration, there were widely advertised and regularly scheduled departures of emigrant ships from such major ports as Hamburg, Bremen, Rotterdam, and Liverpool. Human movement could proceed in massive proportions. Russia also took a passive attitude toward emigration, by unofficially permitting hundreds of thousands of Jews to cross its border. After 1905, the Jewish Colonization Association was permitted to maintain emigrant offices in several cities. Above all, entrance into the United States continued to be nearly unhindered, although immigrants feared the examination at the port of entry (usually Ellis Island, in New York harbor) which disqualified for entry perhaps one percent of arrivals.[21]

Between East European and Germanic Jews there are marked contrasts. The newer arrivals were almost exclusively of traditional Jewish culture. They had no Polish or Russian education—although the Galicians had been required to attend a government school—and few knew the languages of Eastern Europe. A significant

[20]On East European Jewish immigration, in addition to sources cited *supra*, note 5, see Samuel Joseph, *Jewish Immigration to the United States 1881–1910* (New York, 1914), (useful for statistics) and the massive collective work: Walter F. Willcox, ed., *International Migrations*, 2 vols. (New York, 1929, 1931), which contains a useful conspectus on the Jews by L. Hersch (II, pp. 471–521). Lloyd P. Gartner, *The Jewish Immigrant in England 1870–1914* (London and Detroit, 1960), may serve for comparative purposes.

[21]John Higham, *Strangers in the Land: Patterns of American Nativism 1860–1925* (New Brunswick, N.J., 1951), pp. 87–105.

illustration is furnished by the Russian Jewish revolutionary refugees who came to America especially in 1882 and during the post-revolutionary reaction in 1906, 1907, and 1908. Before they could assume leadership in the Jewish labor movement, they had to learn or relearn Yiddish. East European Jewry was undergoing a period of extraordinary ideological development, but most immigrants came from the small towns and villages, far from the centers of thought and agitation. Their ideological experiences were to take place in huge urban colonies in America.

The earlier Jewish immigrants had not much intellectual dynamic. They developed a Judaism which they found suitable and believable, and then tended to hold to it with little change. Well-conceived philanthropy was their strongest urge as Jews. The East Europeans, on the other hand, tended to be intellectually mobile and innovative, in keeping with their regional traditions of intense piety and arduous, sharp-witted Talmudic study. This intellectuality had a pervasiveness rarely equaled in Jewish history. Even quite simple Jews lay under the spell of these traditions, and those who broke with them to pursue newer causes—Zionism, Russian revolutionism, Hebrew or Yiddish revival, entry into Russian, Polish, or American culture—rarely lost the quality of intensity and mobility.

There is a third important contrast. Germanic Jews had spread pretty thinly across the United States, although, like their Christian neighbors, they later left the smaller towns for large cities. The vast majority of East European Jews settled at once in the largest cities, above all New York, and Chicago, Philadelphia, Boston, Baltimore, and Cleveland. If seven or eight smaller metropoli are added, over ninety percent of East European Jews are accounted for.[22]

American Jewry has been shaped by the numbers and traditions and aspirations, and also the envies, jealousies, and mutual dependence, of Germanic and East European Jewries. This will not deny the awareness of their common Jewishness, nor the overwhelming force and attraction of American life in shaping a

[22]Moses Rischin, *The Promised City: New York's Jews 1870–1914* (Cambridge, Mass., 1962), pp. 19–47; Elias Tcherikower, *Geshikhte fun der Yiddisher Arbeter Bavegung in der Faraynikte Shtatn*, 2 vols. (New York, 1943), of which Volume I contains invaluable material on this background (there has been an unsuccessful English translation, abridgment, and revision: Elias Tcherikower and Aaron Antonovsky, *The Early Jewish Labor Movement in the United States* [New York, 1961], pp. 3–74).

Jewish group different from any previously known. How old and new American Jews encountered each other merits closer notice:

> My dear Russian brethren, who have done so much to cast a stigma on the Jewish name, are now adding this new sin to their long list of offenses which we are asked to stand responsible for.[23]

Thus a Reform rabbi in the Middle West; the sin on this occasion was the founding of a Jewish political club for Bryan in 1896. Nine years earlier, Benjamin F. Peixotto addressed a New York City audience:

> I would say here to those who say "send them back, let them stay at home, we don't want them here," I would say you might as well attempt to keep the waves of the old ocean from rushing on our shores, as to keep those from seeking the refuge which this country offers.[24]

The speaker had spent five years in Rumania during the 1870's. Few, if any American Jews had seen Jewish immigrants in their lands of birth or better appreciated why they sought to quit them. Fifteen years, more or less, passed before American Jews—themselves near immigrant origins—appreciated Peixotto's insistence that a high proportion of the 5,000,000 to 6,000,000 Jews of Eastern Europe was bound to leave for America. Since the emancipation and modernization of German Jewry beginning in the eighteenth century, there had been a scornful or condescending attitude to backward, impoverished, persecuted Polish and Russian Jews. For their part, Polish and Russian Jews admired and envied their German fellow-Jews and, like other intelligentsia of their time, some acquired German language and culture at a distance. But there were also many who feared and deprecated the de-Judaization of these favored brethren.[25] All of these heritages were brought to

[23]Swichkow and Gartner, *op. cit.*, p. 151.

[24]Benjamin F. Peixotto, *What Shall We Do With Our Immigrants?* (New York, Young Men's Hebrew Association, 1887), pp. 3–4, quoted in Zosa Szajkowski, "The Attitude of American Jews to East European Jewish Immigration (1881–1893)," *PAJHS*, XL, 3 (March 1951), p. 235.

[25]Cf. S. Adler-Rudel, *Ostjuden in Deutschland* 1880–1940. (Tübingen, 1959), pp. 1–33. The attitudes of some German Jews to first encountering Jews in Eastern Europe are suggestive; e.g., Franz Rosenzweig, *Briefe* (Berlin, 1935), pp. 320–322; Alexander Carlebach, "A German Rabbi goes East," Leo Baeck Institute *Yearbook*, VI (1961), pp. 60–121.

America. Now, German and East European Jews found themselves living next to each other, inhaling and exhaling, one may say, each other's attitudes.

Through the voluminous literature of the decades of large-scale Jewish immigration from the 1880's into the 1920's, several motifs are to be easily discerned in the "uptown" and "downtown" views of each other. To Russian immigrants, the German Jew was hardly a Jew, but a "yahudi," a "deitshuk." His Reform Judaism was a sham as Judaism, little more than a superficial aping of Christianity meant to curry Christian favor. Not only the minority of unswervingly Orthodox among immigrants thought so, but also the much larger mass which failed to recognize anything but old-time Orthodoxy as real Judaism. Probably more damning than the Reform Judaism of the German Jews was the seeming absence among them of folk-feeling, that sense of mutuality, of common fate and kinship, so well developed among poor, oppressed Jews. The immigrants were acutely conscious of the native American Jews' social distance from them, and of their haughtiness and condescension. Even their vaunted charities were cold and impersonal, miscalled "scientific," vacant of sympathy and kindness. It grated them that Jews should hold aloof from other Jews. Among Jewish socialists, this feeling was expressed in the detestation of the Jewish uptowners as capitalist oppressors, although one has the impression that the immigrant Jewish socialists really disliked a much closer target—the climbers to fortune among their own Russian and Polish Jews.[26]

The native German-American Jews had perceptions of their own. The new immigrants were primitive and clannish, unwilling to take on American ways, insistent on maintaining "Asiatic" and "medieval" forms of religion and social life. "Culture" and "refinement" could not be found among them. They demanded charity as a matter of right without any appreciation for what they received. They were unduly aggressive and assertive, and embarrassed the painfully acquired good name of the American Jew. They had a disturbing penchant for unsound ways of thought, especially political radicalism, atheism, Zionism, and held to a form of speech

[26]Rischin, *op. cit.*, pp. 95–111; Harold M. Silver, "The Russian Jew Looks at Charity—A Study of the Attitudes of Russian Jewish Immigrants Toward Organized Jewish Charitable Agencies in the United States in 1890–1900," *Jewish Social Service Quarterly*, IV, 2 (December 1927), pp. 129–144; Arthur Gorenstein (Goren), "The Commissioner and the Community: A Study of the Beginnings of the New York City 'Kehillah'," *YAJSS*, XIII (1965), pp. 187–212.

which could not be called a language.[27] Only slowly did it come to be understood why they were coming en masse, and that pleas to stay home were fruitless. Well into the 1890's, Western—not only American—Jewry pleaded for Russian, Polish, Rumanian, Galician Jews to stay home and await the better times which would surely come in an age of inevitable human progress.[28] Benjamin F. Peixotto was nearly isolated. The few natives who welcomed immigration seem mostly to have been traditionalists who expected reinforcement of their small numbers by Jews arriving from the East European reservoir of religious piety.[29] For those who did come, the policy preferred by native Jews was to develop a class of respectable workingmen. Skilled manual trades in the city and farming on the countryside were to replace peddling and tailoring.[30] How remote this was from the explicit as well as the buried hopes of the immigrants may be seen from the widely known outlines of their social history during the last fifty years.

The real change in the native Jews' attitude occurred around 1903. The Kishinev pogrom of that year, in which high Czarist officials were notoriously implicated, followed by the Russo-Japanese War, the Revolution of 1905 and the pogrom-ridden counterrevolution, proved that the condition of Russian Jews would only deteriorate, not improve. Reluctant American Jewish sympathy replaced the earlier dislike as greater numbers of immigrants than ever poured into the United States during the decade before World War I.[31]

[27]Szajkowski, *op. cit.*, pp. 221–293; Irving A. Mandel, "The Attitude of the American Jewish Community toward East-European Immigration as Reflected in the Anglo-Jewish Press (1880–1890)," *American Jewish Archives*, III, 1 (June 1950), pp. 11–36; Heller, *op. cit.*, pp. 583–586; David Philipson, "Strangers to a Strange Land," *American Jewish Archives*, XVIII, 2 (November 1966), pp. 133–138 (excerpts from his diary); Selig Adler and Thomas E. Connolly, *From Ararat to Suburbia: The History of the Jewish Community of Buffalo* (Philadelphia, 1960), pp. 227–231.

[28]This theme is treated in Zosa Szajkowski, "Emigration to America or Reconstruction in Europe," *PAJHS*, XLII, 2 (December 1952), pp. 157–188.

[29]Davis, *op. cit.*, pp. 261–268.

[30]Herman Frank, "Jewish Farming in the United States," *The Jewish People: Past and Present*, 4 vols. (New York, 1948–1955), II, 68–77; Moses Klein, *Migdal Zophim* (Philadelphia, 1889).

[31]Higham, *op. cit.*, pp. 106–123; Zosa Szajkowski, "Paul Nathan, Lucien Wolf, Jacob H. Schiff and the Jewish Revolutionary Movement in Eastern Europe (1903–1917)," *Jewish Social Studies*, XXIX, 1 and 2 (January and April 1967), pp. 3–26, 75–91; Morton Rosenstock, *Louis Marshall, Defender of Jewish Rights* (Detroit, 1965), pp. 79–89.

This decade also marks the coming of Jews to the political and intellectual forefront among the defenders of free immigration. Of course, other immigrant groups also staunchly defended the right of their families and countrymen to come to America, but of the more recent immigrant stocks the Jews had the best established native element which would press the case effectively. Behind the political and communal leaders were a group of intellectuals both demonstrating and advocating the anthropological and intellectual equality of Jewish and all other newcomers—Israel Zangwill, Mary Antin, Israel Friedlander, Franz Boas, Horace M. Kallen, and others. Moreover, immigrants at the ballot box were now effectively enforcing the doctrines of human equality expounded by these intellectuals.[32] The most favored and seemingly innocuous aid to immigrants remained the dispensing of charity. The old-time charitable societies founded during the 1850's and 1860's–dozens of them named "Hebrew Relief Society" and "Hebrew Ladies Benevolent Society"—took on masses of new clients. How bread and coal and warm clothing developed around the 1920's into family budgets, mental health, and vocational guidance is a story vaguely but widely known in its barest outlines. Again, how the disparate relief societies, orphanges, homes for the aged, and the like united their fund raising and then began to spend and plan in unison, is another story of wide significance. These forward-looking "scientific" institutions were not at all the first resort of the distressed immigrant, who had his own "home town" societies, mutual aid groups, and "lodges" in the hundreds. The tendency to resent charitable patronage was one of the reasons which brought immigrants to found separate institutions. It was stressed that only in their own hospitals and orphanages and homes for the aged was kosher diet and an intimately Jewish atmosphere fostered. Yet it is revealing how "downtown" unconsciously flattered "uptown" by accepting the institutional network founded by the natives and attempting to rival it.[33]

The evolution of other, much more sophisticated institutions is

[32]Higham, *op. cit.*, pp. 123–130, 304–305; Arthur Gorenstein (Goren), "A Portrait of Ethnic Politics: The Socialists and the 1908 and 1910 Congressional Elections on the East Side," *PAJHS*, L, 3 (March 1961), pp. 202–238.

[33]A useful historical anthology is Robert Morris and Michael Freund, *Trends and Issues in Jewish Social Welfare in the United States 1899–1952* (Philadelphia, 1966); Swichkow and Gartner, *op.cit.*, pp, 53–54, 211–212, 215–234; Plaut, *op. cit.*, pp. 140–146; Gutstein, *op. cit.*, pp. 334–360.

instructive. The Educational Alliance was built on New York's Lower East Side in 1889. During its first years, no Yiddish or immigrant cultural expression was permitted within its walls, and the regime was one of an often artificially imposed English culture. By 1914, however, it had become a cultural and social center where young artists and musicians, as well as athletes, trained, where Yiddish was publicly used, and where even youthful Hebraists practiced the reviving language.[34]

The case of the Jewish Theological Seminary suggests still more subtle problems. Jewish natives worried over the young people who rejected the religion of their fathers in favor of radical social doctrines or militant atheism, or drifted into hedonism and seemed criminally inclined. It was virtually postulated that Jewish immigrants would not take to Reform Judaism (actually some of the younger ones became interested in Ethical Culture). In the eyes of native leaders, a traditional but modern form of Judaism for immigrant or immigrants' children was needed, and so the moribund Jewish Theological Seminary was refounded to train "American" rabbis at an institution of higher Jewish learning. A substantial building, considerable endowment, and an outstanding library and faculty were quickly brought together. Yet tensions were never absent between the eminent Solomon Schechter, head of the Seminary, who desired before anything else an institution of learning, and some of the board who seemed to want religiously inspired "Americanization."[35] A suggestive contrast is furnished by the immigrants' yeshiva on New York's East Side. With very meager resources, it was solely a full-time non-professional school for advanced Talmudic study by young men. Long controversy within Yeshivat Rabbenu Yizhak Elhanan preceded the introduction of very modest secular studies. But before 1920, however, the Yeshiva provided full secular secondary training within its own walls, and later established Yeshiva College. This was much to the displeasure of most native Jews, who considered general education under Jewish auspices "ghettoizing." On the other hand, the modernist Jewish scholarship fostered by Schechter at the Jewish Theological Seminary was religiously unacceptable to the Yeshiva's contempo-

[34]Rischin, *op. cit.*, pp. 101–103; *In the Time of Harvest: Essays in Honor of Abba Hillel Silver,* ed. Daniel Jeremy Silver (New York, 1963), p. 3.

[35]Norman Bentwich, *Solomon Schechter* (Philadelphia, 1938), pp. 187–197; *Louis Marshall: Champion of Liberty,* ed. Charles Reznikoff, 2 vols. (Philadelphia, 1956), II, pp. 859–894.

rary leaders. Secular study could be taken in and by some welcomed, but not the modernized, historical study of the sacred tradition.[36]

Immigrant Jews began to acquire uptown esteem. For one, they exhibited an intellectual élan and interest in ideas—especially unconventional ideas—which younger members of staid society found exhilarating. For some Jewish members of proper society the Jewish immigrants seemed to show a more authentic, passionate, somehow appealing way to be a Jew. A second source of esteem derived from the immigrants' greatest short-term achievement, the Jewish labor movement. After a full generation of unsuccessful fits and starts, the movement's surge of vitality and success attracted bourgeois liberals, and drew wide respect and attention. Native Jews repeatedly attempted to mediate strikes of Jewish workers against Jewish employers, on the grounds that they washed Jewish linen in public. The Jewish labor leaders, generally committed to revolutionary rhetoric, refused to regard the strikes as an internal Jewish quarrel but quite often accepted "uptown" mediators anyhow.[37]

World War I was an intense, even decisive experience for both the old and new Jewish stock. Immigrants or their sons wore military uniforms in large numbers, and Army egalitarianism and patriotic fervor proved a superlative "Americanizing" experience. Native Jews were more vigilant than ever in defending immigrants at a time of patriotic xenophobia, against the imputations of disloyalty to which they were vulnerable on account of revolutions and political complexities in their lands of origin and widespread Socialist anti-war sentiment among them. But during World War I also, native Jews became persuaded and in turn became advocates of causes once distasteful to them. Thus they took up the cudgels for Jewish national minority rights in Eastern Europe, toning it down to "group rights" as a more palatable term. The Jewish National Home promised in Great Britain's Balfour Declaration was the other cause. The relief poured out for European Jewry came

[36]*Ibid.*, II, pp. 888–894; Gilbert Klaperman, *The Story of Yeshiva University* (New York, 1968).

[37]Rischin, *op. cit.*, pp. 236–257; Louis Levine (Lorwin), *The Women's Garment Workers: A History of the International Ladies Garment Workers Union* (New York, 1924), pp. 360–381; Hyman Berman, "The Cloakmakers' Strike of 1910," *Essays in Jewish Life and Thought Presented in Honor of Salo Wittmayer Baron* (New York, 1959), pp. 63–94. The slowly rising interest in Yiddish literature may be seen through Morris Rosenfeld, *Briv*, ed. E. Lifschutz (Buenos Aires, 1955), pp. 34–105.

from "uptown" and "downtown," and was distributed mostly by the well-named American Jewish Joint Distribution Committee.[38]

The problems of the 1920's lie beyond the scope of this essay. By that time, the influence of the two segments upon each other was, or should have been, long evident. The old stock's staid conception and practice of Judaism was outmatched and altered by the newcomers' intellectual vigor in that and in other spheres. Indeed, two generations of native Jews, gradually joined en masse by acculturated and prospering immigrant families, focused practically the whole of their communal life and concerns upon the East European immigrant and his transformation. It was the older Jewish stock which long and effectively defended the Jewish newcomers, while chastising them not too privately, and above all helped to keep immigration virtually free before 1925.[39] For the East European immigrants, the example of their predecessors provided a model—for many *the* model—of the way to be an American and a Jew. Adaptation and change were extensive, but those who came first showed those who came later this most significant of lessons. The still sizable numbers of Jews who came after 1925, especially from Germany and Austria during the 1930's, and after 1945 as survivors of the European Jewish Holocaust, found a fully formed American Jewry. Their limited influence on American Jewish life, with the possible exception of its Orthodox religious sector, also shows that the formative years had ended.

[38]Oscar I. Janowsky, *The Jews and Minority Rights 1898–1919* (New York, 1933), pp. 161–190, 264–320; Rosenstock, *op. cit.*, pp. 98–127; Zosa Szajkowski, "Jewish Relief in Eastern Europe 1914–1917," Leo Baeck Institute *Yearbook*, X (1965), pp. 24–56; Naomi W. Cohen, "An American Jew at the Paris Peace Conference: Excerpts from the Diary of Oscar S. Straus," *Essays . . . Baron*, pp. 159–168; for a view of World War I on the local Jewish scene, see Swichkow and Gartner, *op. cit.*, pp. 268–285; see also E. Lifschutz, "The Pogroms in Polland of 1918–1919, the Morgenthau Committee and the American State Department" (Hebrew with English summaries), *Zion*, XXIII–XXIV, 1–2 and 3–4 (1958–1959), pp. 66–97, 194–211.

[39]Higham, *op. cit.*, pp. 264–330; Rosenstock, *op. cit.*, pp. 214–233.

IMMIGRATION AND EMIGRATION / THE JEWISH CASE

by C. BEZALEL SHERMAN

INTRODUCTION

JEWS are distinctive both in the character of their immigration to the United States as well as in the rate of their emigration from American soil. The reasons for this uniqueness lie first in the position occupied by Jews in European countries, and second in the position which Jews came to occupy in the United States.

In their native European countries the Jews generally constituted a group whose rights—if granted at all—were subject to challenge. And in those countries where rights were denied altogether, the Jewish quest for equality met with firm opposition from significant sectors of the population. Furthermore, whatever the legal status of the Jews it was clear that their position in society was controversial: the desire of acculturated Jews to participate in the life of the nation met with resistance. The consequence of these factors was that the impetus which Jews felt to leave their homelands was particularly strong; it did not depend entirely upon economic deprivation. This impetus did not center on single young men, as was the case with other groups; Jewish immigration to the United States (as well as to other "new" countries) included an exceptionally large percentage of women and children.

The push from the native country was complemented by the

pull exerted by America. It is true that Jews, like others, were attracted to the United States by economic opportunity. However, America offered Jews something more than opportunity: it offered unambiguous acceptance as a citizen. Such acceptance also meant that Jews were offered the opportunity to contribute to the national culture on an equal basis. All of this was in sharp contrast to medieval and much of modern Jewish experience.

The result of these welcome and radically new conditions is suggested by the statistics presented by C. Bezalel Sherman. He points out that in addition to its special composition, the Jewish immigrant group is unique in that it shows an extremely low rate of emigration from the United States. Whatever culture-shock or disappointments Jews suffered in the United States, they were not motivated to return to Europe. Jews did not leave the country during depression times, nor did they leave during times of prosperity, as was common among members of other groups who, after achieving some measure of economic security, often returned to their native soil to enjoy the fruits of their labor.

If neither depression nor prosperity loosened the attachment of Jews to America, political developments overseas failed as well. Jews had no desire to return to their European homelands in order to defend them against invasion or rid them of foreign domination. Thus the opportunity which emerged after World War I to participate in building the new national states found no response among Jews who had settled in the United States, although it did provoke such a response—and a substantial rate of emigration—among Gentiles. American Jewish immigrants might wax sentimental about life in the shtetl, but for them the United States was more of a homeland than were the countries which they and their ancestors had inhabited for centuries.

M. S.

IN A NUMBER of significant respects, Jewish immigration into the United States constituted a special situation, quite unlike the one created by all the other groups. A comparison of the number of immigrants who returned home, among the Jews and among the others, offers the first indication of this special situation. Others could, if they so chose, go back to their old countries; for Jews there was generally no way back.

Jews came to the United States to stay. When they left their old countries, they burned all their bridges behind them; and at every opportunity they brought their families with them. Not only did women and children constitute a higher proportion among Jewish immigrants than among others of the "new" immigration—which included . . . a large number of "birds of passage"; the percentage of women and children was also higher among Jews than among others even in the "old" immigration—which was generally a family immigration. "A comparison of the proportion of females and children in the 'old' and the 'new' immigration," writes Samuel Joseph, "with that in the Jewish shows that the Jewish immigration has proportionately almost twice as many females as the 'new' immigration (Jews excepted), and surpasses even the 'old' immigration in this regard. Of children under fourteen the Jewish movement has proportionately more than two and one-half times as many as the 'new' immigration (Jews excepted), and nearly twice as many as the 'old' immigration."[1]

Joseph's study covered immigration up to 1910. Statistics produced by Liebman Hersch show that the situation did not change after World War I. These figures are based, as is Joseph's study, on United States Government statistics (Table 1).

The figures show that the family nature of the immigrants grew substantially in the second quarter of the present century, demonstrating that after World War I the immigration was a permanent one among all groups. The birds-of-passage type virtually disappeared. The tiny role which this type played in Jewish

[1]Samuel Joseph, *Jewish Immigration to the United States from 1881 to 1910* (New York, 1914), p. 132.

TABLE 1

Number of immigrants of a given age among Jews and in general in each 100 immigrants[2]

	Under 14		14–44		45 and older	
Year	General	Jews	General	Jews	General	Jews
1921–24	18.5	29.6	72.3	57.7	9.1	12.7
1925–27	16.0	22.7	74.6	54.1	9.3	23.2
1935–36	19.4	18.0	64.5	65.3	16.2	16.7

TABLE 2

General and Jewish re-emigration for each 100 immigrants[3]

Year	General	Jews
1908–14	30.8	7.1
1915–20	56.6	4.3
1921–24	25.8	0.7
1925–37	40.0	3.8
1908–37	34.6	5.0

immigration can be seen in the above table, in which Hersch registered the extent of re-emigration from the United States (Table 2).

From 1908 to 1937, general reverse migration from the United States was never less than one-quarter of the immigration; among Jews, it was never greater than seven percent. Between 1915 and 1920, reverse migration, under the impact of World War I (during which great numbers of immigrants returned to help their old homelands win the fight), amounted to more than one-half of the

[2]Liebman Hersch, "Jewish Emigration in the Past Hundred Years," *General Encyclopedia* (2nd ed., New York, 1941), I, pp. 465–66. Totals in original text not 100 percent. ("Yidishe emigratsye far di letste hundert yor," *Algemayne Entsiklopedye,* Yidn, Alef.)

[3]*Ibid.*, I, p. 464.

immigration; Jewish reverse migration during this period amounted to only slightly more than four percent. The Jews felt far more obligated to the United States during the war than to their old countries. During the period 1925–37, which included the Depression years in the United States, the general reverse migration was over two-fifths of the immigration. Nowhere else could Jews hope to find better economic conditions; their reverse migration was barely four percent.

As for the "old" immigration, Joseph's figures show that for every 100 immigrants, there were one and one-half times as many returnees among other immigrant groups than among the Jews. His assertion that "the Jewish immigration must thus be accorded the place of distinction in American immigration for permanence of settlement"[4] was correct in 1914, when he made it, and it remains true to this day.

[4]Joseph, *op. cit.*, p. 137.

FROM PAST TO PAST / JEWISH EAST EUROPE TO JEWISH EAST SIDE

by LUCY S. DAWIDOWICZ

INTRODUCTION

EARLIER GENERATIONS of Jewish intellectuals viewed the shtetl*—the East European Jewish town from which many Jewish immigrants to the United States derived—as permeated with such backwardness and superstition that the best thing that could happen to a Jew would be to leave. As suggested in the Introduction, in our own day attitudes have come full circle; the* shtetl *is frequently seen as an attractive—even charming—place, whose virtue resided in the utter integrity and simplicity of its life.*

Lucy S. Dawidowicz, a keen scholar of East European Jewish life, here analyzes the character of life in the Jews' area of first settlement in the United States—the Lower East Side of New York. She demonstrates how the immigrant's shtetl *culture was subjected to severe attack, and how the freedoms which the Jew encountered when he arrived on American soil were responsible for stimulating cultural discontinuity and social change. Having occupied inferior status for so many centuries, the Jew came to hold American freedoms in greater esteem than did others, and these freedoms consequently had a stronger effect upon his communal life; within a single generation the age-old authority of the rabbinate was almost totally subverted.*

In moving toward rapid cultural change, and thus toward

secularization, the immigrants created a problem which was destined to come to fruition at a later time: the problem of Jewish identity. But the immigrant also created a cultural style (its paradigm was the Yiddish theater) and a political style (embodied in the Jewish radicalism of the Lower East Side) that were sufficiently powerful to defer the impact of the identity crisis until the second generation. Dawidowicz's main theme is the vitality of Jewish immigrant culture—a vitality born of sudden exposure to freedoms long denied. There arose among Jewish immigrants an overwhelming desire to take advantage of the freedom to vote, the freedom to express an opinion, the freedom to pursue economic advancement. But, as Dawidowicz suggests, each freedom had its dark side. Education meant further alienation from shtetl *culture and hence an increase in cultural discontinuity; economic opportunity meant the pursuit of mobility to the exclusion of other values. And there was the further fact that the stratification system of the* shtetl *could not be transplanted to American soil. As a consequence, leadership in the American Jewish community was conferred upon individuals who were not strongly committed to traditional values. Furthermore, such individuals lacked experience in exercising authority.*

Yet despite the impact of the new freedoms, the individual Jew did manage to retain a measure of cultural continuity, and the group too succeeded in cohering to an extent. What forces were responsible for this? Some would trace the cause to the vitality of Jewish family life; others believe that it resides more in the character of Jewish culture itself—especially its stress on communalism and on shared responsibility for the general welfare. But whether family bonds or communal traditions, it is clear that however difficult the trauma of the passage from Jewish East Europe to the Jewish East Side, social disorganization remained at minimum levels. To be sure, the culture which the immigrant created did not survive intact; removal to the second area of settlement brought with it further changes. And Jewish life in present-day suburbia seems to have little in common with that of the Jewish East Side. However, if we look beneath the surface we see that even today the culture of the Jewish East Side has not been obliterated: to understand contemporary Jewish voting behavior, religious life, organizational forms, and a host of other aspects of American Jewish life we still must go back to the culture which developed in the Jewish East Sides of the nation.

M.S.

THE JEWISH EAST SIDE was, at the start, Jewish Eastern Europe transplanted. But America added one new element, a catalyst that transformed Old World Jews into New World ones, into American Jews. Its effect was unpredictable—sometimes it produced gold, sometimes trash. It created fantastic new possibilities for Jews, but it also undermined traditional modes and values. It created and destroyed. That element was freedom—freedom to build and freedom to destroy.

For the Jews who came from despotic Czarist Russia, from the autocratic Hapsburg empire, and from the brutally oppressive kingdom of Rumania, the freedom they found in America—in that one square mile on the East Side that was their America—overwhelmed them. That freedom liberated them from the tyrannies of the past. To this Jacob Zvi Sobel, a Hebrew-Yiddish poet, testified in 1877:

Now here am I already in this free land,
Where equal rights exist . . .
Where there are no slaves,
No barons, no counts. [1]

But America was also a land of freedom abused, which swept many immigrants from their moorings and loosened their restraints from interior authority. Thus Isaac Rabinovich, another Hebrew-Yiddish poet from Lithuania, who came to New York in 1893, wrote back home:

> The Jews become much more demoralized here than any other immigrants. The spirit of freedom, which they inhale on their arrival in this new country is changed into a destructive spirit. And Jeshurun waxed fat—and trampled on everything holy, on all sacred traditions.

The Jews who came to America and settled on the East Side

[1]This and the following quotation are taken from Shlomo Noble, "Dos bild fun dem amerikaner yid in der hebreyisher un yidisher literatur in amerike (1870–1900)," *Yivo-bleter*, XXXVIII (1954), pp. 50–77.

were hungry for freedom, for political liberty, and for basic human rights: the right to live (and live in safety), to work, to study, to vote. These rights and liberties they pursued intensely in that crowded, overcrowded square mile on the East Side.

Most highly they valued political freedom—the right to vote, to determine their political fate. That Jews today are the most compulsive voters in the nation is their East Side heritage and that, in turn, is the consequence of earlier political deprivations in Eastern Europe. The East Side Jews registered and voted in greater proportion than any other immigrant group, except perhaps the Irish, and they treated the franchise with greater seriousness than any other group, especially the Irish. At the turn of the century, it was observed that "neither pleasure nor business exigency" prevented Jews from voting, nor did the Jewish voter succumb to "the curious inventions of the Bacchanalians" on election day: ". . . the Russian Jew does not drink anything stronger than tea before he votes and after he has voted he goes about his business without celebrating or rioting."[2] In the main, immigrant Jews voted the Jewish interest and that interest they associated, more often than not, with the Democratic Party, the party of immigration.

But the East Side inherited also another political tradition from Eastern Europe—the politics of revolution. Czarist oppression and Christian anti-Semitism had bred a Jewish brand of political radicalism, a socialist worldview of a universal people and of a cosmopolitan society from which no one would be excluded and in which no one would be despised because of his religion or nationality. This millenarian hope fostered, in Jewish Eastern Europe as on the Jewish East Side, a profound and passionate idealism, but it also encouraged a radical brand of Jewish self-hate and a precipitous flight from Jewish identity, alienation from the Jewish community, and ignorance about one's own roots and origins. That political outlook, too, still persists.

As important to Jews as political freedom was the freedom to live and make a living. In Pobedonostev's long-range tripartite "solution" to the "Jewish problem," one-third of the Jews of Russia were destined to die of hunger. As for Galicia, it was too impoverished and industrially too backward to permit its Jews more than bare subsistence. But America was *di goldene medine* [the

[2]Emanuel Hertz, "Politics: New York," in Charles S. Bernheimer, *The Russian Jew in the United States* (Philadelphia, 1915), pp. 264–265.

golden country] and the streets of New York were paved with gold. Jews were free to work at whatever they wished to work at. The seriousness which Jews applied to politics matched the seriousness which they applied to making a living. Unrestricted from working here or there, in this trade or another, East Side Jews devoted themselves to making money where they could. The freedom to make money became an obsession. To be sure, it was [for a purpose]—money to bring up the children, to spare them the misery of the sweatshop, to provide for the future, to make life better and easier in time to come. But this desire to make a living, to accumulate money, to be secure, became—with some—an end in itself. Their family life was neglected, community was disregarded, tradition abandoned. Jacob Riis, no particular friend of the Jews, yet not an anti-Semite, put it this way:

> Thrift is the watchword of Jewtown. It is at once its strength and its fatal weakness, its cardinal virtue and its foul disgrace. Become an overmastering passion with these people who come here in droves from Eastern Europe to escape persecution, from which freedom could be bought only with gold, it has enslaved them in bondage worse than that from which they flee.

In Eastern Europe, in contrast, successful businessmen seldom managed to evade their familial responsibilities and communal duties. Conforming to older traditions and patterns, they were motivated by a sense of *noblesse oblige*. A rich man gave not only money but time to communal affairs—even if he was vulgar and greedy; for only that way could he win position, prestige, honor. But on the early East Side, none of these counted.

Freedom to get an education, to go to school, was high on the list of rights which the Russian Jews pursued as avidly, energetically, and singlemindedly as making a living. In Eastern Europe the quest for general education accompanied the gradual breakdown of traditional society. Among the upwardly mobile Jewish middle classes, the big-businessmen, merchants and entrepreneurs, contractors, holders of vast land leases, government concessionaires, doctors and lawyers, education was the key to economic success. These people regarded general secular education as a necessity, not a heresy. But at the other end of the East European Jewish social scale, among the Jewish working-class radicals, rebels against Judaism, the quest for education, not revolution, was the real heresy. Julius Martov, who was to become a leader in the Russian Social Democratic Party, discovered this early in his career when he tried to organize Jewish workers in Vilna: "The idea of employing the class struggle to transform the uncultured environment itself . . . was still alien to them. They considered self-education . . . the alpha and omega of the socialist movement."

In America, lavish with its freedom to learn, the Jews' quest for education and self-education became intensified and magnified. The public schools were wide open and hospitable. There was no need to bribe government officials to enroll in high school, and no need to convert to Christianity to be admitted to a university. "The public schools are filled with little Jews," wrote Hutchins Hapgood. "The night schools of the east side are practically used by no other race. City College, New York University, and Columbia University are graduating Russian Jews in numbers rapidly increasing." City College, where the enrollment in those days was about 75 percent Jewish, used to be derisively called "Jews College." The fact that Jews are today as well educated as the high-status old-stock Episcopalians whose ancestors came on the *Mayflower* is owed to these forebears, most of whom came steerage in the ships that plied between Bremen, Hamburg, Rotterdam, Antwerp, and New York.

In addition to these freedoms, America also offered freedom of expression—freedom of speech, press, assembly, thought. Having escaped the stifling Czarist censorship, immigrant Russian Jews rushed to exploit their freedom to write, to talk, to congregate. Between 1885 and 1900 nearly one hundred Yiddish papers were founded in America, and in New York alone there were nearly twenty Yiddish dailies between 1885 and 1917. "The Yiddish newspaper's freedom of expression," a Jewish editor remarked, "is limited by the Penal Code alone." The Yiddish press had a violent and extremist tone, whether politically conservative and Orthodox or radical and antireligious. The irresponsible tone, with slashing accusations directed against government, capital, Jewish institutions, or competing papers, was due partly to the license spawned by American freedom, and partly to the lessons learned from the yellow journalism that William Randolph Hearst was then cultivating.

This untrammeled freedom of expression hatched and multiplied writers, journalists, pamphleteers, poets, speakers, orators, actors, Yiddish King Lears. The period before World War I witnessed an explosion of freedom rather than of talent. Morris

Rosenfeld and Jacob Gordin are the great literary monuments of that era, but upon closer examination they appear like Hollywood foam-rubber boulders, an illusion created by distance and accepted as real because of condescending and indulgent literary standards. The Yiddish theater and Yiddish poets like Rosenfeld fascinated outsiders who were captivated by the energy and intelligence of the Jewish immigrants. No doubt they felt much like Samuel Johnson about a woman preaching—not that it was done well, but surprised that it was done at all, like a dog walking on its hind legs.

Fifty years ago David Pinski, who was to liberate the Yiddish drama and stage from its tawdriness and sensationalism, inveighed against it: "The Yiddish theater has come to denote tomfoolery, clownishness, and degeneracy—the caricature of Jewish life."[3] As for that early East Side Yiddish literature, the best that can be said of it is that it testified to the powerful persistence of folk poetry among the Yiddish-speaking folk. After World War I, Yiddish writing in America emancipated itself from the Rosenfeld-Vinchevsky-Edelshtat primitivism of form and message; the sentimentality and lugubriousness of the earlier era were wrung out. From melodramatic *shund* and/or radical doggerel, Yiddish writing was transmuted into literature.

The freedom of immigrant life spawned more pernicious products than second-rate verse and third-rate theatricals. It produced social demoralization. The Jewish immigration was largely a youthful immigration, of young people—teenagers they would be called today—and men and women in their early twenties, many single and without parents, with perhaps only an older brother or sister *in loco parentis*. They were free—free from parental supervision, from religious obligation, from communal authority. Among some this freedom generated crime and corruption, prostitution and vice, bohemianism and free love. Communal anarchy and the inability of the existing Jewish organizations to cope with these social diseases became shamefully public in 1908 when New York's Commissioner of Police Theodore A. Bingham charged that half the criminals in New York were Jews, though Jews were only a quarter of the population. Four days later the first steps were taken toward creating the Jewish Community,

[3]David Pinski, "The Yiddish Theatre," in *The Jewish Communal Register of New York City, 1917–1918* (New York, 1918), p. 576.

the Kehillah of New York City.[4] It was an attempt to create authority, discipline, and self-control among people intoxicated by freedom—especially religious freedom. By religious freedom, I mean Yom Kippur balls, for instance. In tyrannical Russia, where Jews had been persecuted for being Jewish and rewarded for turning Christian, no Jews held, or attended, Yom Kippur balls.

If Commissioner Bingham's charge was the direct cause of the Kehillah's founding, the lack of religious authority was one of its basic and underlying causes. In his second annual report to the Kehillah in 1911, Judah Magnes stressed that "the problem of religious organization is largely the problem of restoring to the rabbis their authority in matters affecting Judaism as a religion."

Among the immigrants who settled on the East Side, many (how many we do not know—perhaps half, or even more) had been bitten by the bug of modernity. They knew little or no philosophy, nothing of Aristotle or Philo, of Maimonides' proofs of God's existence, but they knew that religion was the opium of the people. They knew that back in the Old Country the keepers of Judaism had been unmoved by the upheavals in the world, which indeed had made them even more repressive and inflexible. Cutting one's earlocks, wearing a coat shorter than the prescribed traditional style, reading "modern" books—these had been the greatest heresies. Consequently in America, where in those days rabbis were few and unheeded, the immigrants seized their religious freedom. Observant East European Jews knew that while America was a *goldene medine,* it was also an "impure" country. After all the Slutsker rabbi had publicly declared that anyone who emigrated to America was a sinner.[5]

To be sure, the fault was not entirely with the immigrants, and the willingness with which they let themselves be seduced by America's freedom to live and work and become educated. The fault was also, here as there, with the rabbis who mistook custom for divine law; who, withdrawing from the real world, sheltered themselves in Talmudic study. They resisted even the introduction of English into the services (perhaps sermonic words of exhortation might have helped—who knows?) and they made no effort to reach

[4]See Arthur Gorenstein, "The Commissioner and the Community: The Beginnings of the New York City 'Kehillah' (1908–1909)," in *Yivo Annual of Jewish Social Science,* XIII (1965), pp. 187–212.

[5]Moshe Davis, *The Emergence of Conservative Judaism: The Historical School in 19th Century America* (Philadelphia, 1963), p. 318.

out among the young to halt the drift into indifference, immorality, or crime. Yet, looking back, we see the rabbis themselves were not to blame. They came here, late in life, finished products of another culture, often baffled by the complexities and inconsistencies in American society. Here is one poignant example: When the Association of American Orthodox Hebrew Congregations began looking for a Chief Rabbi, one of their most promising candidates asked whether the position would be recognized by the *government* as an official permanent position.[6] How could they have understood America?

Here, too, as in Eastern Europe, the rabbis resisted change in the traditional forms of Jewish education, but not quite as adamantly. After all, here the alternative was simple: Jewish children could do without Jewish education and in fact most did. Less than one-forth of the Jewish children in New York before World War I had any Jewish education. In Eastern Europe Rabbi Isaac Jacob Reines was the first to combine rabbinic and secular studies in his yeshiva at Lida. That was as late as 1905. In America the change came sooner, under the pressure of the religious Left. Just as the Reform movement affected the Conservative movement, so the Conservative movement affected Orthodoxy. The Yeshiva Etz Chaim in 1886 and then the Rabbi Isaac Elchanan Theological Seminary—later to merge and become Yeshiva University—paired secular studies with Jewish studies.

The Conservative movement, Marshall Sklare has written, was the product of the second-settlement area. Its equivalent in the first-settlement area—the East Side—was the Young Israel Movement. Young Israel founders were the children of pious and inflexible hasidim, who would not let their clean-shaven, English-speaking sons conduct services or receive [a religious honor]. For these young men, East Side radicalism and secularism were as obnoxious as apostasy. They, too, seized their religious freedom and made an accommodation to America. They shaved their beards and dressed modernly, and to differentiate themselves further from their parents they prayed in *nusach Ashkenaz,* listened to English sermons, and behaved decorously in synagogue.[7]

[6]Abraham J. Karp, "New York Chooses a Chief Rabbi," *Publication of the American Jewish Historical Society,* XLIV (1954–1955), pp. 129–198.

[7]*Young Israel Synagogue Reporter,* 50th Anniversary Issue, March 3, 1962; David Stein, "East Side Chronicle," *Jewish Life* (January–February 1966), pp. 26–39; interview with Rabbi Ephraim H. Sturm, National Council of Young Israel, May 1967.

For decades the East Side lived off the emotional capital of revolutionary Europe. Heine had once observed that "liberty is a new religion, the religion of our age." The Jews of the East Side took a long time to learn that the religion of liberty often turned into idolatry, that the radicalism and atheism which were expected to liberate the human spirit instead suppressed and obliterated it. After the abortive revolution of 1905 a new kind of immigrant started coming to America and gradually began to change (read: improve) the quality of immigrant life. After World War I, that qualitative change became quantitative as well. Maturity, stability, responsibility—personal, familial, communal—came back into style.

AMERICA IS DIFFERENT

by BEN HALPERN

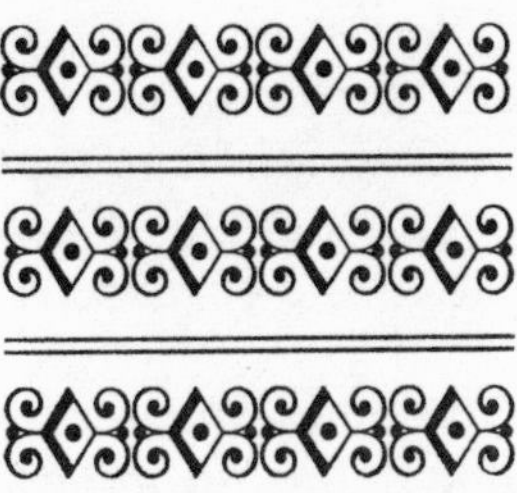

INTRODUCTION

JEWISH IMMIGRANTS knew that America was different from their communities of origin, but it was not immediately apparent why this was so. Ben Halpern's analysis supplies the answer. The fact that American Jewry was formed in the post-Emancipation era, means there was no need for a European-style national debate over whether Jews should be emancipated. Furthermore, the absence of this kind of debate ensured that American anti-Semitism would necessarily have a special character. While European anti-Semitism in the modern period was an integral part of an ideology dedicated to the restoration of a previous era in national history, American anti-Semitism was free of such beliefs.

The post-Emancipation character of American Jewry has affected not only the national ethos in respect to Jews but the internal aspects of American-Jewish life as well. Inasmuch as their own emancipation had never really been questioned, American Jews never felt the need to develop a serious ideological response to the phenomenon of anti-Semitism. European Zionism not only took anti-Semitism seriously, it propounded a specifically Jewish response to the malady; the Zionism which developed on American soil, by contrast, regarded anti-Semitism as more of a Gentile problem than a Jewish one. Similarly, because of their historical situation, American Jews have been uniquely free to determine how extensively they wish to participate in the larger society. Thus "assimilationism" in the United States differs from its European counterpart both in extent and in character. According to Halpern, while the larger society assumes that American ethnic groups will ultimately disappear, it brings only minimal pressure upon them to assimilate. They are free to remain in their ethnic enclaves if they wish to do so.

The value of Halpern's perspectives becomes apparent when the American reaction to Jewish participation in the life of the larger society is contrasted with the European reaction. As Halpern points out, in Europe nationalistic elements viewed such participation " . . . as an illegitimate intrusion, or even [as] a plot by the enemies of the people to corrupt its national spirit." However, in the United States participation in the life of the larger society has generally been welcomed. Such participation is viewed as a tacit acknowledgment of the cultural authority of the dominant group, encouraging evidence of a healthy desire to leave the ethnic enclave in favor of participation in the cultural mainstream. It is not viewed as an illegitimate intrusion or as a corruption of the national spirit.

M. S.

JEWS IN AMERICA at their three-hundred-year mark have their own very strong reasons to underscore the theme that "America is different," and when they orchestrate this music, it is to a counterpoint of peculiarly Jewish *motifs*. America is different —because no Hitler calamity is going to happen here. America is different—because it has no long-established majority ethnic culture, but is still evolving a composite culture to which Jews, too, are privileged to make their characteristic contributions. America is different—it is not Exile, and whatever may be the case with other Jewries, the open doors of the State of Israel do not beckon. With such a rich choice of harmonies, is it any wonder that the tercentenary celebrations [in 1954] of the American Jews swelled to a powerful chorus, elaborately enunciating the single theme, "America is different!"

It seems, however, that the crucial respect in which American Jewry is different was missed altogether in the tercentenary celebrations. That is not surprising, because if this difference were stressed it could have made the whole occasion seem artificial and contrived. American Jewry *is* different from other Jewries. It is younger than any other significant Jewry—with the exception of the State of Israel. In terms of *real,* effective history it is far from being three hundred years old. There is good sense in Croce's contention that only the history of free, rational, creative effort is real history, and that the chronicle of events in which man is passive is a different kind of thing altogether. At any rate, if American Jewry has a truly distinct and individual character, giving it a destiny different from that of other Jewries, there is only one way it can have acquired it: only by freely, rationally, and creatively grappling with the specific problems of its existence, and then handing down its distinctive working hypotheses for elaboration by succeeding generations. American Jewry has had nothing like three hundred years of this sort of history. If there are any native American Jewish institutions that were initiated before the Eastern European immigration of the 1880's, then most of these, too, are creations of the middle nineteenth century. The earliest idea evolved and perpetuated to this day in American Jewry can be nothing younger than the Reform movement, which goes back in this country to 1824. The characteristic American Jewish type today is a second- or third-generation American.

This is, then, one of the youngest of Jewries, one of the youngest even of the surviving Jewries. Its real history begins *after* the "solution" in America of the most critical problem that faced other Jewries in modern times—the problem of the Emancipation of the Jews. This was the problem that other Jewries had to grapple with when they entered the modern world, and the various solutions that they freely, rationally, and creatively evolved for it gave them each their individual character. French Jewry dealt with the issues and problems of Emancipation differently from German Jewry, German Jewry differently from Austro-Hungarian or from Russian Jewry; but all of them had to deal with the problem, and there was a continuity and connection among the solutions they found. What is characteristic of American Jewry, and what makes it different from all of these together, is that it began its real history as a post-Emancipation Jewry. Emancipation was never an issue among American Jews: they never argued the problems it presented in America, nor did they ever develop rival ideologies about it and build their institutions with reference to them.

Because of this, the continuity of European-Jewish ideologies is broken in America. American Jews never had ardent groups of partisans who saw in Emancipation the whole solution of the Jewish problem. In Europe the Zionist movement arose in opposition to this thesis, and proposed "Auto-Emancipation" instead of "Emancipation" as the solution. The theory of "Diaspora nationalism"—the advocacy of minority rights as an answer to the Jewish problem—likewise opposed to the Emancipation principle of individual enfranchisement the view that the Jews must be granted autonomy as a group, as an ethnic entity. All these theories existed in America only as pale copies of the European originals.

There is in America a small group who vociferously defend Emancipation, the American Council for Judaism. The pointlessness of their propaganda is obvious to anyone who asks himself who among the American Jews is opposed to Emancipation. There is no such group or person, for no one proposes to undo what has been the accepted basis of life here since *before* American Jews made any effort to shape their history. Nor does the American Council defend Emancipation as a *solution* for the Jewish problem. Their view would be more accurately expressed by a classic statement of Abraham Cahan's, who declared in 1890:

> We have no Jewish question in America. The only question we recognize is the question of how to prevent the emergence of "Jewish questions" here.[1]

As for the opponents of this view, they, too, do not think in terms of a Jewish question which America has been vainly seeking to solve by the emancipation of the Jews, and for which alternative solutions other than Emancipation must be sought. We are only beginning to see what the Jewish question actually is in America.

Anti-Semitism and Assimilation

From a Jewish point of view, two elements are inseparable from any discussion of the Jewish problem: anti-Semitism and assimilation. For to a Jew the problem essentially is this: how can the Jewish people survive in the face of hostility which threatens to destroy it, and, on the other hand, in the face of a friendliness which threatens to dissolve group ties and submerge Jews, as a whole, by absorbing them individually? Both phases of the Jewish problem are different in America than in Europe, and in both cases the reason is the same: in most countries of modern Europe the questions of anti-Semitism and the Emancipation and assimilation of the Jews were essentially connected with revolutionary crises in their national affairs, while no such connection existed in American history.

All we need do is consider what the Emancipation of the Negroes meant in American political and social history in order to measure the difference between a status that was never really contested, like that of the Jews, and one that it took a civil war to establish. Thus, when we think of anti-Semitism in such countries as France and Germany, Russia and Poland, we must remember that the great revolutions and revolutionary movements in those

[1]Cited in C. Bezalel Sherman's article, "Nationalism, Secularism, and Religion in the Jewish Labor Movement," *Judaism*, Fall 1954 (Tercentenary Issue), p. 355. The statement occurs in a manifesto issued by "Abraham Cahan, Organizer," on behalf of the Hebrew Federation of Labor of the United States and Canada, which was published in *Die Arbeiter Zeitung* (New York), 5 December 1890, two months after the Federation's founding convention. The full text is reproduced in E. Tcherikower's *Geshikhte fun der Yidisher arbeter-bavegung in die Fareynikte Shtatn* (New York, 1945), Vol. II, pp. 499–502.

countries, at critical moments in their national history, placed the emancipation of the Jews upon their agenda for basic reform. Whatever has become part of the program of a national revolution not only divides the people at the first shock, but continues to divide them in the cycles of counterrevolution that always attend such upheavals in a nation's life. Hence, as Jewish Emancipation was an issue raised by the Revolution, so anti-Semitism had a natural place in the programs of European counterrevolutionary parties.

How different it was in America is quite clear. If the American Jews never had to divide ideologically over the issue of Emancipation, one of the reasons is that Emancipation of the Jews never became a revolutionary issue dividing the American people generally. For that matter in the history of America, the Revolution itself did not become a real (rather than academic) issue permanently dividing the people, since it was a revolution against outsiders—and the Loyalists remained in emigration. In England, on the other hand, the Cromwellian revolution was a crux in British history which still serves to determine opposed political attitudes. But at the time of that Glorious Rebellion there were practically no Jews in England. Consequently, at a later time, after the Jews had begun to arrive, the question of their Emancipation was debated in England (just as in America) in a relatively unimpassioned, desultory way. Whatever minor political struggles took place in spelling out the equal rights of the Jews had no inherent connection with, or essential place in, the major upheavals recorded in the national history. To be an anti-Semite in England, as in America, had no obvious, symbolic affinity with a counterrevolutionary ideology opposing the Glorious Rebellion or the American Revolution.

If one examines the American anti-Semitic movements, one cannot fail to appreciate how different they are from their European counterparts. Only in England do we find so anemic, so insignificant an anti-Semitic movement, a movement so unmistakably belonging to the "lunatic fringe."

The anti-Semitic movements of France and Germany, Poland and Russia may also have been fit subjects for psychopathological investigation; but no one will deny that they occupied a place in the forefront of the political affairs of their countries, and moved in (whether with or against) the mainstream of their national history. Far from being "fringe" phenomena, they had political power, or a reasonable chance to attain it. What we have in America in comparison is nothing but an aimless hate-mongering. The kind of anti-Semitism common in America is, and always has been, endemic throughout the Diaspora. It may be found in every social condition and in every political persuasion, from extreme right to extreme left. It is an anti-Semitism of impulse: the most characteristic thing about it is that it is not really organized on the basis of a clearly enunciated program providing what ought to be done about the Jews if the anti-Semites had their way.[2] This is

[2]When American anti-Semites avail themselves of election periods in order to conduct their propaganda, they do, of course, formulate "programs." The provisions relating to Jews in these documents are usually more vituperative than programmatic in character, and they combine obvious, though rather feeble, imitations of European models with some specific American features, reflecting animosity against American Jewish organizations. I owe the following typical examples to the courtesy of Jack Baker of the Anti-Defamation League. "The New Emancipation Proclamation—The Silver Shirt Program" appeared in Pelley's Silver Shirt Weekly of 5 September 1934. It proposed "racial quotas on the political and economic structure" in order to prevent Jewish office-holding "in excess of the ratio of (Jews) . . . in the body politic." All Jews, and all foreign-born persons not "completely naturalized," were to be registered, under severe penalties for evasion. All Jews were to be compelled to "forswear forever . . . Jewish allegiance," and any Jew apprehended in giving support to Jewish nationalism was to be criminally prosecuted for sedition. (Quoted in Gustavus Myers, *History of Bigotry in the United States* [New York, 1943], pp. 405–406).

The 1948 election platform of Gerald L. K. Smith's Christian Nationalist Party called for "the immediate deportation of all supporters of the political Zionist movement" and the outlawry of "this international machine and all its activity." Such "Jewish Gestapo organizations" as "the so-called Anti-Defamation League, the American Jewish Congress, the so-called Non-Sectarian Anti-Nazi League, the self-styled Friends of Democracy" were to be dissolved. Immigration of "Asiatics, including Jews, and members of the colored races" was to be stopped. The partition of Palestine was opposed. The party program published by Smith in 1952, however, had no such specific references to Jews.

The nine point "Program of the National Renaissance Party" (published in the National Renaissance *Bulletin*, October 1953, pp. 3 and 4) proposed, under point 1, to "repudiate the operetta-State of Israel"; in point 2, "to enforce a strict policy of racial segregation in America"; and in point 3 "to bring about a gradual deportation of unassimilable elements . . ." *viz.*, the "Puerto Ricans, Negroes, Jews and Asiatics"; in point 4, to bar Jews "from all political and professional posts" and to forbid marriage between Jews and "members of the dominant White Race"; and in point 6, to base American foreign policy upon a "German-American alliance in Europe; a Moslem-American alliance in the Middle East; and a Japanese-American alliance in Asia" (reproduced in the U.S. House of Representatives, Committee on Un-American Activities, *Preliminary Report on Neo-Fascist and Hate Groups*, Washington, 17 December 1954, pp. 21–22).

See also Richard Hofstadter's comment on the tendency of the political attitudes of the "new American right" to express themselves "more in vindictiveness, in sour memories, in the search for scapegoats, than in realistic proposals for action" ("The Pseudo-Conservative Revolt" in *The New American Right*, Daniel Bell, ed. [New York, 1955], p. 44, and note similar observations in other sources referred to by Hofstadter (*Ibid.*, p. 54, note 7).

something quite different from an anti-Semitism that was primarily political in vision. Modern European anti-Semitism was characterized from the beginning by large and active political aims, and it included, among other far-reaching social revisions proposed in its counterrevolutionary program, precise provisions for making the Jews second-class citizens, expelling them, or exterminating them. In comparison with these movements, American anti-Semitism (and, for the most part, British) has never reached the level of an historic, politically effective movement. It has remained, so to speak, a merely sociological or "cultural" phenomenon.

The question of assimilation also looks different in America, because the Jews never had an established status here other than that of so-called Emancipation: there never were enough Jews here before the nineteenth century to warrant a special, institutionally established status. In Europe, on the other hand, Emancipation came as an effort to alter a hoary, time-honored status in which Jewish communities lived long before the Revolution.

The Emancipation seemed to promise the Jews that the difference between them and the Gentiles would be reduced to the private realm of religion. All public relations with the Gentiles would be carried on in the neutral area of citizenship, where Jews were guaranteed equality. Jews assumed that the public realm was identical with the whole social realm of intercourse between them and the Gentiles, and that in all other than purely Jewish religious affairs they would have full and free contact and equal status with Christians. This they soon found to be a delusion, for in all countries they discovered that Jewishness was a barrier and a disability in a wide range of social relations and that citizenship opened far fewer doors than they had imagined.

In most European countries the areas closed to Jews had been elaborated by centuries of custom and usage. When one had explored the precise extent of new freedoms opened to the Jews by the new status of citizenship, the barred contacts remained clearly and decisively, in fact often quite formally, defined. The army, the higher government service, the magistracy, and the universities were all careers closed to Jews which, by quite explicit understanding, became open immediately upon baptism.

In all of Europe, Jews soon found that even after Emancipation actual relations in society continued to be governed by a series of restrictions taken from the religiously grounded stratifications of the *ancien régime*. To protests that all this was contrary to the new doctrine of citizenship, purporting to open all careers to talent and all doors of social intercourse to individual merit, an answer was soon provided: a still newer doctrine, the doctrine of romantic, organic nationalism, superseded the principle of citizenship. The national idea gave a new justification and pumped new life into practices which had theretofore survived as stubborn relics of feudalism and now all at once became grafted onto the modern idea of democracy. Fixed social positions, traditional folkways and culture, inheritance of privileges and obligations—all that had once been grounded in the divine will—now gained an organic sanction in the national history. The Jews found their assimilation even more rigidly opposed than under the purely religious criterion. If inheritance (that is, ethnic origin) became the key to admission into society and the license for participation in culture, then even the formal step of conversion was of no avail to the Jew.

In the beginning of the present century the actual social conditions that faced the Jew seeking to be part of his European nationality represented a shifting balance between divergent tendencies. One tendency was that of the Revolution, whose principle was to treat the Jew as an individual no different from all the rest. Actual social relations conformed to this principle only to the extent that the Revolution itself, or other forces, had succeeded in atomizing society. The Industrial Revolution and the development of trade allowed Jews to find new opportunities in business and thereby brought them into a new relation of equality with Gentiles. The Revolution succeeded in imposing its own principles in all political relationships except the bureaucracy. But the Jews could not simply move into these new positions unaltered. The grant of equality imposed its conditions and demanded its price. The "clannish" solidarity of the Jews had to be given up so that they could enter the body of citizens as individuals. They could keep their religion as a private cult, but not necessarily the kind of religion that was traditional among them. Jewish tradition was too organic in its own way, it incorporated too much historic distinctiveness and ethnic character, for the rigid individualism of radical revolutionary doctrine. Not that anyone expected to see the full consequences of egalitarian theory rigorously applied to Gentile society. But the revolutionary ardor to liberate the Jews had roots of its own in the anti-Semitism that is endemic in all Gentile society and expresses itself in all its divisions. The Jews might not get all they expected out of Emancipation, but the Emancipators were disposed to watch with a jealous eye how the Jews went about paying its price.[3]

The nobility, the army, the universities, all the corporate embodiments of privilege bearing upon them the stamp of consecration and tradition escaped the leveling influence of Revolution. As Jews rose in society through other channels they found their ultimate elevation blocked at these points. Some fought their way through to these positions as Jews, but most found that access to their goal, otherwise blocked, became magically open through a relatively simple and (in most cases) quite perfunctory operation. So they acquired new "convictions" and became baptized.[4] To the other Jews, this renegadism, as they regarded it, was their first great shocking disillusionment with the Emancipation, the first disclosure of the human degradation which is the price of assimilation.

The most serious strain upon Jewish-Gentile relations was the rise of counterrevolutionary anti-Semitism, which absorbed into an ethnic pattern the basic attitudes to the Jews implied in their old feudal, religiously determined status. Conservative anti-Semitism in an officially liberal society had contented itself with excluding Jews from those areas of corporate traditionalism which the Revolution had not succeeded in atomizing. But now nationalistic counterrevolution, seeking to turn the clock back, opposed the penetration Jews had already made into areas opened up by liberalism. Economic boycotts of the Jews were resorted to in order to bring industry and commerce "back" into the hands of the Germans or the Poles, or whatever the ethnic majority might be.

Particularly did the nationalists resent the great participation of Jews in all cultural activities. The organic doctrine of nationalism sought to overcome a cleavage between culture and tradition that had existed in Europe since the Renaissance. Modern culture had become a secular realm parallel to the traditional beliefs, art forms,

[3]See Graetz's narrative of the "Synhedrion" in Paris and the events leading up to it, *History of the Jews* (Jewish Publication Society translation, Philadelphia, 1895), Vol. V, pp. 474–509.

[4]The quip of the famous Orientalist Chwolsohn—that he was converted out of conviction, the conviction that it was better to be a professor in Petersburg than a tutor in Shnipishok—is only one of a long line of cynical anecdotes (going back at least as far as Heine), which illustrate the psychology of many such conversions.

ceremonials, and etiquette still grounded in religion. The social framework of culture, the *Gelehrtenrepublik,* as the eighteenth-century Germans called it, was a liberal, international, individualistic, and secular intercourse among free spirits, which, even before the Revolution, existed side by side with the corporate social structures where the religious, feudal tradition was fostered. The Revolution was the signal that gave the Jews entrée into this world. It was a liberty that they eagerly embraced, shut out as they were on other sides from assimilation and its rewards. But it was a main object of counterrevolutionary nationalism to bring all culture back into an organic coherence based on the national tradition, even if both the religious and the secular were adulterated as a result. This meant imposing upon all forms of creative expression the same corporate principles and ethnic criteria that regulated participation in the religiously grounded forms. The participation of Jews in any cultural form was henceforth regarded as an illegitimate intrusion, or even a plot by the enemies of the people to corrupt its national spirit.

Thus there were forces in European society determinedly striving to undo even the amount of assimilation Jews had achieved. They were opposed not only to the integration of the Jew into such social relations as were governed by liberal principles but also to the admission of the Jewish convert into social relations still governed by corporate, religiously grounded criteria.

How different was the situation here in America! Here the bare conditions of geography and social statistics made liberalism the dominant principle of social organization. It was not so much revolution against an old regime that opened the door to assimilation for the Jews; it was the large extent of sheer formlessness in American society which allowed Jews and many other heterogeneous groups to live side by side, with the forms of their readjustment to each other to be determined.

Free entry into American society, of course, had its price and also its restrictions, just as did the assimilation of the European Jews after Emancipation. The price of the freedom to let the ultimate forms of mutual relationship between immigrant Jews (like all immigrants) and the whole American community remain for the future to determine was the willingness of the immigrant to give up old inherited forms. Just as settled America was willing, within limits, to be elastic, so it demanded of immigrants wishing to be naturalized that they first of all be elastic and accommodating. Not that there was any haste about the scrapping of outworn Old World customs. America was large enough to set aside "ghettos" in its cities or even whole regions in its broad lands where immigrants could live undisturbed more or less as they had been accustomed to live in the Old Country. But this was a provisional form of living, in effect outside the real America, which everyone expected to be superseded as the forms of true American living were worked out by immigrant and native Americans in a continuing process of give and take.

The willingness to relinquish Old World habits was the *price* of assimilation in America. Its *limits* were defined by the established prerogatives of the older settlers. It is true that the ultimate forms of American life remained—as they still remain—in principle undetermined, and our assumption is that the cultural contributions of all America's components are equally welcome. Yet it is both implicitly and explicitly assumed that those who came here first are entitled to preserve and impose such forms of living as they have already made part of the American way. America is not only in essence free and democratic; it is also, in its established pattern, Anglo-Saxon, religiously multi-denominational, and dominated by the mentality of white, Protestant, middle-class, native Americans. However, this social dominance and cultural predominance are maintained not by delimiting any areas of social life under traditional, religiously grounded, and formally elaborated codes of exclusion which reserve them for particular families or religions, as in Europe. American history has not been long enough for that, perhaps, and in any case it has from the start consecrated the principles of complete social mobility, denying in theory all exclusions. But the claims and privileges of the older settlers are maintained by informal, almost tacit social covenants, which only rarely (as in anti-immigration laws) need to be openly voiced.

Thus if liberal principles fail to be actually observed in America, just as in Europe, and if assimilation stops short at the barriers set up to protect inherited privilege, there is at least this difference: in Europe, the initial status is the historical, quasi-feudal status, and liberalism rules only those areas which it specifically conquers; in America, the initial status is that of freedom, and only experience proves what areas privilege has successfully reserved for itself. Those in America who nurse a nostalgia for historically rooted social status have not been able to swim in the midcurrent of an American counterrevolutionary movement. The American Revolution is the very beginning of real American history, and there is no one who more proudly flaunts it as his symbol than the American conservative. The self-conscious American opponent of the liberal revolution has no real alternative but to become an expatriate.

The result has been that while the history of American Jewish assimilation, too, has been full of disappointment and unanticipated checks, it has run a characteristically different course from the European experience. At the very outset of the European Emancipation, Jews were brusquely confronted with the price they must pay: for freedom of the individual, virtual dissolution of the group. The immigrant to these shores, too, found that the prize of Americanization was to be won at a price: by unreserved elasticity in discarding everything which America might find foreign. In both cases, only religion was reserved as a sanctuary of Jewish tradition. But there were these differences: in Europe, there was a fixed pattern that Jews were expected to adopt in discarding their own customs; in America, the ultimate American way of life was still in principle to be determined, taking into account what of their own immigrants might succeed in "selling" to the whole public. Besides, the demands of the European Emancipation upon the Jews were peremptory, they had to be conceded at once, and even through a formal declaration such as Napoleon extracted from the French Jews. In America, there was no urgency about the procedure. The Jews, like other immigrants, could make their way into the real American community as swiftly or as slowly as they themselves chose. They could, if they preferred, remain in their ghetto seclusion indefinitely.

In Europe, then, the stick; in America, the carrot. A parallel difference existed when the Jews came up against the unexpected barriers to assimilation, the reserved areas not governed by liberal principles. In Europe, the principle of exclusion was clear-cut, traditional—and quite simply overcome, if you wished, by conversion. There was no such clear choice in America. Established privileges were no less alien to this country than an established church. It was neither the accepted practice to demand conversion for specific social promotions, nor to grant them upon conversion. Thus, if American Jews went over to Christianity, it was no such concerted wave as arose in Germany, in the first eagerness to overleap the unexpected sectarian barrier to full assimilation. It was rather a final seal, in individual cases, upon an assimilation otherwise complete.

The Patterns of Modern Jewish Thought

It is clear, then, that the typical situation faced by the American Jew was not the same as that characteristic of the European Continent. The differences apply to both major aspects of the Jewish problem, to anti-Semitism and to assimilation. But modern Zionism, and indeed all modern Jewish ideologies, arose when Jews began to confront, to take account of, and to understand—or try to "reach an understanding" with—the typical situation of Continental Europe. The characteristic American Jewish situation had hardly even begun to be faced—until the establishment of the Jewish State abruptly forced the issue. It need not be surprising, then, if at precisely this time we witness a feverish effort to create a new American Zionism and new American Jewish ideologies generally; nor that these forced-draught efforts should in the beginning often bring more confusion than enlightenment.

What was the historical situation of Continental Jewry in the late nineteenth century, when the modern Jewish ideologies arose? As we have seen, it was characteristically a period of post-revolutionary or, if we may say so, neo-traditionalist nationalism, a period with a living memory of an *ancien régime*, a revolutionary movement, and a wave of post- or even counterrevolutionary reactions. Moreover, the Jewish problem was intimately involved with every phase of that living tradition.

The spirit of that time was critical of the Enlightenment and the Revolution, of rationalism, capitalism, and social relationships based on the undifferentiated equality of citizenship. For the modern European, the Jew became a symbolic embodiment of all these discredited traits. The out-and-out anti-Semites (but not only they) regarded the Jew as the head and fount of everything they despised in the liberal revolution—its rationalism, capitalism, and principle of civic equality. Similarly, of course, the eighteenth-century rebels against the *ancien régime* had seen in the ghetto a symbol of the medievalism they were determined to uproot. And just as the Revolution had proposed the assimilation of the Jews in all respects except as a reformed religious sect, so, by a reversal of history, the critics of the Revolution wanted to solve their Jewish problem by halting or annulling the assimilation that had already taken place and eliminating Jews and Jewish influence from the new order they hoped to set up.

What made one a modern Jew in the late eighteenth century was to understand and accept the attitude of Gentile contemporaries to social problems, and to the Jewish problem among them. The modern Jews of that time accepted the demands of the Enlightenment to change their habits and customs—those relics of medievalism—in order to enter a new enfranchised status; on the other hand, they could not understand or accept the exclusions still practiced against them after they had paid this entry fee. But the modern Jew of the late nineteenth century "understood" fundamentally, however much it may have pained him, why it was that he was not assimilated into full fellowship in his country. He shared with the modern Gentile the feeling that European society had not yet become what it should be, or that it had even gone quite astray from its true path. Thus, integration into society on the basis of the liberal principles of the Revolution no longer seemed to be the solution of his Jewish problem. In fact, the degree to which that integration had already taken place, in culture, in economic pursuits, and even in political participation, began to constitute for him, as for the Gentile, the very crux of the Jewish problem, the false position in which both danger and self-denial dwelled. He, like the Gentile, began to see or foresee other solutions of the Jewish problem as part of a new revolution of the whole structure of European society, in the course of which Jews would either disappear entirely as an entity or regroup in a new segregation from the Gentiles. "Modern" Jews hoped either for a radical revision of the liberal revolution, leading to Socialism and the disappearance of Judaism together with all other religions, or for a new nationalist era in which Jews would live as a distinct national entity, in the places where they then lived or in a new national territory. In other words, either total assimilation in a new, millennial secular society, without the eighteenth-century reservation of freedom to maintain a reformed Jewish religious community, or the total rejection of assimilation and an attempt to establish a new Jewish ethnic independence, in the several countries of Europe or in a new territory to be colonized by Jews.

The rejection of assimilation was a doctrine shared by Zionists with other ethnic autonomists. The failure of Emancipation, from this point of view, demonstrated that there had been a breach of faith by the Gentile Emancipators and an historical error on the part of the Jews; for after the latter had practically reformed themselves out of existence as an historic group, Gentile society had failed to keep its part of the bargain by assimilating the Jews individually. Zionism, however, viewed not only eighteenth-century Gentile liberalism with a disenchanted eye. It also had its reservations concerning those Gentile movements which, like itself, were critical of existing society and hoped to reconstruct it. In this respect, Zionism differed sharply from other modern Jewish movements. Jewish Marxism, regarding the Jewish problem as an expression of capitalism that would disappear in the classless society, implied faith that one's Gentile fellow-Socialists would not break their covenant as had the Gentile liberals. The advocates of national autonomy for minorities in Europe similarly trusted that Gentiles would abide by the covenants that were to embody this principle. Zionism had no faith in the willingness of the Gentiles to extend a welcome to Jews, under any definition, as free and equal brethren in the same land. It was a disillusionment built upon the experience that it was possible for revolutionists to regard Jewish blood spilled in pogroms as merely "grease on the wheels of the revolution."[5]

Zionism took anti-Semitism seriously and expected it to persist. This is the specific way in which it differed from other modern Jewish ideologies. The Socialists, who expected to submerge the Jews in a classless, cosmopolitan society, the Diaspora nationalists, who planned for minority rights—none could hope to succeed unless anti-Semitism vanished. The Zionist (and territorialist) solution of the Jewish problem, contemplating the removal of the Jews from Europe, remained intrinsically possible even if one were pessimistic or prudent enough to reckon with the persistence of anti-Semitism among the Gentiles.

Zionism, like other modern Jewish ideologies, felt it understood the critics of European liberalism (among them, the anti-Semites)

[5]David Shub (in *The Jewish Daily Forward*, New York, 15 May 1955) says that this sentiment was attributed by Zionists to the Jewish Socialist leader Vladimir Medem (1879–1923), and was always denied by Medem and his associates. Whatever the origin of the quotation, which I have not been able to check further, it became a popular byword succinctly expressing an attitude of which Russian and Polish Jews had had several striking evidences among revolutionaries.

A pamphlet inciting to pogroms was issued by the revolutionary *Narodnaya Volya* group, and though it was withdrawn subsequently, there was a continuing discussion of the advisability of using anti-Semitism to foster a revolutionary atmosphere. The shock effect of this event on the Russian Jewish intelligentsia is described in Abraham Liessin's "Episodes," in the Yiddish Scientific Institute's *Historishe Shriften*, Vol. III (Vilna-Paris, 1939), pp. 196–200. It was from this same time that we date the reaction of a significant group of Russian Jewish intellectuals against the ideal of Emancipation and the rise of the counter-ideal of auto-Emancipation.

and their disapproval of the liberal solution of the Jewish problem. Accepting, as they did, the organic, ethnic views of history and nationality, they felt it was a betrayal both of the Gentile and the Jewish national destiny for Jews to make themselves the protagonists of Gentile culture, for example, instead of fostering their own. Moreover, they appreciated that if it were the aim of a group to use all sources of power in a given territory for the preservation and propagation of its distinct national values, its traditional style of life and culture, its own ethnic variant of Christian culture, then it was bound to be resented when political and economic power came into the hands of Jews. Such an attitude left only one possibility for a compact between Jews and Gentiles that the two distinct groups could loyally uphold: those Jews who could not or would not assimilate must have a country of their own where they would be separate and independent.

Two things are characteristic of American Jewish ideologies. The first is that American Jews never faced directly the whole historic complex of problems, centering around Emancipation as a traumatic event, from which modern Jewish ideologies arose. The second is that only in our own time, actually in the years since World War II, has American Jewry been compelled to face its own peculiar situation and to create its own history. One could conclude, then, that American Jewish ideological development may still not really have begun.

Whatever truth there may be in such a conclusion, it need not mean that there have been no differences of opinion, no debates until now. That is obviously untrue, for whatever ideology existed in Europe has had its adherents, few or many, here. Thus American Zionism, for example, arose by understanding and sharing in the typical attitudes, problems, and situation of Zionism in Europe—especially in the degree that American Zionists continued to live the life of the Old Country in America.

Now it was quite generally characteristic not only of American Zionism, or of American Jewry, or even of all immigrants, but of America itself to share and understand the life and thoughts, the trends of modern culture and politics in the Old World. Those newcomers who lived in the immigrant ghettos (at least, the cultural elite among them) shared the life of the Old World most directly and most specifically. Those older settlers (again, the cultural elite among them) who were establishing the permanent forms of American life also continued to live in the current of European political and cultural development, though with greater detachment and in a more general form. It was a more international European culture, and not so specifically a particular national culture, in which they shared. As for the culture arising in America itself, the specific "culture" native to the immigrant ghettos was based not only on an obviously transitory experience but also on an experience of suffering rather than of creation; "permanent" American culture remained intrinsically open and partially unformed, constituting, in a way, a set of defensible hypotheses rather than a body of axioms and absolute values.

It is important to note that only in our own time has the characteristic American Jewish type come to be the native-born American Jew. American Zionism, product of an earlier generation, was to a large extent a movement of the American immigrant ghetto.[6] Thus, intellectually, it shared in and understood the Zionism of the nineteenth-century "modern" European Jew, just as the other immigrant ghettos shared in and understood the social and intellectual movements of the Old Country they came from. The immigrant intellectuals who dominated American Zionism had a more direct and more specific understanding of the situation, problems, and attitudes of the modern European Jew than is possible for the native American Jew. Yet even for them European Zionism was a *vicarious* experience.

It was natural, therefore, that even for the immigrants, new American experiences—the experience of the American immigrant ghetto, and the unfolding experience of the new American society in formation—began to color their Zionism. This tendency was heightened by the influence of native American leaders who were active in American Zionism from the very beginning. The nuances by which American Zionism was touched through its naturalization

[6]See, however, Judd L. Teller's article, "America's Two Zionist Traditions," in *Commentary*, October 1955, pp. 343–352. This article emphasizes the existence of a pre-Herzlian Zionist "tradition" in America, represented by Mordecai Emanuel Noah and Emma Lazarus. It also highlights the difference in attitude between some native-born (or American-educated) early Zionists, like Louis D. Brandeis and Julian W. Mack, and the Eastern European outlook of immigrant Zionism. In common with many writers during the recent Tercentenary celebrations of American Jewry, Teller strains the data perceptibly in an effort to make episodes add up to a native American Jewish tradition; but the differences he emphasizes between the Zionism of the immigrant ghetto and the Zionism of "uptown" Jews is a significant one, in view of the similarity of the latter to the neo-Zionist mood of today. . . .

in America have now, in a time when American Jewry is largely native-born and remains as the major surviving Diaspora, become the dominant coloration of a new American Zionism.

The two major divisions of the Jewish problem, assimilation and anti-Semitism, look different against an American environment. The theory of assimilation as a solution of the Jewish problem was a revolt against an old-established historic status of the Jews in Europe, into which they had sunk vast creative energies. The "ghetto" in Europe was not only an oppression the Jews suffered but a way of life they clung to. And when the reaction against assimilationism came in European Jewry, it paralleled, in a way, the post-revolutionary movements among the Gentiles: it saw itself as the synthetic conclusion of a Hegelian dialectical process. The Emancipation had been an antithesis of an original thesis, the ghetto; and Zionism (like other modern Jewish movements), in transcending the Emancipation, intended to absorb what was valuable not only in the liberal revolution but in the primary status—the ghetto—which assimilationism had rejected.

"Assimilationism" in America was a rejection of life in the immigrant ghetto. But life in the tenements had never been filled with any creative significance, no historic values had been placed upon it and institutionalized through it, it contained no unfulfilled promises, no high demands spontaneously arising from its own context to give historic dimensions to its past and historic perspectives to its future. The immigrant ghetto from the beginning was entered into only to be abandoned. For the Jewish immigrants it represented either the collapse and bereavement of the old values of the true, historic, European ghetto—or, if they had already emancipated themselves from the historic Jewish values, it was a "melting pot," a grimy anteroom to the real America, a sordid extension of Ellis Island.

The generation that entered the immigrant ghetto was confronted by one overwhelming task: to get out, or enable the next generation to get out. This task they accomplished. But the generation that accomplished it had, in a way, stepped out of the frame of history, for history consists in whatever continues over a span of successive generations. The immigrant ghetto was not a continuation of the context of European-Jewish life, whether ghetto or emancipated; it was an interruption of that continuity, a break with that context. Nor did it, nor was it ever intended to, continue into the life of the next generation. It was a specific experience outside the frame of history and hence outside the frame of culture, at least insofar as culture is essentially historic.

There was nonetheless a very active cultural life and a vivid sense of history in the Jewish immigrant ghetto. That generation, in fact, reached an unsurpassed peak of historical awareness as Jews. And, concomitantly, it led a life of high cultural intensity. But the historical movements and cultural trends in which American Jews participated were European-Jewish history and European-Jewish culture, relevant to the situations and problems and expressing the values of European Jewry. The social reality of American Jewry was the one-generation experience of the immigrant ghetto, known from its very inception to be out of the frame of history and culture. Of course, American Jewry could never accept a merely vicarious participation in history and a merely nostalgic participation in culture, however intense these might be. The immigrant generation felt itself to be as much (if not more) a new beginning as a final chapter in the historic and cultural continuity of the Jews. They looked to the day when the threads of vicarious history and cultural nostalgia would weave into a new American pattern of continuity. But every American Jew, whatever his ideological sympathy—religious or secular, Zionist or non-Zionist, "survivalist" or "assimilationist"—knew beyond any question that the new hoped-for continuity that would transmit the American Jewish experience into history and culture must necessarily begin beyond the threshold of the immigrant ghetto.

If, then, "assimilationism" means radically to reject the "institutions" of the ghetto—in America, of the *immigrant* ghetto—then every American Jew, whatever his ideology, is an "assimilationist." And, in fact, the actual process of "assimilation" in the United States *is* the absorption of immigrants out of the immigrant ghettos. This is a movement in social relationships which it is common ground for every American Jew to accept. When "assimilation" served as an issue dividing American Jews it was not the actual process of assimilation out of the immigrant ghetto into the real American society about which they were debating; their argument was about assimilation as it occurred in Europe.

The differences of opinion native to the American Jewish experience are only now beginning to be defined. They arise after assimilation out of the immigrant ghetto has not only been tacitly accepted in principle but carried out in practice. Assimilation can only become an issue, in terms of the actual experience dividing the

American Jews, after the liquidation of the immigrant ghetto. At that point, when he is an "integrated" member of American society, the American Jew—now typically native-born—discovers that he still has a problem of assimilation. The problem is a totally new one, it presents the first challenge whose creative mastery might establish a continuous American Jewish historic tradition. If we may speak in terms of the Hegelian dialectic at all in America, then we are only at the point of establishing a thesis, not, as in Europe, capping an historic antithesis with its synthetic resolution.

In view of this fact it should not be surprising if American Jews are unwilling to begin their history with the disillusioned conclusion that they can come to no satisfactory terms with the Gentiles for the creative survival of the Jewish people in America. Nor should it be surprising that in looking backward for its supports in history, no portion of American Jewry seeks to recapture any values institutionalized and expressed in the characteristic experience of the immigrant ghetto. Nor, finally, should it be surprising—however little gratifying we may find it—that the first attempts to set up American Jewish ideologies are based on a rather empty, almost defiant optimism about Jewish survival in the Diaspora and a somewhat boastful confidence in the values Diaspora Jews will yet produce.

The question of anti-Semitism also looks different when viewed from an American perspective. In the past, to be sure, American Zionists and anti-Zionists have divided ideologically in their reactions to anti-Semitism almost entirely in relation to the nationalistic anti-Semitic movement of Europe. The anti-Zionist view was that, even if the Jewish status of Emancipation liberalism was inadequate, Jewish ideology must have as its premise the full confidence that anti-Semitism must and will disappear in a new Gentile society. The Zionist premise was that modern nationalistic anti-Semitism would not disappear, and that where it had once appeared Jewish life would increasingly become intolerable.

But the characteristic fact about America was that modern nationalistic anti-Semitism had not really appeared here. Moreover, the usual historic grounds for its appearance were lacking. The Jews in America did not come out of a medieval ghetto through an act of emancipation, to find that, as a bourgeois people, they aroused nationalistic anti-Semitism. They filtered out of an immigrant ghetto not as a people but individually. They encountered anti-Semitism in America, but it was not based on a nationalistic reaction, rejecting the emancipation of the Jews. The native American anti-Semitism encountered here was the old perennial anti-Semitism in which Herzl discriminated the elements of "cruel sport, of common commercial rivalry, of inherited prejudice, or religious intolerance." This was a kind of anti-Semitism which neither Zionism nor any other modern Jewish movement could or would understand. It was the type of anti-Semitism with which only the medieval ghetto had provided a certain established basis of understanding.

It is true, on the other hand—and very significant—that European anti-Semitism was able to extend its influence across the Atlantic and demonstrate, on numerous critical occasions, that the fate and destiny of American Jewry were intimately connected with the fate and destiny of European Jewry. But at other times, the global threat to the Jews having subsided, the American Jews who busied themselves with the matter were faced with the problem of their own, specifically American anti-Semitism.

This problem never really became an ideological issue between Zionists and non-Zionists in America any more than did the problem of American assimilation. At most there was a difference in the degree of concern about native anti-Semitism between Zionists and non-Zionists, a sort of temperamental difference rooted quite remotely in differences of ideas. The Zionist attitude, at bottom, assumes anti-Semitism to be ineradicable. With nationalistic secularist anti-Semitism, Zionism once hoped for an understanding through divorce. But where anti-Semitism remains theological, demanding perpetuation of the Jewish Exile until the Second Advent and the subjugation of Jews to Christians in the meantime, Zionism has no understanding to propose. Thus the characteristic attitude of American Zionism to this problem—that is to say, to native American anti-Semitism—is not to take it too seriously, to feel that it is essentially a Gentile, not a Jewish, problem. On the other hand, it is characteristic of non-Zionism to take precisely this problem seriously. Non-Zionists are inclined to turn a blind eye to the seriousness of nationalistic anti-Semitism such as we saw in Europe, rejecting the notion that Jews should attempt any "understanding" with Gentiles through emigration. The basis for this attitude is an underlying belief that anti-Semitism is not really a "modern" movement, with more vitality and contemporaneity than the Emancipation of the Jews, but only a medieval survival that should expire with the inevitable increase of rationality. Among the "missions" which non-Zionism has proposed for the Jewish Diaspora, one taken up with great earnestness in every country, and in America as well, is to cure the Gentiles of their vestigial anti-Semitism and so to consummate fully the Jewish Emancipation. But whether this is at all conceivable, assuming that Jews remain a distinct entity in the Diaspora, is a problem the non-Zionist ideologists still have to face.

The crucial difference which has been brought about in the Jewish problem in the past generation is not only the rise of the State of Israel, but perhaps even more the destruction of European Jewry. This is a factor whose significance is likely to be overlooked because it is a negative factor —and one, of course, which it is anything but pleasant to remember. Without European Jewry, the face of the Jewish problem as it appears to American Jews is radically altered, and in a way simplified. Hitherto, views on the Jewish problem, in its two aspects of assimilation and anti-Semitism, were based on European traditions and, no less, upon involvement with the European-Jewish situation. But now American Jews live in a Jewish world where, essentially, they see only two main constitutents: themselves—American Jewry—and the State of Israel. In Israel, the Jewish problem of assimilation and anti-Semitism does not exist, or only in the most indirect and transmuted forms. It continues to exist in America. But the problems of assimilation and anti-Semitism must now be approached in the forms native to America, without the overtones of significance previously lent them by their involvement with the developments in Europe. That simplifies the situation considerably.

We cannot say as confidently that it clarifies it as well. The nature of the Jewish problem characteristic of America has not yet been considered with the degree of rigor and incisiveness that were typical of European-Jewish ideologies. That was natural so long as the American situation was regarded as an atypical and not too significant variant of the Jewish problem. It now becomes the major exemplification of that problem in our times. That fact requires, as it is beginning to produce, a new focus in the direction of Jewish thought.

SOCIAL CHARACTERISTICS OF AMERICAN JEWS

AMERICAN JEWRY, 1970
A DEMOGRAPHIC PROFILE
by SIDNEY GOLDSTEIN

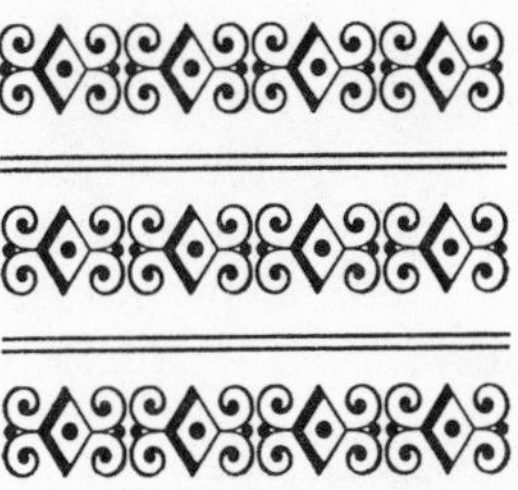

INTRODUCTION

*SIDNEY GOLDSTEIN'S analysis of demographic trends among American Jews highlights the uniqueness of the Jewish demographic situation. It also demonstrates how this uniqueness has affected group identification, how this uniqueness is in the process of diminishing, and how recent demographic changes may affect Jewish identity as well as the viability of the Jewish community. Goldstein's historical portrait of the Jewish community emphasizes that the Jewish group has been concentrated in a very few urban communities, that within these communities Jews have settled in strongly ethnic neighborhoods, that Jews have followed a restricted number of occupations (especially those in which success depends on the individual's initiative and merit), and that Jews have been strongly motivated to achieve a high level of secular education.**

*Goldstein's analysis constitutes the most recent summary of research in the field. It should be noted that data from the National Jewish Population Study, conducted under the auspices of the Council of Jewish Federations and Welfare Funds, are not included in his article. While several reports (designated as "working papers") of the NJPS became available late in 1972, further analysis is required before NJPS data can be incorporated into the existing body of knowledge. The working papers present percentages only; no numerical values are given. They also lack information on the extent to which the sampling design was realized, as well as an explanation of weighting procedures.

Goldstein highlights the emergence of factors which are operating to modify these older patterns. One such set of factors has to do with changes originating in the general community—changes which will result in a general demographic profile more closely approximating that of the Jewish community. Thus, the trend toward urbanization results in a reduction of Jewish-Gentile differentials in place of residence. Another example, the nationwide trend toward increasing the number of years which the individual spends in the classroom, similarly will result in a reduction of Jewish-Gentile differentials.

A second set of factors is the obverse of the first—namely, changes in the Jewish community which result in a Jewish demographic profile closely approximating that of the general community. These changes include the movement of Jews to new geographical areas, as well as the relocation of Jews to cities located within the same geographical area. In this connection the recent trend in the Jewish community toward suburbanization is significant, for it is a shift which further works to reduce Jewish-Gentile differentials. Of equal significance are occupational changes, especially the movement among Jews away from proprietorship and toward employment as salaried professionals or managers.

Goldstein's interest in Jewish-Gentile convergence—whether originating from the direction of the general or the Jewish community—is motivated both by scientific considerations and by a concern with the implications of demography for group identity and survival; this concern explains Goldstein's focus on the distinctiveness of the Jewish demographic profile as well as on trends working toward its reduction. In the course of his analysis Goldstein emphasizes little-recognized factors which may have significant implications for group cohesion, for example the role of migration as a weakening factor (Goldstein believes it to be of equal or even greater importance than intermarriage) and the ironic role played by secular education. The effect of traditional Jewish culture on the individual was what made possible the achievement of an extraordinarily high level of secular learning, and the result has been that although many Jews are no more than second- or third-generation Americans, the educational profile of the Jewish group resembles that of the most favored Protestant denominations of the old immigration.

Currently, the educational achievement of Jews is being

subjected to challenge; the task of lifting the educational level of significant segments of the population has raised the possibility of restrictions on the opportunities of a small and "overachieving" group like the Jews, and of a consequent slowdown in the rate of Jewish advance on the educational front. But however this question may eventually be resolved, the current situation is one of an extraordinarily high educational profile among American Jews, and this in turn has had important implications for group identity and cohesion. Thus, higher education may have the effect of reducing family solidarity, and reduced family solidarity may produce a weakened group identity. Higher education may also have the effect of raising the rate of intermarriage. Furthermore, it may mean the pursuit of occupations which lack continuity with historic Jewish experience, especially those which involve the individual in a kind of quasi community drawn from a wide variety of religious and ethnic groups. Ironically, then, the individual may become alienated from the same Jewish community whose culture initially impelled him to pursue educational attainment.

M. S.

BASIC TO AN EVALUATION of the current status and future prospects of the Jewish community in the United States is an analysis of the group's demographic structure: its size, distribution, and composition, and factors affecting its future growth and character. The demographic structure of the American Jewish population, like that of the United States population as a whole, has been undergoing steady change under the impact of industrialization and urbanization. An evaluation of the Jewish community therefore requires an assessment of changes which are a function of the total American experience, as well as those which may be unique to the Jews. At the same time, the changing demographic structure also calls for continuous further adjustment in the behavior of individual members of the Jewish community and in the structure of the community as a whole. Thus, the socio-demographic structure is both a product and a cause of change in Jewish life in the United States. . . .

In the most recent definitive work of the world's Jewish population, Professor U. O. Schmelz of the Hebrew University points out that "the task of drawing even a rough outline of the present demographic situation of world Jewry is greatly complicated by vast lacunae in our knowledge."[1] This is especially true in the United States. Because of the high premium placed on separation of church and state, a question on religion has never appeared in a decennial U.S. census, nor, with the exception of the marriage records of two states, does it appear in any vital registration records.[2] In the general absence of official and comprehensive information on religion, social scientists concerned with research in which religious differentials are a key focus have had to rely largely on specialized sample surveys to obtain their data. But in most instances, because these surveys focus on the total population, the

[1]U.O. Schmelz and P. Glickson, *Jewish Population Studies, 1961–1968* (Jerusalem: Hebrew University, Institute of Contemporary Jewry, 1970), p. 13.

[2]Conrad Taeuber, "The Census and a Question on Religion" (paper presented at a conference sponsored by the National Community Relations Advisory Council, the Synagogue Council of America, and the Council of Jewish Federations and Welfare Funds, New York: 23 October 1967).

sample seldom includes more than several hundred Jews, and often considerably less, thereby making comprehensive analyses of the Jewish subgroup difficult, if not impossible. For needed information, Jewish groups have therefore had to collect their own data on the size, distribution, composition, and vital processes of the Jewish population.

Since 1955, more than 20 Jewish communities have undertaken surveys. Yet, because most of the communities have been of moderate size, legitimate questions have been raised about their typicality in relation to the Jewish population of the United States as a whole, and, in particular, about their representativeness of Jewish communities in such large metropolitan centers as New York, Chicago, and Philadelphia. Both to satisfy the need for national data and to insure coverage of large communities, the National Jewish Population Survey (NJPS) is currently in the process of collecting data that will permit the first comprehensive assessment of the Jewish demographic situation in the United States. Until the results of this study are complete, however, insights must rely heavily on the information provided by the individual community surveys and by the limited number of national surveys focusing on demographic characteristics by religion.

For an understanding of the dynamics of change characterizing the Jews in the United States, a brief outline of the demographic and socio-historical setting is essential.[3] Two interrelated factors set into motion the social forces which have determined the pattern of Jewish life in the United States. First, from 1880 to the mid-1920's, the size of the Jewish population increased rapidly, from less than a quarter of a million to an estimated 4.2 million. This phenomenal growth converted the Jewish population in America from an insignificant minority, too small to establish anything more complex than localized Jewish communal life, to a substantial and vibrant national American subsociety. At the beginning of the 1970's the American Jewish community, numbering about 6 million, constitutes the largest concentration of Jews in the world, more than two-and-one-half times the number of Jews in Israel, and accounts for nearly half of world Jewry. Yet, although Jews are considered

[3]For a fuller discussion of the socio-historical setting of contemporary American Jewry, see Sidney Goldstein and Calvin Goldscheider, *Jewish Americans: Three Generations in a Jewish Community* (Englewood Cliffs, N.J.; Prentice-Hall, Inc., 1968); also C. Bezalel Sherman, *The Jew Within American Society* (Detroit: Wayne State University Press, 1965).

one of the three major religious groups in the United States, they are less than 3 percent of the total population, and, in fact, are undergoing a continuous decline in proportion, as the total population grows at a faster rate than do the Jews.

The second major factor transforming the American Jewish community is the source of its population growth. The tremendous increase in number was not the result of natural growth—the excess of births over deaths; nor was the growth evenly spread over the nine decades. Rather, the increase was primarily the consequence of the heavy immigration of East European Jews between 1870 and 1924. Before 1870, the American Jewish community was composed largely of first- and second-generation German Jews who had immigrated in the 50 preceding years. Of the remaining number, some were of Sephardi origin, descendants of the original Spanish-Portuguese settlers of the colonial period; others were from Central Europe, descendants of pre-nineteenth-century migration. By the 1920's German and Sephardi Jews no longer constituted the dominant Jewish subcommunity in America, but were submerged in the overwhelming numbers of East European immigrants, 2.5 million of whom arrived between 1870 and 1924. The immigration quota laws of the 1920's ended the mass influx of East European Jews, and since then the growth of the American Jewish population has been remarkably slow. As a result, the conditions defining the character of the American Jewish community at the beginning of the 1970's evolved out of the Jewish immigration at the turn of the century. Increasingly, however, the character of the American Jewish community is the result of internal changes among native-born American Jews. And the growing dominance of this segment of the population has set the stage for the significant social and cultural changes within the Jewish population, which will take place in the closing decades of the twentieth century. The transition from a foreign-born, ethnic immigrant subsociety to an Americanized second- and third-generation community has had, and increasingly will have, major consequences for the structure of the Jewish community and for the lives of American Jews. . . .

Population Growth

From a small community of only several thousand persons at the time of the American Revolution, the Jewish population of the United States has increased to about 6 million persons in 1970. But this growth has been very uneven. In the mid-nineteenth century, the Jewish population still numbered only 50,000 persons; and by 1880, the year before the major immigration from Eastern Europe set in, Jews in America were estimated to number only 230,000 (Table 1). Out of a total United States population of 50 million, Jews represented less than one-half of 1 percent. Within the next ten years the Jewish population almost doubled, and by 1900 it numbered just over 1,000,000 persons. Thus, in a twenty-year period, when the total United States population increased only by 50 percent, the Jewish population increased fourfold. As a result, at the turn of the century Jews constituted 1.4 percent of the American population. Rapid growth continued through the first years of the twentieth century, interrupted only by World War I. By the mid-1920's, when national-origins quota laws restricted further large-scale immigration from both Southern and Eastern Europe, Jews in the United States numbered 4,250,000 persons, or 3.7 percent of the total population.

Since then, except for a slight increase in immigration after the rise of Hitler, when our laws were relaxed to permit the entrance of refugees, immigration has not been a major factor in the growth of the American Jewish community. Between 1964 and 1968, for example, an estimated total of only 39,000 Jews, or 2.3 percent of all immigrants,[4] entered the United States as permanent residents. Jewish population increase now depends largely on an excess of births over deaths. And since the Jewish birth rate is below that of the general population, the rate of increase of Jews has been below that of the total American population. Thus, whereas the United States population has increased by almost two-thirds between 1930 and 1970, the Jewish population has grown by only 40 percent. According to the latest estimate prepared by the *American Jewish Year Book,* the Jewish population in 1968 was 5,869,000, or 2.94 percent of the total American population.[5] If the rate of growth characterizing the 1950's and 1960's has persisted, the Jewish population will have reached 6,000,000 by 1970. Because of the differential rates of growth of the Jewish and the total populations, the proportion of Jews in the total, after peaking at about 3.7 percent in the 1920's, has declined to below 3 percent. It is likely to

[4]Jack J. Diamond, "Jewish Immigration to the United States," *American Jewish Year Book* Vol. 70 (1969), pp. 289–294.

[5]Alvin Chenkin, "Jewish Population in the United States," *ibid.*, Vol. 71 (1970), pp. 344–347.

TABLE 1
Jewish population growth, United States, 1790–1970

Year	Number	Percent of total U.S. population
1790[b]	1,200	0.03
1818[a]	3,000	0.03
1826	6,000	0.06
1840	15,000	0.1
1848	50,000	0.2
1880	230,000	0.5
1888	400,000	0.6
1897	938,000	1.3
1900	1,058,000	1.4
1907[b]	1,777,000	2.0
1917	3,389,000	3.3
1927	4,228,000	3.6
1937	4,771,000	3.7
1950[c]	5,000,000	3.5
1960	5,531,000	3.1
1968	5,869,000	2.9

[a]Estimates for 1818–1899 are based on "Jewish Statistics," *American Jewish Year Book.* Vol. 1 (1900), p. 623.
[b]Estimates for 1790 and 1907–1937 are from Nathan Goldberg, "The Jewish Population in the United States," in *The Jewish People, Past and Present,* Vol. 2 (New York: Jewish Encyclopedia Handbooks, 1955), p. 25.
[c]The 1950–1968 estimates are from *American Jewish Year Book,* Vol. 70 (1969), p. 260.

continue to decline as long as the Jewish birthrate remains below that of the rest of the nation.

This decline in relative numbers may not be very significant, since Jews have never constituted a numerically large segment of the population. If anything, it is noteworthy that, despite their small numbers, they are generally afforded the social position of the third major religious group in the country. There seems little reason to expect that this situation will change even though their percentage in the total population declines further, particularly since Jews, both as a group and individually, will undoubtedly continue to play significant roles in specific spheres of American life, such as cultural activities, education, and urban politics. From the demographic point of view, more important factors may be influencing the position of the Jewish community within the total American community, among them changes in the geographical concentration of Jews in certain parts of the nation as well as their disproportional representation in selected socio-economic strata of the population. But before turning to these considerations, some attention must be given to the operation of the vital processes in the growth of the Jewish population, since this is a key to understanding the total pattern of Jewish growth in the future.

Mortality

. . . Although the specific findings differ somewhat, the data permit the general conclusion that differences exist between the age-specific death rates, life expectancy, and survival patterns of Jews and of the total white population, generally more so for males than for females. . . . Jewish age-specific rates are below those of the white population at younger ages, and higher at older ages. The differences for males tend to be sharper than for females at all ages. . . . There has been some speculation that proportionately more Jews with physically impaired lives may survive until later years, when the effects of chronic disease may take higher tolls, thereby raising the age-specific death rates of older Jews above those of the general population. For example, the data by cause of death for Providence lend support to such a contention; for Jews aged 65 and over, the death rates from all major chronic diseases were higher than for the total white population.

Comparison of life tables for Jews and total whites suggests that average life expectancy at birth favors Jewish males, but shows little difference for females. The advantage of Jewish males declines, however, with advancing age and actually becomes less than that of all whites beyond age 65. For females, the life expectancy of Jews remains below that of total whites throughout the life cycle, and the differential tends to become increasingly higher from middle age onward. Because the proportion of individuals surviving to a particular age reflects the effects of mortality only up to that age, the lower Jewish mortality in childhood, as well as in the early and middle adult stages of the life cycle, accounts for higher proportions of Jews surviving into middle age and, in the case of males, even into the lower range of old age.

Since the studies on which these conclusions are based cover a range of 25 years, it appears that identification as a Jew has continued to affect the life chances of individuals. But two points must be stressed: 1) the life table data are cross-sectional, i.e., they are based on the mortality experience of the population at a given point in time rather than on the longitudinal mortality experience of a given birth cohort as it passes through the life cycle. As such, the current experience of the older generation probably does not reflect the patterns which will characterize the younger population at older ages; nor do the current patterns of the younger groups necessarily represent the mortality experience of the older population at earlier ages. Relatively small differences already exist between Jews and the total white population, and these will most likely diminish still further as the socio-economic environment of Jews and non-Jews and their utilization of health services become more similar in the years ahead. 2) The existing differences are not large enough to account for the overall differences in the rate of natural increase of the Jewish population, compared to the total population. To a much greater extent, that differential is attributable to variations between Jews and non-Jews in levels of fertility.

Fertility

Whatever the source of information, fertility research in the United States has consistently found a lower birthrate for Jews than for members of other religious groups. As early as the late nineteenth century, a study of over 10,000 Jewish families in the United States revealed that the Jewish birthrate was lower than the non-Jewish.[6] In the Rhode Island census of 1905, the only state census that obtained information on religion and related it to family size, the average family size of native-born Jewish women was 2.3, compared to an average of 3.2 for native-born Catholics and 2.5 for native-born Protestants.[7] Similarly, the birthrates of Jews in the 1930's were shown to be lower than those of economically comparable Protestant groups; Jews also were found to have a higher proportion using contraceptives, planning pregnancies, and relying on more efficient methods to achieve that goal.[8] The

[6]John S. Billings, "Vital Statistics of the Jews in the United States," *Census Bulletin*, No. 19, 30 December 1889, pp. 4–9.

[7]*Rhode Island Census of 1905*, Tables VII and VIII, pp. 550–553.

[8]R. K. Stix and Frank Notestein, *Controlled Fertility* (Baltimore: The William and Wilkins Co., 1940), p. 29; Raymond Pearl, *The Natural History of Population* (New York: Oxford University Press, 1939), pp. 241–242.

Indianapolis fertility study conducted in 1941 included Jews only in the screening phase of the investigation, which was designed to focus exclusively on Protestant couples; but even here the fertility rates, standardized for age, were about 18 percent higher for Catholics than for Protestants and about 25 percent lower for Jews than for Protestants.[9]

Beginning in the 1950's, a series of important surveys were undertaken to investigate the fertility behavior of the American population. Among these were the Growth of American Families Studies (GAF), the Princeton Fertility Studies, and investigations based on the Detroit Area Studies.[10] In each of these, Jews constituted only a small proportion of the total sample, thereby precluding detailed investigation of Jewish fertility. Yet the data on Jews yielded by these studies were clear-cut in pointing to lower Jewish fertility. The results of the GAF study indicate, for example, that in 1955 the average family size of Catholic and Protestant couples was 2.1, compared to an average of only 1.7 for Jewish couples.[11] Also, Jews expected significantly fewer children (2.4) than either Protestants (2.9) or Catholics (3.4). Overall, the GAF study found that Jews had the smallest families, married later, expected and desired to have the smallest families, had the most favorable attitudes toward the use of contraception, were more likely to have used contraception, were most successful in planning the number and the spacing of all their children, and were most likely to use the most effective methods of birth control.[12] The 1960 GAF study recorded similar patterns . . . .

Although focusing on a somewhat different population, and

[9]Pascal K. Whelpton and Clyde V. Kiser, "Differential Fertility Among Native-White Couples in Indianapolis," *Social and Psychological Factors Affecting Fertility, I, Milbank Memorial Fund Quarterly,* July 1943, pp. 226–271.

[10]Ronald Freedman, Pascal K. Whelpton, and Arthur A. Campbell, *Family Planning, Sterility and Population Growth* (New York: McGraw-Hill, 1959); Pascal K. Whelpton, Arthur A. Campbell, and John E. Patterson, *Fertility and Family Planning in the United States* (Princeton: Princeton University Press, 1966); Charles F. Westoff, Robert G. Potter, Jr., Philip C. Sagi, and Eliot G. Mishler, *Family Growth in Metropolitan America* (Princeton: Princeton University Press, 1961); Charles F. Westoff, Robert G. Potter, Jr., and Philip C. Sagi, *The Third Child* (Princeton: Princeton University Press, 1963); David Goldberg and Harry Sharp, "Some Characteristics of Detroit Area Jews and Non-Jewish Adults," in Marshall Sklare, *The Jews: Social Patterns of an American Group* (New York: The Free Press, 1958), pp. 108–110.

[11]Freedman, Whelpton, and Campbell, *op. cit.,* pp. 608–610.

[12]Whelpton, Campbell, and Patterson, *op. cit.,* pp. 71–72; 247–252.

using a follow-up approach to their original sample rather than an independent cross-section of the population in successive rounds of interviews, the Princeton Fertility Studies of 1960 and 1967 reached the same conclusions as those reported by GAF. Jews, when compared to Protestants and Catholics, desired fewer children and more successfully planned their pregnancies. Over 90 percent of the Jewish couples used the most effective contraceptive methods, compared to only 66 percent of the Protestants, and 35 percent of the Catholics.[13] These patterns persisted even when metropolitan residence, social class, and other significant variables were controlled.

In its 1957 sample population survey, the United States Bureau of the Census collected information on the number of children ever born. With this information, it is possible to calculate fertility rates expressed as the number of children ever born to women within specific age groups. Here, too, the results obtained confirmed the lower fertility of Jews. The cumulative fertility rate of Jewish women 45 years of age and over was 2.2, compared to 3.1 for Catholic women and 2.8 for Protestant women. Lower fertility also characterized Jewish women at younger ages. Moreover, controlling for area of residence, the fertility rate for Jewish women in urban areas was 14 percent below that of urban women of all religions combined. Finally, the evidence available from over a dozen Jewish community studies points to similar lower Jewish fertility (Table 2). In Providence, for example, there were 450 Jewish children under five years of age for every 1,000 women aged 20 to 44. This was significantly lower than the fertility ratio of the total population in the metropolitan area (620) or the total white urban American population (635). A similar differential characterized Springfield.

The low Jewish fertility is significant for Jewish population growth because the average number of children born is so close to the minimum number needed for replacement. Replacement level is generally cited as 2.1, taking into account that a small proportion of adults will never marry and that a small percentage of those who do will not produce children. The importance of fertility is accentuated as the rate of intermarriage increases, contributing to possible losses in the population through both conversion of the Jewish partner away from Judaism and the socialization of children

[13]Westoff, Potter, and Sagi, *op. cit.*, p. 89.

TABLE 2
Jewish fertility-ratio: Number of children under age 5 to number of women aged 20–44, selected communities

Community[a]	Year	Fertility ratio
New Orleans, La.	1953	496
Lynn, Mass.	1955	528
Canton, Ohio	1955	469
Des Moines, Iowa	1956	596
Worcester, Mass.	1957	525
New Orleans, La.	1958	510
Los Angeles, Cal.	1959	560
South Bend, Ind.	1961	494
Rochester, N.Y.	1961	489
Providence, R.I.	1963	450
Camden, N.J.	1964	480
Springfield, Mass.	1966	418
Columbus, Ohio	1969	444
U.S. white population	1960	667
U.S. white population	1969	523

[a]See appendix at end of chapter for citation of individual community studies.

of mixed marriages either in non-Jewish religions or in an entirely nonreligious environment.

Within the Jewish group itself, research, particularly on the Providence community, has shown considerable variations in birth levels among groups differing in religious identifications (Orthodox, Conservative, Reform), social class, and generation status. In particular, the Providence data emphasized the importance of generation changes in the relation of social class to fertility. The data clearly indicate the trend toward convergence and greater homogeneity in the fertility patterns of socio-economic groupings within the Jewish population, with distance from the first generation. This contraction of socio-economic differentials may be regarded as the result of the widespread rationality with which the majority of contemporary Jews plan their families, the absence of rapid upward mobility characteristic of earlier generations, and the greater homogeneity of the contemporary Jewish social structure.

Third-generation American Jews are largely concentrated in

the college-educated group and in high white-collar occupations. The lack of wide social class distinctions for this generation may account for the absence of striking fertility differences within this segment of the Jewish population. It may thus be fortunate from the point of view of Jewish population growth that such a large proportion of the younger generation are concentrated in the higher education and higher socio-economic groups. Reflecting a reversal in the older pattern of high fertility among the lower socio-economic segments of the population, the fertility data from the Springfield survey show that it is the higher educated among the younger groups within the Jewish population who have the highest fertility levels.[14] Had the lower fertility characterizing the more educated segments of the Jewish population of earlier generations persisted and become dominant in the younger generations, the problem of demographic survival facing the Jewish community today would be accentuated. For the immediate future, all available evidence continues to point to inadequate birth levels among Jews, insuring little more than token growth. This being so, the total Jewish population is not likely to increase rapidly beyond its present six million level.[15]

Marriage and the Family

The family, as one of the primary institutions of society, not only functions to reproduce and maintain the species, but acts as one of the major agents of socialization in the transmission of values, attitudes, goals, and aspirations.[16] Any investigation concerned with the future of American Jewry must give some consideration to the composition, structure, and nature of the American Jewish family, particularly at a time when broader changes in the society as a whole have had an important effect on family and marriage patterns.

The Jewish family is generally characterized as having strong

[14]Sidney Goldstein, "Completed and Expected Fertility in an American Jewish Community," *Proceedings of the Fifth World Congress of Jewish Studies, Jerusalem, 1969*.

[15]For a fuller review of patterns and trends in Jewish fertility see Calvin Goldscheider, "Fertility of the Jews," *Demography*, No. 4, 1967, pp. 196–209; Calvin Goldscheider, "Trends in Jewish Fertility," *Sociology and Social Research*, No. 50, 1966, pp. 173–186.

[16]William J. Goode, *The Family* (Englewood Cliffs, N.J.: Prentice-Hall, Inc., 1966), pp. 1–7.

ties, tightly knit kinship relations, and great stability. Yet, despite the importance Jews have traditionally attached to the family, few community surveys have given much consideration to it. Attention has generally been restricted to the percentage of individuals in the Jewish population who are married, widowed, or divorced. Only recently have surveys also focused on the type and size of the family unit, age of marriage, and frequency of remarriage. Two sets of data are available for examination of demographic aspects of the Jewish family in America: First, the 1957 census survey contains a limited amount of information on marital patterns by religion. Second, insights into family and marriage patterns can be gained from selected community surveys, particularly that of Providence.

The 1957 census survey data confirm that Jews, compared to the general population, are more apt to marry at some point in their life cycle, to marry at a somewhat later age, and to have more stable marriages (Table 3). These statistics show that 70 percent of the men 14 years and over in the total population were married, compared to 73 percent of the Jewish males. Concomitantly, lower proportions of Jewish men were widowed and divorced. The gross data, however, reflect the differential age structure of the Jewish and total male populations. Examination by specific age group is more revealing.

Among males aged 25 to 34, for example, only 17.9 percent of those in the total population were still single, but this was true of 29.8 percent of the Jewish males, attesting to the later marriage age of Jewish men. By age 35 to 44, however, this differential disappeared and, in fact, was to some degree reversed. Among men aged 65 and over, 7 percent in the total population were still single, compared to only 4.8 percent of the Jewish men. Although these data are cross-sectional, they do indicate that by the end of the life cycle a somewhat higher proportion of Jewish men than of males in the general population were married, although in both cases the proportions reached over 90 percent.

Regretfully, the census statistics by age do not distinguish between the widowed and divorced. Because the two were grouped together, the percentage increased consistently with rising age, from 0.5 percent of the total male population aged 20 to 24, to just under one in four males of those aged 65 and over. For all age groups, however, the percentage in this particular marital category was considerably lower for the Jewish male population than for all males. The census statistics do not permit us to determine categorically whether this reflects differences in divorce or in survival. But because these differences hold for all age groups including the younger, which are not likely to be affected by mortality to a very great extent, they may reflect differences in divorce rates as well as a greater tendency for Jewish males to remarry after divorce or widowhood. For all age groups combined, a category for which the census data distinguishes between widowed and divorced, Jewish men had proportionately fewer of both, but the relative difference was greater for the divorced than for the widowed.

The census does present standardized statistics on marital status, which show what the marital status of the Jewish population would be if its age composition were that of the total male population, while retaining its own age specific marital characteristics. Reflecting later age at marriage, the percentage for single Jews is greater than was actually the case, but the percentage of widowed and divorced remains well below the corresponding percentages for the total male population. Comparable analyses can be made for the female population. Overall, differences between Jewish women and women in the total population seem to be less marked than those characterizing the men; and the similarities extend to the age specific characteristics.

The value of the census data is limited because it determines only marital status. Also important for an evaluation of the Jewish family are questions of stability of marriage, as judged by number of times ever-married persons have been married, changes in age at first marriage, and changes in household types.

The one fact emerging from the various community studies which collected information on marital status is the high proportion of the Jewish population that is married, usually three-fourths or more. Also, judging by those studies which present the percent married and ever-married by age group, almost all Jews (95 percent or more) marry at least once. Three other observations emerge from the data: 1) In the Jewish population, as in the general population, the proportion of widows is considerably higher than the proportion of widowers, reflecting the higher mortality rates of men. 2) The average Jewish male marries later in life than does the Jewish female. 3) The rate of remarriage is higher for widowers than for widows.[17]

[17]Ronald M. Goldstein, "American Jewish Population Studies Since World War II," *American Jewish Archives*, April 1970, p. 14.

TABLE 3

Percent distribution by marital status, Jewish and total population, by sex and age, United States, 1957[a]

Age and sex	Total population				Jewish population			
	Single	Married	Widowed and divorced	Total	Single	Married	Widowed and divorced	Total
Males								
14–19	97.5	2.5		100.0	99.4	0.6	—	100.0
20–24	51.8	47.7	0.5	100.0	c	c	c	c
25–34	17.9	80.3	1.8	100.0	29.8	69.3	1.0	100.0
35–44	8.6	88.5	3.0	100.0	5.3	92.6	2.1	100.0
45–64	7.7	86.2	6.1	100.0	7.2	90.0	2.9	100.0
65 and over	7.3	68.4	24.2	100.0	4.8	80.0	15.2	100.0
Total unstandardized	23.9	70.5	5.6[b]	100.0	23.5	73.0	3.5[b]	100.0
Total standardized for age	23.9	70.5	5.6	100.0	27.9	68.9	3.2	100.0

TABLE 3 *(Continued)*

Age and sex	Total population: Single	Total population: Married	Total population: Widowed and divorced	Total population: Total	Jewish population: Single	Jewish population: Married	Jewish population: Widowed and divorced	Jewish population: Total
Females								
14–19	87.0	12.8	0.2	100.0	96.8	3.2	—	100.0
20–24	29.0	69.1	1.9	100.0	c	c	c	c
25–34	9.1	87.6	3.2	100.0	9.1	88.6	2.3	100.0
35–44	6.4	86.7	6.9	100.0	7.7	87.5	4.8	100.0
45–64	7.1	73.2	19.7	100.0	8.6	75.0	16.4	100.0
65 and over	8.0	36.5	55.5	100.0	1.1	42.5	56.4	100.0
Total unstandardized	18.6	66.7	14.9[b]	100.0	17.7	67.4	14.8[b]	100.0
Total standardized for age	18.6	66.7	14.9	100.0	20.8	65.8	13.4	100.0

[a]**U.S. Bureau of the Census, "Tabulation of Data on the Social and Economic Characteristics of Major Religious Groups, March 1957."** (Unpublished)

[b] *Percentage of population widowed and divorced, by sex*

	Widowed	*Divorced*		*Widowed*	*Divorced*
Jewish males	2.5	1.0	Jewish females	13.4	1.4
Total males	3.8	1.8	Total females	12.6	2.3

[c]Percent not shown where base is less than 150,000.

The data collected in the Providence survey lend weight to the assumption that the high value placed by Jewish tradition on marriage and the family leads to both a high marriage rate for Jews and a greater stability of Jewish marriages.[18] In Greater Providence, among both males and females, a higher percentage of the Jewish population was married. . . . On the other hand, the percentages of separated and divorced persons were below those in the general population. The differential pattern generally persists even when age is controlled. The differences in the proportion divorced in the total and Jewish populations are affected by the extent of remarriage, as well as by the different age structures of the two populations. Attesting to the higher stability of Jewish marriages is the fact that the proportion of persons married more than once in the Jewish population was one-third lower than in the general population.

In the Providence Jewish population, as in the total population, certain sex differentials in marital status are noteworthy. The percentages of single and married males were greater than comparable proportions in the female population. On the other hand, the percentages of divorced and widowed women exceeded the comparable values for the men. These sex differences are attributable to several factors. Males tend to marry several years later than females. Sex-selective mortality favors the female, which means that the married woman, on the average, outlives her husband by a number of years. With a larger proportion of older persons projected for the Jewish population, the percentage of widowers and, particularly, of widows will increase. The somewhat lower percentage of separated and divorced males may stem from the greater tendency of men to remarry.

Several national studies have found that Jews marry at later ages than do either Protestants or Catholics.[19] The 1957 census survey found the median age at first marriage of Jewish women to be 21.3, compared to 19.9 for Protestants, and 20.8 for Catholics. The Providence data also revealed such differentials. The average age of Jewish males at first marriage was 26, compared to 23 for the total population; Jewish women, on the average, were married at age 23,

[18] Goldstein and Goldscheider, *op. cit.*, pp. 103–104.

[19] Ronald Freedman, Pascal K. Whelpton, and John W. Smit, "Socio-Economic Factors in Religious Differentials in Fertility," *American Sociological Review*, August 1961, p. 610; Whelpton, Campbell, and Patterson, *op. cit.*, p. 321.

compared to age 20 for the total female population. Moreover, grouping women according to the date of their first marriage suggests that later age of marriage has characterized Jewish women since at least 1920. Age at first marriage has been declining since World War II, after having risen between the 1910 and the 1935–39 marriage cohorts from 19 to 23. The decline in the average marriage age of Jewish women parallels a development in the general population, but the change has been greater for Jewish women, resulting in a narrowing of the differences in the average marriage age between women in the Jewish and the total populations. The pursuit of higher education has often been cited as a reason for delayed marriage among Jews. Although this is undoubtedly a factor, it may not be the only explanation, since the decline in the average age at marriage has taken place at a time when the proportion pursuing higher education has been reaching new peaks. Changes in the general social and economic environment and the greater reliance of Jews on birth control, and its more efficient practice, may be factors in explaining the more rapid decline in the marriage age of Jews.

A related dimension of family structure is household composition, that is, whether the Jewish household contains only the immediate family of husband-wife-children or other relatives, such as grandparents. In Providence, the average size of Jewish households was 3.25 persons, similar to the average found in a number of recent Jewish community studies, most varying between 3.1 and 3.3. This reflects both the low level of fertility characterizing Jewish families and the very great tendency for Jewish households to be organized as nuclear rather than extended household units. In Greater Providence, 85 percent of all households consisted only of the immediate family of husband, wife, and children. Only 8 percent included other relatives. An equal proportion were one-person units, but almost all of these were concentrated in the older age groups. That the trend is clearly in the direction of nuclear households is evidenced by the generational differences in the percentage of nuclear household units, which rose from 85 percent of households headed by a first-generation person, to 97 percent headed by a third-generation individual. Part of the differences stems from the different age composition of the generations, but even when age is held constant, the increase in nuclear households among third-generation Jews remains.

In organizing their families in nuclear units, Jews are

conforming to the pattern characterizing families in the United States as a whole. Such a development is consistent with the trend toward greater geographical separation of childrens' from parents' residences. This has significant implications for the strength of Jewish identification as it is reinforced through the extended family unit. It also has a number of immediate and practical implications for the burdens that the community may be asked to assume as nuclear families break up through the death of a spouse, leaving single individuals who will not be absorbed into the household units of children or other relatives. Coupled with the trend toward an aging population, the predominance of the nuclear family among Jews takes on added significance.

Intermarriage

Increasing concern with the demographic growth and survival of the Jewish population in the United States is based not only on the low fertility of the Jews; low growth rates or actual decline can also result from excessive losses to the majority group through assimilation. A consistent threat, not only to the maintenance of Jewish identification but also to the demographic maintenance of the Jewish population, is interfaith marriage. If marital assimilation takes place at a high rate, the Jewish group faces demographic losses both through the assimilation of the Jewish partner to the marriage and through the loss of children born to such a marriage. In recent years, concern with the "vanishing American Jew" has reached considerable proportions as a variety of evidence has suggested an increasingly high rate of intermarriage. In the face of earlier evidence that the Jewish group had been remarkably successful, compared to other groups, in maintaining religious endogamy, the disquiet caused by this new evidence is understandable.[20] It has generated considerable research in Jewish community surveys on the extent of intermarriage, both as an indication of the possible impact of intermarriage on Jewish demographic survival and as an index of the extent of group conformity, loyalty, and cohesiveness among Jews.

No definite assessment of the level and character of Jewish intermarriage and of changes over time can be made without the development of a considerably better body of data than is currently

[20]Milton M. Gordon, *Assimilation in American Life* (New York: Oxford University Press, 1964), pp. 181–182.

available. Although statistics on rates of intermarriage are available now from a number of community surveys, the quality of the data varies; their use must be preceded by careful attention to the type of community studied, to the comprehensiveness of the study's population coverage, and to the way intermarriage was measured. The rate of intermarriage tends to be considerably higher in areas where Jews constitute a smaller percentage of the population. The rate of intermarriage is also higher if the data are based on a study in which both Jewish and non-Jewish households in the community are surveyed, since such surveys are most apt to find those families which are on the fringes of the Jewish community. Finally, care must be given to the manner in which intermarriage itself is measured. Studies relying exclusively on the current religious identification of marriage partners run the serious risk of undercounting intermarriages, since those partners to a mixed marriage who changed their religion in conjunction with the marriage would not be identified as having intermarried.

There is general agreement that the rate of Jewish intermarriage has increased, but because of the lack of data by which to measure trends, as well as serious questions about the quality of available statistics, the extent of the increase has not been clearly determined. A study of intermarriage in New Haven, Connecticut, showed, for example, that Jewish intermarriages increased from zero in 1870 to 5.1 percent in 1950;[21] but New Haven is one of the very few communities where statistics are available over such a long period of time. Most of the other statements concerning increased rates of intermarriage are based on general comparisons of the current levels of intermarriage in various communities with those in a different set of communities at an earlier time.

For example, in a series of communities cited by Nathan Goldberg, where surveys were taken during the 1930's, the rates of intermarriage generally ranged between 5 and 9 percent.[22] These included such communities as Stamford and New London in Connecticut, Dallas, and San Francisco, But during the same period, Duluth, Minnesota, showed an intermarriage rate of 17.7

[21]Ruby Jo Reeves Kennedy, "What Has Social Science to Say About Intermarriage?" in Werner J. Cahnman, ed., *Intermarriage and Jewish Life* (New York: Herzl Press, 1963), p. 29.

[22]Nathan Goldberg, "The Jewish Population in the United States," in *The Jewish People: Past and Present* (New York: *Jewish Encyclopedia Handbooks*, 1955), Vol. 2, p. 29.

percent. A number of communities surveyed in the late 1950's and 1960's also showed levels of intermarriage between 5 and 10 percent: Camden, New Jersey, Rochester, Los Angeles, Jacksonville, Florida, Long Beach, California, and San Francisco. Judging by the similarity between these levels and those noted for a number of communities in the 1930's, one could conclude that there has been no significant rise in the level of intermarriage. Also, in the March 1957 nationwide sample survey, the United States Census found that 3.8 percent of married persons reporting themselves as Jews were married to non-Jews and that 7.2 percent of all marriages in which at least one partner was Jewish were intermarriages; but both these figures are probably somewhat low, since no information was collected on the earlier religion of the marriage partners. Couples with one converted spouse were therefore not enumerated as mixed marriages. However, in the late 1950's and the 1960's, other estimates of the rate of Jewish intermarriages based on local studies ranged as high as from 18.4 percent for New York City, 37 percent for Marin, California, and 53.6 percent for Iowa.[23] Judging from these latter studies, recent intermarriage rates were higher, but the typicality of these high rates remains questionable.

Other data used to document the rising trend in intermarriage are those comparing differentials among either the various age segments or the various generation levels of the population in a given community. An analysis of this kind by Erich Rosenthal for the Jewish population of Washington, D.C., in 1956 found that the rate of intermarriage was directly related to distance from the immigrant generation.[24] Whereas the mixed marriage rate was 11.3 percent for the total Jewish population, it increased from 1.4 percent among foreign-born husbands to 10.2 percent among native-born husbands of foreign parentage, up to 17.9 percent of native-born husbands of native parentage. Questions have been raised, however, about the typicality of the Jewish community of Washington, and whether findings based on it can be generalized to more stable communities.

Rosenthal's more recent research on Indiana, using marriage

[23]New York data are taken from Jerold S. Heiss, "Premarital Characteristics of the Religously Intermarried in an Urban Area," *American Sociological Review*, No. 25, 1960, pp. 47–55. Iowa data were analyzed by Erich Rosenthal, "Studies of Jewish Intermarriage in the United States," *American Jewish Year Book* Vol. 64 (1963), pp. 34–51.

[24]Rosenthal, *ibid.*

records and covering the years 1960–1963, cites an extraordinarily high rate of intermarriage, 48.8 percent of all marriages occurring in that period.[25] The data indicate that intermarriage increases as the size of the Jewish community decreases. In Marion county, containing Indianapolis, the intermarriage rate was 34.5 percent; in counties with very small Jewish populations it rose to 54 percent. Rosenthal suggests that "the larger the Jewish community, the easier it is to organize communal activities, to effect the voluntary concentration of Jewish families in specific residential neighborhoods, and to maintain an organized marriage market."[26] The key variable is the number of potential marital partners. Although the Indiana situation again cannot be considered typical of United States Jewry, the high rates in themselves are alarming. They do confirm the much greater probability that intermarriage will occur in those regions of the country and in those communities where the Jewish population is of inadequate size to encourage and to permit high levels of in-marriage.

Another small Jewish community illustrating the high level of intermarriage is that of Charleston, West Virginia. In 1959 Charleston had a Jewish population of 1,626. By 1970 it had declined to 1,295. In 1958–1959 the Charleston Jewish community's birthrate was just above its death rate, to provide a small natural increase. By 1969–1970 the death rate in the community was twice that of the birthrate. Of the original Jewish residents in Charleston in 1959, only 939 were left in 1970. The excess of deaths over births, coupled with the loss through out-migration of almost 300 Jews, contributed to this reduction. But particularly noteworthy is the heavy rate of intermarriage. In 1959, 18.4 percent of all couples living in the Charleston Jewish community were intermarried. By 1970 the proportion had reached 26.8 percent. Of the 12 marriages which took place in the community during 1969, five were intermarriages. Here, as a case in point, is the drastic decline of a small Jewish community due, it would seem, to its very small size, its high degree of isolation, and the particular economic problems of West Virginia. In this process, intermarriage has played a complementary role to net losses through out-migration and the excesses of deaths over births. This is not to suggest that such a

[25]Erich Rosenthal, "Jewish Intermarriage in Indiana," *American Jewish Year Book* Vol. 68 (1967), p. 263.

[26]*Ibid.*, pp. 263–264.

development will become characteristic of United States Jewry as a whole. Yet fear of this kind of development, based on the statistics for such communities as Washington and Indiana, has given rise to the very great concern about the impact of intermarriage on the survival of American Jewry. This kind of relationship also leads to the suggestion that greater mobility among American Jewry may lead to increased rates of intermarriage. For if such mobility takes Jews into communities where the size and density of Jewish population are small, the result may differ little from the one noted for Indiana or Charleston, West Virginia.

In assessing our current knowledge of intermarriage, it must be recognized that several important areas of research concerning marriages between Jews and non-Jews have been largely neglected. Not all cases of intermarriage necessarily lead to the loss of the Jewish partner. Conversion of the non-Jew to Judaism may actually add to the Jewish population and also increase the likelihood that the children of such a marriage will be raised as Jews.[27] In order to ascertain the extent to which this happens, surveys focusing on intermarriage must obtain information on the extent of conversion, as well as on the religion in which the children of mixed marriages are raised. Both the Providence and Springfield surveys collected such information. Although these are limited by their reliance on master lists, steps were taken to insure maximum opportunity for inclusion of all Jewish households. While no claim is made that the resulting statistics have identified all intermarriages, the findings probably do not depart excessively from the real level of intermarriage. This probability, coupled with the opportunity provided by these data for examining both extent of conversion and extent to which children of mixed marriages are raised as Jews, argues in favor of their brief examination here.

The Providence survey identified 4.5 percent of all marriages as intermarriages, that is, a marriage in which one of the spouses was not Jewish by birth. In the vast majority of these cases, the husband was Jewish and the wife non-Jewish by birth. Only 0.1 percent represented the Jewish wife whose husband was born non-Jewish. This pattern of sex differentials, in which more Jewish men than women marry non-Jewish partners, is typical of almost all communities for which data were collected. Compared to the

[27]Marshall Sklare, "Intermarriage and Jewish Survival," *Commentary*, March 1970, pp. 51–58.

statistics cited for Washington, San Francisco, and Indiana, the intermarriage level in Providence was quite low. Yet it was not atypical, being comparable to levels of intermarriage noted for Rochester, Camden, Springfield, Los Angeles, and New Haven. Since these communities do vary in both size and location, no obvious common denominator helps explain their similar levels of intermarriage.

Of all the intermarried couples, 42 percent had experienced the conversion of one partner to Judaism, thereby creating religious homogeneity within the family unit. The survey could not fully ascertain the number of Jewish partners to a mixed marriage who converted away from Judaism, canceling out the gains made through conversion of the non-Jewish partner to Judaism. But the survey data do suggest that, in a considerable proportion of intermarriages, conversion to Judaism does occur, thereby enhancing the chances that the family unit will remain identified as Jewish, and that the children will be raised as members of the Jewish community.

For Providence, as for Washington, insights into the trend in level of intermarriage can be gained only by cross-sectional comparison of the intermarriage patterns of different age and generation groups within the population. With the exception of the 30-to-39-year age group, the Providence data pointed to an increase in the rate of intermarriage among the younger segments of the population; the highest percent intermarried (9 percent) characterized the youngest group. On the other hand, the proportion of persons who converted to Judaism consistently increased with decreasing age, from none of the non-Jewish spouses in the 60-and-over age group, to 4 out of 10 among those aged 40 to 59, to 7 out of 10 among those under age 40. This clear-cut pattern is consistent with a conclusion reached by Gerhard Lenski, based on a Detroit study, that the probability of mixed marriages leading to a conversion is considerably greater among younger persons.[28]

Like the Washington studies, the Providence data indicate that generation status affects the rate of intermarriage; however, they also show that it affects the extent of conversion. Among the foreign-born, only 1.2 percent were reported intermarried. Among third-generation Americans, this proportion was almost 6 percent.

[28]Gerhard Lenski, *The Religious Factor* (Garden City, N.Y.: Doubleday and Company, 1963), pp. 54–55.

Moreover, the pattern of differentials by generation status operated within the respective age groups. Only one-fourth of the mixed marriages of the foreign-born resulted in a conversion of the non-Jewish spouse, compared to over half of the intermarriages involving third-generation males. This pattern of generational differences remains even when age is held constant. While confirming that the rate of intermarriage has risen among third-generation, compared to first-generation, Jews, the Providence levels are well below those observed for Washington, D.C. The Providence data also show a higher rate of conversion of the non-Jewish spouse to Judaism among the third, compared to the first, generation.

Comparisons of the level of intermarriage among the children of the heads of households surveyed in the Providence study support the higher rates for younger segments of the population. Whereas the intermarriage rate of Jews in the survey was 4.5 percent, that among the children of these households was 5.9 percent. Since the children enumerated here included those living outside Greater Providence, the higher rate may reflect not only their younger age but also a tendency for persons who intermarry to move away from their family's community. Although this may partially represent an attempt at anonymity, it is more likely related to the fact that the child was already living away from home and from parental control, thus enhancing the possibility of courting and marrying non-Jews. Most likely presenting a more correct image of the sex differential in levels of intermarriage, the data for the children of the survey units indicate that almost 8 percent of the male children intermarried, compared to only 4 percent of the females.

The Providence data were also used in an attempt to assess the effect of intermarriage on fertility levels.[29] Comparison of the fertility of the intermarried with that of the nonintermarried shows that for both women 45 years old and older, who had completed their fertility, and those under 45 years of age, who may still have additional children, intermarried couples had lower fertility than the nonintermarried. Intermarried couples had a lower average number of children ever born; they had a much higher percentage of childlessness; and they had a lower percentage of families with four or more children. Quite clearly, intermarriage resulted in lowered fertility; but the differences were not as great among the

[29]Goldstein and Goldscheider, *op. cit.*, pp. 166–169.

younger women in the population as among the older, suggesting that whatever factor served earlier to restrict the fertility of intermarried couples operated to a lesser degree for the younger couples.

Finally, the Providence survey ascertained the religious identification of all children in households of intermarried couples. Of the 280 children in this category, 136 were children of couples in which the non-Jewish spouse had converted to Judaism and were therefore being raised as Jews. Of the 144 children belonging to families in which the non-Jewish spouse had not converted, 84 children were being raised as Jews, and 60 as non-Jews. The fact that only 22 percent of the 280 children of intermarriages were being raised as non-Jews is in strong contrast to the findings of the Washington survey that 70 percent of the children of mixed marriages were being raised as non-Jews. Too few studies have explored this relationship, and more research is essential to obtain meaningful data on a national level.

The Springfield survey collected data comparable to that of Providence, and its findings, including an overall intermarriage rate of 4.4, are so similar that presentation of the detailed results would be repetitious. Finally, mention must be made of the Boston survey of 1965 because of its very comprehensive coverage of the population and because it represents a Jewish community of about 200,000 persons. This survey found that 7 percent of the marriages represented intermarriages. Although higher than the level noted for Providence and Springfield, this percentage is still markedly below the high levels noted in some other communities. However, the Boston data do suggest a sharp rise in the level of intermarriage among the very youngest segment of the population. Intermarriage characterized only 3 percent of the couples in which the age of the husband was 51 and over, and only 7 percent of those with the husband between ages 31 and 50; but 20 percent of the couples in which the husband was 30 years old, or younger, were intermarried. Regretfully, the Boston study did not report how many of the intermarried persons had converted, or in what religion the children of such marriages were being raised.

Another recent investigation of intermarriage, by Fred Sherrow, based its findings on data collected from 1964 follow-up interviews of a national sample survey of 1961 college graduates.[30]

[30]Reported in Arnold Schwartz, "Intermarriage in the United States," *American Jewish Year Book* Vol. 71 (1970), pp. 101–121.

The study thus refers to a young population. By 1964, 57 percent of the Jewish respondents had married. Of these, between 10 and 12 percent married non-Jews by birth. The data further show a conversion rate of less than 20 percent by the non-Jewish spouse to Judaism. This rate is considerably below that found in a number of Jewish community studies, but in the absence of comparable data for older cohorts of college graduates, it is not possible to determine whether conversion is increasing among the young. Sherrow suggests that the low rate of conversion he identified may reflect a weakening of the proscription against intermarriage. In addition, the data reveal that 55 percent of the Jews who intermarried retained their Jewish identification. Combining this retention rate with the gains from conversion to Judaism indicates an estimated overall net loss of 30 percent of the population involved in intermarriages. On this basis, the conclusion seemed justified that the rates are not yet high enough to signal the imminent dissolution of the American Jewish community through intermarriage.

What is the overall picture that emerges? No simple answer to this seems possible. Quite a heterogeneous pattern characterizes the United States depending on the size, location, age, and social cohesiveness of the particular community. Yet, within these variations in level of intermarriage, the analysis of the data in terms of age and generation status does suggest that the intermarriage rate is increasing among young, native-born Americans. Eventually, intermarriage rates in the United States may reach a plateau around which the experience of individual communities will fluctuate. But for the immediate future, the overall rate of intermarriage is likely to rise further, as an increasing proportion of the population becomes third-generation Americans and moves away from older areas of dense Jewish population to newly developed, more integrated areas within both the cities and suburbs, and to more distant communities with fewer Jews and less organized Jewish life. At the same time the data for several communities suggest that although the rate of intermarriage may be increasing among the third generation, a high proportion of these intermarriages result in the conversion of the non-Jewish spouse to Judaism: the rate of conversions is higher among the very groups having a higher intermarriage rate. Moreover, a significant proportion of children in such marriages are being raised as Jews. And finally, among the young, the fertility patterns of intermarried couples also resemble more closely those of the nonintermarried than in the older age groups. These changes suggest that the net effects of intermarriage on the overall size of the Jewish population may not yet be as serious demographically as suggested by several Jewish community studies. What their effect is on Jewish identification and religiosity is beyond the scope of this evaluation. There can be little doubt that the problem of intermarriage warrants considerable concern on both policy and research levels, but, from a demographic point of view, there is also much need to focus on questions of Jewish fertility and Jewish population redistribution.

Population Distribution

In considering the future of the American Jewish population, attention must be given to its geographical distribution among the various regions of the United States, as well as within the large metropolitan areas where so many of the country's Jews live. That New York City and the Northeastern region contain the greater part of the Jewish population of the United States is well known. Yet this concentration has not always been as great as in recent decades, nor is it likely to remain so.

The 1900 *American Jewish Year Book* estimates (Table 4) indicate that, at that time, 57 percent of American Jewry lived in the Northeast, in contrast to only 28 percent of the total American population;[31] and virtually all these Jews were in New York, Pennsylvania, and New Jersey, with New York alone accounting for about 40 percent of the national total. The North Central region accounted for the next largest number of Jews—about one-fourth —with most concentrated in Illinois, Ohio, Indiana, Wisconsin, and Michigan. By contrast, one-third of the total United States population lived in this region in 1900. Compared to the general population, Jews were also underrepresented in the South, where 14 percent were located, largely in Maryland. Florida at that time had only 3,000 Jews. The proportion of Jews in the West in 1900 was identical to that of the general population, just over 5 percent.

The decades following 1900 saw continued mass immigration from Eastern Europe, resulting in a fourfold increase of the Jewish population between 1900 and 1930. Reflecting the tendency of the immigrants to concentrate in the large cities of the Northeast, and especially New York, considerable change occurred in the regional distribution of the American Jewish population. The *American*

[31]"Jewish Statistics," *American Jewish Year Book* Vol. 1 (1899–1900), p. 283.

TABLE 4

Distribution of total United States and Jewish population, by regions, 1900, 1930, and 1968

	1900		1930[c]		1968[d]	
Region	Jewish[a]	United States[b]	Jewish	United States	Jewish	United States
Northeast	56.6	27.7	68.3	27.9	64.0	24.2
New England	7.4	7.5	8.4	6.6	6.8	5.7
Middle Atlantic	49.2	20.3	59.9	21.3	57.1	18.5
North Central	23.7	34.6	19.6	31.4	12.5	27.8
East North Central	18.3	21.0	15.7	20.5	10.2	19.8
West North Central	5.4	13.6	3.9	10.9	2.3	8.0
South	14.2	32.2	7.6	30.7	10.3	31.2
South Atlantic	8.0	13.7	4.3	12.8	8.1	15.0
East South Central	3.3	9.9	1.4	8.0	0.7	6.6
West South Central	2.9	8.6	1.9	9.9	1.5	9.6
West	5.5	5.4	4.6	10.0	13.2	16.8
Mountain	2.3	2.2	1.0	3.0	0.9	4.0
Pacific	3.2	3.2	3.6	7.0	12.2	12.8
Total United States						
Percent	100.0	100.0	100.0	100.0	100.0	100.0
Number (in 1,000's)	1,058	75,994	4,228	123,203	5,869	199,861

[a]"Jewish Statistics," *American Jewish Year Book*, Vol. 1 (1900), pp. 623–624.
[b]U.S. Bureau of the Census, *1960 Census of Population*, Vol. 1, *Characteristics of the Population* (Washington, D.C.: Government Printing Office, 1961), pp. 1–16.
[c]H. S. Linfield, "Statistics of Jews," *American Jewish Year Book*, Vol. 33 (1931), p. 276.
[d]Alvin Chenkin, "Jewish Population in the United States," *American Jewish Year Book*, Vol. 70 (1969), p. 266.

Jewish Year Book estimates for 1927 place over two-thirds of the Jewish population in the Northeastern region, with 60 percent in New York, New Jersey, and Pennsylvania;[32] New York State alone accounted for 45 percent of the Jews in the United States. This considerable increase in the number of Jews in the Northeast, from 57 percent in 1900 to 68 percent in 1927, contrasts with the stability of the American population as a whole; both the 1900 and 1930 censuses found 28 percent of all Americans living in the Northeast. The percentage of Jews living in each of the other regions declined. In 1927 only one in five lived in the North Central region, only 8 percent in the South, and just under 5 percent in the West. As a result, the overall differential between the distribution patterns of the Jewish and the total population increased. The sharpest changes were in the South and West. The South's share of the total Jewish population declined from 14 to 8 percent, while it continued to account for about 30 percent of the total population. The West increased its share of the total population from 5 to 10 percent in these 30 years, but its Jewish population declined from 5.5 to 4.6 percent of the national total.

For the United States population as a whole, the period between 1930 and the present showed a continuous westward shift. The proportion of Americans living in the Western region had increased to 17 percent by 1968; and both the Northeastern and North Central regions accounted for smaller proportions of the total American population than they did in 1930. The South's share increased a little, but this was entirely attributable to the greater population concentration in the South Atlantic states, particularly Florida.

With the cutoff in large-scale immigration, changes in the distribution of the Jewish population of the United States in the period between 1930 and 1968 became largely a function of their geographic mobility. These changes were considerable; in fact, Jewish redistribution represented to a somewhat accentuated degree the general redistribution of the population as a whole. For example, between 1930 and 1968, the proportion of all American Jews living in the Western region increased from under 5 to 13 percent. Similarly, the proportion of Jews living in the South increased from under 8 percent of the total to 10 percent. By contrast, the proportion living in the North Central region declined

[32]H. S. Linfield, "Statistics of Jews," *ibid.*, Vol. 33 (1931–1932), p. 276.

from one out of five in 1927, to only 12 percent in 1968. And by 1968 the Northeastern region, including both New England and the Middle Atlantic states, although containing almost two-thirds of all American Jews, had a smaller proportion of the total American Jewish population than it did in 1930.

This decline in the proportion living in the Northeast may be indicative of developments that will become more accentuated in the future: 1) as Jews increasingly enter occupations whose nature requires mobility because of the limited opportunities available in particular areas; 2) as family ties become less important for the third-generation Jew than they had been for the first- and second-generation; 3) as more Jews no longer feel it necessary to live in areas of high Jewish concentration. In short, the available data suggest the beginning of a trend toward the wider dispersal of Jews throughout the United States.

Assuming that such a pattern develops, the Jewish population in the future will not only be an increasingly smaller proportion of the total American population, but it will also be increasingly less concentrated in the Northeastern part of the United States. In an ecological sense, therefore, the population will become more truly an American population, with all this implies regarding opportunities for greater assimilation and less numerical visibility. Although this may be a trend of the future, it must be emphasized that the Northeast, and New York in particular, will remain a very large and obviously dynamic center of American Jewry. At the same time, its population will probably grow increasingly older because more and more of the younger Jews will leave this section of the country to become part of the mainstream of American life through the process of geographic mobility.

Urban-Rural Residence

Closely related to the concentration of Jews in the Northeast is their distribution between urban and rural places of residence. Jews in the United States are unique in their exceptionally high concentration in urban places, particularly in very large ones. The best source of information for this, the 1957 Bureau of the Census survey, found that 96 percent of the Jewish population 14 years old and over lived in urban places, compared to only 64 percent of the total American population (Table 5). Moreover, 87 percent of all Jews in the United States 14 years old and over lived in the large urbanized

TABLE 5

Urban-rural residence of persons 14 years old and over, Jewish and total civilian population, United States, March 1957[a]

Residence	*Total*	*Jewish*
Total urban	63.9	96.1
Urbanized areas of 250,000 or more	36.6	87.4
Other urban	27.3	8.7
Rural non-farm	24.4	3.6
Rural farm	11.7	0.2
Total percent	100.0	100.0
Total number (in 1,000's)	119,333	3,868

[a]U.S. Bureau of the Census, "Religion Reported by the Civilian Population of the United States: March 1957," *Current Population Reports,* Series P-20, No. 79 (2 February 1958), Table 3.

areas of 250,000 population or more, in contrast to only one out of every three persons in the general population. The high concentration of Jews in New York City is, of course, a major factor in this differential.

The census data also show that under 4 percent of American Jewry live in rural places, and almost all of these in nonfarm residences. The reasons for the heavy concentration in large urban places are well known and require no discussion here. However, it is noteworthy that though Jews constituted only 3 percent of the total American population, they comprised almost 8 percent of the total urban population; in all other types of residence Jews accounted for 1 percent or less of the total. In this respect, the experience of the Jews may foreshadow that of the total population, for one of the major demographic and ecological developments in the United States over the last several decades has been the increasing concentration of the American population in metropolitan areas. As this trend continues, the proportion of Jews in the metropolitan population will decline, as more of the total American population comes to live in such areas. Since the American Jewish population is so highly concentrated in major metropolitan areas, a key focus must be on what is happening to the population within such areas.

Suburbanization

There is a considerable sociological literature on the Jewish ghetto in the United States.[33] Yet, from a demographic point of view, there are few reliable statistics for documenting either the character of the ghettos into which the immigrant populations moved or for measuring the speed with which such ghettos broke down. For few cities have there been demographic studies of the Jews of either adequate historical depth or sufficient comparability over time to permit such documentation. In very few communities has more than one population survey of the Jewish community been undertaken, so that opportunities of measuring trends in residential patterns are quite limited. Yet, given the very high concentration of Jews in urban areas and the fact that they tended to live in a very segregated fashion, an analysis of the distribution of the Jewish population must take note of this situation and attempt to suggest the future pattern of development.

The pattern of Jewish settlement in large cities by no means remains stable. The radical shifts in distribution are clearly evident, for example, from estimates of the Jewish population in New York City in 1930 and 1957, and a projection for 1975.[34] Although the New York data are only crude estimates, they do point to the pattern of development in the single largest American Jewish community, and therefore have special significance.

By 1930 the large area of Jewish population density on the Lower East Side had already passed its peak: only 16 percent of New York City's Jews lived in all of Manhattan (Table 6). By contrast, one-third lived in the Bronx and almost one-half in Brooklyn; less than 5 percent of the total Jewish population of New York City lived in Queens. Within one generation, a sharp redistribution occurred. In 1957 only one in four Jews in the city lived in the Bronx, whereas Queens now accounted for one in five. Manhattan continued as the residence of 16 percent of New York City's Jews, but the proportion living in Brooklyn had decreased. While the projections for 1975 must be taken as very tentative, they indicate a continuation of the trends already observed for the 1930–1957 period: relatively fewer Jews living in the Bronx and Brooklyn, and more in Queens.

[33]See, for example, Louis Wirth, *The Ghetto* (Chicago: University of Chicago Press, 1928); Peter I. Rose, ed., *The Ghetto and Beyond* (New York: Random House, 1969).

[34]C. Morris Horowitz and Lawrence J. Kaplan, *The Jewish Population of the New York Area, 1900–1975* (New York: Federation of Jewish Philanthropies of New York, 1959).

TABLE 6
Jewish population of New York area, 1923–1975[a]

Distribution of New York City Jews among 5 boroughs

Area	*1923*	*1930*	*1957*	*1975*
Manhattan	37.4	16.3	16.0	15.1
Bronx	20.3	32.1	23.3	21.1
Brooklyn	39.3	46.6	40.3	38.6
Queens	2.7	4.8	20.0	24.8
Richmond	0.2	0.2	0.3	0.4
Total percent	100.0	100.0	100.0	100.0
Total number (in 1,000's)	1,882	1,825	2,115	2,133

Distribution of New York area Jews between city and selected suburbs[b]

Area	*1957*	*1975*
New York City	81.9	78.5
Nassau	12.8	14.6
Suffolk	0.8	1.2
Westchester	4.5	5.7
Total percent	100.0	100.0
Total number (in 1,000's)	2,580	2,715

[a] C. Morris Horowitz and Lawrence J. Kaplan, *The Jewish Population of the New York Area, 1900–1975* (New York: Federation of Jewish Philanthropies of New York, 1959), Table 9.
[b] A revised estimate prepared for the *American Jewish Year Book* Vol. 64 (1963), shows a total Jewish population of 1,836,000 for New York City in 1960 and a total of 2,688,000 for the N.Y.-Northeastern N.J. Standard Consolidated Area: 68.4 percent in N.Y.C., 20.2 percent in Nassau, Suffolk, and Westchester and 11.3 percent in Rockland, N.Y. county and 8 counties of New Jersey.

What these data do not show is the considerable development of Jewish communities in the suburban sectors of the New York metropolitan area. Although the data for the larger area are restricted, both in the area covered and in the method of estimates, they do, in a crude way, point to the nature of developments. According to the statistics, the total Jewish population in 1957 in the New York area, including both the city and adjoining Nassau, Suffolk, and Westchester counties, numbered 2,580,000 persons, of whom 81.9 percent lived in the city proper. While the number of Jews in the city between 1957 and 1975 is estimated to remain relatively stable at 2.1 million persons, it is expected to grow for the total area from 2.58 million to 2.72 million. Thus, the proportion of Jews living in the suburbs will increase from 18.1 percent in 1957 to 21.5 percent in 1975. The New Jersey and Connecticut segments of New York's suburbs are not included here; if they were, much sharper changes would doubtless be noted.

Even more dramatic changes occurred in the distribution of the Jewish population of Chicago. In 1931, 47.6 percent of Chicago's Jews were concentrated on the West Side. According to 1958 estimates, only 5.5 percent remained in that area of the city, a decline from an estimated 131,000 to 12,000 persons. By contrast, the North Side of Chicago had increased its Jewish population from 56,000 persons in 1931 to 127,000 in 1958, or from 20 to 57.7 percent of the total. In 1958 an estimated 62,000 of the Chicago area's 282,000 Jews were living in the suburbs.

A somewhat similar picture emerges from a comparison of the 1949 and 1959 residential patterns in Detroit. In 1949 Dexter, the largest single area of residence, accounted for almost half of the Detroit area's total Jewish population; the second largest was the North West, accounting for one-fourth. In 1949 no Jews lived in the suburban Oak Park and Huntington Woods sections. By 1959, 18 percent of the Detroit area's total Jewish population had moved to the suburbs. The old center of Dexter was virtually abandoned as an area of Jewish settlement, with only 10 percent of all Detroit Jews remaining. It was replaced as a leading center of residence by the North West, with 50 percent of the total. In fact, by that time research had identified a new residential area, the New Suburbs, which extended beyond the older suburban areas; 3 percent of the Jewish population already lived there, and future growth was expected. Overall, the Detroit area data point to a pattern quite common in many of the metropolitan areas with Jewish communities. The total geographic area in which Jews live has become much larger. Their dispersion within that larger area has increased considerably, yet distinct areas of Jewish concentration remain identifiable; even as the older areas disappear, newer concentrations are emerging. The resultant strain on Jewish institutions represents a major adjustment problem which many Jewish communities must face as they undergo significant population redistribution. . . .

The developing pattern seems to be even greater dispersion and more general residential integration of the Jewish community. As a result, institutions become located at quite widely separated points in the metropolitan area, and the community finds it increasingly difficult to decide upon a central location for those institutions serving the community as a whole. In the past, residential clustering has been an important variable in helping to perpetuate traits, values, and institutions important to Judaism. In metropolitan areas with large Jewish populations such clustering undoubtedly will continue to characterize a number of Jewish settlement areas both within the central cities and in some of the suburbs. But greater dispersal and greater integration seem likely to be the more common developments in the future, becoming critical factors in explaining changes in the extent and character of ties to Judaism.

In a recent investigation, Serge Carlos analyzed the influence of the urban and suburban milieu on religious practices.[35] Although his study focuses on Catholics, it may have some significance for religious behavior in general. Carlos found that the level of church attendance increases as people move from the central area of the city to the periphery. He interprets this pattern as an effect of the need for community identification and integration, both largely missing in suburban communities. At the same time he notes that the higher rates of suburban church attendance represent mainly nominal religious participation, with the result that the proportion of churchgoers who engage in devotional religious practices is lower in the suburban areas. As a reflection of the older age structure of the Jewish population living within central cities, as well as the higher proportion of Orthodox and Conservative, one would expect a higher degree of devotional religious practice in urban than in suburban places of residence. Indeed, research on Greater Providence, where an attempt was made to measure residential differences in religious assimilation, suggests a pattern of greater assimilation for suburban residents.[36] They have higher intermar-

[35]Serge Carlos, "Religious Participation and the Urban-Suburban Continuum," *American Journal of Sociology*, March 1970, pp. 742–759.

[36]Goldstein and Goldscheider, *op. cit.*, pp. 161–163, 181–183, 190–191, 208–210, 241–242.

riage rates, lower scores on indices of ritual observance, higher rates of nonaffiliation and higher proportions with no Jewish education. These appear even after controlling for generation status, suggesting both that the migration to the suburbs may be selective of those not eager to maintain as strong Jewish identity as those in the cities, and that the greater residential dispersion of Jews within the suburbs removes the reinforcement of traditional patterns formerly provided by the older, more densely populated urban areas. Depite this weakening, a high percentage of suburban Jews do continue to identify as Jews and to follow selected religious practices. In short, residential differences exist, but they are not so sharp as to lead to the conclusion that suburbanization itself will cause high rates of assimilation. Similar changes in identification and practice are also occurring to a considerable degree in the older urban areas, as the generation composition of their population changes.

Jewish communities in the United States vary considerably in their patterns of residential distribution. We have inadequate information on why, despite redistribution, some communities in both suburbs and central cities continue to maintain areas of considerably higher Jewish concentration than do others. Little is known about the extent to which, or the way in which, high density of settlement substitutes, as it seems to do in the New York area, for high levels of organizational affiliation and participation as the mechanism for Jewish identification. Research in depth, like that undertaken by Carlos, is needed to ascertain how the communal orientation of Jews living in the cities and in suburbs of differing Jewish density varies and what meaning the various activities have for the individuals, particularly as they relate to the larger question of Jewish identification and survival.

Migration

. . . The importance of migration in the future development and growth of the American Jewish community has been seriously underrated. Data on both the national regional distribution of population and the increasing suburbanization of the Jews suggest that population mobility is a major development in the United States and may have significant impact on the vitality of the local Jewish community. As indicated before, more widespread distribution within the metropolitan area will have an impact on rates of intermarriage, on the degree of integration of Jews into the local community, on the ease with which Jewish identity can be maintained, and on the strength of Jewish institutions themselves, as the population they serve becomes more dispersed. On the national scene, a higher rate of redistribution may also be occurring as Jews, in increasing numbers, enter the salaried professional and executive world and transfer, or are transferred, to branch firms located in places where large Jewish communities do not exist. Moreover, the repeated movement associated with such occupations may well be a new phenomenon on the American Jewish scene, one that may lead to less stable family and communal ties.

What does the evidence available from local Jewish community surveys indicate? The 1963 Detroit study, which ascertained the place of birth of the resident population, found that only one-third of the total Jewish population of Detroit was born in the city; another 28 percent were foreign-born; 36 percent had come to Detroit from other places in the United States, a little over half of these from other cities or towns in Michigan, and the rest from other states. A somewhat similar picture emerges from comparable statistics on Camden, New Jersey, where one-third of the residents were born in the Camden area, and almost 60 percent had moved there from other places in the United States; a small percentage were foreign-born. Using the state as a unit, the Providence study found that 60 percent of all Jews living in Greater Providence were born in Rhode Island. Of the 40 percent who were born elsewhere, 16 percent were foreign-born and the remaining 24 percent were equally divided between natives of New England and of other states Virtually identical patterns emerged for Springfield, Massachusetts. Comparison of the mobility of Jews with that of the general population is best achieved by examining the proportion of the native-born who were living in their state of birth. For Greater Providence, 76 percent of the general population, compared to 72 percent of the American-born Jews, were born in Rhode Island. Judged by state of birth, therefore, the Jewish population closely resembles the total population in its migration level. It also resembles the general pattern in that most of the movement of native-born Jews to the state is from nearby areas.

Mobility can also be judged by length of residence in the area. The Milwaukee study, for example, found that 60 percent of the city's Jews had been living at their current address for less than ten years, and 40 percent for less than five years. These data suggest a high degree of residential mobility among Jews, although they do not specify whether it took the form of intra-urban mobility or migration across larger distances. The recent Boston study also suggests a high degree of mobility. Half the population had lived at their present address for under ten years, and 31 percent for five years or less. These percentages varied considerably by age. Among those 21 to 29 years of age, 70 percent were at their present addresses for less than five years; by contrast, at the other end of the age hierarchy, only 10 percent of those 60 to 69 years old were living in their present homes under five years. Further reflecting the high mobility of Boston's Jews is the finding that 34 percent intended to move within the next two years. Thus a high turnover is indicated both by the recency of the in-move and by the high percentage intending to move in the near future. A very high proportion of the intended mobility is within the Boston metropolitan area itself, and the projected patterns indicate a heavy movement to the newer suburban areas. At the same time, the decline of the older areas in Boston is underscored by the very low percentage of persons moving into them, and the high percentage of those still living there who indicated an intention to move out. For example, less than 25 percent of those living in Central Boston came in the last five years, but 42 percent planned to move out during the next two years. In contrast, of the population living in the south suburbs, 32 percent moved in within the last five years, and only 12 percent indicated an intention to move out within the next two. . . .

The 1968 Columbus, Ohio, survey distinguished between Jews living in areas of high-Jewish density and those living in areas where the Jewish population was more dispersed. Examination of a variety of characteristics for these two populations indicates that the Jews living in the more concentrated areas of settlement were older, were more likely to have been born in the community itself, had a lower education, included a higher proportion of businessmen and a lower proportion of professionals, and inclined toward more traditional religious beliefs and practices. These findings suggest, as do the data for Providence, that although within the larger community some degree of segregation still occurs among Jews, the importance of religion as a basis for selecting neighborhood of residence is diminishing in favor of other socio-demographic criteria.

The Columbus survey also examined the religous composition of the neighborhood in which Jews lived and asked respondents what type of neighborhood they preferred (Table 7).

The results document quite clearly that only a small minority of Jews was living in neighborhoods that were at least 75 percent

TABLE 7
Jewish composition of present neighborhood and preferred composition, Columbus, Ohio, 1969[a]

Percent Jewish	*Present composition*	*Preferred composition*
About 100	1	3
At least 75	8	8
About 50	20	48
25 to about 50	31	25
Under 25	30	2
No other Jews	6	0
Don't know	4	14
Total percent	100	100

[a]Albert J. Mayer, *Columbus Jewish Population Study, 1969* (Columbus: Columbus Jewish Welfare Foundation, 1970), p. 87.

Jewish and little more than one-quarter of the Jewish population in sections that were as much as 50 percent Jewish. In fact, 30 percent were in neighborhoods where less than one in four of the population was Jewish. Yet, respondents expressed preference for neighborhoods with higher proportions of Jews, generally in a 50-50 balance. The overall conclusion therefore points to the desire on the part of Columbus Jews to live in an integrated neighborhood, but one having a substantial number of other Jewish families.

These data refer only to a single community and quite obviously cannot be generalized to the total American Jewish population. They do suggest, however, that in the process of movement, many Jews will, if possible, seek out areas where other Jews are living and which have Jewish institutions to meet their religious and educational needs. Problems will arise if movement occurs to areas where these opportunities do not exist. The degree to which such considerations will in the future influence whether or not Jews move from one section of a city to another and, more particularly, from one metropolitan area to another, or from one region of the United States to another, will be an important factor in the extent to which increased population mobility represents a serious threat to the cohesiveness of the Jewish community.

Migration and population redistribution are important for the development of an area. They affect not only its size, but also the characteristics of its residents if they are selective of particular age, education, occupation, and income groups. At the same time, migration may have an important effect on the migrant himself, particularly on the degree of his integration into the community. A large turnover of population may also have a significant impact on community institutions. To the extent that community ties within the Jewish population are expressed through membership in temples, enrollment of children in educational programs, participation in local organizations and philanthropic activities, a high degree of population movement may either disrupt such patterns of participation or weaken the loyalities they generate. More seriously, they may result in the failure of families and individuals to identify with organized life in the local community. Sociological research has suggested, for example, that recent migrants to a community are much less active in its formal structure than are longtime residents.[37] Although their participation eventually increases, the adjustment has shown to take at least five years, and sometimes migrants never reach the same level of participation, as persons who grew up in the community. Obviously, if a significant proportion of immigrants know in advance that their residence in the community is not likely to be permanent, tendencies toward lower rates of participation and affiliation may be even stronger.

We have a minimum of historical evidence for the Jewish population to document whether the level of mobility is increasing. The available data, both on mobility and on changes in the educational level of Jews and the type of occupations they are entering, suggest that one of the major changes taking place in the American Jewish community is an increasing rate of population movment. For example, some recent statistics from Toledo, Ohio, indicate that one-fifth of the city's Jews move each year. The study reports that national chain operations have brought to Toledo a surprisingly large number of Jewish men in managerial positions, and that the university had a substantial increase in the number of Jewish faculty. At the same time, the study reported that 45 to 60 percent of young Jews raised in Toledo seek, and find, permanent residence in distant cities after graduation from college. This

[37]Basil Zimmer, "Participation of Migrants in Urban Structures," *American Sociological Review*, 1955, pp. 218–224.

pattern is likely to be more typical of the general American scene, resulting not only in the increasing migration of Jews within the United States, but also in an increasingly higher rate of repeated movement by the same persons. We know from general migration studies that higher than average mobility rates have always characterized professionals and highly educated individuals because of the more limited demands for their talents in particular localities. Also, as Toledo shows, in recent years many national firms have adopted a company policy of repeated relocation of their executives and professionals to different branches of their firms. As the proportion of Jews holding such positions increases, the rate of Jewish population mobility is likely to increase.

As Glazer and Moynihan observed: "The son wants the business to be bigger and better and perhaps he would rather be a cog in a great corporation than the manager of a small one. He may not enjoy the tight Jewish community with its limited horizons and its special satisfactions—he is not that much of a Jew any more."[38] In short, they suggest that status may be the drawing force of third-generation Americans as financial success was the major consideration of second-generation Americans. Finally, as discriminatory practices diminish and executive postions formerly closed to Jews open up, this too will be conducive to the greater geographic dispersal of Jews willing to develop occupational careers outside the communities where they grew up.

Some evidence of this trend is already available through limited statistics from Providence. That study collected information on the residence of all children of family units surveyed, permitting comparison of place of residence of children in relation to that of their parents living in the Providence area. Lenski noted that one of the best indicators of the importance attached to family and kin groups by modern Americans is their willingness to leave their native community and migrate elsewhere.[39] Since most migration is motivated by economic or vocational factors, he suggests, migration serves as an indicator of the strength of economic motives compared to kinship ties. In modern society the continual removal of economic rewards out of the hands of kinship and extended family groups lessens the dominance of Jewish families over the

[38]Nathan Glazer and Daniel P. Moynihan, *Beyond the Melting Pot* (Cambridge, Mass.: The M.I.T. Press, 1963), p. 150.

[39]Gerhard Lenski, *The Religious Factor,* (Garden City, N.Y.: Doubleday and Company, 1963), p. 214.

placement of its young within the socio-economic world. The changing kinship relations, coupled with more fluid labor markets, contribute to higher mobility rates.

If this interpretation is correct, the Providence data suggest that kinship ties of Jews have been weakening. Among all Providence families surveyed, there were 748 sons 40 years old and over, of whom one-third were living outside Rhode Island. Compared to this, just one-half of the 1,425 sons between ages 20 and 39 were living outside the state. Moreover, a higher proportion of the younger group were living outside New England. Further accentuation of the trend is suggested by the fact that almost two-thirds of children under age 20 who were living away from their parental home were outside Rhode Island, and 42 percent of the total were outside New England. Although fewer daughters lived away from their parental community, the basic age pattern was the same as for males.

These data lend weight to the assumption that the American Jewish community is increasingly mobile and that such mobility must be taken into account in any evaluation of Jewish life in the United States. Mobility is not a new facet of Jewish life. But whereas at a number of points in Jewish history it may have served to strengthen the Jewish community and indeed to insure its very survival, there is serious question whether this is generally true of increased internal migration. Such mobility may still serve a positive function in a given situation. Small Jewish communities may benefit considerably from the influx of other Jews who are attracted by nearby universities or modern, technological industries. Such in-migration may be crucial in creating the critical mass prerequisite to initiation and maintenance of the institutional facilities essential for continued Jewish identification. Migration may thus constitute the "blood transfusion" which greatly enhances the chances of the community's survival.

More often, however, and especially in the case of repeated movement, mobility may weaken the individual's ties to Judaism and to the Jewish community, which in turn weakens the community as it becomes more difficult to call upon the individual's loyalty to local institutions. For all too long the local Jewish community has assumed that most Jews remain within it for a lifetime, and that they are therefore willing and obligated to support it. This may no longer be true for many Jews. An increasing number may be reluctant to affiliate with the local community, not so much because they do not identify with Judaism, but because they anticipate that they will not remain in the local area long enough to justify the financial investment required. All this suggests the need for greater concern with the role of migration than of intermarriage in the future of American Judaism. The latter may largely be only a by-product, along with other undesirable consequences, of increased mobility.

Generational Change

Of all demographic characteristics of the Jewish community perhaps the one with the greatest relevance for its future character is the changing generation status of the Jews, i.e., how many are foreign-born, how many are children of foreign-born, and how many are at least third-generation Americans. In the past, a major factor in the continued vitality of the American Jewish community has been the continuous "blood transfusions" it received through the massive immigration of Jews from the ghettos of Eastern Europe. Now, for the first time in the community's history, a third-generation Jewish population faces the American scene without large-scale outside reinforcement; at the very same time, it enjoys much greater freedom than ever before. The Jewish community in the United States is increasingly an American Jewish community in every sense of the word.

Information on the generation status of American Jews must be gleaned from local community studies. These show beyond any doubt that the vast majority of America's Jews today are native-born (Table 8). Of all community studies presenting information on the nativity of the Jewish population, the one of Dade County, Florida, reported the highest percentage of foreign-born, 33 percent in 1961, and the one of Camden, New Jersey, the lowest, reporting 9 percent in 1964. But these extremes largely reflect the differential age composition of the population of the two areas. For most communities the percentage of foreign-born ranges between 20 and 25. Yet, even this range is somewhat high because the surveys in many of the communities were conducted in the 1950's. If one considers only those communities where surveys were taken in the 1960's, the proportion of foreign-born was generally under 20 percent. In several communities comparable data were collected at two different points in time, indicating the pattern of change. For example, the 1953 Los Angeles survey reported 32 percent

TABLE 8

Nativity of Jewish population, selected communities

		Nativity		
Community[a]	*Year of study*	*U.S. born*	*Foreign born*	*Total*[c] *percent*
Trenton, N.J.	1949	77	24	100
New Orleans, La.	1953	81	17	100
Los Angeles, Cal.	1953	68	32	100
Canton, Ohio	1955	77	23	100
Des Moines, Iowa	1956	78	22	100
Washington, D.C.	1956	83	17	100
Memphis, Tenn.	1959	81	18	100
San Francisco, Cal.	1959	72	26	100
Los Angeles, Cal.	1959	75	25	100
Rochester, N.Y.	1961	79	21	100
South Bend, Ind.	1961	80	20	100
Trenton, N.J.	1961	85	15	100
Providence, R.I.	1963	83	17	100
Detroit, Mich.[b]	1963	62	38	100
Pittsburgh, Pa.	1963	88	12	100
Camden, N.J.	1964	91	9	100
Milwaukee, Wis.[b]	1964	65	35	100
Springfield, Mass.	1966	85	14	100
Boston, Mass.	1966	83	15	100
Columbus, Ohio[b]	1969	74	26	100

[a]See appendix at end of chapter for citation of individual community studies.
[b]Head of household.
[c]Includes small percent of unknown nativity.

foreign-born; by 1959, the proportion had fallen to 25 percent. The Trenton, New Jersey, survey of 1949 reported 24 percent of the population as foreign-born; by 1961 the percentage was only 15. In 1937 the foreign-born in Des Moines comprised 35 percent of the Jewish population; in 1956, only 22 percent were foreign-born. An even sharper decline in the foreign-born characterized Pittsburgh in the 25-year period between 1938 and 1963, from 38 to 12 percent.

Evidence of the growing Americanization of the Jewish

community is also provided by the comparative data on the percentage of foreign-born in different age segments of the population. Here, the Greater Providence statistics provide a useful example. They have the added advantage of not only distinguishing between the foreign-born and native-born segments of the population, but of subdividing the latter into second and higher generations. Of the total 1963 Jewish population of Greater Providence, only 17 percent were foreign-born. The remaining 83 percent were almost equally divided between second-generation Americans (that is, with either one or both parents foreign-born) and third- or fourth-generation Americans (both parents born in the United States). The statistics on generation status by age indicate that not only was the percentage of foreign-born in the population declining, but that of second-generation Jews as well; at the same time, the proportion of third- and fourth-generation persons was increasing. . . .

The New York community represents a unique situation. Stemming from the city's role as a port of entry, it still has a disproportionately large foreign-born population, estimated at 37 percent of its 1963–1964 adult population. This contrasts with about 20 to 25 percent of all adults in most other communities. Attesting to its attraction for new immigrants, 11 percent of all New York Jews between ages 20 and 34 were foreign-born, compared to only 1 percent in other places. As a result, the changes in the generation composition of New York's Jewish population will lag behind that of the balance of the United States.[40]

Because of the importance of generational change for the structure of the Jewish community, Dr. Goldscheider and I based our analysis of Jewish Americans on a comparison of the demographic, social, economic, and religious characteristics of three generations in the Jewish community.[41] That study emphasizes that the future of the American Jewish community depends to a great degree on how its members (largely third-generation) are reacting to the freedom to work toward integration into the American social structure as an acculturated sub-society, or toward complete assimilation and loss of Jewish identification. Whether they are reversing or accelerating certain trends toward assimilation, initiated by their second-generation parents or by the smaller

[40]*American Jewish Year Book* Vol. 69 (1968), p. 273.

[41]Goldstein and Goldscheider, *op. cit.*

number of older third-generation Jews, provides the insights for the detection and projection of the patterns of generation change.

The physical dispersal and deconcentration of the Jewish population were rapid. They marked for many not only a physical break from the foreign-born, but symbolized the more dramatic disassociation of American-born Jews from the ethnic ties and experiences that had served as unifying forces in the earlier generation. The degree of identification with Judaism of the third-generation Jews who participate in this dispersal has become a key issue. At the same time, sharp rises have taken place in secular education, as distance from the immigrant generation increased. This provided the key to Jewish participation in the professions and, more recently, in high executive positions.

Dispersal of the Jewish population and its greater exposure to public education increased the interaction between Jews and non-Jews and, as later analysis will document, has resulted in higher intermarriage rates with increasing distance from the immigrant generation. These generational changes in residential location, social class structure, and marriage patterns have been accompanied also by redirections of the religious system. Striking shifts were observed between first- and third-generation groups in identification and membership from Orthodox to Conservative and Reform, as well as declines in regular synagogue attendance, observance of kashrut, Jewish organization affiliation, and use of Yiddish as a spoken language. Yet, these trends were counteracted by a clear tendency toward increased Jewish education for the young, as well as increases in selected religious observances. Overall, some aspects of religiosity appeared to be strengthened, others declined, and some remained stable over the generations. Religious change among three generations of Jews is a complex process involving the abandonment of traditional forms and the development of new forms of identity and expression more congruent with the broader American way of life. Our generational analysis suggests, that evolving out of the process of generational adjustment, the freedom to choose the degree of assimilation was exercised in the direction of Jewish identification.

Age Composition

. . .the age structure of the American Jewish community is clear: On the whole, the Jewish population is older than the total United States white population; and over time, both because of its lower fertility and because it has in most places such a large proportion of individuals in the 45-to-64 age group, the Jewish population can be expected to become increasingly older. In American society the problems associated with an aged population are many. During the next few decades such problems may become even more serious for the Jewish community than for the population as a whole. This can be illustrated by projections made for the age composition of the Jewish population of Greater Providence for 1978, fifteen years after the survey. It must be emphasized that these projections assume that fertility and mortality will continue at the 1960 levels and that the total metropolitan area's population will not be affected by migration. The resulting projections definitely point to an aging of the population: a rise from 10 to 17 percent in the proportion of the persons 65 years of age and older. In actual numbers, there will be a 70 percent increase in the number of aged. At the same time, the percentage under 15 years of age will decline from 25 in 1963, to 19 in 1978. Reflecting both the low fertility rates of 1960 and the fewer women of childbearing age, the absolute number of children under 15 will be 20 percent lower in 1978 than in 1963, affecting the community's task in educating and providing leisure activities for youngsters. But changes will also occur in the middle segment of the age hierarchy, as the reduced number of persons resulting from the especially low Jewish birthrate during the depression move into the 45-to-54 age range. The percentage of this group is projected to decline from 16 of the total in 1963, to only 10 in 1978. In actual numbers, there will be a decline of almost one-third. This may create some serious problems for the community, as the pool of persons to whom it can turn for leadership and financial contributions is greatly reduced. Given the possibility of these developments, Jewish communities may want to reevaluate and reorganize their services, deciding, in particular, which to retain for the Jewish community because of their Jewish component, and which to relegate to the larger community because of their secular character.

Overall, therefore, the dynamic character of the Jewish age structure requires continuous monitoring, not only for the demographic impact it will have on births, deaths, migration, and socio-economic structure, but also because of its broader social implications.[42] While recognizing the general trend toward an aging population, with its associated problems of housing for the aged,

[42]See Gosta Carlsson and Katarina Carlsson, "Age Cohorts and the Generation of Generations," *American Sociological Review*, August 1970, pp. 710–718.

financial crises resulting from retirement, more persons in poor health, one must also be aware that changes are taking place at other points in the age hierarchy and that the need for schools, playgrounds, camps, and teenage programs also vary as the age profile changes. Too often the Jewish community has been guilty of planning its future without taking account of the basic considerations of the probable size, distribution, and age composition of the population.

Education

For a large majority of the Jews who emigrated to America in the late 1800's and early 1900's, the major incentive was the supposed equal opportunities permitting significant social and economic mobility. But lacking secular education, adequate facility in English, and technical training, many found that rapid advancement proved an unrealistic goal. For others, both educational and occupational achievement were made difficult, if not impossible, by factors related to their foreign-born status or, more specifically, to their identification as Jews. Frustrated in their own efforts to achieve significant mobility, many Jews transferred their aspirations to their children. The first-generation American Jew recognized the special importance of education as a key to occupational mobility and higher income, and made considerable effort to provide their children with a good secular education. Reflecting the great value placed by Jews on education, both as a way of life and as a means of mobility, the Jews of America have compiled an extraordinary record of achievement in this area. . . . In recognition of the important effect of education on the social position of the Jew in the larger community, as well as its possible influence on the degree and nature of Jewish identification, most recent surveys have collected information on education. All these clearly document the high educational achievement of the American Jewish population (Table 9). . . .

. . . A college education is becoming virtually universal to younger segments of the Jewish population. Within the Jewish population itself, the important educational differential will thus be between those who had only some college education and those who went on to postgraduate work. At least one caveat should be added to the conclusion concerning virtually universal college education for Jews in the future: If the current emphasis on recruitment of minority-group members and underprivileged students persists,

TABLE 9

Educational distribution of adult Jewish population, selected communities[a]

Community	Year	Educational distribution[b] (percent)				
		8 grades and less	*1–3 high school*	*4 high school*	*1–3 college*	*4 or more college*
Trenton, N.J.	1949	22	7	32	9	18
Canton, Ohio	1955	21	10	33	18	8
Des Moines, Iowa	1956	18	7	32	19	19
Washington, D.C.	1956	10	8	27	16	36
New Orleans, La.	1958	10	8	18	20	28
Los Angeles, Cal.	1959	9	15	– 49[c] –		23
South Bend, Ind.	1961	17	8	33	18	22
Rochester, N.Y.	1961	21	12	30	30	23
Providence, R.I.	1963	15	8	34	16	25
Detroit, Mich.	1963	9	– 37[c] –		– 54[c] –	
Camden, N.J.	1964	11	9	34	18	28
Milwaukee, Wis.	1964	11	11	28	23	27
Springfield, Mass.	1966	11	7	33	19	27

[a] See appendix at end of chapter for citation of individual community studies.
[b] Table omits the "Unknowns."
[c] Figures refer to sum of 2 columns.

especially to the point of meeting certain enrollment quotas, the higher rates of enrollment by members of other segments of the population may necessarily be reduced. Jews, in particular, might be affected by such a development because of their very high enrollment rates.

As part of a larger survey of inequality in educational opportunity in the United States, the Bureau of Census Current Population Survey of October 1965 gathered information about school-age children.[43] A 1970 report, limited to white boys and girls aged 14 to 19 who were enrolled in elementary or secondary public or private schools, reviewed the college plans of the sample

[43] A. Lewis Rhodes and Charles B. Nam, "The Religious Context of Educational Expectations," *American Sociological Review*, April 1970, pp. 253–267.

respondents. Since religion was one of the three key variables for which information was collected (the other two were race and national origin), this analysis provides an opportunity to compare the college intentions of Jewish teenagers and teenagers in general.

The religious composition of the student body was based on the principal's estimate of the percentage of Protestants, Catholics, and Jews in his school. Of the estimated 330,000 Jewish students enrolled in public and private elementary and secondary schools, 74,000, or 22.4 percent, were enrolled in schools with half or more of their students Jewish; 118,000, or 35.8 percent, were in schools where less than half of the students were Jewish; an additional 41.8 percent were in schools for which no religion composition could be obtained.

The study found that 86 percent of the 330,000 Jewish students planned to attend college, compared with only 53 percent of the general student body. Interestingly, the percentages differed strikingly between those teenagers who were receiving their education in schools with heavy Jewish populations and those in schools with less than 50 percent Jewish students. Among the former, 94 percent planned to attend college; among the latter, only 80 percent did.

Other variables obviously affect plans for college. The study attempts to control for the effects of intelligence, mother's education, occupation of household head, and family income. Adjusting for all these factors reduced the differences among the various religions in the percentage of students with college plans. Yet, part of the religious differences persisted; and even after controlling for all these variables, 70 percent of all the Jewish students, compared to the general average of 53 percent, had college plans. Even within the high-IQ subgroup, comparisons between Jews and other segments of the population showed that Jews continued to have the highest proportion planning for college education.

The authors conclude:

> The high rate of college plans (86 percent) for pupils with Jewish mothers is particularly noteworthy, especially when the effect of religious context is added to the analysis. If the majority of the student body is Jewish the college plans rate for Jewish students is fourteen percentage points higher than the rate for Jewish students in schools where Jews are in the minority. The rate is fifteen percentage points higher even when the intelligence, mother's aspiration, occupation,

and income are included in the analysis. The same results are observed for high-IQ Jews. The results suggest that it would be worthwhile to test the hypothesis that exposure of a Jewish student to the norms and values of a Jewish subcommunity is important in formation of educational expectations.[44]

These data have a number of implications for the types of demographic developments considered in this paper: First, they clearly confirm the projection that college education will be virtually universal among Jewish students, if they can realize their aspirations. Second, because plans for attending college are still quite low for a number of other religious groups, ranging in the 40 to 50 percent level, it will be some time before college attendance becomes universal among the non-Jewish population. As a result, some of the differences noted with respect to education can be expected to persist for a number of decades, and indirectly continue to affect occupation and income differentials. Also important is the finding that the proportion planning to go to college differed significantly (14 percentage points) between those receiving their elementary and secondary education in a largely "Jewish environment" and those doing so in more heterogeneous schools. If the Jewish population becomes more generally dispersed and tendencies toward migration increase, a much higher proportion of Jewish youth may be attending schools that are less densely Jewish. If either residence or school environment is so important for motivating individuals toward higher education, increased population redistribution may lower somewhat the proportion of Jewish youth planning to go to college. This must, however, remain speculative, pending more research on the role of the Jewish subcommunity, as compared to the role of the family, in forming education expectations.

In the meantime, high level of educational achievement significantly affects several areas of Jewish life in the United States. To the extent that education is highly correlated with occupation, an increasing proportion of college graduates in the Jewish population will affect its occupational composition. More Jews will be engaged in intellectual pursuits and in occupations requiring a high degree of technical skill. Concomitantly, there also will probably be a reduction in the number of self-employed, both because small, private business will not provide an adequate

[44]*Ibid.*, pp. 263–264.

intellectual challenge and because patterns of discrimination, which thus far have excluded Jews from large corporations, are likely to continue to weaken. However, the impact will go beyond occupation.

In order to obtain a college education, particularly at the postgraduate level, a large proportion of young Jews must leave home to attend colleges in distant places. As a result, their ties to both family and community will weaken. A high proportion of these college-educated youths probably never return permanently to the communities in which their families live and in which they were raised. Thus education serves as an important catalyst for geographic mobility and eventually leads many individuals to take up residence in communities with small Jewish populations, to live in highly integrated neighborhoods, and to work and socialize in largely non-Jewish circles. The extent to which such a development occurs needs to be closely followed during the decade of the 1970's.

Finally, Jews with higher education may have significantly higher rates of intermarriage and greater alienation from the Jewish community. This involves not only the possible impact of physical separation from home and the weakening of parental control on dating and courtship patterns, but also the general "liberalization" a college education may have on the religious values and Jewish identity of the individual. It would be ironic if the very strong positive value that Jews traditionally have placed on education and that now manifests itself in the very high proportion of Jewish youths attending college may eventually be an important factor in the general weakening of the individual's ties to the Jewish community.

Occupation

. . . The 1957 census sample survey provides data on. . . the occupational composition of the Jewish population and permits us to compare their patterns with those of the general population. . . . Sharp differentials characterized the occupational composition of the Jewish group, compared to the general population (Table 10). Three-fourths of all Jewish employed males worked in white-collar positions, compared to only 35 percent of the total white male population of the United States. These large differences were to a very great extent attributable to the much greater concentration of Jewish men in professional and managerial positions. Of the total Jewish male labor force, one in five was a professional, compared to only one in ten in the general population; and one out of every three Jews was employed as manager or proprietor, compared to only 13 percent of the total male population. The proportion in clerical work was similar for Jews and the total labor force, but in saleswork it was almost three times as high for Jews as for total males. Conversely, the proportion of Jews in manual work was very small: only 22 percent, compated to 57 percent of the total male labor force.

Compared with males, women in the labor force were much more concentrated in white-collar positions, but the differentials between Jewish women and all women were less marked than those for the men. Just over four out of every five Jewish women were in white-collar jobs, compared to just over half of the total female labor force. A similar pattern emerged from examination of the specific occupational categories. Among professionals, for example, the proportion of Jewish women was 15.5 percent, compared to 12.2 percent for the total female labor force. Like men, Jewish women were considerably underrepresented in manual labor categories: only 17 percent, compared to 44 percent of the total female labor force. . . .

The different occupational composition of Jews compared to the general population has often been attributed to their higher concentration in urban places and to their higher educational achievement. The census tabulations enable analysis of the occupational data for the urban population, while controlling for years of school completed by religion. By restricting the data to a more homogeneous social and economic environment and by holding constant the wide differences in educational achievement, it becomes possible to ascertain more clearly to what extent occupational differences are directly related to religious affiliation and to what degree they may simply be a reflection of differential opportunities available to Jews because of their places of residence and levels of education.

With residence and education controlled, 70 percent of the Jewish males were white-collar workers, compared to 41 percent of the general male population. Thus, the concentration of Jews in white-collar positions remained far above that of the total population; but the difference was no longer in the ratio of two to one, as indicated by the unstandardized data. Moreover, for selected occupational categories there also was a dramatic change. For example, with residence and education controlled, only 10 percent of the Jewish males were professionals, compared to 12

TABLE 10

Percent distribution of employed persons 18 years old and over by major occupation group, Jewish and total population, by sex, total and urban United States[a], 1957[b]

Major occupation group	*Total United States*				*Urban United States*			
	Males		*Females*		*Males*		*Females*	
	Total population	*Jewish*	*Total population*	*Jewish*	*Total population*	*Jewish*	*Total population*	*Jewish*
Professional	9.9	20.3	12.2	15.5	11.5	9.9	12.5	8.9
Farmers & farm managers	7.3	0.1	0.7	0.2	0.4	—		—
Managers & proprietors	13.3	35.1	5.5	8.9	14.6	36.8	5.3	8.9
Clerical workers	6.9	8.0	30.3	43.9	8.6	8.0	33.5	41.3
Sales workers	5.4	14.1	6.9	14.4	6.3	15.0	7.1	19.0
Skilled laborers	20.0	8.9	1.0	0.7	21.3	11.7	1.1	1.0
Semi-skilled laborers	20.9	10.1	17.1	11.2	21.7	14.0	17.7	15.1
Service workers	6.1	2.3	22.7	5.1	7.7	3.4	22.1	5.9
Farm laborers	2.5	0.1	3.0	—	0.3	0.1	0.1	—
Unskilled laborers	7.7	0.8	0.6	—	7.7	1.1	0.5	—
TOTAL	100.0	100.0	100.0	100.0	100.0	100.0	100.0	100.0
Total white-collar	35.5	77.5	54.9	82.7	41.0	69.7	58.4	78.1
Total blue-collar	57.2	22.2	44.4	17.0	58.7	30.3	41.5	22.0

[a]Standardized by years of school completed.

[b]U.S. Bureau of the Census, "Tabulations of Data on the Social and Economic Characteristics of Major Religious Groups, March 1957." (Unpublished)

percent of the total male population. What originally was a two-to-one differential completely disappeared and was even reversed. On the other hand, differentials in the managerial and the sales categories remained about the same. Similar conclusions held for occupational differentials for females after the data were restricted to urban residence and standardized by education. Overall, therefore, controlling for both education and residence suggests that both these factors explain some, but not all, variations in occupational differentials between Jews and the total population. . . .

The 1957 census data obviously are outdated by now. For evidence of the occupational composition of the Jewish population in the 1960's, one must turn to the various community surveys taken during that period. In 1960, 45 percent of the American white urban male population was engaged in white-collar work, but in such communities as Providence, Camden, Springfield, Rochester, and Trenton the percentage for Jews ranged from a low of 80 to a high of 92 percent. While the percentages in specific occupational categories varied among communities, depending on the character of the community and the nature of occupational opportunities, the proportion of professionals among Jews was from two to three times greater than among the general population, and the differentials in the proportion of managers and proprietors were even larger.

Some indication of the changes that may be taking place in the occupational composition of Jews can be gained from statistics on occupation by age for Providence (Table 11). These point in the direction of a reduced percentage of Jews in the managerial and proprietor group, and an increasing proportion in the professions and in saleswork. For example, among males the proportion of professionals increased from 17 percent of those 65 and over, to 25 percent of those 25 to 44; and conversely, the proportion employed as managers declined from over half of the oldest group to just about one-third of the 25–44-year group. At the same time, the proportion of sales personnel increased from 11 percent of the oldest to almost one-fourth of the 25–44 year group. The concentration of older males in managerial positions must be interpreted within the context of the high percentage of self-employed who tend to remain in the labor force, while those in the white-collar and manual-labor group must retire. Yet, as many as 17 percent of the aged segment of the employed population still held manual jobs, compared to only 13 percent of those in the

45-to-64-year group and 8 percent of those aged 25 to 44. In general, the same pattern by age characterized the employed females, although the differentials were not always as sharp.

Survey data on the occupation of heads of Jewish families for Detroit covering 1935, 1956, and 1963 provide a unique opportunity to compare changes over 28 years in the occupational composition of the Jewish population. The evidence clearly points to a pattern of occupational concentration. In 1935, 70 percent of the heads of Jewish families were employed as white-collar workers. By 1963 their percentage had risen to 90. The most striking changes characterized the professionals, who increased from 7 percent in 1935 to 23 percent in 1963, and the manager-owners, who grew from 31 to 54 percent of the total in that period. At the same time, the proportion of lower white-collar workers, that is, sales and clerical workers, declined from 32 to only 13 percent. Using the 1940 and 1960

TABLE 11

Occupational status by age and sex, Jewish population of Greater Providence, 1963 (Percent)

	Occupation				
Age	*Professionals*	*Managers*	*Clerical workers*	*Sales workers*	*Manual laborers*
Males					
15–24	12.3	24.6	13.9	24.6	21.5
25–44	24.6	37.9	4.8	24.3	9.2
45–64	19.0	43.6	3.5	19.5	13.4
65 and over	17.2	50.5	4.0	11.1	17.2
TOTAL	20.7	41.0	4.5	20.9	12.1
Females					
15–24	22.0	4.0	64.0	2.0	6.0
25–44	32.3	10.3	34.8	16.1	5.8
45–64	8.9	15.3	42.8	22.9	7.6
65 and over	1.3	31.6	21.5	26.1	16.4
TOTAL	17.9	12.9	41.6	18.4	7.2

censuses as bases for comparing changes in the general population, the data also show some upward concentration. In 1940, 31 percent of the population was in white-collar occupations; by 1960 this had risen to 38 percent. The proportion of professionals also grew considerably, from 5 to 12 percent, and that of managers-owners increased slightly, from 9 to 10 percent, compensated by a small decline in the proportion of lower white-collar workers, from 17 to 16 percent. Again, the patterns for the Jews and the total population were parallel, but the occupational movement of Jews has been much more accentuated. The conclusion seems warranted that, in time, increasing occupational concentration will also take place in the population as a whole, and differentials between Jews and the total population will decline. But in the short run, the discrepancies may be greater as Jews move up more quickly.

The Detroit data by age for 1963 also confirm occupational shifting within the white-collar segment of the occupational hierarchy. For example, only 19 percent of the 45-to-64-year age group were professionals, compared to 42 percent of the 20-to-34-year age group. As in Providence, a lower proportion of younger men were managers-owners: 40, compared to 56 percent. Particularly noteworthy is the decline in the proportion of independent businessmen within the managerial-proprietor group, from 42 percent among those aged 45 to 64, to only 30 percent of the younger group. Even if a considerable portion of those currently engaged as managers or sales and clerical workers should become owners at a later stage of the life cycle, the total percentage is not likely to exceed the proportion in the 45-to-64-year group classified as owners in 1963. Again, the data analyzed here suggest, that in the years ahead, business ownership is likely to decline among the Jewish population.

What do these varied data suggest for future trends in Jewish occupational composition? Although restricted because of their cross-sectional character, they point to a continuing increase in the proportion of Jews engaged in professional work, and to either stability or actual decline for the managerial and proprietor group. Possibly, a number of younger persons currently classified as salesworkers will at later stages of their life cycle move into managerial and proprietor positions, but evidence for Providence indicates that half or more of these younger individuals were working for others, outside of family businesses. With the gradual disappearance of small businesses, an increasing proportion of these

Jewish men may turn to executive positions in business corporations instead of operating their own firms, as did many of their parents and grandparents.

It seems reasonable to assume, that with the general rise in educational level, educational differentials among members of the various religious groups will lessen; and as discriminatory restrictions on occupational choice weaken, occupational differentials will also decline. The very high proportion of Jews in white-collar occupations . . . will persist; but within this concentration, there may in fact be more diversity in the future than there was in the past. At the same time, the total population will also concentrate more in higher occupational categories, with a decline in occupational differentials as the net result.

In commenting on educational and occupational changes within the Jewish population, Albert Mayer, the author of the 1968 Columbus, Ohio, study, made a most important observation. He stressed that the organized Jewish community must come to recognize that its constituency is now almost entirely high white-collar as well as college-educated. Unless the community takes full recognition of this crucial fact in all its activites, it will find much difficulty in gaining the loyalty, interest, and support of its membership. The reaction of the organized community to its membership may very well still be in terms of earlier twentieth-century stereotypes, i.e., a largely foreign-born, immigrant group in need of welfare and social services. This is a false image in view of generation changes, education, and occupational mobility; and any approach ignoring these changes runs the risk of serious failure. Such an attitude on the part of the community may be compounded by changes in identification patterns within the population itself. More Jews in scientific and executive positions may well lead to increased channeling of self-identification through the professional or intellectual subsocieties rather than through the Jewish community. Increased geographic mobility would reinforce such a development and pose still further challenges for the organized Jewish community.

Income

The demographer probably encounters greater difficulty in collecting information on income than on any other standard variable that interests him. Not until 1940 was the first income question included in the federal census. Social surveys focusing on fertility in the

United States today often find it harder to obtain accurate information on income than on such intimate matters as birth control practice and sexual activity. Not surprisingly, therefore, few among the large number of Jewish community surveys collected such information; and if they did, the data are often either of questionable quality or limited because there are no comparable figures for the general population. Yet, in a consideration of the position of Jews in American society, it is important to look at Jewish income levels, to ascertain whether they differ from those of the general population and, if so, why. For such purposes three sets of national data are available: the findings of the 1957 census surveys; the Lazerwitz study based on survey research statistics from the University of Michigan; and Bogue's analysis of the National Opinion Research Survey data. . . . However, the Lazerwitz and Bogue materials are limited in that they present only gross comparisons. The census data have the advantage of permitting more detailed analysis to document the influence of other factors on differences in income between Jews and the total population. For each person in the 1957 census sample, information was solicited on the amount of money income received in 1956 (Table 12). This included income from such varied sources as wages and salaries, self-employment, pensions, interest, dividends, and rent. Since both high education and high white-collar employment are highly correlated with income, the fact that the \$4,900 median income of Jewish males was well above the \$3,608 median for the male population as a whole comes as no surprise. This sharp differential was also reflected in the more detailed statistics of distribution by income class. Incomes of \$10,000 and over were reported by 17 percent of the Jewish males, compared to only 3.6 percent of the males in the total population. On the other hand, just over one-fourth of the Jews, but 41 percent of the total male population, had incomes under \$3,000. These differences extended to females as well, as evidenced by the 50 percent higher median income of Jewish women, compared to that of the total female population.

Controlling the census statistics for urban residence and major occupational groups eliminated the sharp differentials noted for the unstandardized data. For males, the standardized data showed a median income for Jews of \$4,773, just slightly above the \$4,472 median for the total population. Narrowing of differentials also extended to the overall distribution by income level. For the standardized data, 18 percent of the Jewish males, compared to 23 percent of the total male population, had incomes under \$3,000;

TABLE 12

Percent distribution of persons 14 years old and over by income in 1956, Jewish and total population, by sex, total and urban United States[a]

Income	*Total United States*				*Urban United States*			
	Total population	*Jewish*	*Total population*	*Jewish*	*Total population*	*Jewish*	*Total population*	*Jewish*
	Males		*Females*		*Males*		*Females*	
Under $1,000	17.2	10.0	46.9	39.0	5.6	4.1	23.2	22.5
1,000–1,999	11.7	9.0	19.3	16.6	6.1	6.4	20.6	18.8
2,000–2,999	12.1	7.4	15.7	15.2	10.8	7.6	24.3	24.7
3,000–3,999	14.8	11.0	11.0	15.1	17.4	13.9	19.6	19.1
4,000–4,999	15.9	14.0	4.3	6.5	21.4	23.3	7.8	9.7
5,000–5,999	11.9	13.4	1.5	3.6	16.0	17.0	2.7	2.8
6,000–9,999	12.7	18.0	0.9	2.3	17.6	18.9	1.4	1.7
10,000 and over	3.6	17.2	0.2	1.5	5.0	8.7	0.3	0.7
Total percent	100.0	100.0	100.0	100.0	100.0	100.0	100.0	100.0
Median income	$3,608	$4,900	$1,146	$1,663	$4,472	$4,773	$2,255	$2,352

[a]Standardized for major occupation group; U.S. Bureau of the Census, 1957 sample survey unpublished data.

and the proportion with incomes of $10,000 and over was 8.7 and 5.0 percent, respectively. The same narrowing of differentials appeared for women, as evidenced by the reduction of the difference between the median incomes of Jewish women and all women to less than $100.

Clearly, then, the considerably higher income level characterizing Jews, compared with the general population, is a function of their concentration in urban areas and in high white-collar positions. This suggests, that as educational differentials between Jews and the rest of the population narrow and as increasing proportions of non-Jews enter higher white-collar positions, the existing income differentials between Jews and the general population will diminish. Such a conclusion seems justified by additional information showing that for Jews, as for the total population, the median income level consistently rises with increasing education (Table 13). For example, for Jews with less than an eighth-grade education, the average median income was $2,609; but for those with a college degree, it was $8,041. If Jews and the total population with similar levels of education are compared, however, the differences in median income are generally less than 10 percent for all educational categories below the college level. For the college groups, and particularly for those with a college degree, the differences increase. In all likelihood, the sharp differential

TABLE 13

*Median income in 1956 of Jewish and all United States urban men 14 years old and over by years of school completed**

Years of school completed		*Total*	*Jewish*
Elementary	0–7	$2,654	$2,609
	8	3,631	3,844
High school	1–3	3,858	4,672
	4	4,563	4,913
College	1–3	4,526	5,026
	4 or more	6,176	8,041

*U.S. Bureau of the Census, 1957 sample survey unpublished data.

within the college-graduate group reflects the higher proportion of Jews who have postgraduate education and are in high-income professional and executive positions. As proportionately more persons in the general population obtain a postgraduate education, differences in income level between the Jewish and the total population will probably diminish. . . .

Overview of Future Demographic Trends

From existing information on the demographic history of the American Jewish community and on its structure in 1970, what patterns of development can be anticipated?

Numbering about 6 million in 1970, after slow growth during all but the first several decades of this century, the Jewish population is likely to continue its slow increase. The low rate of growth results particularly from the low level of Jewish fertility, which is below that of Protestants and Catholics and hovers close to the minimum needed for replacement. Limited data suggest that death rates of Jews are slightly below those of the general population, but the overall death rate of the Jewish population is likely to rise as the average age increases. This, together with possible larger losses from intermarriage, will contribute to maintenance, if not accentuation, of the slow growth rate. As a result, the Jewish population, even while growing slightly, will come to constitute an increasingly smaller proportion of the total American population, having already declined from the peak of 3.7 to less than 3 percent by 1970.

While declining as a percent of the total population, Jews will also become more dispersed throughout the United States. As a result of continuously higher education and changing occupations, lower levels of self-employment, weakening family ties, and reduced discrimination, Jews are likely to migrate in increasing numbers away from the major centers of Jewish population. This will operate on several levels. Regionally, it will lead to fewer Jews in the Northeast. Jews will continue to be highly concentrated in metropolitan areas; but, within the metropolitan areas, ever increasing numbers will move out of the urban centers and former ghettos into the suburbs. In doing so, the Jewish population will become much more geographically dispersed, even while distinct areas of Jewish concentration remain.

At the same time that its overall numbers and distribution change, the Jewish population will also undergo significant changes in selected aspects of socio-economic composition. In others, it will show less change; but, because of changes in the general population, differences between Jews and non-Jews may narrow.

As a result of the significant reduction in Jewish immigration to the United States since the 1920's and the subsequent aging and death of the immigrants, the most striking compositional change characterizing American Jewry is the reduction in the percent of foreign-born. Indeed, even the proportion of second-generation American Jews will increasingly diminish as third- and fourth-generation persons become an even larger proportion of the Jewish population, with all this implies for questions of Jewish identification and assimilation. Reflecting their lower fertility, the Jewish population, already six years older on the average than the general population, is likely to undergo further aging. This will mean a considerable increase in the proportion of older persons as well as of the widowed, especially women.

Already unique in their high concentration among the more educated, high white-collar and high income groups, the Jews may undergo still further changes. College education will be an almost universal phenomenon among them, and an increasing proportion will pursue graduate studies. At the same time, continuously rising education levels among non-Jews may narrow educational differentials between Jews and non-Jews. The high proportion of Jews who obtain specialized university training, their tendency to move out of small family businesses and into salaried employment, and their increasing willingness to seek and take positions away from their community of current residence may bring an increase in the number of Jews in technical and executive occupations within the top professional and managerial occupational categories, where they already are heavily concentrated. At the same time, the general upward shift in the occupational level of the general population will narrow existing differences in the occupational structure of the Jewish and non-Jewish populations. In turn, this narrowing in both educational and occupational differences will lead to reduction in the income differences currently characterizing Jews and non-Jews. Such a development is strongly suggested by the fact, that with control for education and occupation, income differences between Jews and non-Jews have been shown to be greatly reduced, and sometimes reversed.

These demographic changes point to a number of challenges which the American Jewish community must face. In the last three decades of the twentieth century, increasing Americanization will continue, as judged by greater geographic dispersion, a higher percent of third- and fourth-generation Americans, and narrowing of such key socio-economic differentials as education, occupation, and income. To what extent will the diminution in the distinctive population characteristics of Jews and their greater residential integration lead to behavioral convergence? The risks or opportunities for this to occur, depending on how one views the situation, are increasingly present. Recent research suggests, that while growing similarity on the behavioral level is likely, structural separation and the continuity of Jewish identification will persist.[45] The direction of changes appears to be the adjustment of American Jews to the American way of life, creating a meaningful balance between Jewishness and Americanism.

APPENDIX

Jewish Community Studies

All About Us! (Jacksonville, Fla.: Jewish Community Council, 1954).

Axelrod, Morris, Fowler, Floyd J., and Gurin, Arnold, *A Community Survey for Long Range Planning: A Study of the Jewish Population of Greater Boston* (Boston: Combined Jewish Philanthropies of Greater Boston, 1967).

Baum, Samuel, *The Jewish Population of Des Moines* (Des Moines: Jewish Welfare Federation, 1956).

Beckenstein, Esther, *Report on the Jewish Population of Metropolitan Chicago* (Chicago: Jewish Federation of Metropolitan Chicago, 1959).

Bigman, Stanley K., *The Jewish Population of Greater Washington in 1956* (Washington, D.C.: The Jewish Community Council of Greater Washington, 1957).

Chenkin, Alvin, and Goldman, Benjamin B., *The Jewish Population of New Orleans, La.* (New York: Council of Jewish Federations and Welfare Funds, 1953).

Goldstein, Sidney, *The Greater Providence Jewish Community: A Population Survey* (Providence, R.I.: General Jewish Committee, 1964).

———, *A Population Survey of the Greater Springfield Jewish Community* (Springfield, Mass.: Jewish Community Council, 1968).

The Jewish Community of Pittsburgh: A Population Survey (Pittsburgh: United Federation of Pittsburgh, 1963).

The Jewish Population of Canton, Ohio (Canton: The Jewish Community Federation of Canton, Ohio, 1955).

[45]Goldstein and Goldscheider, *op. cit.*, pp. 232–243.

The Jewish Population of Charleston, W. Va. (Charleston: B'nai Jacob Synagogue, 12th Annual Report, 1970).
The Jewish Population of Greater Lynn, Mass. (Lynn: The Jewish Community Federation of Greater Lynn, 1956).
The Jewish Population of Rochester, New York (Monroe County), *1961* (Rochester: Jewish Community Council, 1961).
The Jews of Worcester (Worcester, Mass.: Jewish Federation, 1958, 1961).
Kaplan, Saul, *Jewish Births and Jewish Population in Cook County, Illinois—1963* (Chicago: Jewish Federation of Metropolitan Chicago, 1966).
Massarik, Fred, *The Jewish Population of Los Angeles* (Los Angeles: Jewish Federation—Council of Greater Los Angeles, 1959).
———, *The Jewish Population of San Francisco, Marin County and The Peninsula* (San Francisco: Jewish Welfare Federation, 1959).
———, *A Report on the Jewish Population of Los Angeles* (Los Angeles: Jewish Federation—Council of Greater Los Angeles, 1959).
———, *A Study of the Jewish Population of Long Beach, Lakewood and Los Alamitos* (Long Beach, Cal.: Jewish Community Federation, 1962).
Mayer, Albert J., *Columbus Jewish Population Study:* 1969 (Columbus, Ohio: Jewish Welfare Federation, 1970).
———, *The Detroit Jewish Community Geographic Mobility: 1963—1965, and Fertility—A Projection of Future Births* (Detroit: Jewish Welfare Federation, 1966).
———, *Estimate of the Numbers and Age Distribution of the Detroit Metropolitan Area: 1956* (Detroit: Jewish Welfare Federation, 1959).
———, *Flint Jewish Population Study,* 1967 (Flint, Mich.: Jewish Community Council, 1969).
———, *Income Characteristics of the Jewish Population in the Detroit Metropolitan Area: 1956* (Detroit: Jewish Welfare Federation, 1960).
———, *Jewish Population Study: 1963, Number of Persons, Age and Residential Distribution* (Detroit, Jewish Welfare Federation, 1964).
———, *Milwaukee Jewish Population Study, 1964–1965* (Milwaukee: Jewish Welfare Fund, 1966).
———, *Movement of the Jewish Population in the Detroit Metropolitan Area: 1949–1959* (Detroit: Jewish Welfare Federation, 1964).
———, *Social and Economic Characteristics of the Detroit Jewish Community: 1963* (Detroit: Jewish Welfare Federation, 1964).
Robison, Sophie M., *Jewish Population Study of Trenton, New Jersey* (New York: Office for Jewish Population Research, 1949).
Rosen, Harry R., "Jewish Population Survey 1/70," *Toledo Jewish News,* April 1970, p. 17.
Shapiro, Manheim S., *The Bayville (Dade County, Florida) Survey of Jewish Attitudes* (New York: American Jewish Committee, 1961).
———, *The Southville (Memphis, Tenn.) Survey of Jewish Attitudes* (New York: American Jewish Committee, 1959).

Sterne, Richard S., *A Demographic Study of the Jewish Population of Trenton, New Jersey and Vicinity* (Trenton: Jewish Federation of Trenton, 1961).

We See Ourselves: A Self Study of the Jewish Community of St. Joseph County, Indiana (South Bend, Ind.: Jewish Community Council of St. Joseph County, 1961).

Westoff, Charles F., *A Population Survey* (Cherry Hill, N.J.: Jewish Federation of Camden County, 1964).

THE JEWISH FAMILY

THE STRATEGY OF THE JEWISH MOTHER

by ZENA SMITH BLAU

INTRODUCTION

OF ALL of the topics of sociological interest relating to the American Jew none has received as much attention as the Jewish family. Most of the wide literature on the Jewish family emanates from Jews themselves and generally concerns a family composed of immigrant parents and their second-generation children. While there are also treatments of families composed of second-generation parents and their third-generation offspring, most works on the Jewish family portray individuals who retain some linkage with an immigrant past.

The literature on the American Jewish family includes treatments which are warmly sentimental in tone, as in the writings of Sam Levenson and Harry Golden. But the dominant mood, especially in the fictional literature and more especially in that which emanates from the more recognized writers, is sharply critical of the Jewish family. Parents are seen as threatening figures who induce guilt in the child when he attempts to achieve independence. Because of the parental heritage even the child who persists in his efforts to achieve independence is bound to fail. Excessively dependent on his parents, he is a born loser: Even if he should succeed in the struggle to be himself his victory is fated to be won at an excessive emotional cost.

The large number of fictional works which portray the American Jewish family (together with the growing nonfiction literature written in a popular vein) attests both to the productivity of Jewish writers as well as to the freedom which they feel in revealing their personal background. Yet despite the abundance of such self-revelation our knowledge about the American Jewish family is severely limited—a result of the fact that fictional and popular treatments have not been complemented by a growing body of scientific literature. As a result Zena Smith Blau's contribution is especially welcome, providing insights into the Jewish family that have been missed by novelists and popular writers.

Blau's focus is on the same Jewish mother whom others have singled out for attack. But rather than sketching a neurotic parent-child relationship she emphasizes the positive consequences of Jewish child-rearing practices. She develops the argument that Jewish mothers—at least those of the recent past—promote a strong ego structure in their children. As a result of their efforts the child finds the strength to cope with an environment in which he may encounter assaults upon his feelings of self-worth, as in the case of exposure to anti-Semitism. But Blau sees the intense parent-child relationship as having even more important consequences than this, of giving the Jewish child a strong belief in his own ability to achieve success in the classroom and ultimately in his career.

Instead of viewing Jewish nurturant behavior as harmful to the child Blau maintains that it is a positive benefit. She believes that the alternative to close family relationships—namely, dependence upon peer-group relationships—is at best a mixed blessing which produces difficulties avoided by the structure of Jewish family life. Reliance on peers can create limited horizons, expecially in the type of working-class and lower-middle-class neighborhoods where American Jews lived before they moved to suburbia. Finally, Blau sees the relationship with the mother as indispensable to the building of loyalty to the ethnic group. Although Blau's primary emphasis is on the parent-child relationship, she views this relationship against the wider canvas of the group and suggests that the growth of identification with the mother during early childhood is crucial to the retention of Jewishness during adulthood.

M. S.

A WIDESPREAD BELIEF in America, shared by Jews as well as by non-Jews, is that Jews are "smart but neurotic." The Jew's intellectual aptitudes and interests are usually attributed to the cultural values transmitted by the Jewish fathers for whom learning and study were traditionally a religious obligation. As for the neurosis, that is blamed on the Jewish mother. The role that Jewish immigrant mothers played in the achievements of their children has been obscured by the uncritical acceptance of the view that their distinctive pattern of maternal behavior engendered a special affinity for neurosis in their children.

That high scholastic and occupational attainment has been more characteristic of second-generation Jews than of other religious and ethnic groups is confirmed by the available empirical evidence. Whatever indices have been employed to measure achievement—I.Q. scores, school grades, years of schooling, occupational level, and social mobility—Jews, on the average, exhibit higher levels of performance than the non-Jews to whom they have been compared.[1] But the proposition that neurosis is significantly more widespread among Jews than among non-Jews is a matter of conjecture rather than of fact, because the evidence required to test this proposition has not been available until recently. That Jews exhibit greater acceptance of psychiatry and are more likely to seek this form of professional service is not necessarily an indication that they are sicker than non-Jews. For the decision to seek therapy is influenced by social attributes and attitudes quite independent of the nature and degree of illness manifested by

[1]See, for example, Gerald S. Lesser, Gordon Fifer, and Donald Clark, "Mental Abilities of Children from Different Social-class and Cultural Groups," *Monographs of the Society for Research in Child Development,* Vol. 30, No. 4 (1965), pp. 82–83; also, Fred L. Strodtbeck, "Family Interaction, Values and Achievement," in David McClelland and Associates, *Talent and Society* (Princeton: D. Van Nostrand Co., Inc., 1958), pp. 135–194; Ben B. Seligman and Aaron Antonovsky, "Some Aspects of Jewish Demography," and S. Joseph Fauman, "Occupational Selection among Detroit Jews," in Marshall Sklare, ed., *The Jews: Social Patterns of an American Group* (Glencoe: Free Press, 1958), pp. 83–86, pp. 119–137.

individuals.[2] The *true* prevalence and severity of emotional disorders in the *general* population, therefore, cannot validly be inferred from ascertaining the characteristics of psychiatric patients. Some standardized test must also be applied to a systematically drawn sample of untreated people to determine whether the nature and degree of emotional disturbance among Jews actually differs from that among non-Jews.

Such a study, based on a sample of 1,660 respondents in midtown Manhattan, published in 1962, provides the first reliable data on this question. Leo Srole and Thomas Langner report that neurotic symptoms were common in all three major religious groups: Respondents rated as "well" constituted only 20.2 percent of Protestants tested, 17.4 percent of the Catholics, and 14.5 percent of the Jews. But when the authors classified people according to the *severity* of their symptoms and the degree to which these interfered with their ability to carry on normal activities, they discovered that *impairing* forms of emotional disorder were significantly lower among Jews (17.2 percent) than among either Protestants (23.5 percent) or Catholics (24.7 percent). Further, Jews were concentrated in the mental health category of "mild symptom formation," exhibiting far fewer cases of incapacitating disorder than Protestants and Catholics. Interestingly, the Jewish immunity from psychological impairment was most pronounced among respondents from working-class families, where mental illness is generally most prevalent.[3]

In view of this evidence that Jews are not more but less prone to emotional *impairment* than non-Jews, a reassessment of the characteristics and effects of Jewish maternal practices is necessary. Instead of being a pathogenic agent, as is commonly assumed, the mode of socialization practiced by Jewish immigrant mothers may have promoted a strong ego structure in their children that enabled them to cope successfully with the emotional strains to which low-status minority groups are subject, and in doing so made a

[2]For a discussion of the cultural and social factors that predispose Jews to seek psychotherapy, especially psychoanalysis, more than other groups see Jerome Myers and Bertram Roberts, "Ethnic Origins and Mental Illness," in Marshall Sklare, *op. cit.*, pp. 551–560.

[3]Leo Srole, Thomas Langner, et al., *Mental Health in the Metropolis* (New York: McGraw-Hill, Inc., 1962), Vol. 1, pp. 305–306. The distributions shown have been standardized by age and sex to eliminate any biases arising from differences in the composition of the three religious groups in the sample.

significant contribution to the remarkable record of educational and occupational attainment of second-generation Jews in America.

Not all Jewish immigrant women, of course, exhibited identical maternal behavior, but there can be little question that the constellation of maternal traits commonly referred to as "the *Yiddishe Mameh*" was the modal maternal pattern among Jewish immigrants from Eastern Europe; that it was different from the typical maternal behavior found among non-Jews in America;[4] and that it was both appropriate and effective for realizing the child-rearing goals of Jewish parents.

Jewish mothers were active, responsible, stable, expressive, and verbal women for whom *naches fun die kinder* [Joy from children] represented the highest form of self-fulfillment and achievement for a woman. They perceived the child as a fragile creature whose body and spirit needed to be carefully and assiduously nurtured and protected not only in infancy but throughout childhood and even adolescence. Coming as they did from a society in which child mortality rates were high, they exercised the utmost vigilance over the health and nurturance of their children. They went to inordinate trouble and expense to provide their children with the "best and freshest" food, the best medical care, the warmest clothing—at considerable sacrifice of other needs and wants. That their high standards of child care were effective is attested to by the fact that infant and child mortality rates were lower among Jews than in the rest of the American population during the earlier decades of this century, despite the fact that the majority of Jewish immigrants were in the working class where the mortality risks are greatest.[5]

Strong bonds of love and mutual dependency between mother and child are traditional among Jews. For most of their history they have occupied the position of a beleagured minority exposed to hostility, as well as to the pressure to abandon their faith and take up the ways of the majority. Various practices evolved among diaspora Jews to strengthen and fortify the child to cope with these pressures. The responsibility for establishing the bulwark of this fortification

[4]A striking similarity exists between the mode of maternal behavior of the *Yiddishe Mameh* and that found among women in the new middle class in contemporary Japan, who, like the Jews, are strongly committed to high educational attainment for their children. See Ezra Vogel, *Japan's New Middle Class* (Berkeley: University of California Press, 1963).

[5]Seligman and Antonovsky, *op. cit.*, pp. 63–68.

system is assigned to the mother,[6] and the task begins at birth of building a healthy body, a strong ego, and a strong primary identification with the mother which is perceived as the essential *motivating* force for learning the ways of Jews and for adhering to them, even under adverse conditions.[7]

The traditionally strong emotional bonds between Jewish mothers and their children were further intensified in America by the pattern of small families that rapidly became established among Jewish immigrants, a pattern markedly different from non-Jewish immigrants.[8] In general, lower birthrates facilitate upward social mobility, and this is the effect they had in the case of the Jews. With fewer mouths to feed Jewish immigrants could invest a larger proportion of their scarce economic resources in small business enterprises and thereby achieve middle-class status in much higher numbers than non-Jewish immigrants; this, in turn, materially enhanced the chances of high educational attainment for their children. But even among Jews who remained in the working class, the small family pattern enabled a mother to concentrate more effort and care on each of her children throughout childhood and adolescence. The payoff, of course, was higher educational attainment and higher social mobility among second-generation Jews than among non-Jewish immigrants.

In America, the Jewish mother appeared far more permissive, indulgent, and self-sacrificing than the typical Anglo-Saxon or immigrant mother, at least in the years prior to the 1940's. For example, they were a good deal more tolerant of whining and

[6]Accordingly, Jewish religious law defines the progeny of mixed marriages as Jews only if the mother is Jewish.

[7]The transmission of traditional learning and ritual, serving as a role model for sons in the home, and acting as the representative of the family in the religious community are responsibilities of the father. A relatively egalitarian power structure *within* the family was traditional among Eastern Jews long before the migration to America, a reflection of the recognition of the importance of both parents in the perpetuation of Judaism from one generation to the next.

[8]For comparative data concerning family size and fertility rates of Jewish immigrants see Seligman and Antonovsky, *op. cit.*, pp. 63–68; also David Goldberg and Harry Sharp, "Some Characteristics of Detroit Area Jewish and Non-Jewish Adults," in Marshall Sklare, *op. cit.*, pp. 107–118. My current research, based on a sample of 1,100 black and white mothers of fifth-and sixth-graders in the Chicago metropolitan area, suggests that Jews continue to have fewer children than Catholics and Protestants, and that they and their husbands come from smaller-sized families than non-Jews. (The Jewish subsample [109 cases] is two-thirds third generation and one-third second generation.)

crying, and of dependency behavior generally. They exerted little pressure on their children to control explosions of feeling and temper, and demanded only that they refrain from engaging in physical forms of aggression—*nit mit die hendt* [Not with the hands] was a common admonishment in the Jewish home. Toward his father and other grown-ups a Jewish child was expected to behave with respect, but toward his mother he was allowed considerably more leeway to express negative as well as positive feelings. Jewish mothers erected no status distance between themselves and their children. They did not stand on ceremony; they did not protect their pride or their self-respect. With no other human being did the Jewish child develop as close, as trusting, as free and fearless a relationship as with his mother, and therein lay the secret of her power to gain his compliance ultimately in those areas of behavior in which she chose to exert pressure during the entire period of maturation.[9]

Identification with the mother is the cornerstone of the entire socialization process: Jewish mothers understood that once firmly established—but not before—it would be possible to gain the *voluntary* compliance of their children to those basic social norms to which they as Jews were committed, and to which they were determined their children should also permanently adhere—whatever later pressures they might encounter to deny or violate them. That Jews as a rule retain their Jewish identity, and have done so over the centuries, however ambivalently, is largely due, although not entirely, of course, to the strength of the primary identification with the Jewish mother, and to the profound fear of the guilt that denial of her would engender.

Jewish mothers seemed singularly unconcerned with "discipline" and "independence training." They allowed their children a greater degree of latitude in acting out at home than was customary among Gentiles, and readily acknowledged that their children were *zelosen,* that is, pampered, demanding, spoiled, not well-behaved the way Gentile children seemed to be in the presence of their mothers. The Anglo-Saxon code of stoic endurance and suppressed emotion was alien to Eastern European Jews. Of course, *Yiddishe Mamehs* had their boiling point, which varied a good deal depending on their individual temperament, but generally they

[9]See Henry Roth's novel, *Call It Sleep* (New York: Cooper Square Publishers, Inc., 1934), for a sensitive portrayal of interaction between an immigrant Jewish mother and her first-born child.

preferred controlling their children *mit guten,* that is, by explanation, reasoning, distraction, and admonishment. As a rule, they were "naggers" or "screamers" rather than disciplinarians. They gained compliance from their children by entreaties repeated so often that finally the child would comply voluntarily, albeit wearily, with their requests. The Jewish mother avoided methods of control that aroused fear of herself in the child, and regarded such methods as morally wrong as well as inexpedient for cultivating inner control in her children.

This is not to say that Jewish women endured all misbehavior with perfect equanimity. They were volatile, expressive women who, if other methods of control failed, would flare up, scream at their children, and occasionally slap them, usually taking care to avoid the region of face and head. But they did not nurse their anger. The outburst quickly subsided, the child was embraced and comforted, and peace was restored. Such scenes were commonplace in Jewish homes, and added to the liveliness of the atmosphere.

Jewish fathers as a rule were more controlled and reserved in their dealings with their children, but they were usually not any more harsh with them. However, their silence when they became angry with a child created more discomfort and readier compliance than the mother's outburst. But in both cases it was the discomfort—anxiety and guilt—that parental disapproval induced rather than fear of coercion that led Jewish children at a relatively tender age to internalize those norms of behavior which are of paramount importance to Jews.

But if the Jewish mother was permissive with respect to the acting out of wilfulness, anger, tension, or fearfulness in children—appreciating the cathartic value of such behavior—she was not at all permissive on the question of moral training. Teaching of the basic precepts of Judaism began virtually in infancy for Jewish children whether they were brought up in religious or in secular homes. The kind of appeal that Jewish immigrant women employed to motivate their children to eat, for example, was often couched in normative terms. They did not simply impress on their children that eating was an act of self-interest—that by doing so they would grow up big and strong—but they also invested this mundane activity with moral significance and transformed it into an act of altruism by urging the child to eat *for* others—for mama, for poppa, for other members of the family and inevitably, the appeal was made to eat for "the poor, starving children of Europe." Similarly, as their children grew older Jewish mothers represented learning as not only being in the child's own self-interest, but also as a means of fulfilling his obligations to his parents, to his people, and to humanity.

For all their warmth and indulgence Jewish mothers were demanding, determined women who spared neither themselves nor their husbands and children. Their standards and expectations were extremely high, and they insisted on "the best" whether they were shopping for food or selecting a doctor. Their ambition for the future achievements of their children was anything but modest. When her son began to make the first feeble sounds on his violin a Jewish mother already envisioned another Elman or Heifetz. If he showed scientific proficiency she foresaw another Einstein. At any signs of flagging effort or undue interest in activities that might divert their children from serious pursuits, Jewish mothers would inquire with withering contempt, "So what you want? To be a nothing?" In public, however, Jewish women shamelessly bragged about the achievements of their children, and took enormous pride in them.

The scholastic and occupational achievements of their children was, in fact, a major area of status competition among Jewish immigrant women, and there was no social activity that they carried on with more liveliness and zest than bragging about their children. Even relatively diffident, quiet, modest women felt constrained to engage in this pattern of *berimen sich mit die kinder* [Bragging about one's children]. To say nothing about the accomplishments of her own children when others did so was tantamount to publicly admitting that there was nothing extraordinary about them, which to a Jewish mother was unthinkable. This ubiquitous social pattern served two important functions in the Jewish immigrant community: It was a highly effective social mechanism first for reinforcing parental ambitions, and second for diffusing information and knowledge about paths of achievement and mobility open to Jewish youth. Immigrants had little knowledge initially about the American occupational structure and even those men who possessed extensive religious learning did not, as a rule, have the secular education necessary to enter professional and managerial positions. Fathers, therefore, could not draw on their own experience to prepare their children for occupational ascent. In this kind of context the gossip that Jewish mothers exchanged about the educational achievements and career plans of their children became an important informational resource in the Jewish immigrant community. Mothers with older children transmitted information about career lines to mothers with younger children, who, in turn, relayed it to their husbands and children. Every distinction that a Jewish child earned, every step that he traversed in his educational career, every career decision, and every advancement was duly reported by his mother to her circle of friends and acquaintances, and she, in turn, brought back their reports to her own family.

This vast information exchange, operated primarily by mothers in the Jewish immigrant community, bolstered parental ambitions and reinforced the pressure on their children to strive for high educational and occupational goals. It also served to disseminate concrete and realistic knowledge among both generations concerning the barriers, the costs, and the sacrifices involved in the achievement of these goals. The triumphant accounts circulated by proud mothers of the rewards won by their sons through long, arduous, educational preparation even in the face of widespread anti-Semitism, encouraged the spread of optimism tempered by realism among the Jewish masses. A Jew, parents would repeatedly remind their children, had to be twice as qualified as a Gentile in order to garner the same rewards, and it was this kind of hardheaded realism, and not simply their respect for learning, that led them to stress educational attainment and excellence so heavily.

Jewish immigrants were no better off economically when they settled in America than other immigrants; they lived in the same squalid neighborhoods; their children attended the same schools and learned from the same teachers. But, as a rule, they exhibited a greater aptitude for learning and a greater will to learn than non-Jewish children. Learning, of course, has traditionally commanded respect even among the Jewish masses who, as a rule, had only a meager amount of secular or religious education. Every indication of intellectual curiosity and verbal precocity in their children was received with pleasure and delight by Jewish parents, and long before their formal schooling began Jewish youngsters understood that there was no more effective way to win approval and praise from adults. Even an impudent question or a naughty remark, if clever, was received with amused tolerance by parents and proudly relayed to friends and relatives as evidence of *chochma,* which is the Hebrew word for wisdom, but also is used colloquially to denote brightness, cleverness, or wit.

Another stimulus to intellectual aptitude was the amount of verbal exchange that took place in the Jewish home. It is now recognized that exposure to this factor in their early formative years increases the learning readiness of children, and it has long been known that verbal skill is an important component of I.Q. and achievement-test performance. That Jewish women, in particular, were talkative, any Jewish male will ruefully confirm, but it is not generally recognized that this notorious attribute of theirs gave their children a head start in learning. Whatever Jewish mothers did for their children—and they did a great deal—was accompanied by a flow of language, consisting of rich, colorful, expressive words and phrases. Their vocabulary of endearments alone could fill a modest-sized paperback, but they also had a superb store of admonishments, curses, imprecations, explanations, songs, and folk sayings that they effortlessly invoked as they went about ministering to the needs of their children and their husbands. The freedom that they exhibited with the spoken word invited a similar response from their children in the home and it carried over into school despite the fact that Yiddish, and not English, was their mother tongue. This helps account for the fact that learning aptitude was demonstrated not only by Jewish children whose fathers had extensive religious learning but also by those from homes where learning and cultivation were largely absent.

The determined struggle of Jewish mothers to delay the emotional emancipation of their children is well known and often criticized but it was nevertheless a significant factor in the high educational attainment of second-generation Jews in America. It is to their credit, I think, that they recognized that the basic conditions required to fashion a Talmudic scholar are very much the same as those needed to achieve any other career requiring a high order of intellectual skill. In both cases a prolonged period of time and arduous work must be devoted to the acquisition of a complex body of knowledge, during which time the child must be provided encouragement and emotional support as well as insulation from influences which might lure him into abandoning long-term plans for more immediate pleasures and rewards. Jewish mothers achieved this by denying the legitimacy of their children's declarations of independence. *Mainst as du bist shoin a ganzer mensch* [You only think you are a mature human being] was their stock retort to youthful emancipation proclamations. They employed every stratagem to remain as indispensable to their children in later childhood and adolescence as they had been earlier in life. The concept of early independence training was foreign to their thinking. According to their view a child was a child whether he was five or fifteen and required much the same order of care, devotion, and protection in adolescence as in childhood. With respect to learning and intellectual matters generally, they encouraged the development of self-reliance and autonomy but they were reluctant to grant their children other forms of independence or to impose any serious responsiblity on them until they had completed their education and were ready to assume the obligations of marriage and career.

A signal of their readiness to relinquish control was the application of pressure on their sons to find "a nice Jewish girl" and marry her. But until they saw their mission safely accomplished they doggedly resisted their children's perennial attempts to assert independence. The second generation learned to value independence not by being pressured to become self-reliant but by struggling against these formidable adversaries. Second-generation Jews lost a good many skirmishes with their mothers but ultimately they won the war, just as their mothers intended.

An important consideration in the sustained protectiveness of Jewish mothers and their determination to delay the emotional emancipation of their children was their fear that the children would fall prey to the social influence of Gentile peers, particularly those from low-status immigrant families with rural origins in which parents did not value education. Non-Jewish immigrants generally wanted their children to grow up quickly, to get out and earn a living so that they might help relieve the family burden of poverty. In this setting, Jewish parents did not encourage their children to seek the companionship of others, preferring that they pursue solitary pastimes at home rather than enjoy the freedom of the streets.

There is some grim humor in the fact that these efforts by Jewish mothers to insulate their children from peer-group influences antithetical to educational attainment and to the maintenance of Jewish values generally were aided and reinforced by the anti-Semitism that was so widespread in those days in Gentile society. There was, of course, a considerable amount of hostility and rivalry among the Gentile children too—between the Irish,

Italians, Poles, and WASPs—who had in common an antipathy to Jews. Some Jewish boys fought it out with the Gentiles on the streets but many others retreated from the street to the sanctuaries of home, library, and settlement house and discovered there enjoyment in solitary pastimes—study, reading, playing an instrument, and listening to music—which enabled them to develop competence and to derive satisfaction. Children with enjoyable pastimes of their own develop a degree of personal autonomy generally not found among children always in the company of other children.

Jewish youth often occupied a marginal status in the social system of the American high school in the pre-World War II era. Barred from competing successfully in this social arena, they were more likely than non-Jewish youth to concentrate their energies on schoolwork and on extra-curricular activities of a more intellectual nature, areas of activity in which the dispensation of rewards were less subject to the intrusion of prejudices over which they could exercise no control. Competition in athletics and in social leadership became the domain of Gentile youth while that of the Jews typically was in scholarship, journalism, debating—activities that commanded little esteem in the adolescent social system but constituted good preparation for intellectual achievement in adult life. Excluded from the contest for popularity in the larger social system of the school, Jewish adolescents could better afford to ignore the anti-intellectual norms that dominated the social systems of most American high schools, and operated to discourage scholastic excellence.[10] They were tagged as "competitive," "greasy-grinds," and "eggheads." But these unpopular youthful social types—not the athletic heroes and the social stars—often grew up to become the doctors, lawyers, writers, college professors, and the scientific and intellectual innovators of their generation.

The hostility of Gentiles and exclusion from their fun and games led Jewish youth, either as a matter of preference or because they had no other option, to form social ties primarily with their fellow Jews, with whom they could feel at ease not only because they were Jews but because they shared the same aspirations, the same values and interests, and the same need to submerge the

[10]For a detailed analysis of how the social system in American high schools operates to discourage high scholastic achievement see James S. Coleman, *The Adolescent Society* (New York: The Free Press, 1961).

consciousness of the social rejection that each individually had experienced at the hands of the Gentiles. If their "clannishness" violated the democratic ideal it also operated to sustain and reinforce the influence of Jewish parents. This alliance of sustained parental influence with that of Jewish peers fortified Jewish youth against the anti-Semitism and the anti-intellectualism that surrounded them in the working-class and lower middle-class neighborhoods in which they were born and grew up.

The success of the Jewish immigrant mothers in educating their children and immunizing them from severe emotional disorders warrants study by those interested in the way maternal strategies affect intellectual achievement, particularly of children in low-status groups. It is one thing for a parent to stress the importance of education as the means of escaping poverty, it is quite another, as the Jewish mother knew, to implement these objectives. Most lower-class parents who stress the value of education (one thinks of many black parents today) must contend with the fact that their children's friends and associates under-value education, so that a parent who values education and at the same time encourages early independence (as most lower-class families do) is caught in contradictory strategies. Children trained to be independent at an early age only become independent of parental influence and more dependent upon their peers.

A different and more demanding child-rearing strategy is required for upward mobility than for status maintenance: Children of poor but ambitious parents must achieve and sustain a level of scholastic competence and a set of future expectations like those of middle-class children for an extended period of time, but do so without the benefit of contact with middle-class peers who share and support their aspirations. In short, in order to live up to high parental aspirations, working-class children must be *more* autonomous from peer-group influences than middle-class children, for they must sustain a deviant set of expectations and behavior relative to their peers.

Moreover, under the best of conditions, the chances of working-class children to reach college are more uncertain, because they cannot count on financial support from parents. Finally, the greater cognitive stimulation and cultural enrichment provided in the middle-class home combine to promote and sustain higher scholastic competence among middle-class children, as compared with children from the working class. A child rearing strategy for social mobility, to be effective, must promote sustained and significant compensations to the working-class child because of the obstacles that he must overcome. The strategy of the Jewish immigrant mother did just that.

The most common criticism of Jewish mothers is that they were "overprotective." "Overprotection" implies the existence of an objectively defined norm according to which it is possible to rank maternal behavior irrespective of maternal objectives and of the social context in which a child is being reared. Many people believe that overprotection has adverse effects on children and on their subsequent life adjustment, but the little empirical research that exists suggests that just the opposite may be the case. David Levy's well-known study, for example, of twenty "overprotected" children first seen at about the age of ten and followed up in late adolescence reports that they were better than average in their pattern of physical growth, their freedom from accidents, serious illness, enuresis, and in their heterosexual development, classroom adjustment, and scholastic ability, and that, almost without exception, they outgrew the behavior problems—acting out at home, eating problems, and difficulties in forming friendships—they had exhibited in childhood.[11]

With respect to infancy and early childhood there has been a long-term trend, more marked in the middle class than in the working class, toward the more permissive, more love-oriented strategies of socialization practiced by Jewish immigrants. At the same time parents today fear that their milder, less coercive behavior will have the effect of prolonging emotional dependency on the mother and thereby create problems for the child in the area of school and peer-group adjustment. Consequently, they begin to discourage dependency behavior at a very early age by promoting contact with other children as a means of loosening the emotional ties to the mother.

Furthermore, pressures on the child to exhibit independence and self-control at home mount considerably just at the time that he enters school and is undergoing the strains of adjustment to the formal requirements of the school and to the experience of

[11]David M. Levy, *Maternal Overprotection* (New York: Columbia University Press, 1943).

becoming a member of a new, more complex social system. Instead of counteracting the new fears and strains that accompany the transitional period of later childhood by maintaining a supportive, nurturant stance toward the child and being reasonably permissive with respect to the acting out of these strains at home parents often do the opposite—they add to the burden of pressure on the child during this period of life by ignoring or responding negatively to dependency behavior, especially in the case of boys.

The mother who denies her child the right to express his fears and anxieties, who is indifferent or critical or punitive in the face of childish appeals for help, reassurance, comfort, and support does not promote independence of mind or of character. The refusal to countenance dependency behavior seems, in fact, to have quite the reverse effect. Thus, Sears, Maccoby, and Levin who deal with this issue in their important study, *Patterns of Child Rearing,* report their finding that

> The more the mother behaved in [a] negative way when the child was dependent, the more dependent he was likely to be. . . . Dependency did not appear to be increased either by a sympathetic attitude . . . or by the mother's responding positively to the child's dependency demands.[12]

The same study also indicates that children who exhibit stronger attachment to their mothers in early childhood more readily internalize parental norms of conduct, and take earlier responsibility for *self*-control than more independent children of the same age.

The mother who continues to respond positively to dependency needs over the entire period of elementary *and* high school is in a better position to influence the achievement motivation of her child than the one who stresses early independence.[13] The greater need

[12]Robert R. Sears, Eleanor E. Maccoby, and Harry Levin, *Patterns of Child Rearing* (Evanston: Row, Peterson, 1957), p. 172.

[13]Skepticism about the favorable effects of "independence training" appears to be spreading among behavioral scientists. For example, in a report of a recent conference on socialization for competence this comment appears: "Actual independence on the part of the child may not be correlated with independence training. True independence may emerge more often than not in opposition to parental pressure. Parents who try to inculcate independence deliberately may produce a docile child rather than a truly independent one. . . ." *Social Science Research Items,* Vol. 19 (June 1965), p. 20. (Brewster Smith's summary of Robert W. White's comments.)

for maternal approval and reassurance motivates the emotionally attached child to work harder at the task of learning. If the mother stresses its importance the child will exert himself to meet her expectations within the limits of his capacity. Pressure does no harm if, at the same time, the child has the reassurance of parental help and emotional support, and the freedom to act out anxiety, tension, and frustration that are the *normal* accompaniments of any kind of serious intellectual work. There is no reason to regard "babyish" forms of acting out as pathological. Demands for attention, tears, and temper in later childhood are to be expected because the child, as a rule, has not yet developed more genuinely mature ways of dealing with anxiety and tension. Moreover, judging from Levy's findings concerning the school adjustment of his subjects, the child who is permitted to act out emotional tensions at home where they can be dealt with in an accepting and reassuring way is less likely, *not* more likely, to exhibit behavior problems in school.

The child whose dependency needs are met in the home has less need to rely heavily on peers for affection and emotional support, and can, therefore, exercise more autonomy in relation to them. All children want acceptance from peers but they differ according to the price they are willing to pay for social acceptance, just as adults do. The child who can safely depend on parents for warmth, understanding, and response, will be less inclined to comply to peer expectations that violate parental norms, because he values parental approval so highly initially, and after further maturation, because the norms themselves become internalized and the threat of guilt feelings their violation would engender becomes more painful than the social disapproval of peers.

In contrast, pressure on the child to become self-reliant at home, before there has been time for him to internalize high achievement norms, and to establish a reliable pattern of scholastic competence in school makes a child fearful of failure, less persistent, and more vulnerable to the influence of peers.[14]

Children for whom the peer group becomes a mainstay of emotional gratification and support become less closely bound to their parents *not* by becoming more emotionally self-reliant, but by

[14]For experimental evidence that high-achievement motivation in boys is positively related to maternal warmth and pressure for high achievement but negatively related to independence training see Bernard C. Rosen and Roy D'Andrade, "The Psychosocial Origins of Achievement Motivation," *Sociometry*, Vol. 22 (1959), pp. 185–218.

becoming more reliant on their peers and therefore more subject to their control. This form of dependence is most marked among lower-class children. Owing to poverty, low education, high birthrates, and the fatalism that poverty breeds, parents in this stratum are less attentive, less nurturant, more authoritarian, more critical, and more coercive in raising children than the middle class. Pressure for early physical self-reliance goes hand in hand with obedience training, enforced by heavy doses of punishment. Under such conditions, close bonds to peers soon take precedence over parental ties, and peer norms rather than parental aspirations form the child's orientation toward school and toward the future, which generally forecloses the possibility of status mobility.

The power of the peer group in later childhood and adolescence, however, has also mounted rapidly over the past few decades in the middle classes, but for different reasons. Middle-class mothers promote strong attachment toward themselves in infancy and early childhood much as Jewish immigrant mothers did. But unlike the latter, they fear that the child's attachment to them will hinder the development of independence and "successful social adjustment." This belief is part of an ideology that has attained widespread acceptance in the middle class in recent decades. According to this view the prototype of the healthy, wholesome, normal child is the one who is happy, extroverted, free of tension, sociable, athletic, and popular. To counteract attachment to the mother (and also, incidently, to win more freedom for themselves), children are encouraged to do things with other children, leading them to become excessively dependent on peers. Once established, children avoid activities that are best carried on in solitude. Studying, reading, practicing an instrument seem a waste of precious time spent away from the company of other children. And mothers themselves, not as strongly committed to intellectual values as to sociability, are loath to set limits on the social life of their children, fearing that doing so would undermine their children's "popularity."

Middle-class parents accept with amused tolerance their children's preoccupation with every fad of teenage culture, because these are part of a social ritual shared with other children, and are taken as evidence of their children's "good social adjustment," which translated into teenage argot means "being popular." This preoccupation of young people with being well-liked by everyone, with being "in" is fostered by too many middle-class parents, and is one of the roots of conformism and of the "other-directedness" so often observed in American character.[15] Early marriage, dropping out of school, drug-use are phenomena that in the past were mainly found among youth from deprived homes. In recent years, these same phenomena are also appearing with increasing frequency in segments of the middle class in which parents have embraced the social-adjustment ideology. This ideology provides a rationale for sparing parents' time and effort in child rearing, and for abdicating the responsibility of guiding and influencing children to youthful peer groups.

The effectiveness of alternative strategies of child rearing can best be judged by their outcomes in adulthood. Every mode of child rearing entails some risks, especially when carried to extremes. It is necessary to determine the nature of these risks and to avoid those practices associated with failure in major adult social roles. In modern societies, educational attainment, more than any other factor, determines socio-economic status and chances of adults to gain access to the great variety of other resources—material *and* non-material—that exist in complex, industrial societies. It is therefore important to discover what strategies of socialization foster intellectual motivation and competence without undermining other attributes of a well-integrated personality—the ability to love and be concerned for others; to command love and concern from others; the ability to exercise freedom and self-discipline; to play and to work; and, the ability to be stable and to change. To produce a well-balanced adult requires a *balanced* strategy of socialization in childhood *and* youth.[16]

[15]A number of studies, based mostly on high-school and college students, indicate that high scholastic achievers exhibit less need for social affiliation and lower conformity to peer-group standards than less successful students. For a review of these findings see David E. Lavin, *The Prediction of Academic Performance* (New York: Russell Sage Foundation, 1965), pp. 64–121.

[16]Although systematic longitudinal research relating alternative patterns of socialization to adult behavior does not yet exist, empirical data of various kinds on adults, comparing Jews to other groups in American society, can be found. In such comparisons, Jews, as a rule, rank high on positively valued behaviors and low on negatively valued ones. Thus they are not merely high achievers—scholastically and occupationally—but also score high on creativity in science, literature, and the performing arts; family stability; voluntary association membership; political interest and participation; philanthropy; attendance at cultural events, such as theater and concerts; and exposure to serious books and magazines. Conversely, Jews are low compared with other ethnic and religious groups on alcoholism, disabling emotional impairment, drug addiction, and homicide.

Sustained parental pressure is necessary but not sufficient to establish the internalization of high aspirations and high principles in the developing child. My current research on maternal strategies and scholastic ability in later childhood shows, for example, that other things being equal, mothers with higher aspirations for their children do produce children with higher ability. At the same time, mothers who are more nuturant, more responsive, more stimulating, more affectionate, and more tolerant of criticism and temper outbursts, and, in general, who interact more with children in positive ways produce higher achievers. In contrast, reliance on the use of physical punishment—in toilet training, for misbehavior, and for poor grades—shows a negative correlation with achievement.[17]

The Jewish maternal strategy combined elements of firm control with permissiveness. Jewish women demanded a great deal of their children intellectually and morally. For this reason, they limited the social activity of their children well into adolescence. They did not confuse social precocity with the social competence that develops with maturity, as many modern mothers do. They communicated their expectations clearly and consistently by verbal expressions of approval and disapproval, not by punishment. As *compensation* for the demands they made in these strategic areas, they were generous and permissive in other ways. They were nurturant, warm, indulgent, and tolerant of criticism and outbursts of hostility toward themselves. In short, they worked to establish self-discipline in intellectual moral spheres of conduct in their children but otherwise allowed their children a great deal of freedom of thought and action within the home.

Authoritarian parents, in contrast, attempt to impose conformity to their aspirations and standards by generalized restrictiveness and by punishment. But intellectual motivation is one attribute that cannot be forced. Indeed, fear of punishment appears to have a stupefying effect on children. Great anxiety about failure impedes learning. And failure ultimately produces indifference or avoidance of intellectual tasks. A "bad" report card is treated not as a weakness but as a vice; neither help nor sympathy for the child is forthcoming. Such parents offer few positive compensations to counterbalance the pressure and pain they impose on their

[17]For the first published report on these results see Zena Smith Blau, "Maternal Aspirations, Socialization and Achievement of Boys and Girls in the White Working Class," *Journal of Youth and Adolescence*, Vol. 1 (March 1972).

children. Coercive methods of control without protective or permissive elements, produce either timid, fearful children or hostile, aggressive ones, who act out when they can escape adult surveillance.

Laissez-faire, permissive parents follow still a third strategy. They do not pressure or direct their children in a sustained, consistent way to work at intellectual tasks either because of their own indifference to intellectual values or because they fear that parental pressure is bad for children's psyches. They make few demands, set as few limits as possible on social play on the assumption that "social adjustment" should be accorded the highest priority in childhood. They are indulgent, particularly in material ways, if they can afford it, and avoid imposing restrictions of any kind upon their children. There are two kinds of permissive parents. Those who are affectionate and concerned, and the others who are remote, too preoccupied with their own lives to notice or care much what their children do as long as they do not make demands on their time and attention. With the latter type of parent it is difficult to say where permissiveness shades off into emotional neglect.

Such children do not learn the self-discipline required to do *any* kind of work, intellectual work included. They get easily bored and lack the persistence to complete those tasks they undertake. Lacking parental guidance or intervention, they are highly vulnerable to the influence of "other kids." Often, permissively reared children, if they are not also neglected, have high intellectual ability but they lack staying power for any task that is not also "fun." Middle-class children reared in this way are not accustomed to pressure. As long as there is none they get along fine. But even the most permissive upper-middle-class parents expect their children to go to college. The trouble in such homes starts when parents begin applying pressure on high-schoolers to work for grades good enough to get into college. Many young people from such homes have no immediate interest in going to college, and they feel much aggrieved that their parents, having let them do what they pleased for so long, suddenly change their tune. To start demanding conformity to standards from children in adolescence which had been largely ignored during childhood is to invite conflict and rebellion. Having had no direction in how to develop self-discipline, such children often feel overwhelmed by anxiety when first confronted with the pressure of work. In some cases such children "drop out" or "crack-up" in adolescence. But, as a rule, this is a temporary phenomenon, at least in the middle class. Reality eventually catches up with them. The necessity of a college education for getting a job that is interesting and allows self-direction becomes self-evident. They return to college under their own volition with a determination to learn to work, at least to the extent necessary to acquire a college degree.

A protective strategy like that of the Jewish mother, is most likely to produce excellence; the outcome of the permissive strategy is more apt to produce mediocrity; and the authoritarian strategy entails the greatest risk of failure in any sphere of adult life that requires intellectual discipline and skill. A comparison of the way mothers from various religious sub-groups in the communities I am currently studying rear their children reveals, not surprisingly, that to be a "Jewish mother" one does not have to be Jewish. A strategy similar, but not identical, to that of Jewish immigrant women is most frequent among high-status Protestant denominations such as Episcopalians and Presbyterians, Unitarians, and among Ethical Culturists and non-believers. Such women along with the Jews (two-thirds of whom are third generation and the rest second generation) have high expectations for their children, stress general moral principles and at the same time are warm, attentive, tolerant of criticism and temper, place few restrictions on their children within the home, and seek to control their children in non-punitive ways. Typically, these women have middle-class origins, higher education, are married to men in higher middle-class occupations. Their children exhibit the highest scholastic achievement in our sample. Compared to their own upbringing, they tend toward lessened restrictiveness, less use of physical punishment, and delayed pressure for independence.

Fundamentalist Protestants and white Catholics, in contrast, continue to follow a child-rearing strategy most *unlike* that of Jewish immigrant women. Their social origins and present status are working class, and they, along with their husbands, typically have the least education in the sample. Although themselves raised with the most strictness and punishment, they too show some tendency away from these practices. From the standpoint of economic position, social status, and educational status, the latter group of women are most similar to Jewish women of the immigrant era. But there is a world of difference between them in their strategies of child rearing. Among such women, Jewish immigrants were indeed deviant in their ways of rearing children. But history shows, that given their aspirations, they were right. When deviant patterns of behavior become adopted by higher status groups in a population they are called innovators. That, in essence, is what Jewish immigrant mothers turned out to be. Recognition of this fact, I believe, is long overdue.

DESCENT GROUPS AMONG NEW YORK CITY JEWS

by WILLIAM E. MITCHELL

INTRODUCTION

WILLIAM E. MITCHELL'S paper on descent groups complements Blau's contribution on the mother-child relationship. Despite its importance the extended-family relationship which Mitchell analyzes has received much less attention than has the nuclear family.

Mitchell centers his discussion on Cousins' Clubs and Family Circles among Jews in New York City. As an anthropologist he was struck by the novelty of these structures; it was unexpected that they should exist and be viable in what Mitchell terms a "Western urban industrialized setting." Mitchell's surprise is understandable—the tendency in modern society is to form bonds on the basis of mutual interest and congeniality, whereas the Cousins' Clubs and Family Circles embody an older principle whereby the closest bonds and the most fulfilling relationships are seen to be those which are established among kin.

Modern society subjects kin relationships to great strain. As the rate of social mobility among members of an extended family is not uniform, the group comes to include individuals on different class levels. The same is true for education—not everyone achieves the same educational level. "Brow-level" distinctions also emerge. The end result is that members of the same extended family come to occupy very different statuses.

If the cohesion of the extended family is complicated by these differences, it is further disrupted by geographical dispersion—from one neighborhood to another, from city to suburb, and from one community to another. Furthermore, given the individuation which occurs in modern society, even if relatives reside in the same city or neighborhood, they may not encounter each other in the ordinary round of their activities. Modern economic organization, in addition, rewards individuals who free themselves from the restrictions which come with strong kinship involvement. Thus the kinship principle seems to be assailed from all quarters.

The emergence and proliferation of Cousins' Clubs and Family Circles suggest that the extended family is aware of the threat to its viability and is acting to combat the forces which endanger its continuity. The family does so by forming itself into a kind of voluntary association meant to substitute for the older informal bonds which previously served to maintain cohesion.

It is difficult to say whether Cousins' Clubs and Family Circles are a transitional or a permanent phenomenon. Family members have the option of joining a wide variety of other Jewish voluntary associations, based upon ethnic rather than family bonds and drawn, as a rule, from a single class, status, or "brow-level." Not only do such groups offer a more homogenous environment than do the descent-group associations, but they have less potential for creating negative or hostile relationships among their members. Another possibility which threatens the Cousins' Clubs and Family Circles is that their members may be attracted to non-family cliques. When such cliques are composed only of Jews they do not pose problems of ethnic solidarity. They do, however, diminish the solidarity of the extended family. Finally there is the possibility that individuals may sever their bonds with Jewishness and the Jewish community; since the Cousins' Club and the Family Circle are based upon a shared Jewishness they are vulnerable when assimilation occurs, for assimilation breaks the linkage with the past as well as the symmetry of the group. To break with the past is to destroy the base on which the vitality of the Cousins' Clubs and Family Circles depends.

M. S.

THE FOLLOWING advertisement appeared in the *New York Sunday Times* July (1960):

> Cousins' Clubs, Family Circles, club benefits, anniversaries. We have modern facilities and pleasant surroundings to make your affair a success within a modest budget . . .Write Deerpark Farms, Cuddebackville, N.Y.

And this one was in the New York *Post* (1959):

> Family Circles, Societies, and Cousins' Clubs are invited to affiliate. Ask us how to become a Workmen's Circle branch. Phone or write for details.

The Cousins' Clubs and Family Circles to which the managers of Deerpark Farms and the Workmen's Circle were appealing . . . are two types of corporate descent groups which apparently are unique to American Jewry.[1] Anthropologists and friends to whom I have written abroad inform me that there are no similar kinds of kinship organizations existing among the Jews of England, France, Israel, South Africa, or Australia. I do not as yet have a similar distributional check for other nations with a big Jewish population. In the United States these descent groups exist in all of those cities where there is a large Jewish Community, e.g., Los Angeles, Chicago, Pittsburgh, Philadelphia, and New York.

The comparatively recent emergence in the United States of these descent groups among one of the most urbanized cultural groups in the world poses some intriguing problems for theorists in the areas of urban kinship, acculturation, social mobility, formation of descent groups, and comparative structure of nonunilineal descent groups, of which the Family Circle and Cousins' Club are heretofore unreported examples. Since they are unreported in the

[1]My use of the term "corporate" is that of Fried's (1957:23), i.e., "A group is corporate if it maintains continuity of possession to an estate which consists of things, persons, or both."

anthropological literature . . . and since I frequently have met with such marked scepticism among colleagues as to the possible existence of these descent groups, my comments will be primarily of an ethnographic nature.

The study of these kin groups is being carried out in the New York City area in connection with a social science project sponsored by the Jewish Family Service of New York and the Russell Sage Foundation.[2] We have collected data on over a score of Family Circles and Cousins' Clubs, including tape-recorded interviews with officers and members, genealogies, and copies of records such as constitutions, minutes of meetings, correspondence, family histories, and financial records. My wife and I also have attended numerous gatherings of these kin groups as participant observers. Unfortunately, as is so often the case in fieldwork, it has not been possible to study each group in comparable terms of depth and range of coverage.

Nonunilineal descent groups have only recently developed into a specialized area of inquiry in the field of kinship studies as such workers as Goodenough (1955), Firth (1957), Davenport (1959), Sahlins (1959), Ember (1959), and Solien (1959) have focused attention on this problem area by their theoretical and ethnographic contributions. Firth (1957:6) has suggested that we call these descent groups "ramages" and Davenport (1959:562) has proposed "sept." However, since the definitions of these terms are not appropriate for describing the structural properties of Cousins' Clubs and Family Circles, for the purposes of this paper at least, I am using the term "ambilineage" as the rubric under which to classify both types of descent groups, although there are marked structural differences between them.[3]

[2]The project is entitled "Studies in Social Interaction" and the research staff includes Hope Leichter, Director, Judith Lieb, Alice Lin, Candace Rogers, and formerly, Fred Davis and Diane Pendler. I am indebted to each of them as well as to my wife, Joyce S. Mitchell, for relevant research material.

[3]Firth (1957:6) describes his use of "ramage" as follows: "In former publications I have used ramage to include the Tikopia descent group. This, I think, is better described functionally as a lineage, keeping the term ramage for those descent groups which are not unilineal. Ramage would then be defined as a corporate descent group of a nonunilinear (ambilineal) character, membership being obtained ambilaterally, i.e., through either parent according to circumstances. Such a group ethnographically is normally found to be nonexogamous." However, in a Family Circle or Cousins' Club membership is obtained not only through parents but through spouses as well.

Ember (1959:573), following Davenport's (1959:562) use of "sept," gives us the clearer definition: "Corresponding to the unilinear term "sib," the term "sept" is

An ambilineage may be defined as a corporate descent group with lineal transmission of affiliation rights through both males and females from an apical ancestor or ancestors to whom each cognate can genealogically trace his relationship.

In any discussion of Family Circles and Cousins' Clubs one point should be made at the very start. These are not Landsmanschaft Vereins, i.e., a type of Jewish voluntary association which includes as members those individuals and their descendants who emigrated from a common territory in Europe, usually defined according to a town, city, or county. Whereas these Vereins are organized around the unifying tie of a former common residential territoriality, the Family Circles and Cousins' Clubs are organized exclusively on the basis of kinship.

The majority of the five and a quarter million Jews in the United States today are the immigrants, or the descendants of immigrants, who came to this country from Eastern Europe. . . . The Landsmanschaft Verein was their social invention for providing a system of mutual cooperation among individuals whose kinship ties had been broken by immigration.[4] I as yet have not established when the Family Circle as a structural type first appeared within the New York Jewish community but its formal structure seems to be modeled in part on that of the Vereins. I do have information on a few Family Circles that originated in the 1920's but there are others which are undoubtedly older. The only published statistics on Family Circles in New York are in a book written by a WPA Writer's Project (Yiddish Writers' Group of the Federal Writer's Project: 1939) which lists the names of over a hundred such organizations. Nor do I know exactly when the Cousins' Club first appeared except that it is antedated by the

proposed for the nonunilinear descent group whose members acknowledge a bond of common descent but are unable to trace the actual genealogical connections between individuals (see Murdock 1949:47 for the definition of a sib)." Since Family Circles and Cousins' Clubs trace the connecting links to a common ancestor or ancestral conjugal pair, they are not "septs" according to the above definition. Instead, they are a type of lineage, i.e., a descent group whose members actually can trace, genealogically, links to a common ancestor or ancestors. Unlike "unilineages" where membership rights are transmitted exclusively through either men (a patrilineage) or women (a matrilineage), the Family Circle and Cousins' Club type of lineage structure could be distinguished by the term "ambilineage," since membership rights are transmitted through both men and women, while actual affiliation is through either parents or spouse.

[4]For more detailed discussions of voluntary associations see, for example, Komarovsky (1946), Dotson (1953), and Little (1957).

Family Circle. It also has been very difficult to get any accurate estimate on the number of these kin groups in the New York City area today. In an informal telephone check with the United Jewish Appeal and the Jewish National Fund, I found the former has "several hundred" and the latter "about 300" such groups listed on their rolls as contributors. However, since only two of the groups I have studied to date give to Jewish philanthropies, the existing number must greatly exceed the 300 mark.

With this introduction in mind, I should like to describe these ambilineages in general terms. If the descent group is our reference unit—whether Family Circle or Cousin Club—there are four possible modes of affiliation, *viz.* matrilateral, patrilateral, virilateral and uxorilateral.[5] In other words, an ego may affiliate with the descent group if his mother, father, husband, or wife is a member or eligible for membership. Thus while some individuals have no descent group with which they may affiliate, there are many instances where an individual belongs to two or three such groups. One of the most interesting facts about these kinship organizations is that regardless of the mode of ego's affiliation or his sex, the rights and duties of all members are the same. Affines as well as cognates, women as well as men, are not only eligible to hold offices within the group, but frequently hold the highest offices. For example, one of my informants is the secretary of her husband's Cousins' Club on his mother's side and the president of the Family Circle on her husband's father's side. Incidentally, there are no ambilineages among her own cognates.

The members of most Family Circles and Cousins' Clubs are

[5]Since anthropologists only recently have begun to recognize the structural implications of the inclusion of cognate's spouses as members in some descent groups, e.g., Southall (1959), we have no terms for stating an affine's mode of affiliation to a descent group. I am suggesting "virilateral" to describe the mode of affiliation for a woman to her husband's descent group and "uxorilateral" to describe the mode of affiliation for a husband to his wife's descent group.

I also wish to propose a distinction between descent groups which restrict membership to cognates only and those which incorporate affines. The first type could be called "cognatic descent groups" as distinguished from "composite descent groups" where the spouses of cognates are incorporated as members. The most precise designation of a Family Circle or Cousins' Club would then be a "composite ambilineage" as distinct from a "cognatic ambilineage" where affines of cognates would be excluded from membership. A similar distinction could be made for other forms of lineage and sib structures. This differentiation between "cognatic descent groups" and "composite descent groups" should not be confused with Murdock's (1949:65–66) "consanguineal kin groups" and "compromise kin groups" since the structural criteria involved are different.

residentially scattered throughout the metropolitan area including the suburbs in New Jersey, Connecticut, Westchester, and Long Island. Some even live as far away as Hartford, Atlanta, Miami, and Detroit. The socio-economic status of members also varies and a group might include among its members a lawyer and university professor as well as a cabdriver and bartender.

Elected officers usually include a president, vice-president, treasurer, recording secretary, and social secretary. Some groups also have a corresponding secretary, a trustee responsible for the care of the organization's documents, or a sergeant-at-arms who is sometimes empowered with the right to levy fines from those members who become too vocally dominant during a meeting. The election of officers is usually held every one or two years.

The amount of the yearly dues varies from group to group as do the other details of organization, but all that I have studied impose some financial obligations on their members. Persistent failure to pay dues results in excluding the delinquent member from the organization. Aside from dues, many groups also have a "Good and Welfare Fund" or "Sunshine Club" which raises money at each meeting by donations or a raffle, the funds being used as cash presentations or to buy gifts for members celebrating some important family event, e.g., a wedding anniversary, birth of a baby, Bar Mitzvah, or a graduation from high school or college.

All of these descent groups keep some records with a constitution, minutes of meetings, and financial records as the minimum. Others may have a recorded family history complete with information on all known ancestors including a genealogy and maps showing from where they emigrated. Some also regularly issue a newsletter to members which is also sent to relatives who are geographically dispersed.

The attention and emphasis given to these different documents varies again with the group. For example, a constitution might be written in ungrammatical English on notebook paper or typed on legal bond and phrased in the elegant jargon of the lawyer who as a member of the Family Circle was drafted to write its constitution.

One of the Family Circles I have studied—we can call it the Goldman Family Circle—has an eight-page constitution of the formal-legal type. This Family Circle is 32 years old and had 83 members of whom 58 are cognates and 25 are affines. There are also at least 33 lineal descendants of the ancestral pair who, although aware of the group's existence, have not affiliated for reasons of geographical distance, disinterest, or personal enmity to the Family Circle or some of its members. The following are a few excerpts from the Goldman Family Circle's constitution:

> The object of the organization is to create a close relationship between the members and to carry into effect programs that will mutually benefit the entire family.
>
> Any person is eligible for membership who is a descendant of Itzik and Malka Goldman according to the Family Tree on file with this Constitution, their offspring and their spouses.
>
> Dues shall be as follows: $8.50 per year for a single member; $12.00 per year for a married couple.
>
> The financial records of the Family Circle are to be audited every two years by a committee of 3 members appointed by the president; within 30 days from the expiration of the term of the treasurer.
>
> The Cemetery Committee shall have charge of the Family Circle burial grounds; shall attend funerals and unveilings of monuments, and shall visit the families of the bereaved during the period of mourning.
>
> The Family Circle shall at all times contract for, lease or own a cemetery for the burial of its deceased members or those of their families entitled thereto, as herein provided.

Most Family Circles and Cousins' Clubs meet regularly once a month from September to May or June, either in the different homes of members or in a private room at a centrally located hotel. The preferred meeting times are Saturday night or Sunday afternoon. The first part of the afternoon or evening is occupied with the business meeting, often a raucous, anarchistic affair in spite of the president's earnest attempts to follow *Robert's Rules of Order*. I have seen the chair reduced to absolute impotence as his relatives in great high humor or heated indignation debated and argued the current family issues, quite oblivious to his gavel-pounding and pleas for quiet. Here is a statement from the minutes of a Cousins' Club:

> Due to all the hollering and noise, our newly elected president wanted to throw in the sponge and call it quits, but we moved her down.

This poses an interesting paradox. Although many of these groups have adopted the structural trappings of a formalized government including a constitution, parliamentary procedure, and the election of a chief executive, the actual business of the group is conducted in an egalitarian and intensely personal manner with little regard for the elaborate formal structures they have created.

Occasionally an argument in the business meeting will become so serious that a member and his family will resign, and it may be years, if ever, before they will return to the group. In one Family Circle a conflict had developed between an affinal member and his wife's siblings. He was angry because they would not donate money to buy their aged mother—his mother-in-law—a television set. Hoping to shame his wife's non-contributing brothers and sisters in front of their own relatives, he asked the Family Circle at its business meeting to help buy the set. A great debate ensued. It was finally decided that the Family Circle had no funds to provide luxuries for its members although they would grant the protagonist a loan if he wished to buy the set for his mother-in-law. His proposal having backfired, he resigned from the organization, taking his wife and children with him.

Once the group has completed its business meeting—and this may take an hour or longer—the rest of the evening is a party. Refreshments, often elaborate, are served and there is modest drinking. Some groups, however, limit the amount of money that the hostess or social committee may spend on food as well as define the kind of food to be served. This is especially true of the Cousins' Clubs which consciously want to reduce competition among their members.

During the party there is always much visiting among members and some joke-telling. If children are allowed to attend, they might be asked to perform for the group. In some groups the older folks play poker and the younger people might dance. Here is one informant's description of her Family Circle meeting:

> We sit and talk mostly—sit and talk, play the piano, sing, dance; that's what we always do when we get together after we have the meeting, which is a formal meeting with everyone shouting at each other. But it's lots of fun. We like it.

Besides these regular meetings, the group usually sponsors several other activities during the year, and at some of these the cognates of affinal members are invited to attend. Many groups have a spring or summer outing at a park or at a small country resort like Deerpark Farms. In December there probably is a "Chanukah Party" for the children . . . .

Although I have been making ethnographic generalizations regarding both Family Circles and Cousins' Clubs, there are some very definite structural differences between them. In a Family Circle all of the lineal descendants and their spouses of the acknowledged ancestral pair are eligible to affiliate regardless of age or generation, whereas the Cousins' Club restricts its membership horizontally to a set of first cousins and their spouses. Their children, however, may also become members at the age of 21 or when they marry, if this is earlier. The original group of first cousins who founded the descent group are usually the children of some six or seven siblings who immigrated from Europe. The cousins, for the most part, are born in the United States. One of the principal reasons for this rare type of horizontal kin organization is undoubtedly the intergenerational value conflicts which sometimes separate the immigrant generation from their more Americanized offspring. The Cousins' Club is apparently one way to maintain and proclaim the traditional Jewish value of family solidarity by organizing generationally while at the same time excluding an older and sometimes troublesome generation whose viewpoints and life-styles are so different.

Another important structural difference between the Family Circle and Cousins' Club is their degree of corporateness. Some Family Circles are actually incorporated by the State of New York, maintain a large and active loan fund for members, and own their own burial ground. Whereas the functions of the Family Circle are economic as well as social, the Cousins' Club is more exclusively a social group which attempts to maintain its integration by theater parties, cook-outs, or an inaugural dinner-dance.

In summary, I have tried to present a general image of two unique types of nonunilineal descent groups which I have called ambilineages. Although the picture is incomplete, it should serve as a further reminder that kinship relations in a Western urban industrialized setting can be considerably more structured than we have assumed.

REFERENCES CITED

William Davenport, (1959) "Nonunilinear descent and descent groups," *American Anthropologist,* Vol. 61, pp. 557–572.

Floyd Dotson, (1953) "Voluntary associations in a Mexican city," *American Sociological Review,* Vol. 18, pp. 380–386.

Melvin Ember, (1959) "The nonunilinear descent groups of Samoa," *American Anthropologist,* Vol. 61, pp. 573-577.

Raymond Firth, (1957) "A note on descent groups in Polynesia," *Man,* Vol. 57, pp. 4-8.

Morton H. Fried, (1957) "The classification of corporate unilineal descent groups," *Journal of the Royal Anthropological Institute,* Vol. 87, pp. 1-29.

Ward H. Goodenough, (1955) "A problem in Malayo-Polynesian social organization," *American Anthropologist,* Vol. 57, pp. 71-83.

Mirra Komarovsky, (1946) "The voluntary associations of urban dwellers," *American Sociological Review,* Vol. 11, pp. 686-698.

Kenneth Little, (1957) "The role of voluntary associations in West African urbanization," *American Anthropologist,* Vol. 59, pp. 579-596.

George P. Murdock, (1949) *Social Structure,* New York.

New York *Post,* 15 March 1959; p. M 13.

New York Sunday Times, 10 July 1960, p. xx7.

Marshall D. Sahlins, (1958) *Social Stratification in Polynesia.*

Nancie L. Solien, (1959) "The nonunilineal descent group in the Caribbean and Central America," *American Anthropologist,* Vol. 61, pp. 578-583.

Aidan W. Southall, (1959) "A note on local descent groups," *Man,* Vol. 59, pp. 65-66.

Yiddish Writers Group of the Federal Writers' Project, *Jewish Families and Family Circles of New York.*

JEWISH RELIGION AND THE AMERICAN JEW

JEWISH RELIGIOSITY
IDEOLOGICAL AND RITUALISTIC DIMENSIONS

by SIDNEY GOLDSTEIN and CALVIN GOLDSCHEIDER

INTRODUCTION

THE IMPACT of American culture and social structure, together with the thrust of Jewish tradition, has had the effect of magnifying the religious component in the group identification of the American Jew. This magnification has occurred despite the tendency for each generational group to be more highly acculturated and secularized than its predecessor.

The data presented by Sidney Goldstein and Calvin Goldscheider on the Jews of Providence, Rhode Island, provide insight into changing patterns of religiosity among American Jews. As with all small communities, Providence tends toward consensus and therefore it does not exhibit the wide variation in Jewish religious practice encountered in larger communities. For example, both ultra-Orthodox and ultra-Reform groups are poorly represented in the community. But despite the fact that the Jewish population of Providence is comparatively small and therefore atypical of American Jewry, Providence has the advantage of being located in the Northeastern section of the nation—the area where the concentration of Jewish population is the highest in the country.

Goldstein and Goldscheider find that attendance at religious services is at a very moderate level. But despite the degree of secularization implicit in this finding the great majority of Providence Jews are willing to accept the label of either "Reform," "Conservative," or "Orthodox." We can only speculate as to what these labels mean to those who accept them—what is impressive is that they are accepted so readily.

Like other investigators, Goldstein and Goldscheider devote concentrated attention to what they term the "ritualistic dimension." Their attention to this factor grows out of their familiarity with traditional Judaism, in which the ritualistic element tends to overshadow other dimensions of religiosity. Their finding is that a significant proportion of Providence Jews fail to observe the norms of the group with which they are seemingly affiliated. But despite such latitudinarian behavior most Providence Jews evince a desire to observe some Jewish rituals.

As with the pseudonymous communities of Riverton or Lakeville, the Jews of Providence are moderate in their level of religious observance. * *But what is particularly impressive about the Providence findings is evidence which can be interpreted to mean that the drift toward nonobservance (or what the authors designate as "secular" in contrast to "moderate" or "traditional" levels of ritual observance) has been arrested. The rise in the moderate level of observance among Reform Jews who are second- or third-generation Americans is a case in point. It is possible to interpret this finding conservatively, by maintaining that the descendants of old-line Reform or secular families have assimilated, leaving behind a hard-core group which is represented in the survey population. It is also possible to claim that highly secular Jews do not settle (or remain) in communities like Providence. But it seems more valid to take the increase in the moderate-observance category (and the fact that only 15 percent of the households fall into the "secular" category) to mean that there is a continuing ritualism in Providence. It appears that a pattern of Jewish identification in which the ritual element is absent finds few supporters.*

Providence Jews are not only moderate observers, they are highly selective observers as well. Consequently the pattern of ritual performance which they have created does not follow traditional

*Cf. Marshall Sklare and Marc Vosk, *The Riverton Study: How Jews Look at Themselves and Their Neighbors* (New York: The American Jewish Committee, 1957), pp. 9–13, and Marshall Sklare and Joseph Greenblum, *Jewish Identity on the Suburban Frontier: A Study of Group Survival in the Open Society* (New York: Basic Books, 1967), pp. 45–59.

norms. As an example, from the traditional perspective their pattern places undue emphasis on celebrating the minor festival of Chanukah and on the lighting of the menorah even as it underemphasizes the observance of the Sabbath. If the pattern is incongruous from the standpoint of traditional norms it becomes understandable when we keep the following factors in mind: 1) the Jews of Providence are the inheritors of a tradition in which ritualism is accorded priority; 2) they constitute a minority group which practices a deviant religion; and 3) they wish both to retain their ethnic and religious distinctiveness and to participate in the larger society.

M. S.

ALTHOUGH ALL JEWS may share core values of a religio-cultural complex, within the Jewish group, as within other religious groups, there are variations in the degree of commitment to and identification with its religious value system. Even casual observers of the American Jewish community are aware of the different patterns of Jewish religious identification, of variation in the performance of religious rituals, and of the variety of ways Jews maintain religious and cultural attachments. The religiosity continuum ranges from the traditional-observant Jew, actively participating in the Jewish community, to the unaffiliated, nonobservant, secular Jew, with the overwhelming majority between these extremes. Moreover, in the process of integrating into American society, Jews have altered the forms of their religious expression and the degree of their religious commitments. . . .

Facets of Religiosity

Religiosity is a complex phenomenon involving a number of dimensions. This complexity stems from the nature of religion in general. According to Lenski, religion encompasses a system of beliefs about the nature of forces shaping man's destiny and the practices associated therewith; religious group involvement may be communal or associational and religious orientations vary in "doctrinal orthodoxy" and "devotionalism."[1] In a more elaborate definition of religion and religious systems, Talcott Parsons identifies at least five dimensions: 1) an integrated set of beliefs; 2) a set of symbols, acts, and persons which have the quality of sacredness; 3) a set of prescribed activities which is interpreted as important and often obligatory in the light of the beliefs involved; 4) a sense that those sharing common beliefs constitute a collectivity; and finally, 5) a sense that man's relation to the supernatural world is connected with his moral values.[2]

[1]Gerhard Lenski, *The Religious Factor* (Garden City, N.Y.: Doubleday & Company, Inc., 1963), pp. 18–26, 330–336.

[2]*Religious Perspectives of College Teaching in Sociology and Social Psychology* (New Haven: The Edward W. Hazen Foundation, n.d.), p. 7.

Discussions concerning the nature of religion lead to the inevitable conclusion that commitment to and expressions of religion, i.e., religiosity, must also be viewed multi-dimensionally Some suggest that a comprehensive study of the religious experience and expression encompasses three dimensions: 1) theoretical expression—doctrine; 2) practical expression—cultus; and 3) sociological expression—communion, collective, and individual religion.[3] Others specifically concerned with the problem of the several dimensions of religiosity have outlined five dimensions: experiential, ideological, ritualistic, intellectual, and consequential.[4]

What are the common elements of these various typologies of religion and religiosity and how can these be applied to the study of religiosity among Jews? The first relevant[5] dimension of religiosity that will be examined is religious ideology as manifested in institutional identification. . . .

The Ideological Dimension

Identification and membership with one of the three religious divisions within Judaism—Orthodox, Conservative, or Reform—reflect the degree of association with religious doctrine, Orthodox being the most traditional and Reform the least. Historically, Jews settling in the Providence community were originally Orthodox, as were the majority of the Jews who migrated to the United States at the turn of the century. However, early in the community's history a Reform congregation was established (1877) and, following the national pattern, a Conservative congregation was organized in the early 1920's. The central role of the synagogue in Jewish communal life as a place for prayer, study, and assembly is attested to by the manifold increase in the number of congregations during the late nineteenth and early twentieth centuries. Between 1855 and 1910 no less than 23 separate synagogues were chartered, and probably a number of others existed on a less formal basis. Many of these early

[3]Joachim Wach, *Sociology of Religion* (Chicago: University of Chicago Press, 1944), pp. 19–34.

[4]Charles Y. Glock and Rodney Stark, *Religion and Society in Tension* (Chicago: Rand McNally & Co., 1965), pp. 20–38.

[5]We will be concerned with religious behavior rather than beliefs and attitudes, and the typology developed is therefore not intended to be exhaustive. Rather, it serves to organize the ensuing data analysis and discussion. The measures that will be used for each of these dimensions will be discussed when we focus on specific dimensions.

congregations have since disappeared as neighborhoods lost their Jewish population, or as ethnic ties which bound their members together weakened; other congregations merged to form larger and stronger organizations; and still others have recently emerged to meet the needs resulting from the shifts of Jewish population to the suburbs as well as changes in religious affiliation. At the time of the survey [1963], there were 18 synagogues and temples in the community: 8 were Orthodox, 8 were Conservative, and 2 were Reform.[6]

Two measures of religiosity will be used as indicators of the ideological dimension. The first is religious self-identification: how do members of the Jewish community define themselves, given the alternatives Orthodox, Conservative, Reform or Other.[7] Second, synagogue membership data were obtained and the respondents were classified as Orthodox, Conservative, or Reform according to their affiliation with specific congregations. Religious self-identification and congregational affiliation may reveal different patterns and are thus separated. Their interrelationship will be discussed later.

The overwhelming majority of the adult Jewish population, 95 percent, identify themselves as either Orthodox, Conservative, or Reform (Table 1). Within this threefold division, persons identifying with Conservative Judaism far outnumber the other two segments; more than half of the Jewish population identify as Conservative, 20 percent as Orthodox, and 21 percent as Reform. The small percentage of the Jewish population who are not identified with one of the three religious divisions testifies to the very strong tendency

[6]Sidney Goldstein, "The Providence Jewish Community After 125 Years of Development," *Rhode Island History,* XXV (April, 1966), pp. 51-52; the history of the Jewish community may be found in *Rhode Island Jewish Historical Notes,* Vols. I-III (Providence: Rhode Island Jewish Historical Association, June 1954–May 1962). For discussions of the immigrant Orthodox community and the emergence of Conservative Judaism see Moshe Davis, *The Emergence of Conservative Judaism* (Philadelphia: Jewish Publication Society of America, 1964); Marshall Sklare, *Conservative Judaism* (Glencoe, Ill.: The Free Press, 1955); Charles S. Liebman, "Orthodoxy in American Jewish Life," *American Jewish Year Book* (Philadelphia: Jewish Publication Society of America, 1965), LXVI, pp. 21–92; Charles S. Liebman, "A Sociological Analysis of Contemporary Orthodoxy," *Judaism,* XIII (Summer, 1964), pp. 285–304.

[7]The survey asked the respondent, "What do you consider yourself?"; besides Orthodox, Conservative, and Reform the choices included Yiddishist, Secular, Unitarian, Christian, and Other. The overwhelming majority considered themselves members of one of the three major religious divisions. The small percent who identified themselves with the remaining categories have all been grouped as "Other" in this analysis of religiosity.

toward some denominational affiliation and clear-cut lines of religious categorization.

An examination of the data by generation and age reveals the dramatic shifts that have occurred with respect to religious identification. The proportion identifying as Orthodox has declined sharply from over 40 percent among the foreign born to 6 percent among third-generation Jews. Conversely, the proportion who identify with Reform Judaism has almost trebled in three generations—from 12 to 35 percent. The Conservative group is the largest in any generation but the proportion identifying with Conservative Judaism declined from the second to the third generation after increasing from the first to the second. The shift in identification appears to be from Orthodoxy among the immigrant generation to Conservative among the second generation and some

TABLE 1

Religious identification, by generation and age

Generation and age	*Orthodox*	*Conservative*	*Reform*	*Other*	*Total Percent*
All ages					
First generation	41.1	42.4	11.6	5.0	100.0
Second generation	14.9	61.0	20.1	4.0	100.0
Mixed parentage	7.1	56.7	34.0	2.2	100.0
Third generation	6.3	49.0	35.3	9.4	100.0
TOTAL	19.8	54.1	21.2	4.9	100.0
25–44 age group					
First generation	22.6	50.0	19.0	8.3	100.0
Second generation	12.5	63.8	20.7	3.0	100.0
Mixed parentage	7.7	62.4	27.6	2.3	100.0
Third generation	4.5	51.9	36.7	6.8	100.0
45–64 age group					
First generation	35.1	49.1	11.1	4.7	100.0
Second generation	16.0	61.3	18.6	4.0	100.0
Mixed parentage	5.9	42.4	49.4	2.4	100.0
Third generation	18.4	32.7	28.6	20.4	100.0
65 & over age group					
First generation	51.8	33.5	10.2	4.5	100.0
Second generation	17.9	45.5	28.6	8.0	100.0

greater shift toward Reform in the third generation. This pattern can most clearly be seen in the differential gains and losses within each generation. In the first generation Orthodox and Conservative identification was equally divided, and it accounted for over 80 percent of the total. Among second-generation Jews, Conservative and Reform gained at the expense of a declining Orthodoxy, with over a 40 percent difference between Conservative and Reform identification in favor of the former. However, among third-generation Jews the difference between the Conservative and Reform was only 14 percent, indicating that gains in Reform identification resulted from losses to both Orthodox and Conservative Judaism. . . .

Attendance at Religious Services

In order to evaluate the scope of religious practices among Jews two aspects of the ritualistic dimension will be examined: 1) attendance at religious services and 2) ritual practices in the home. We will first turn to an analysis of the number of times each adult member of the household had attended religious services during the previous year. This section deals with generation changes in regularity of religious service attendance among Jews and non-Jews and then examines in more detail the pattern of synagogue attendance among several groupings within the Jewish community. . . .

A detailed look at generation changes in synagogue attendance reveals several striking points (Table 2). First, only a small proportion of the adult Jewish population never attend the synagogue. Although the third generation has the highest proportion of those who never attend, there are no systematic patterns of increase, and the percentage is, for all generation categories, less than 15 percent.[8] Second, there is a regular pattern of decline in synagogue attendance of once a week or more with distance from the immigrant generation. Among the foreign born, 22 percent attend the synagogue once a week or more but less than 4 percent among the third generation do so. Third, the modal

[8]The lack of change in nonattendance and, if anything, slight increases in nonattendance among both age groups of the third generation are in contrast to a report of a Gallup Public Opinion Poll sponsored by the *Catholic Digest*. The poll revealed that among Catholics and Jews, nonattendance at religious services declined between 1952 and 1966; among Jews the decline was from 56 to 39 percent. Reported in *The New York Times*, 14 July 1966, p. 18.

category of synagogue attendance for each generation is attendance four to eleven times a year rather than the stereotyped image of attendance just at High Holiday services (the Jewish New Year and the Day of Atonement). More than one out of every three Jews apparently attends religious services on the High Holidays as well as on a number of occasions throughout the year: probably a few times on Friday evening, Bar or Bat Mitzvahs, some holidays, or to recite the memorial prayer on the anniversary of a relative's death or at memorial services on specified holidays (Yiskor). Both the "four to eleven times a year" and the "one to three times a year" models have increased with distance from the first generation at the expense of more frequent attendance. These data on generation changes suggest a continual and striking decline in synagogue attendance but only a small increase in nonattendance. Together with indicators of the ideological dimensions, reduction in the frequency of synagogue attendance has occurred without signs of total nonaffiliation or nonattendance.

In traditional Judaism women are excused from a number of religious commandments in order to do full justice to their family and home responsibilities. Embedded in the Jewish cultural tradition has been the association of men with the synagogue.[9] Moreover, studies have pointed to the importance of analyzing men and women separately when examining generation changes in church attendance among Catholics.[10] Yet, behaviorally, differences between Jewish men and women in synagogue attendance are minimal. Although slightly more women never attend and fewer women attend once a week or more, differences for all other categories are small. In addition, the pattern of decline in synagogue attendance with distance from the first generation characterizes both sexes; differences between the sexes are most pronounced among the foreign born and diminish steadily among the native born. Together with the trend toward family as opposed

[9]In describing Eastern European shtetl life, Zborowski and Herzog point out: "The man's area is the Shul as House of Study, as House of Prayer and as House of Assembly. . . . The woman's area is the Home . . ."; Mark Zborowski and Elizabeth Herzog, *Life Is With People* (New York: Schocken Books, 1962), p. 124 and pp. 125–141. See also Marshall Sklare, "Aspects of Religious Worship in the Contemporary Conservative Synagogue," in *The Jews*, ed. Marshall Sklare, pp. 358–361.

[10]Bernard Lazerwitz and Louis Rowitz, "The Three-Generations Hypothesis," *American Journal of Sociology*, LXIX (March 1964), pp. 529–538.

TABLE 2
Frequency of synagogue attendance, by generation and age

Generation and age	*Frequency of synagogue attendance* Never	1–3 times a year	4–11 times a year	Once a month	2–3 times a month	Once a week	Several times a week	No information	Total percent
All ages									
First generation	12.7	18.8	32.9	7.9	5.0	13.5	8.5	0.7	100.0
Second generation	11.3	23.7	39.4	7.4	6.9	7.7	2.5	1.0	100.0
Mixed parentage	9.3	29.3	41.5	8.0	4.2	5.5	2.3	0.0	100.0
Third generation	14.6	29.5	43.8	5.1	2.5	2.5	1.1	0.8	100.0
TOTAL	11.8	23.7	38.4	7.4	5.7	8.3	3.8	0.9	100.0
25–44 age group									
First generation	7.2	24.1	48.2	6.0	4.8	4.8	4.8	0.0	100.0
Second generation	12.3	26.8	42.1	5.6	5.2	5.0	2.6	0.2	100.0
Mixed parentage	9.1	31.8	39.1	8.2	4.1	5.5	2.3	0.0	100.0
Third generation	13.8	31.9	42.4	4.9	2.6	3.0	1.0	0.3	100.0
45–64 age group									
First generation	8.5	18.8	37.5	8.5	4.1	16.1	5.9	0.6	100.0
Second generation	10.3	23.0	37.8	8.6	7.6	9.1	2.6	1.0	100.0
Mixed parentage	9.4	24.7	45.9	8.2	4.7	4.7	2.4	0.0	100.0
Third generation	14.9	17.0	53.2	6.4	2.1	0.0	2.1	4.3	100.0
65 and over age group									
First generation	18.4	17.5	24.4	7.8	6.0	13.0	12.0	0.9	100.0
Second generation	14.3	15.2	40.2	7.1	8.9	8.9	0.9	4.5	100.0

to male synagogue membership noted earlier, these data suggest a change in the traditional role of women in terms of synagogue attendance. . . .

Judged by these statistics, the high rates of synagogue membership and formal religious identification are not directly transferred to high rates of participation in religious services. Jews may well be following the model set by their non-Jewish neighbors in displaying an increased rate of identification with religious institutions. Nevertheless, the data on generation changes in synagogue attendance suggest that identification and membership do not necessarily involve an intensification of religious behavior as evidenced by synagogue attendance. Rather, they seem to be part of a larger complex wherein the contemporary Jew, secure in Americanism, feels no reluctance about identifying himself with institutionalized Judaism and thereby affirming his Jewishness. In fact, such identification becomes virtually compelling since it is the only way, outside of the intellectual subsociety, in which the American Jew can locate himself in the larger community. To this extent, the data support the conclusion of other studies showing the large proportion of Jews belonging to and identifying with synagogues. The conclusion that increased identification represents increased concern with religious practice as manifested by synagogue attendance is not, however, warranted.

Furthermore, the decline in synagogue attendance characterizes persons in each of the residence, education, and religious identification categories. Consequently, among third-generation Jews there appears to be a greater homogeniety toward less regular synagogue attendance. Not only has Orthodox Judaism declined but synagogue attendance (religious practices) of third-generation Jews who identify as Orthodox has also declined.

Observances in the Home

Together with the synagogue, the home has traditionally been a stronghold of Judaism. In fact, many religious practices associated with Judaism are focused on the home and the everyday life of Jews rather than on synagogue worship. In attempting to assess the nature of religiosity and generation changes along the ritualistic dimension, inquiry into Jewish ritual practices in the home is essential. Five religious rituals will be examined:[11] 1) lighting Sabbath candles Friday night; 2) having or attending a seder on Passover; 3) buying kosher meat; 4) using separate dishes for meat and dairy foods; and 5) lighting Chanukah candles.

Based on whether each of the five rituals was observed always, usually, sometimes, or never, a composite ritual performance index was constructed and each household was classified as being "traditional," "moderate," or "secular." One point was assigned for a response of "always," 2 points for "usually," 3 points for "sometimes," and 4 points for "never." Each question on ritual practices was equally weighted in importance. Thus, the family who always performed all five rituals received a score of 5 points; the family who never performed any of the rituals received a score of 20. Families receiving a score of 5 through 9 points were classified as traditional; at the other extreme, those receiving a score of 16 through 20 points have been classified as secular; the intermediary group, ranging in score from 10 through 15, has been classified as moderate.

According to the classification, slightly less than one-half of the households were moderate in their ritual practices, over a third were traditional, and 15 percent practiced the rituals so seldom as to be categorized as secular (Table 3). As with Orthodox identification and regular synagogue attendance, sharp declines are noted in the proportion of households classified as traditional. Among the foreign born[12] 58 percent were traditional in their ritual practices; among the third generation the proportion declines to less than 20 percent. However, the major decline in traditional practices has not led to a significant increase in the proportion of households that are secular in ritual practices. Rather the major shift has been toward the center, as were the sharp increases in Conservative membership and identification. Families classified as secular gained slightly in three generations (13 to 17 percent), while families classified as moderate more than doubled (29 to 64 percent). Without exception, these patterns persist with age controls. Furthermore, among the

[11]In contrast to other measures, the questions regarding home rituals focus on the household unit rather than the individual. The native born of mixed parentage were eliminated because of their small number.

[12]Generation status as well as the other characteristics to be discussed are based on the characteristics of the head of the household.

TABLE 3
Ritual performance index, by generation and age

	Index of ritual performance			
Generation and age	*Traditional*	*Moderate*	*Secular*	*Total percent*
All ages				
First generation	58.2	28.7	13.0	100.0
Second generation	32.3	52.4	15.3	100.0
Third generation	19.0	64.1	17.0	100.0
TOTAL *	37.3	47.6	15.1	100.0
25–44 age group				
First generation	38.7	54.8	6.5	100.0
Second generation	33.7	57.7	8.6	100.0
Third generation	18.7	65.7	15.7	100.0
45–64 age group				
First generation	59.3	28.6	12.1	100.0
Second generation	31.3	50.6	18.1	100.0
Third generation	25.0	56.3	18.8	100.0
65 & over age group				
First generation	60.3	24.7	14.9	100.0
Second generation	33.8	45.9	20.3	100.0

*Includes a small number of native born of mixed parentage.

first generation the youngest age group differs significantly from the oldest age group in the direction of less traditional ritual practices (60 versus 39 percent), but within the second and third generation variation by age is minimal. As suggested earlier, among the third generation greater homogenization in terms of religious behavior appears to have taken place. . . .[13]

Both Orthodox and Conservative Judaism call for strict conformity to the five rituals measured here. Reform Judaism does not demand either the use of kosher meat or the maintenance of separate meat and dairy dishes. For the most part, however, sharp differences in ritual practices characterize the three religious

[13]Although the number of female heads of households is small and is concentrated in the first and second generation, similar patterns of decline in traditional ritual practices were observed.

groupings (Table 4). Three-fourths of the Orthodox Jewish households were traditional, compared to 35 percent of the Conservative and only 10 percent of the Reform. Conversely, one-fourth of the Reform Jewish households were secular, compared to 12 percent of the Conservatives and 5 percent of the Orthodox. These patterns are maintained for each of the generations without exception. Investigation of the changes in religious rituals for each religious division indicates several significant points. First, with distance from the immigrant generation, declines in religious ritual adherence occur for each of the three religious divisions. Even among the Orthodox, traditional ritual observance declines from 85 percent of the first generation to 50 percent of the third generation. Second, the decline in traditional ritual observance among Conservative and Reform households has not resulted in a concomitant increase in secular households. In fact the proportion who perform religious rituals so rarely as to be classified as secular has declined slightly among Conservative Jews and declined even more among Reform Jews with increased Americanization. Moreover, among the Orthodox the proportion of households that are secular has increased slightly. As before, what emerges is the growth of moderate adherence to ritual practices with the avoidance of both extremes. Fully three-fourths of the third generation who are Reform are classified as moderate in the extent of their ritual practices. As a consequence of generational shifts, there is greater similiarity in the amount of ritual practices among the religious divisions of the third generation than among either the first or second generation.[14]

In order to provide additional insight into generation changes in ritual practices, each of the five rituals will be examined separately by generation. Two distinct patterns emerge out of the five rituals considered (Table 5). On the one hand, always lighting candles Friday evening and adhering to kashrut (both purchasing kosher meat and keeping separate dishes) have minimal adherence and their practice has radically declined in three generations. On the other hand, attending a seder on Passover and lighting Chanukah candles are very popular, with little or no change by generation.

[14]Because of the small number of persons who identified themselves as Other, a detailed analysis was not possible. The data on Others nevertheless show the decrease in traditional and increase in secular ritual practices. Almost two-thirds of this group were secular, 27 percent were moderate, and 8 percent were traditional.

TABLE 4
Ritual performance index, by generation and religious identification

Ritual index and religious identification	*First generation*	*Second generation*	*Third generation*	*Total**
Orthodox				
Traditional	84.4	64.7	50.0	75.6
Moderate	12.7	26.9	40.0	19.2
Secular	2.9	8.4	10.0	5.2
Total percent	100.0	100.0	100.0	100.0
Conservative				
Traditional	47.9	33.8	23.8	34.8
Moderate	38.5	55.1	65.5	53.7
Secular	13.6	11.1	10.7	11.5
Total percent	100.0	100.0	100.0	100.0
Reform				
Traditional	11.8	11.5	3.8	9.5
Moderate	56.9	66.5	75.5	65.7
Secular	31.4	22.0	20.8	24.8
Total percent	100.0	100.0	100.0	100.0

*Includes a small number of native born of mixed parentage.

The proportion lighting candles every Friday night declines with generation from 61 percent to 26 percent and, conversely, the proportion never lighting Sabbath candles has more than doubled in three generations. Even more radical changes characterize kashrut adherence. Among first-generation Jews 62 percent always buy kosher meat and 53 percent have separate dishes; among the third generation only 19 percent always buy kosher meat and a mere 16 percent have separate dishes.[15] As a further indication of the

[15]Of the households who reported buying kosher meat "usually" or "sometimes," many did so for nonreligious reasons, either because one of the household members liked a particular cut of meat or because the housewife thought that the meat was of a better quality than that available in a nonkosher store. Some persons who usually bought kosher meat were tempted to take advantage of a sale of nonkosher meat in the local supermarket. Reflecting the religious inconsistencies in their practices, several were careful to indicate that they "koshered" (salted) the meat purchased in supermarkets.

TABLE 5
Five selected rituals, by generation

Selected rituals	*First generation*	*Second generation*	*Third generation*	*Total*
Sabbath candles				
Always	60.6	37.2	25.5	42.4
Usually	5.8	10.1	16.3	9.4
Sometimes	15.3	25.1	24.2	22.1
Never	16.5	25.3	34.0	24.3
Total percent*	100.0	100.0	100.0	100.0
Passover seder				
Always	82.5	77.6	72.5	78.6
Usually	5.6	5.8	11.1	6.2
Sometimes	6.3	8.1	8.5	7.5
Never	4.1	7.2	7.8	6.6
Total percent*	100.0	100.0	100.0	100.0
Kosher meat				
Always	62.0	33.8	19.0	39.7
Usually	4.9	6.5	3.9	5.7
Sometimes	17.3	27.6	32.7	25.2
Never	13.6	30.5	43.8	27.7
Total percent*	100.0	100.0	100.0	100.0
Separate dishes				
Always	53.0	25.2	15.7	31.7
Usually	1.7	0.7	0.0	0.9
Sometimes	2.7	3.4	1.3	2.9
Never	39.7	68.3	81.7	62.1
Total percent*	100.0	100.0	100.0	100.0
Chanukah candles				
Always	74.5	74.0	76.5	74.1
Usually	2.4	3.3	4.6	3.2
Sometimes	4.4	6.8	3.9	5.8
Never	16.3	13.9	15.0	15.1
Total percent*	100.0	100.0	100.0	100.0

*Percentage may not add up to 100 percent owing to the small number of cases for whom no information was available.

striking declines in these ritual practices, the proportion who never buy kosher meat and do not maintain separate dishes for meat and dairy increases consistently with distance from the first generation; the former increases from 15 to 44 percent and the latter from 40 to 82 percent.

Attending a Passover seder and lighting Chanukah candles differ significantly from this pattern. Although there have been slight decreases in attendance at seder, almost three-fourths of the third generation always attend and only a small minority of the Jewish population never attend. Always lighting Chanukah candles has slightly increased among the third generation to 77 percent. The youngest ages within each generation are even more likely to have a seder and light Chanukah candles in contrast to patterns observed for each of the other rituals.[16]

The increased and sustained popularity of Chanukah and Passover may stem from the emphasis given to these practices in both the Jewish educational system and the community at large. In particular, the treatment of Chanukah along with the Christmas holiday in many public schools, as well as its use by some parents as a substitute for Christmas, accounts for the high proportion of families who adhere to this ritual. Similarly, sustained popularity of the Passover seder may be related to the increasing de-emphasis of its religious or historical significance and its use as an occasion for family reunions. At the same time, the much greater publicity given to the seder in recent years in the mass media, particularly television, and its coincidence with Easter must be considered. . . .

The data on specific ritual practices suggest that religious rituals are increasingly adhered to by the third generation in those instances where children are involved, where the ritual is family oriented, and where pressures for conformity are exerted by both the Jewish and non-Jewish community. However, adherence continues to decline in day-to-day rituals (kashrut) or weekly activities (Sabbath candles and synagogue attendance) that are somewhat demanding and on which no strong emphasis for

[16]For similar findings regarding the decline in kashrut, see Albert Gordon, *Jews in Transition* (Minneapolis: University of Minnesota Press, 1949), p. 90; Howard Polsky, "A Study of Orthodoxy in Milwaukee: Social Characteristics, Beliefs and Observances," in *The Jews*, ed. Marshall Sklare, pp. 332–333. On Chanukah practices, see Arthur Hertzberg, "Religion," *American Jewish Year Book* (1958), LIX, pp. 118–120; Herbert Gans, "The Origins and Growth of a Jewish Community in the Suburbs," in *The Jews*, ed. Marshall Sklare, p. 220.

conformity is placed either in the religious school or in the public image of what constitutes being a Jew.

Analysis of specific ritual practices also helps to explain the decrease in the proportion of family units in the traditional category of ritual practice and the sharp increases of the third generation in the moderate group. The change noted stems from the net effects of a decline in adherence to such practices as Sabbath candlelighting and kashrut and an increase and stability in Chanukah and Seder observance. Again, these data on the changing components of ritual practices and the changing nature of religious identification within the context of Judaism suggest that the identification of Jews with the Jewish community is not so much the result of increased religiosity; rather, the changes appear to have resulted in a new form of religious expression among third-generation American Jews which reflects the acceptance of external symbols that identify the Jew as Jew in conformity with the patterns of religious identification stressed by the larger American community.

THE RELIGION OF AMERICAN JEWS

by CHARLES S. LIEBMAN

INTRODUCTION

CHARLES S. LIEBMAN takes us backstage, as it were, in order to detail the inner workings of American Jewish religion. His analysis consequently differs from the usual portraits of Jewish religious life, whether of Reform, of Conservatism, or of Orthodoxy. Furthermore, Liebman's perspective makes him particularly critical of the portrayals of Jewish religiosity which have appeared in the mass media. He suggests, however, that false portrayals may create their own truth: they may motivate individuals to conform with stereotypes projected about them.

Liebman's analysis of the kind of immigrants who came to the United States and the social situation with which they were confronted is crucial to his argument, as is the distinction which he draws between elite religion and folk religion. He stresses that both the German Jewish immigration of the mid-nineteenth century and the East European immigration of the late nineteenth and early twentieth century were dominated by followers of folk religion.

Because America was different and emancipation was not a problem, the kind of Reform Judaism that evolved in the United States differed from its European prototype. As Liebman puts it: "American Reform at its outset was the folk religion of the German-American Jew." The European-trained Reform rabbis who came to the United States later succeeded in formulating an elite version of Reform Judaism, but in any case the folk content of Reform Judaism was destined to be reshaped by the East European Jew, whose gradual infiltration of the movement caused Reform to take on the folk patterns of East European rather than of Western Jewry. To be sure, such patterns had themselves been extensively reshaped by the confrontation with American culture.

Liebman is particularly acute in his analysis of American Orthodoxy. He stresses that the leaders of the elite religion of Orthodoxy remained in Eastern Europe until after World War I, and in fact did not arrive in substantial numbers until World War II. America gave Jews the freedom to construct their own Judaism and ". . . to a greater extent than ever before the folk now set their standards independently of the elite." Thus it came about that American Orthodoxy was an Orthodoxy pervaded with folk religion. Furthermore, the acculturation which Jews underwent meant that the Orthodox norms of Eastern Europe were widely disregarded. Yet, given its structure, Orthodox Judaism never lost its elite tradition, which maintained a foothold even during the chaotic days of mass immigration. In recent decades the elite version of Orthodoxy has reasserted itself with the arrival of new immigrants fully committed to Orthodoxy and more particularly with the settlement in the United States of a group of religious leaders of East European Jewry. In Liebman's view the rise of Conservatism, and to a lesser extent of Reform, provided a haven for those dissatisfied with Orthodoxy and helped make possible the rise of a new elitist leadership within Orthodoxy.

It is Liebman's contention that Conservatism represents the purest expression of the folk religion of the American Jew (though there is an elite version of Conservative Judaism as well). He emphasizes that Conservatism appealed to traditionally minded East European Jews who were seeking a way to combine their traditionalism with the American cultural patterns which they had adopted. The folk religion which they created had a particularly strong emphasis on the ethnic aspect of Jewishness. Liebman believes that the stress on ethnicity under the umbrella of religion, and as institutionalized in the American synagogue, was responsible for the rapid growth of Conservatism. He describes the individuals who proceeded to establish hundreds of Conservative synagogues across the nation as ". . . quite concerned with group survival, not very interested in religion, and in search of institutions which expressed values of both communal survival and integration or acculturation to middle-class American standards."

If the folk religion of American Jewry has had a strong ethnic-communal thrust in contrast to a universalist-pietistic thrust, then the Reconstructionist movement initiated by Mordecai M. Kaplan should not only have constituted a fourth religious group but should have achieved primacy over its competitors. No one has been more of an admirer of folk religion than Kaplan. He has been unique in his ability to reconceptualize the essence of American Jewish folk religion, giving it ideological justification and thus conferring intellectual respectability. But Reconstructionism never became a fourth wing of American Judaism. Liebman is obliged to account for its failure as an institutionalized movement, for his theoretical perspective would lead us to believe that a Reconstructionist triumph was inevitable. His explanation of Reconstructionism's failure constitutes a significant extension of his theory of folk religion versus elite religion and should provoke an interesting debate among students of the religion of American Jews.

M. S.

. . . IN ORDER to understand fully the religion of American Jews we must . . . define two concepts: "folk religion" and "elite religion." Folk religion is the religion of a community which delineates the peculiarity of the particular group and which is generated by the community itself. . . . The popular religious culture of folk religion can be better understood if we first understand elite religion. The term religion refers here to a formal organized institution with acknowledged leaders. Within the institution, symbols and rituals are acknowledged as legitimate expressions or reenactments of religious experience, and a set of beliefs is articulated as ultimate truths.[1] Elite religion is the symbols and rituals (the cult) and beliefs which the leaders acknowledge as legitimate. But most importantly, elite religion is also the religious organization itself, its hierarchical arrangements, the authority of the leaders and their source of authority, and the rights and obligations of the followers to the organization and its leaders.

For various reasons—the evolution of religion, the conflict of different cultures, differentiated levels of religious and even nonreligious education, and psychological propensities—large numbers of people may affiliate with a particular religious institution, and even identify themselves as part of that religion, without really accepting all aspects of its elitist formulation. What is more, a kind of subculture may exist within a religion which the acknowledged leaders ignore or even condemn, but in which a majority of the members participate. This is called folk religion. Why consider folk and elite religion to be two aspects of the same religion? Why not call them two separate religions? The answer is that both share the same organization and at least nominally recognize the authoritative nature of the cult and beliefs articulated by the elite religion. Folk religion is not self-conscious; it does not articulate its own rituals and beliefs or demand recognition for its informal leaders. As far as elite religion is concerned, folk religion is

[1]This discussion follows O'Dea's treatment of institutional religion, in which he distinguishes three levels: cult, belief, and organization; Thomas O'Dea, *The Sociology of Religion* (Englewood Cliffs, N.J.: Prentice-Hall, Inc., 1966), pp. 36–51.

not a movement but an error, or a set of errors, shared by many people.

Folk religion is expressed primarily though rituals and symbols. These rituals may be rooted in superstition; they may originate from an older localized religion which has been replaced by the elite religion; or they may arise from a need on the part of people for the sanctification of certain social, economic, or even sexual activity which elite religion refuses to legitimize. Folk religion tends to accept the organizational structure of the elite religion but to be indifferent to the elite belief structure. Of course, its rituals and symbols imply a belief system, but this tends to be mythic rather than rational and hence not in opposition to the more complex theological elaboration of the elite religion. Where the beliefs of the folk religion are self-conscious and articulated, they tend to be beliefs about which the elite religion is neutral. . . .

The potential for folk religion to become institutionalized always exists; if it does, it will become a separate religion or an official heresy. The history of Catholicism is filled with such examples. Yet folk religion permits a more intimate religious expression and experience for many people, and may, in fact, integrate them into organizational channels of the elite religion. It is a mistake to think of folk religion as necessarily more primitive than elite religion. While its ceremonies and sanctums evoke emotions and inchoate ideas associated with basic instincts and primitive emotions, it is also more flexible than elite religion. Hence it is also capable of developing ceremonial reponses to contemporary needs which may be incorporated into the elite religion. Much religious liturgy arises from the folk religion and is incorporated into the elite religion.

The absence of an elaborate theology within folk religion and the appeal of folk religion to primal instincts and emotions does not mean that folk religion is less attractive to intellectuals than is elite religion. Quite the opposite may be true under certain circumstances. In secular America, elite religion has been forced to retreat before the challenge of science, biblical scholarship, notions of relativism implicit in contemporary social science, and the whole mood of current intellectual life. . . .

The problem for the religious elite has been that most intellectuals cannot accept dogmatic formulations which purport to be true or to have arisen independent of time and place. Hence intellectuals have special difficulty with elite religion. But the same intellectual currents which challenge religious doctrine can also serve to defend behavioral and even organizational forms against the onslaught of such secular doctrines as twentieth-century positivism or eighteenth- and nineteenth-century deism. Thus folk religion, with its stress on customary behavior and traditional practices, may be legitimized functionally without an elitist prop. An intellectual today may well be attracted to folk religion because it provides him with comfort and solace, a sense of tradition, a feeling of rootedness, a source of family unity. His worldview may remain secular, and from the point of view of elite religion his beliefs will therefore be quite unsatisfactory. But it is, at least in the first instance, elite religion, not folk, which is challenged by his worldview.

In traditional Judaism, folk religion has always existed side by side with elite religion. Many of its ceremonies and rituals were incorporated into the elite religion; others were rejected; still others achieved a kind of quasi-incorporation. They were and are widely practiced and even have a certain liturgical legitimacy; but they are still outside the boundaries of elite religion. Such ceremonies, for example, are associated with Jewish holidays. Best known, perhaps, are Jewish New Year rituals of eating apple and honey and the ceremony of *tashlich*, at which Jews throw crumbs representing their sins into a body of water. The essentially healthy relationship between the folk and elite religion in traditional Judaism is exemplified by the fact that Jews who participate in *tashlich* feel the need to accompany the act with the recitation of a traditional psalm. That is, the sanctums of the elite religion must accompany a purely folk religious act.

Every religious group has both its folk and elitist aspect. They may differ from one another, and, as we shall see, branches or denominations within Judaism do differ from one another as to the extent to which the folk and elite formulations are in tension with each other. But first some historical background is necessary.

AMERICAN JUDAISM BEFORE THE TURN OF THE CENTURY

In 1880 there were approximately 250,000 Jews in the United States. During the next forty years over 2,000,000 Jews immigrated, the great majority from Eastern Europe. The intensity of the immigrants' Jewish identification and Jewish concerns, and even more, their large numbers and the problems created by such a vast lower-class segment of people, overwhelmed the existing Jewish institutions and transformed the very nature of American Judaism. Consequently, the turn of the century is a convenient starting place for anyone who wishes to understand the roots of the contemporary Jewish community.

Early Reform

Before the arrival of the East Europeans, most American Jews were German in origin and Reform in religious orientation. But there was a great difference between American Reform and German Reform. . . . German Reform represented a conscious break with the Jewish tradition. Under the influence of the European Enlightenment and concerned with the requirements for Jewish emancipation, it defined itself in opposition to the traditional patterns of Jewish belief and practice. It was a new elitist formulation of Judaism. In contrast, American Reform was the religious organization of the German-American Jew who came searching for personal liberty and economic advancement. That Jew was neither ideologically oriented nor purposefully assimilationist. He had no need to rebel consciously against the tradition, because there were no traditional institutions in the United States which were of any concern to him. American Reform at its outset was the folk religion of the German-American Jew.

Jews had lived here prior to the large German immigration, which began in the 1840's. They included Sephardic Jews . . . and Germanic Jews, who came in numbers small enough to be assimilated into Sephardic institutions. But these institutions, centered around the synagogue, were confined mostly to the East

Coast, were wealthy, followed traditional Sephardic practices quite different from those of the Germans, and were indifferent, if not hostile, to the new German immigrants.

The new immigrants, many of whom settled away from the older Sephardic communities, naturally established their own synagogues. At least, those who bothered about Judaism did so. But they did not think of these institutions as particularly denominational. The new German synagogues were not established in deliberate opposition to any other synagogue or ideology. With the arrival of German rabbis, preeminently Isaac Mayer Wise, who was already identified with German Reform, some deliberate and successful efforts were made toward organizing these synagogues into a central body with a uniform liturgy and a single ideology.

In 1857 Wise published a prayerbook which he hoped would meet the needs of these congregations. He called it *Minhag America,* The Custom of America. To Wise, Jewish denominationalism was not the division between Reform and Orthodoxy. At this period in his life Wise believed that the only type of synagogue which would survive was the indigenous American congregation, which he saw as Reform in orientation. Wise did not fear the opposition of Orthodox or traditionalist Jews. The great Jewish problem in America was not to fight the tradition but to retain the Jewish allegiance of the immigrants and their children. Consequently, Wise thought of his prayerbook and liturgy as reflecting, not so much Reform, but rather the needs of American Jews.

In 1873 Wise founded the Union of American Hebrew Congregations and in 1875, Hebrew Union College (HUC) for the training of American rabbis. The word Union in the name is significant because it suggests the absence of schism. As Samuel Cohon has noted, the term Union expressed the founder's hope "to have one theological school for all Jews of the country,"[2] at least for all but the "ultra-Orthodox," to use Cohon's formulation. Certain segments of American Judaism found the practices of HUC "too Reform," however, and in 1886 they founded the Jewish Theological Seminiary Association to organize a more traditional institution to train rabbis. Even then an Orthodox leader, Judah David Eisenstein, objected to the new seminary, and argued that if HUC

[2]Samuel S. Cohon, "The History of Hebrew Union College," *Publications of the American Jewish Historical Society* 40 (September 1950), p. 24.

was indeed too Reform, one solution was for the non-Reform to identify themselves with it and change its character.[3]

American Reform, however, had already begun to take shape as a distinctive movement with its own ideological position. In 1885 a group of Reform rabbis met in Pittsburgh and adopted the famous statement of principle known as the Pittsburgh Platform. These rabbis represented the more radical and ideological wing of Reform. Wise himself was not present at the meeting. But after 1885 and until the repudiation of the Pittsburgh Platform in 1937 by the Central Conference of American Rabbis (the Reform rabbinical organization), this statement represented, one might say, the elitist formulation of American Reform.[4] It repudiated the binding character of "Mosaic legislation," that is, Jewish law and its divine revelation. It is doubtful, however, if this rejection of traditional Jewish law and dogma was more shocking to the sensibilities of the East European immigrant than the assertions that Judaism was *only* a religion; that "we consider ourselves no longer a nation but a religious community"; and that "we recognize in Judaism a progressive religion, ever striving to be in accord with the postulates of reason." This was the spirit of American Reform which the East European Jew found upon his arrival in the United States.

The New Immigrants

Who were the new immigrants? The important fact to be noted is that a disproportionately large number of them, relative to a cross-section of East European Jewry, were nontraditionalists, secularist Jews, Socialists, and Zionists. A few of them, particularly the Socialists, were militantly antireligious. Most, however, were not ideologically oriented. They were traditionalist in orientation but without the political, economic, or ideological stake that many East European Jewish leaders had in traditionalism. They were adherents of the folk, rather than the elite, religion of traditionalism.

Within traditional Judaism, folk religion and elite religion may be distinguished from each other by their orientation to change.

[3]Judah David Eisenstein, *Ozar Zikhronothai* (New York: Published by the author, 1929), pp. 206–211. The pages are reprinted from an article by Eisenstein in the *New York Yiddish Zeitung,* 1886.

[4]The text of the Pittsburgh Platform is reprinted in Nathan Glazer, *American Judaism* (Chicago: University of Chicago Press, 1957), pp. 151–152.

Traditional society differs from modern society, not in the occurrence of change (all societies change), but in its orientation to the concept of change.[5] Traditionalists accept only change which can be legitimized by past values and practices. The hallmark of the elite religion of traditional Judaism is the fact that the touchstone of legitimacy is the sacred textual tradition and the codes of Jewish law. The traditional elite are represented by the Talmudic scholars and sages. The traditionalist folk, on the other hand, find the touchstone of legitimacy in the practices of the community. In this sense the traditionalist folk are more innately conservative than the elite but are more susceptible to a radical break with the past, once the consensus within the community is broken.

The first traditionalist immigrants found themselves surrounded by a disproportionate number of nontraditionalists. Not only were the vast majority of new immigrants adherents of folk, rather than elite, traditionalism, but there was also a decided absence of distinguished scholars and rabbis. Israel Rosenberg, one of the leading Orthodox East European rabbis in America, noted the miserable state of Jewish education and commented at the 1924 convention of the Union of Orthodox Rabbis (Agudat Horabbonim): "To a certain extent the Jews of Europe are also responsible for this situation. When they saw that the stream of emigration to America was increasing, it was incumbent among them to send us the spiritual giants, those who had it in their powers to influence and to work."[6]

Although most of the estimated fifty thousand Jews who immigrated to the United States from 1881 to 1885 settled in New York, the leading East European congregation of the city had only a part-time rabbi of meager scholarship. When twenty-six Orthodox congregations met to choose a joint leader for New York Jewry, no American rabbi was even considered. In 1887 the secretary to Rabbi Isaac Elhanan Spektor, the outstanding rabbinic authority from Russia, referred to American rabbinical leaders as "improper men."[7] The few Talmudic scholars who did come "were without honor or

[5]The distinction and some application to contemporary Judaism is made by Jacob Katz, "Traditional Society and Modern Society," *M'Gamot* 10 (March 1960), pp. 304–311 (Hebrew).

[6]Agudat Horabbonim, *Jubilee Volume* (New York: Arius Press, 1928), p. 110.

[7]Cited in Abraham J. Karp, "New York Chooses a Chief Rabbi," *Publications of the American Jewish Historical Society* 45 (March 1955), pp. 129–198.

support even in their own poor communities."[8] One contemporary, commenting on the Talmudic saying that "the sages are kings," noted that in America this should read "the shoemakers, tailors, and usurers are the sages."[9]

The absence of a religious elite meant that the traditionalist immigrants were especially susceptible to a breakdown in religious consensus. To a greater extent than ever, the folk now set their own standards independently of the elite. The traditionalist immigrants were certainly not irreligious, nor did they wish to conceal their Jewish identity. But they did desire to be accepted and integrated into American society. . . . And while they were not irreligious, neither were they religious in the elitist sense in which one's life is bounded and guided by a legal textual tradition. Their piety was what Leo Baeck called *Milieu-Fromigkeit,* and what we have called a manifestation of folk religion. Willing as they were to take extended leave of family and home, they were less committed to tradition and more accepting of new values than their relatives and neighbors who came much later.

When the rabbi of Slutsk visited America and appeared at a public meeting of the Union of Orthodox Jewish Congregations during the first wave of immigration, "he chastised the assemblage for having emigrated to this *trefa* [impure] land."[10] Similarly, would-be emigrants were warned by such renowned rabbinic authorities as the Hafetz Hayim, Rabbi Israel Meir Hacohen, to stay home and not endanger their Judaism.[11] Those who did emigrate

[8]Ezekial Lifschutz, "Jewish Immigrant Life in American Memoir Literature," *YIVO Annual of Jewish Social Science* 5 (1950), p. 232.

[9]Shlomo Noble, "The Image of the American Jew in Hebrew and Yiddish Literature in America, 1870–1900," *ibid.*, 9 (1954), p. 87. A Yiddish story relates how Jews in a small East European town raised money to send a young man to America to prevent him from marrying a Gentile: Isaac Metzker, "To the New World," *A Treasury of Yiddish Stories*, ed. Irving Howe and Eliezer Greenberg (New York: Meridian Books, 1958), pp. 504–515. Milton Himmelfarb has noted: "After all, who went to America? Overwhelmingly, it was not the elite of learning, piety, or money but the *shnayders,* the *shusters* and the *ferdgenevim*"; Milton Himmelfarb, "The Intellectual and the Rabbi," *Proceedings of the Rabbinical Assembly of America,* 1963, p. 124. See also Mark Zborowski and Elizabeth Herzog, *Life Is With People* (New York: Schocken Books, 1952), pp. 260–261, and Arthur Hertzberg, "Seventy Years of Jewish Education," *Judaism* 1 (October 1952), p. 361.

[10]Moshe Davis, "Jewish Religious Life and Institutions in America," *The Jews: Their History, Culture, and Religion,* 2d ed., ed. Louis Finkelstein (Philadelphia: Jewish Publication Society, 1955), I, p. 539.

[11]Lloyd P. Gartner, *The Jewish Immigrant in England, 1870–1914* (Detroit: Wayne State University Press, 1960), p. 30.

were unable to separate the distinctively religious or legally essential elements from the nonessential elements of Judaism. We find that the "religious" practices which persisted among the immigrants were those most closely associated with the cultural life-style of Eastern Europe and were irrelevant to the process of American acculturation. In contrast, practices which were more deeply rooted in the textual religious tradition were readily abandoned.

Among the most important set of rituals in Jewish law are those surrounding Sabbath observance. The Torah commands the Jew, under penalty of death, to refrain from work on the Sabbath. The Sabbath rest is connected to creation itself. By resting on the Sabbath, the Jew refreshes and renews his spirit through prayer, study, good food, and even sexual intercourse, to which he is commanded. In the elitist formulation the Jew also affirms, by abstinence from forbidden work, his belief in God the Creator, who also rested on the Sabbath. But Sabbath observance entailed economic hardship for the immigrants and often did not survive the voyage across the Atlantic. A survey of Jewish workmen on the Lower East Side revealed that only 25 percent rested on the Sabbath; 60 percent of the stores owned by Jews were open. . . .[12]

Kashrut, the laws pertaining to permissible and forbidden foods, survived longer than Sabbath observance, though in an attenuated form. The parts which survived were rooted in the folk, rather than in the elitist, aspects of Judaism. The laws of kashrut govern which animals may be consumed, as well as which cuts of meat may be eaten, and prohibit mixing dairy and meat dishes. Kashrut resulted, therefore, in certain styles of food. Long after most Jews ceased to observe kashrut they continued to eat "kosher style." Among the animals which are forbidden to the Jew is the pig. In the elitist formulation eating pork products is sinful, but no more sinful than eating shrimp. Further, the laws make no distinction between consuming forbidden foods in one's home and consuming them in a restaurant. But the folk religion made both these distinctions. Pig was anathema, and it is not uncommon today to find Jews who will eat all nonkosher food except pork. Similarly, a newly emerging folk religion of American Judaism gave special sanctity to the home and forbade eating certain foods in the intimacy of the family but not outside. Many new immigrants in

[12]Cited in Moses Rischin, *The Promised City* (Cambridge, Mass.: Harvard University Press, 1962), pp. 146–147.

particular would have been shocked at the thought of eating nonkosher meat at home *or* outside long after they ceased observing the Sabbath. Behind all this is the special association between eating and cultural or life-style patterns which the Jew retained.

An elitist Jew might be expected to provide extensive Jewish education for his child, but as late as 1916 there were only two religious elementary schools (*yeshivot*) in the United States. According to an educator of that period, Jews opposed parochial schools, which they felt were harmful to democracy.[13] Less than 24 percent of the estimated number of Jewish children of elementary school age in New York received any form of Jewish education in 1917, and less than 1 percent received any training at the high school level.[14] It was primarily the elderly or the very poor who studied the Talmud, and then only at a very low level.

Jewish law extends to the most initimate details of family life—laws of family purity—and requires a married woman to immerse herself in a lustral bath (mikvah) at a specified time following each menstrual period. Writing in 1928 about the immigrant era, an observer commented that lustral baths were simply unavaliable and that "the daughters of Israel had ceased to guard their purity."[15] The Union of Orthodox Rabbis, in the first issue of their publication in 1918, noted that family purity had been "erased from our lives." Requirements of family purity did not involve economic hardship, but they were an anachronism in the values of middle-class American culture toward which the immigrants aspired.

Many Jews did retain an attachment to the synagogue, but this was a broadly cultural, rather than a specifically religious, commitment. As early as 1887 one commentator noted that when the immigrants had built beautiful synagogues they felt they had fulfilled their obligation to Judaism.[16] The large majority of Jews attended a synagogue only on Yom Kippur, the most sacred day in the Jewish calendar.

The new immigrants did found countless small synagogues almost immediately upon arrival, but that in itself was no evidence

[13]Alexander M. Dushkin, *Jewish Education in New York City* (New York: Bureau of Jewish Education, 1918), p. 21.

[14]*Ibid.*, p. 156.

[15]Agudat Horabbonim, *Jubilee Volume*, p. 16.

[16]Moses Weinberger, *Ha-Yehudim Vehayahadut B'New York* (New York: 1887), p. 2.

of religiosity. If the function of the synagogue was primarily for worship there was no need for such proliferation. But if its primary purpose was to meet the social and cultural needs of small groups originating in different European communities this proliferation is more understandable. The synagogues were social forums and benevolent societies adapted to the requirements of poor, unacculturated people. The evidence suggests an absence of religious, as distinct from ethnic, commitment on the part of the East European immigrants to the United States. But the older Jewish community made no such distinctions. To them the bulk of the immigrants were very religious unacculturated Jews. . . .

THE RISE OF CONSERVATIVE JUDAISM

We are now in a position to understand the emergence of a distinctly American brand of Judaism. American Judaism in its religious aspects is not quite synonymous with Conservative Judaism, but it is intimately connected with its growth.

In 1902 the Jewish Theological Seminary was reorganized, and Solomon Schechter was brought from England to head it. Its new financial benefactors were primarily nontraditionalists (Reform Jews) who hoped that the institution and its future rabbinical graduates would Americanize and acculturate the East European immigrants. It is most interesting that the Reform Jews sought to use a nominally traditionalist institution to reach the new immigrant. However, their own status in American society was threatened by the masses of Jewish immigrants.[17] Indeed, the rising anti-Semitism in this period was attributed to the nonacculturated character of the immigrants which reflected unfavorably on the native American Jews.[18] They apparently believed that the seminary could reach the new immigrants since it shared their commitment to religious tradition. . . .

In its infancy, the Conservative movement (with some

[17]Marshall Sklare, *Conservative Judaism* (New York: Free Press, 1955), pp. 161–165, 191–193.

[18]*Ibid.*

exceptions) represented an upper-class formulation of elitist traditional Judaism. But its synagogues were more adaptable to the changing needs of American Jews than were those of Orthodoxy. Some Conservative rabbis were themselves in the forefront of those clamoring for change. But the changes which the rabbis sought were rooted in ideological convictions about the nature of Judaism. The masses sought change for very different reasons.

The alliance between the masses of East European immigrants or their descendants and the Conservative movement finally took place as the East Europeans abandoned the traditional folk religion of Orthodoxy and sought new forms of Jewish expression. Conservatism became predominant in areas of "third settlement." This was the most fashionable ethnic settlement and typically was located near the city limits, where residence "symbolized the attainment of solid middle-class position or better and is indicative of a relatively high level of acculturation."[19] Here Jews constituted a distinct minority of the population and were surrounded, not by other ethnic groups over whom they might feel a sense of status superiority, but rather by Protestants and "old Americans" to whom they were subordinate in status. "The importation of the Orthodox synagogue to areas of third settlement would not have helped to reduce this status hiatus; it would in fact only have served to underline it."[20]

It is not surprising, then, that Jews sought to develop a new form of worship. The surprise is that Conservative synagogues still conformed so closely to traditional Orthodoxy. The content was not changed because the new Conservative Jews had no interest in content. They were folk traditionalists or "reformed" secularists with a communal or ethnic definition of Judaism. They were quite concerned with group survival, not very interested in religion, and in search of institutions which expressed values of both communal survival and integration or acculturation to middle-class American standards.

To the upwardly mobile, status-conscious, economically successful East European Jews of the second or even first generation, there was a tremendous socio-economic cost in being Orthodox. The economic cost came from not working on the Sabbath and the holidays. A social-status cost resulted from

[19]Sklare, *Conservative Judaism*, p. 217.

[20]*Ibid.*, p. 67.

affiliation with an institution lacking in decorum, unconcerned with physical amenities, and chaotic in worship. There was an intellectual cost in paying lip service to a faith burdened with real and imagined superstition which was out of keeping with the prevailing spirit of rationalism and secularism. Hence the immigrant sought new institutional outlets for his Judaism. These outlets had to be outwardly religious, since this was the most legitimate expression of Judaism in America; but they also had to provide a focus for expressing his essentially communal concerns.

The growth of Conservatism in turn took the pressure off Orthodoxy to accommodate itself rapidly to the American environment. Conservative Judaism provided a safety valve for discontented Orthodox Jews and reduced the demand for radical innovation within Orthodoxy, leaving it relatively unconcerned with integration. However, this also changed with the growth of an American-born rabbinate and laity.

Conservative Judaism is the primary Jewish expression of the East European immigrant and his descendants. It is fair to say that the folk religion of the contemporary American Jew is more adequately expressed through Conservatism than through any other movement. But it was not just shaped by the Jewish folk religion; it developed its own elite religion, its own ideology and practices which were shared by its leadership but not by the masses of Conservative Jews. In Conservatism, far more than in Orthodoxy or Reform, there is a sharp division between folk religion and elite religion. The original adherents of Orthodox folk religion have died out or become Conservative. Reform is experiencing a crisis in its own formulation. In fact, considerable numbers of Reform Jews, especially in the East, and many of its leaders share the folk religion of Conservative Judaism. Some nominally Orthodox Jews (though none of its leaders) also participate in the folk religion characteristic of Conservatism. Consider first, however, the elite religion of Conservative Judaism.

The Elite Religion of Conservative Judaism

Conservative Judaism traces its intellectual origin to the Historical School of Judaism in nineteenth-century Europe.[21] It represents a commitment to the historical traditions of Judaism, which it

[21]Moshe Davis, *The Emergence of Conservative Judaism* (Philadelphia: Jewish Publication Society, 1963).

acknowledges as primarily legalistic and textual. Unlike Orthodoxy, however, Conservative Judaism sees the Jewish people and their history—through which God acts—as the source of authority, rather than the sacred texts—through which, according to the Orthodox, God speaks. Thus Conservative Judaism opens the theoretical possibility for reform and even radical change in Jewish law, depending upon how one interprets Jewish history and law, the needs of the time, and the mix between past and present authority. The elitist ideology of Conservatism is shared by most of the nine hundred or so members of the Rabbinical Assembly (the rabbinical arm of Conservatism) and by a few hundred, perhaps as many as a few thousand, Conservative educators and Jewishly literate laymen.

The center of Conservative Judaism for this small community of elite is the Jewish Theological Seminary (JTS). JTS is more traditional in orientation than even its elitist constituents, and its leaders have opposed the introduction of changes in Jewish law. This opposition has been generally successful (somewhat less so in the last few years), because the Talmudic scholars who might introduce the changes or reforms with textual or legal justifications are on the JTS faculty and are generally the more traditional element within the Conservative movement.

But more significantly (for many Conservative rabbis would accept change even if it could not be legitimized by textual exegesis of some kind), JTS as an institution maintains a strong hold over its graduates and friends. This is due in part to the interpersonal relationships developed during student days between future rabbis and the JTS leadership, and in part to the enormous prestige of JTS as a center for scholarly research. In addition, many Conservative rabbis harbor feelings of guilt toward JTS. While this last point is highly speculative, it is based on the observation that many JTS graduates are disturbed by the kinds of compromises they have made with lay leaders of their congregations and feel that they have thereby betrayed the seminary. Many Conservative rabbis have very ambivalent feelings toward JTS, to whom they relate as sons to a father. The same individuals who are willing to follow its leadership on matters of religious reform often express a sense of bitterness and even hostility toward the institution.

In recent years the faculty, curriculum, and standards of conduct within JTS have become even more traditional. This has produced some serious strains among the elite themselves, particularly between the rabbinical students and the JTS leadership.

The problem is that JTS, whose students at one time came primarily from Orthodox homes, now recruits its students from homes where the prevailing atmosphere is Conservative folk religion. Before they come to JTS these students are socialized somewhat to the elite religion by the youth and camping movements of Conservatism. However, these institutions are staffed by individuals whose ideology is less traditional than that of the JTS leadership.

There is one central value, however, which is shared by both the elite religion and the folk religion of Conservatism: the value of integration into American life and a rejection of the notion that integration can only be sought at the expense of survival.

THE FOLK RELIGION OF AMERICAN JUDAISM

First- and second-generation American Jews of East European origin created the folk religion of American Judaism. Its adherents, as noted earlier, included virtually all the nominally Conservative Jews, many Reform, and some Orthodox.

Ritual of the Folk Religion

It is clear that the immigrant was willing to sacrifice a great deal that was basic and fundamental to the Jewish religion. He quickly denuded Judaism of much basic ritual. The laws of the Sabbath, kashrut, and family purity—the basic elements of Jewish ritual life—were abandoned by most of the first- and second-generation Jews. (Kosher-style, however, replaced kosher, a substitution which, as we noted, suggests that we are dealing with a choice for the sake of convenience, not a deliberate variation of life-style in an effort to conceal or lose one's identity.)

Despite the abandonment of the basic Jewish ritual, objections to intermarriage were retained. Why? Many of the early Reform rabbis raised no objections to intermarriage; indeed, they welcomed it. It is certainly consistent with Reform's definition of Judaism as a religion stressing morality and ethics which the Jew is obligated to diffuse among non-Jews. Why is intermarriage any more horrendous than violation of the Sabbath? In the catalog of ritual Jewish sins, there is hardly anything worse than desecration of the Sabbath. But obviously in the catalog of Jewish communal sins there is nothing worse than intermarriage. Countless Jewish mothers and fathers have cautioned their children before they left for college: "Forget Sabbath observance or kashrut if you must, but just make sure you don't fall in love with or marry a non-Jewish student." The proper ritual advice should be: "Marry a non-Jewish person if you must, but remember to observe the Sabbath." Of course, such advice sounds ludicrous. And the fact that it is ludicrous says something about the ritual, as opposed to communal, priorities of Jews.

The pattern of ritual which Jews have maintained is supportive of Jewish communalism and ethnicity, of the Jewish home and peoplehood. The seder, now celebrated as an annual festive family meal, is the most widely observed Jewish practice. The rites of passage—circumcision, bar mitzvah, a Jewish marriage, and a Jewish funeral—all serve to integrate the Jew into the community of fellow Jews. Chanukah was elaborated by American Jews to protect the child and to defend Judaism against the glamour and seductive power of Christmas. These holidays are the major points of contact between the Jew and his ritual traditions. Obviously, even these celebrations have undergone considerable distortion as they developed. The joyful and child-centered aspects were stressed and the more historically symbolic and existential theological aspects de-emphasized. Of somewhat lesser, though still considerable, importance is the celebration of the High Holy Days inaugurating the Jewish New Year. These days, Rosh Hashana and Yom Kippur, have acquired particular religious significance as memorials for departed parents and as the holidays of Jewish affirmation.

Some East European immigrants, forced by economic circumstances to work on the Sabbath, attended religious services in the early morning and then went to work. Second- and third-generation American Jews have reversed the process for the High Holy Days (the Sabbath is totally ignored). The folk religion enjoins the Jew from working on these days, regardless of whether he attends the synagogue or not and regardless of whether he prays or not. At least a token appearance at the synagogue is a desideratum, particularly at the time when memorial prayers for the dead are said. But the stress is not so much on prayer, and certainly not on hearing the shofar (the ram's horn blown on Rosh Hashana), which is central to the religious service. Rather, the stress is on staying away from work and thereby publicly acknowledging one's Jewish identity.

One does not have to believe with Emile Durkheim, the seminal French Jewish sociologist, that all religion is the celebration and ritualization of communal ties to observe that this is the major function of Jewish folk religion in America. It is not without significance that Mordecai Kaplan, whose philosophy of Reconstructionism was an effort to provide an ideological and elitist framework for Jewish folk religion, was influenced by Durkheim's theory of religion.

In a number of community studies, Jews were asked what they considered essential for a person to do in order to be a good Jew. The answer most frequently given was "Lead an ethical and moral life." Close behind and affirmed by over three-quarters of the respondents was "Accept his being a good Jew and not try to hide it."[22] Less than half, however, thought it was essential for one to belong to a synagogue or temple, and less than one-quarter thought that it was necessary to observe the dietary laws or attend weekly services in order to be considered a good Jew.

Associationalism

The Jewish folk religion includes a commitment to Israel . . . and to group survival, but its essence is one's social ties to other Jews. The distinguishing mark of American Jews is less and less how they behave and is certainly not what they believe; it is that they associate primarily with other Jews. Gerhard Lenski, in his Detroit area study, found that ties binding Jews to their religion are weaker than those of Protestants or Catholics, but ties binding them to one another are much stronger. More than other religious groups, "the great majority of Detroit Jews find most of their primary relationships within the Jewish subcommunity."[23] Even the highly acculturated and assimilated, wealthy, predominantly third-generation suburban

[22]Marshall Sklare and Joseph Greenblum, *Jewish Identity on the Suburban Frontier* (New York: Basic Books, 1967), and studies of Jews in Miami, Baltimore, Kansas City, and White Plains, conducted by Manheim Shapiro for the American Jewish Committee.

[23]Gerhard Lenski, *The Religious Factor*, rev. ed. (New York: Doubleday, Anchor Books, 1963), p. 37.

American Jews studied by Sklare and Greenblum continue to make their friends almost exclusively among other Jews.[24] They noted that "87 percent of the parents had most or all of their close friendships with Jews; the same holds true for 89 percent of our respondents."

Schools

Most Jewish parents who send their children to Jewish schools do so because they expect the school to serve those functions which the acculturated, Jewishly ignorant parent can no longer fulfill, "to reinforce Jewish identification through learning about Jewish history and traditions."[25] In his study of the growth of a new Jewish community, Herbert Gans notes that the community organized a school before a synagogue because the school was necessary as "an institution which transmits norms of ethnic culture and symbols of identification, whereas the home and the family are run by secular, middle-class behavior patterns."[26]

A synagogue bulletin carried the following argument by the principal of the congregation's supplementary Hebrew high school, urging parents to enroll their children:

> Our adolescent youngster, for instance, begins to evaluate the Synagogue he once accepted unthinkingly. Does he really need worship or home observances? Does Jewish living do him or the world any good? Do Bible stories about tribes and miracles deserve all this fuss? These are really adolescent problems, not Jewish ones. If a child did not continue on to public high school, he would be assailed by the same doubts concerning the value of his secular elementary education. Such problems do not usually trouble a child who carries on his Jewish education through the high school level.

The writer's rationale for the child's continuing his Jewish education is worth noting. Jews traditionally educated their children in order to teach them how to live as good Jews. Now parents are urged to enroll their children so that the school may transmit to them the *value* of being Jewish. . . .

[24]Sklare and Greenblum, *Jewish Identity*, pp. 269–290.

[25]Herbert Gans, "The Origin and Growth of a Jewish Community in the Suburbs: A Study of the Jews of Park Forest," *The Jews: Social Patterns of an American Group*, ed. Marshall Sklare (New York: Free Press, 1958), pp. 217–218.

[26]*Ibid.*, p. 217.

The Synagogue

The synagogue plays a crucial role in the folk religion of the Jews. Statistics are difficult to ascertain, but the combined estimates of members of all Orthodox, Conservative, and Reform congregations suggest that about 60 percent of American Jews are affiliated with a synagogue. According to the most recent community surveys, less than 20 percent of the Jews reported attending synagogue services oftener than once a month.

But the synagogue is far more than a religious center. It tends to be the center for all Jewish activity. . . . It provides recreational and educational facilities, lectures, art classes, social outlets, golden age clubs, and a meeting place for other nonsynagogal Jewish organizations in the area. It raises funds not only for its own needs but for Jewish philanthropic purposes as well. The synagogue-based campaign provides a major source of funds for federations of Jewish philanthropies and for assistance to Jews abroad, particularly in Israel. Furthermore, secular Jewish organizations such as B'nai B'rith and the American Jewish Congress are not alternatives to the synagogue. Most members of the major Jewish communal organizations are synagogue members. Indeed, Jewish organizational membership tends to be a supplement rather than an alternative. Those who are affiliated with Jewish organizations are most likely to identify themselves with the religious community. According to Bernard Lazerwitz, "the two dominating factors of Jewish identification which are also strongly associated with one another are the religio-pietistic and Jewish organizational factors."[27]

The synagogue is the institutional center of Jewish life. Its public image is religious, its ostensible director is a clergyman, and its activity is therefore legitimate. The official ideology of the synagogue and the rabbi is that of an elite religion, but its content is that of the Jewish folk religion.

Reconstructionism

There was one effort, characteristically arising out of the Conservative movement, to reformulate the essence of American Jewish folk religion in ideological terms, and hence to institutionalize it and provide it with a formal leadership. This was the

[27]Bernard Lazerwitz, *A First Report on the General Components and Consequences of Jewish Identification*, mimeographed (Waltham, Mass.: National Jewish Welfare Board, 1968), p. 19. . . .

Reconstructionist philosophy and movement founded by Mordecai Kaplan in the 1920's. Kaplan's major work is *Judaism as a Civilization: Toward a Reconstruction of American-Jewish Life,* a title which suggests both a traditional view of Judaism and at the same time its reformulation in contemporary terminology.[28] The Reconstructionists challenged the notion of God as a Being. They redefined Him as a power and force in man and nature which makes for salvation, by which they mean freedom, justice, love, truth, and creativity. Under the influence of Durkheim and Dewey, Kaplan sought to explicate or make manifest in religion what others had seen as its latent function: social solidarity and the strengthening of peoplehood. Kaplan sought to retain the form of many traditional observances by reinvesting them with contemporary humanist meaning or national-historical significance.

The most remarkable feature of Reconstructionism is its failure as an institutionalized movment. Kaplan taught at the Jewish Theological Seminary from 1909 to 1963, serving also as dean of its Teachers Institute. He was a very popular teacher and for many years the most influential instructor there. Two generations of Conservative rabbis and educators came under Kaplan's influence. Since 1934 the Jewish Reconstructionist Foundation has published a lively biweekly periodical, *The Reconstructionist,* which has attracted many outstanding Jewish intellectuals as contributors and subscribers. And yet Reconstructionism has made few inroads into organized Jewish life. Only a handful of synagogues are associated with it, it has little money, and since the 1950's it has failed to gain the affection of young intellectuals, particularly within the Conservative movement.

Kaplan was not saying anything very new. He articulated in a provocative and intellectual manner the folk religion of American Jews. Why did his movement strike such a small chord if most Jews consciously or unconsciously are really Reconstructionists? The answer rests in the fact that to label one's religion explicitly as Reconstructionism is to identify it as a sham. Jews have preferred to deceive themselves and others about the nature of their faith and commitment. For the intellectuals of the 1930's, Reconstructionism had a more positive image. The Jewish Theological Seminary student, for example, knew he had lost the traditional Jewish faith in

[28]First published in 1934 by Macmillan, the volume has been reprinted by the Reconstructionist Press and most recently (1967) by Schocken Books in a paper edition.

God and belief in the divine authority of religious law. Coming as he generally did from an Orthodox home and attending an institution of Conservative Judaism, he was quite self-conscious about his divergence from tradition. But he did not want to break with Judaism. He not only wanted to remain Jewish but to believe that he could function as a rabbi within the traditional Jewish fold. Kaplan offered him a rationale and a justification. Reconstructionism had an appeal to Jewish intellectuals, particularly rabbis, as long as there were young men who wanted to be rabbis and did not want to be—or found they could not be—"religious." But the number of such young men, particularly in the Conservative rabbinate, is declining.

The institutional weakness of Reconstructionism lies partly in the fact that if one wants to be Jewish and not religious, there are secular Jewish organizations which can occupy one's energy and attention. Jewish philanthropic organizations, Zionist organizations, B'nai B'rith, the American Jewish Congress, the American Jewish Committee, and other groups provide outlets for one's Jewish identification outside a religious context. These secular Jewish organizations tend to specialize in one aspect of Jewish life or to concentrate on one type of Jewish problem. But they maintain secondary activities in the hope of appealing to all Jews, regardless of their particular interest.

Pure Jewish secularism has no legitimacy in America (witness the demise of Jewish secularist labor and Yiddishist schools, and the inability of Zionists to establish a network of schools, as they have done in a number of other countries). Consequently, the secular organizations themselves have increasingly incorporated religion into the structure of their activity. They generally have one or more rabbis on their staffs, they often introduce some minor religious service into their meetings or conferences, and they articulate their special interests—whether they be Jewish-Christian relations, defense against real or imagined anti-Semitism, support for Israel, or even battling for strict separation of church and state—in quasi-religious terminology. Thus even Jewish secular organizations are "religious." Many spokesmen for these organizations deny that they are secular. To many Jews they differ from Orthodox, Conservative, and Reform synagogues only in their nondenominationalism.

A second factor which has handicapped Reconstructionism is the increased "religiousness" of the American Jew. We have suggested all along that religion is the public façade for the essentially communal content of Jewish identification. But as Jews become increasingly acculturated they take the façade of their public image more seriously. This is the paradoxical result of the fact that more and more Jews learn about themselves from the outside world, particularly the mass media. Newspapers, magazines, and television are probably the primary sources of information for Jews about Judaism. But the mass media obtain their information from the façade of Jewish life, not from the inner content. . . .

The process of acculturation has led an increasing number of Jews to believe that Judaism is a religion. Consequently, if Jews are nonreligious, they more readily lose a sense of Jewish identification. But if they desire a continuing identification, they must be religious. For such Jews, God must be more than the impersonal force or power that Reconstructionism asserts.

Reconstructionism, then, has lost much of its appeal for Conservative Jews, particularly rabbinical students. These young men now come from Conservative backgrounds. They never broke with Orthodoxy; they have no nostalgia for replicas of East European life-styles, no guilt feelings about their religious beliefs or behavior. Furthermore, they are not attracted to the rabbinate by a depression economy which offers no occupational alternatives. They want to become rabbis because they believe Judaism has something to say of religious and social significance.

Reconstructionism has enjoyed some increase in popularity, however, among Reform Jews, though not among its theological spokesmen. Reform theologians either are far more committed to religious existentialism and belief in a personal God or, at the other extreme, are far more radical than Kaplan. The radical Reform Jews deny the utility of the God concept or the existence of meaningful Jewish tradition. Nevertheless, Reform, like every other American Jewish institution, was engulfed by the East European immigrant. This was not only true among the laity but also among the Reform rabbinate, and resulted in the introduction of more traditional symbols among the Reform, a greater emphasis on traditional observance, and greater sympathy toward Zionism. David Philipson, a member of the first graduating class of Hebrew Union College in 1883, viewed these developments at the 1931 meetings of the Reform rabbis with chagrin, and attributed them to "the large number of young rabbis who came from Zionistic and Orthodox environments."[29]

As Reform found an East European Jewish identity, Kaplan's notion of peoplehood and his justification of many ritual practices as folkways had special resonance for some. In a recent survey of first- and last-year students at rabbinical seminaries, respondents were asked to check the name of an individual who best reflected their religious, philosophical, or theological position. Between the first and the last year, the number of Jewish Theological Seminary students choosing Kaplan decreased, but at the Reform schools the number increased. To many Reform Jews of East European background, classical Reform Judaism appears schismatic. For them, Kaplan represents the route back to the unity of the Jewish people.

Religious Elitism and the Growth of Jewish Denominationalism

The religious definition of Judaism strengthens elitist religion within Conservativism and Reform as well as within Orthodoxy. Within Orthodoxy, the religious right wing and the Talmudic scholars—those most at home in the sacred textual tradition and those, therefore, with the greatest stake in the present system of religious authority—have assumed the leadership. In Conservatism and Reform, the influence of the rabbi, the bearer of their elitist religion, has been enhanced because only the rabbi has the requisite knowledge and "authority" to manipulate the symbols of the religion and organize its cult. Of course, this notion of rabbinic authority was borrowed from Christianity by the modern Jew, who, religious though he may be, tends increasingly to be religious in a Christian rather than in a traditional Jewish sense.

One result of the growth of elitism has been the development of Jewish denominationalism. Religious denominationalism among Protestants has often been associated with differences in social class. It might be well to explore the question of social change and question whether certain Jewish religious developments might not be ascribed more properly to change in social conditions.

The identification of individual Jews with Orthodoxy, Conser-

[29]David Philipson, *My Life as an American Jew* (Cincinnati: John G. Kidd & Son, 1941), p. 128.

vatism, and Reform in America is indeed associated with differential social characteristics. In view of the fact that a substantial segment of all three denominations shares in the Jewish folk religion, one might even argue that social and life-style differences have been the major source of differentiation among the denominations. Reform Jews were the wealthiest and best educated, Orthodox the poorest and least educated; indeed, many of the ritual and behavioral differences between Orthodoxy and Reform do reflect differences in social class. (Since Orthodox Jews tend to be older than other Jews and of more recent immigration, they are naturally the poorest and least educated. Whether differences in the social characteristics of the denominations will remain the same in the future is problematical.)

But if the major distinguishing features of the three Jewish branches are their social characteristics, then one might anticipate a lessening of Jewish denominationalism and perhaps even a merging of the three groups should their members become socially homogeneous. This is, after all, the process that has taken place among Protestants. Jews who rise in social class might simply leave one denomination, Orthodoxy, and switch their affiliation to Conservative or Reform. This unquestionably has happened. But the experience of Protestantism has been that not all members of a lower-status denomination change to a higher-status one as they rise in social class. Instead, whole groups or denominations tend to respond to changes in their members' social status by changes in their prescribed religious practices and beliefs. These changes help account for the growing ecumenism among Protestants.[30]

In order to examine changes in the social characteristics of Orthodox, Conservative, and Reform Jews, synagogues in the Greater New York area were examined during two periods: 1948–1952 and 1958–1962.[31] Synagogues were located by census tract, and the median income of the residents of each tract was examined. The assumption was that a new synagogue reflected the social characteristics of the area in which it was located, and that the relative class composition of Jews was proportional to that of the other residents within a given census tract. The study found that, on the average, Reform Jews have been and continue to be in the

[30]Robert Lee, *The Social Sources of Church Unity* (Nashville: Abingdon Press, 1960).

[31]For details of the study, see Charles S. Liebman, "Changing Social Characteristics of Orthodox, Conservative and Reform Jews," *Sociological Analysis* 27 (Winter 1966), pp. 210–212.

highest income bracket, Orthodox Jews in the lowest, and Conservative Jews between the two but closer to Reform. However, since World War II the overlap between the three groups is considerable. Reform Judaism is no longer confined to Jews of the highest income and Orthodoxy to those of the lowest. Instead, the social distance among Orthodox Jews themselves, or Conservatives, or Reform Jews, is growing. . . .

This overlapping may in the long run lead to increased cooperation between the three groups. But it is dangerous to make such a prediction without taking into account the growth of elite religion. Jews who share a folk religion may readily move from one denomination to another if the distinctions are based only on acculturation, style, and taste. But should elite religion continue to develop more rapidly than changes in the class composition of the three groups, there is no reason to believe that social homogeneity would inevitably lead to religious unity. In fact, Orthodoxy, which has the most highly developed elitist leadership and which has been most successful in repressing its folk elements (partly because its adherents of the folk element abandoned Orthodoxy for Conservatism), has become more sectarian with its rise in social status. The elite religion of Orthodoxy must be more sectarian than the folk religion because communal consensus carries much less weight in its scale of values. The increase in income among Orthodox Jews has simply meant that its elite leadership now has greater resources and is better able to strike out on an independent path from Conservatism and Reform.

Conservative and Reform leaders in turn have sought to delineate the particular boundaries differentiating their own groups from Orthodoxy. In part this has been a response to Orthodoxy's denial of their religious legitimacy in a period when religious legitimacy is increasingly important. In part it has been a response to the threat posed by the synagogues' peripheral nonworship activity which engulfs the religious center and reduces the rabbis' authoritative platform. This threat has always existed and has been an inherently unsatisfactory condition for the rabbi, who is now in a position to fight back. But most of all, the Conservative and Reform leaders have had to define their particular boundaries in response to the increasing sense of religious (as distinct from communal) Jewish identity among many young people. This identity requires that the rabbi assert a religious definition of his own denomination if his synagogue is to have any meaning.

But once boundaries are asserted in elitist terms, differences between the groups become significant. The folk religion also distinguished between Orthodoxy, Conservatism, and Reform—Reform being modern, Orthodoxy old-worldly, and Conservatism between the two. To the third- or fourth-generation American Jews, to whom the conflict over acculturation is a fight long past and for whom Judaism is a religion, these distinctions are trivial and hardly enough to sustain or justify independent religious establishments. The elitist distinctions in theology and practice appear to be of greater substance. In their efforts to impose elitist definitions on the masses of synagogue members, each group has paid increased attention to the development of synagogue-based youth groups and summer camps. Part of the impetus was to recruit young men for the elite ranks, particularly the rabbinate, but the enterprise can also be seen as an effort on the part of each movement to socialize the future synagogue members to the values and definitions of the elite.

PROSPECTS FOR THE FUTURE

The self-definition of Judaism in religious rather than communal-ethnic terms has been a major tendency in American Jewish life. But there are forces operating against this trend which might well become dominant in the future. These include the decline of Christian churches and the deterioration of organized religion's reputation, which may result in Jews being more comfortable with a different structural façade. In addition, there is the increasing significance of the role of Israel in the life of the American Jew, and the Jewish identity which is aroused by threats to Israel's safety. Support for and interest in Israel by some Jews represents a secular and ethnic outlet for Jewish expression which is not necessarily religious in nature. Should there be increasing manifestations of anti-Semitism in the United States, Jews will be drawn together across denominational lines. Anti-Semitism, like perils to Israel, will activate religiously uninterested Jews who might otherwise have left the community.

JEWISH IDENTITY
SELF-SEGREGATION
ACCULTURATION
ASSIMILATION

JEWISH ACADEMICS IN THE UNITED STATES

by SEYMOUR MARTIN LIPSET and
EVERETT CARLL LADD, JR.

INTRODUCTION

THE ENTRANCE of Jews into the professoriat is a recent development in the history of American Jewry and a significant aspect of its changing occupational structure. After a long period of exclusion and discrimination Jews began joining university faculties in significant numbers in the post-World War II era. They achieved an extraordinary record of success, quickly overcoming the handicap of recent arrival on the academic scene and despite occasional manifestations of lingering discrimination. According to Lipset and Ladd: "By every criterion of academic accomplishment, Jewish faculty as a group have far surpassed their Gentile colleagues." Perhaps the most revealing evidence of Jewish success is their finding that some 32 percent of Jewish academicians are on the faculties of schools in the highest-quality category. This compares with only 9 percent of their Gentile colleagues.

The extraordinary rise of Jewish academicians—achieved without recourse to preferential hiring or other artificial practices—raises the question of the possible relation of Jewishness to academic success. Two possibilities suggest themselves in this regard: that the status occupied by Jews as a group predisposes them to academic success, or that Jewish culture impels them to it. These need not be mutually exclusive; it is entirely possible that both factors have been present and have operated to reinforce each other.

The Jewish rise in the academy has meant that the Jewish contribution to American scholarship, research, and intellectual life—already noticeable before World War II—has increased enormously in recent decades. Since the academy is now undergoing rapid change this trend may not continue in as marked a fashion as before, but, barring sharp reversals in hiring practices, the contribution of Jews should become even greater as years go by since (on account of past discrimination) Jewish academics tend to be younger than their Gentile colleagues and thus have a longer period of productivity ahead of them.

The role of the Jew in the academy, and in American intellectual life generally, is an important topic in the sociology of the Jews. Nevertheless, the Lipset and Ladd article should be read not only for what it says of the impact of the Jew on the academy, but equally for what it says of the impact of the academy upon the Jew—and especially upon his Jewish identity. The academic life typically involves something more than making a living. It demands commitments—to an institution, to a discipline, and, as the phrase "the academic community" suggests, to an entire way of life. Some scholars have strong ties beyond the academy. Those whose loyalty is centered in the academy vary in the degree and type of communitarianism which they espouse. Some have a strong loyalty to the institutions which they serve while others are cosmopolitan—their loyalty is to a wider academic community, and in some cases to a community which is international in scope. In any case membership in the academic community is capable of reducing, if not replacing, the significance of inherited membership in a religious or ethnic group. The conditions of academic life complicate the holding of such inherited memberships, for not only does academia have a communitarian aspect but it also places great stress upon creativity and critical intellectuality—orientations which are not easily reconciled with inherited loyalties to religious and ethnic groups.

Given the character of academic life we must conclude that even if American universities were dominated numerically by Jews and thus constituted a "Jewish" occupation—a condition beyond the realm of possibility—the potentiality for academicians to be alienated from the Jewish community would still exist. On the face of it such alienation does not appear to be crucial to the continuity of the Jewish community. Despite the sharp increase in the proportion who are academicians, the overwhelming majority of American Jews are in other occupations. However, academics are influential out of all proportion to their numbers; while many do not aspire to influence outside the confines of their discipline, we would expect that Jewish academicians have a special potential for influencing their fellow Jews. This potential is compounded by the Jewish affinity for, and admiration of, intellectuality. To the extent that the Jewish academic is alienated from the Jewish community he creates a model of marginal affiliation which other Jews are free to emulate.

The survey which Lipset and Ladd utilize as the central source of their data did not focus on the problem of ethnic identity. Since it included only some general items on religious behavior it is difficult to pinpoint the degree of Jewish alienation of their respondents. But the finding that 29 percent of the academicians who reported that their parents were Jewish considered their own religion to be "none" (or "other") suggests that there is a strong potentiality for alienation. It is difficult to say to what extent this group has assumed what the authors call an "ethnocultural" Jewish identification which would substitute for a religious identification, but the findings of Lipset and Ladd (together with those of other investigators) lead to the conclusion that academia constitutes a kind of frontier area in the emergence of the phenomenon of alienation from Jewish identity.

M. S.

INTELLECTUALISM has long been associated with Jewishness. Many have commented on the major contribution of Jews to learning and intellectual life. Even in societies which have discriminated in various manifest ways against them, Jews have formed a disproportionately large segment of those attending higher schools. *Numeri clausi* designed to limit Jewish access to privileged positions in both Czarist and Soviet Russia have allowed for a slightly larger percentage of Jews in universities than in the general population, but much fewer than would qualify in an open competition.[1] And whenever discriminatory barriers against them have broken down, within one generation Jews have poured into educational institutions and formed a major segment of the intellectuals.

The United States has been the most important example of a free society from the point of view of the Jewish community. But even here, Jews were held back from educational and job opportunities within the university system. Important private universities had quotas limiting the number of Jewish undergradu-

[1]In 1881, before the *numerus clausus* took effect in Russia, at a time when the great mass of Jews did not yet speak Russian, "8,200 Jewish boys accounted for 12 percent of all the students in the gymnasiums and progymnasiums": Patrick L. Alston, *Education and the State in Tsarist Russia* (Stanford: Stanford University Press, 1969), p. 122; see also pp. 130–132, 139 for data on the effect of government policies in reducing Jewish enrollments. The quotas were temporarily lifted after the Revolution of 1905, but were restored in 1908. During this brief period "the influx of Jews to the higher schools had been very great, so that their number was now vastly in excess of the established norm, [thus making it] necessary [for the higher schools] to bar completely all new candidates. . . . Once more, bands of 'martyrs of learning' could be seen wending their way toward the universities in foreign lands"; S. M. Dubnow, *History of Jews in Russia and Poland,* Vol. 3 (Philadelphia: Jewish Publication Society of America, 1920), p. 158. For Soviet policies and Jewish educational statistics, see Alec Nove and J. A. Newth, "The Jewish Population: Demographic Trends and Occupational Patterns," in Lionel Kochan, ed., *The Jews in Soviet Russia Since 1917* (London: Oxford University Press, 1970), pp. 145–148, 154–157.

Note: We wish to acknowledge our debts to Dr. Clark Kerr, Chairman of the Carnegie Commission on Higher Education, the sponsor of the survey on which this article is based; to Professor Martin Trow of the University of California, Berkeley, who directed the administration of the survey; and to their colleagues. The interpretations expressed here are solely the responsibility of the authors. . . .

ates until the end of World War II.[2] Relatively few Jews were able to secure employment on the faculty of these schools. The change in favor of Jewish participation at the summit of American higher education in the past 25 years has been so extensive and totally accepted that some indication of how different the situation was at the beginning of the careers of the current generation of senior professors would seem to be in order.

Overt anti-Jewish prejudice within academe seemingly was at a high point in the 1920's and 1930's, when large numbers of the children of immigrants began to enter college. This pressure led many schools to impose quotas on the admission of Jews to both undergraduate and professional schools. A. Lawrence Lowell, as president of Harvard, and Nicholas Murray Butler, when president of Columbia, openly defended Jewish quotas.[3] And as late as 1945 Ernest M. Hopkins, then president of Dartmouth, justified the use of a quota at his institution on the grounds that "Darmouth is a Christian college founded for the Christianization of its students."[4] These restrictions carried over even more intensely to faculty appointments.[5] Ludwig Lewisohn reported in his *Memoirs* how he was prevented from teaching English; Edward Sapir was told by his graduate-school professors that as a Jew he could not expect an appointment and had to go to Canada; Lionel Trilling recalled in an article in *Commentary* that he was the first Jew appointed to the English department in Columbia; the Harvard Law School did not appoint another Jew after Felix Frankfurter until 1939, when Paul Freund and Milton Katz were named assistant professors. The City College of New York became one of the first schools to open its doors to Jews, but even CCNY was charged with discrimination at the beginning of the 1930's. Heywood Broun and George Britt pointed out that "only five [Jews] have the rank of full professors. . . . All five are men of exceptional attainments. The percentage of Jews in the lower orders . . . is much higher than

[2]Heywood Broun and George Britt, *Christians Only* (New York: The Vanguard Press, 1931), pp. 72–124.

[3]Carey McWilliams, *A Mask for Privilege: Anti-Semitism in the United States* (Boston: Little, Brown, 1948), pp. 38–39; Broun and Britt, *op. cit.*, pp. 88–89; Dan W. Dodson, "College Quotas and American Democracy," *The American Scholar*, Summer 1945, pp. 270–271.

[4]Lawrence Bloomgarden, "Our Changing Elite Colleges," *Commentary*, February 1960, p. 152.

[5]C. B. Sherman, *The Jew Within American Society* (Detroit: Wayne State University Press, 1961), pp. 174–178.

among the more desirable positions. Even in a friendly college, the openings for Jewish professors are distinctly limited."[6] Seven years later, a report in the *American Jewish Year Book* described the national situation in dramatic terms:

> It is very difficult these days for Jews to become full professors in the leading universities. In order to attain such rank, they must have achieved distinction in their respective fields of national and international character. While Jews constitute a considerable proportion of the student bodies in the colleges and universities throughout the land, certainly much more than their numerical proportion, they represent but an insignificant proportion of the faculties.[7]

The limitations in the academic job market were often used by graduate departments as a justification for admitting few Jewish students to graduate work. The old (vicious) circular reasoning legitimated the refusal to enlarge the body of Jewish graduate students on the grounds that to do so would mean training people who would not get jobs. Soon after the end of World War II, Albert Sprague Coolidge of Harvard told a Massachusetts legislative committee, "we know perfectly well that names ending in 'berg' or 'stein' have to be skipped by the board of selection of students for scholarships in chemistry." And he explained this practice as stemming from the department's understanding that there were no jobs for Jews in chemistry.[8]

Since that time, however, the situation has changed startlingly on both student and faculty levels. Schools which were notorious among Jews for their restrictionist policies suddenly opened their doors.[9] And now, at the beginning of the 1970's, Jews form a heavy proportion of academe.[10] The large national sample (60,000) of

[6]Broun and Britt, *op. cit.*, p. 105.

[7]Maurice J. Karpf, "Jewish Community Organization in the United States," in *American Jewish Year Book,* Vol. 39 (1937), pp. 61–62. See also Broun and Britt, *op. cit.*, pp. 179–187.

[8]McWilliams, *op. cit.*, pp. 138–139.

[9]Nathan Glazer and Daniel P. Moynihan, *Beyond the Melting Pot* (2nd ed., Cambridge, Mass.: M.I.T. Press, 1970), pp. 156–159.

[10]Administrative positions were the last to be opened to Jews, but during the late 1960's, these restrictions were also broken. Chicago, Cincinnati, Dartmouth, MIT, Pennsylvania, and Rutgers recently appointed Jewish presidents. In line with the Broun-Britt complaints about CCNY, it did not get a Jewish president until 1969. The first Jewish dean of the Harvard Law School, and the first in the university's history, was designated in 1971.

faculty who filled out questionnaires for the Carnegie Commission on Higher Education in 1969 contained close to 6,000 who reported that their parental family was Jewish. Jews constituted 9 percent of the weighted sample.[11] Their proportion has increased dramatically over time, as evidenced by the data in Table 1. The professorial generation which entered academe in the 1920's is today less than 4 percent Jewish; by the first post-World War II generation, however, the Jewish proportion had climbed to 9 percent, at which point it leveled off. The most recent group of young faculty, those under 25, include 12 percent Jews. Whether this represents a new major increase, or possibly reflects the fact that Jews are able to complete their graduate work and enter teaching earlier than their Gentile compeers, cannot be determined from our data.

The increase in Jewish faculty has been even greater at the more important centers of learning, as Table 2 indicates. At Ivy League schools, one group of the elite colleges, the proportion of Jews among professors in their fifties (18 percent) is over twice that among faculty in their sixties, while about a quarter of those under 50, all of whom entered the professoriate after World War II, are Jewish.

Location of Faculty

The entry of Jews into academe has followed, in part, along certain traditional lines. Their geographic distribution shows the same pattern as the Jewish population generally. Most Jewish professors are located in the Northeast. They are the most underrepresented in the South, and are relatively strong in the West. . . .

[11]In 1969 the Carnegie Commission on Higher Education initiated several large-scale national surveys of students, faculty, and administrators. These studies were administered by the Survey Research Center of the University of California, Berkeley, with advice and technical assistance from the Office of Research of the American Council on Education. Financial support was provided by the Carnegie Commission and the United States Office of Education, Department of Health, Education and Welfare. A disproportionate random sampling procedure was used to select colleges and universities, to obtain adequate numbers of institutions of various types and characteristics. The 303 schools thus chosen included 57 junior colleges, 168 four-year colleges, and 78 universities. Next, a six-in-seven random sample of faculty was drawn from the rosters of the included institutions, yielding a sample of 100,315. A very high return of 60,028 completed questionnaires (60 percent) was achieved. The return questionnaires, finally, were differentially weighted, adjusting the data for the disproportionate sampling of institutions and the unequal rates of response. Tabulations from the weighted data of this survey, then, may be taken as reasonably representative of the entire population of teaching faculty at colleges and universities in the United States.

TABLE 1
Religious background of American professoriate, by age

	Number	Percent				
		Jewish	Catholic	Protestant	Other and none	Total
65 years & over	1,446	3.8	13.7	79.0	3.6	100
60–64	3,067	4.9	13.6	77.1	4.3	100
55–59	4,028	6.7	16.3	73.2	3.8	100
50–54	5,648	7.3	17.2	70.8	4.7	100
45–49	7,569	9.1	16.6	67.6	6.7	100
40–44	8,831	9.7	18.3	63.9	8.1	100
35–39	9,971	9.4	20.0	62.6	8.1	100
30–34	10,212	9.3	19.6	63.1	8.0	100
26–29	7,990	9.6	21.6	62.2	6.5	100
25 years & under	1,266	11.9	21.3	60.7	6.1	100
All Faculty	60,028	8.7	18.6	66.0	6.8	100

More interesting is the distribution of the different religious groups among the various disciplines (Table 3). The largest concentration of Jews is in the two major free professional fields, medicine and law.[12] Clearly, the early penchant of Jews for these two areas, which have been both prestigious and least subject to the prejudices and whims of employers, has carried over into teaching and research. It is noteworthy that within the natural sciences they are most heavily represented in the two fields having the strongest links to medical problems, biochemistry and the complex of bacteriology: molecular biology, virology, and others. This finding is paralleled by the very heavy involvement of Jews in clinical psychology, perhaps the closest field to medicine among the social sciences.[13] It is impossible to tell from the data how much of the attraction of these "health"-linked fields has been a substitute for

[12]On Jewish overrepresentation in these fields, see Ernest van den Haag, *The Jewish Mystique* (New York: Stein and Day, 1969), p. 23.

[13]Proportionately there are more Jews in psychiatry than in any other medical speciality. *Ibid.*, p. 23.

TABLE 2
*Religious background of American professoriate, by age, elite colleges and universities only**

	Number	Percent				
		Jewish	*Catholic*	*Protestant*	*Other and none*	*Total*
65 years & over	439	9.3	9.1	74.8	6.6	100
60–64	1,012	10.4	9.0	73.2	7.4	100
55–59	1,317	14.4	9.5	69.5	6.1	100
50–54	1,756	16.1	10.9	66.2	6.8	100
45–49	2,425	20.0	11.7	58.3	10.0	100
40–44	2,749	22.6	11.6	54.8	11.0	100
35–39	3,322	20.3	14.9	54.4	10.5	100
30–34	3,398	20.2	15.4	54.4	10.0	100
29 years & under	2,673	20.6	18.7	51.8	8.8	100
All faculty in elite colleges and universities	19,092	19.0	13.4	58.3	9.3	100

*An institution was classified as *elite* on the basis of a three-item index, including selectivity (Scholastic Aptitude Test scores required for admission), affluence (revenue per student), and research activity (research expenditures per student).

fulfilling the Jewish dream of becoming a "doctor." Probably, many Jews who were unable to attend medical school picked such subjects as a "second choice."

The considerable presence of Jews in social science departments (and schools of social work), in comparison to most of the humanities and natural sciences, may be related to the disposition of secularized Western Jews for reform-oriented politics, to be discussed later. A variety of studies of undergraduate career choices indicate that the more left-disposed students are more inclined than others to an academic career, particularly in the politically relevant social sciences.[14] As the newest group of disciplines, the social

[14]Ian D. Currie, *et al.*, "Images of the Professor and Interest in the Academic Profession," in Ronald M. Pavalko, ed., *Sociology of Education* (Itasca, Ill.: Peacock, 1968), pp. 540–541, 549–550; Martin Trow, "Recruitment to College Teaching," in A. H. Halsey *et al.*, eds., *Education, Economy and Society* (New York: The Free Press, 1961), pp. 609–617.

sciences have been less discriminatory, more committed to universalistic principles than the humanities. The latter, as the oldest and least "practical" fields, have tended to be identified with high status, and hence were more restrictive in their admission policies.

The underrepresentation of Jews in the humanities and history may reflect the continuation of a distinction frequently made in Wilhelminian and even Weimar Germany. Some who supported the appointment of Jews to professorships in the sciences and social sciences argued that they could not be professors of German literature or history. These subjects were at the heart of the *Volkswesen,* the national essence, while the Jews (obviously) were *wesenfremd,* alien to the national essence. Suspicions about the *Volkswesen* suitability of Jews in English and history have not completely vanished in the U.S. In his presidential address to the American Historical Association, in 1962, Carl Bridenbaugh lamented that "many of the younger practitioners of our craft . . . are products of lower middle-class or foreign origins and . . . find themselves in a real sense outsiders to our past and feel themselves shut out. This is certainly not their fault, but it is true." By "products of . . . foreign origins," we would hazard the guess, Professor Bridenbaugh was not thinking primarily of Albanians.[15]

Fittingly, in view of the historic limitations on Jews in agriculture in Christian Europe, they are largely absent from the faculties of agriculture schools, and are heavily underrepresented in fields linked to the soil or agriculture, e.g., geography, earth sciences, botany, and zoology. The absence of Jews in religion and theology undoubtedly reflects the fact that there are only two Jewish supported universities, and that all university-affiliated schools of theology are Christian.

Caliber

Over fifty years ago, Thorstein Veblen addressed himself to the issue of the "intellectual pre-eminence of the Jews," describing their contribution in highly laudatory terms:

> It is a fact which must strike any dispassionate observer that the Jewish people have contributed much more than an even share to the

[15]Carl Bridenbaugh, "The Great Mutation," *The American Historical Review,* January 1963, pp. 322–323.

TABLE 3
Respondent's principal teaching field [a]

	Number	Percent			
		Jewish faculty	*Catholic faculty*	*Protestant faculty*	*Other and none*
Social sciences	6,845[b]	14.6	16.9	60.5	8.0
Anthropology	444	12.2	9.0	67.3	11.5
Economics	1,469	15.0	16.7	60.0	8.3
Political science	1,230	12.6	14.4	65.3	7.7
Psychology	2,046	16.5	17.8	58.5	7.2
Sociology	1,004	12.7	20.0	58.5	8.8
Humanities	9,546[b]	7.5	24.5	61.6	6.5
English language & lit.	3,307	7.4	21.3	64.9	6.5
Modern European languages and literature	1,601	7.2	29.5	56.4	6.9
History	1,955	8.8	20.2	66.2	4.7
Journalism	308	5.9	10.5	72.5	11.1
Philosophy	761	7.6	36.4	49.9	6.1
Religion and theology	523	1.0	30.9	65.3	2.7
Fine arts	3,732	7.2	15.5	70.6	6.7
Architecture	499	9.2	20.5	63.4	6.9
Art	808	4.4	22.7	65.0	7.9
Drama and speech	933	9.3	13.0	72.9	4.9
Music	1,317	6.5	11.0	76.7	5.7
Physical Sciences	7,599	8.2	16.7	66.8	8.3
Chemistry	1,834	6.3	17.9	69.1	6.8

intellectual life of modern Europe. So also is it plain that the civilization of Christendom continues today to draw heavily on the Jews for men devoted to science and scholarly pursuits. It is not only that men of Jewish extraction continue to supply more than a proportionate quota to the rank and file engaged in scientific and scholarly work, but a disproportionate number of the men to whom modern science and scholarship look for guidance and leadership are of the same derivation. . . . They count particularly among the vanguard, the pioneers, the uneasy guild of pathfinders and

TABLE 3 *(Continued)*

	Number	*Percent* Jewish faculty	Catholic faculty	Protestant faculty	Other and none
Earth sciences	786	3.6	13.2	74.8	8.3
Geography	390	2.3	15.1	75.3	7.2
Mathematics & statistics	2,831	8.6	18.5	65.0	7.9
Physics	1,662	13.8	14.2	60.1	11.9
Biological sciences	4,403	9.8	14.3	67.7	8.2
Bacteriology[c]	788	14.1	15.8	60.7	9.4
Biochemistry	643	20.6	10.9	58.6	9.8
Botany	339	3.7	14.7	75.0	6.7
Physiology	927	9.4	16.8	65.5	8.3
Zoology	391	3.6	8.9	81.4	6.0
Law	593	24.9	17.9	52.7	4.6
Social work	497	16.3	17.2	60.3	6.2
Education	3,277	6.2	17.4	72.0	4.4
Medicine	2,312	22.4	12.8	59.1	5.7
Business	2,080	7.5	18.4	69.3	4.7
Engineering	4,165	9.0	16.5	65.1	9.4
Agriculture	1,348	.7	8.5	84.1	6.6

[a]The number of faculty in the various fields included in this table does not equal 60,028 because: 1) some faculty members (7,664) did not specify their "principal teaching field"; 2) some fields included in the survey have not been listed; and 3) some respondents did not answer the question on their religious background.
[b]The total number of cases for the social sciences or the humanities is more than the total of those listed for the separate disciplines because they include individuals who were listed as "social scientists" or under categories like "other foreign languages including linguistics," etc.
[c]Molecular biology, virology, microbiology.

iconoclasts, in science, scholarship, and institutional change and growth.[16]

Other writers have even pointed to evidence that Jews played a major role in science and scholarship long before the modern era. Thus, drawing on George Sarton's classic studies in the history of

[16]Thorstein Veblen, "The Intellectual Pre-Eminence of Jews in Modern Europe," in his *Essays in Our Changing Order* (New York: The Viking Press, 1934), pp. 221, 223–224. The essay was first published in 1919.

science, Weyl and Possony reported that, for the first 1,400 years of Christendom, Sarton listed 1,897 scholars of whom 10.6 percent were Jewish, at least three times their proportion in the population of Europe.[17] For more recent times, a variety of analysts of intellectual creativity have emphasized the very heavy representation of Jews of varying nationalities among Nobel Prize winners. Lewis Feuer noted that out of 40 Germans who received such prizes up to 1940, 12 (30 percent) were Jewish.[18] Ernest van den Haag pointed to the fact that 18 of the 67 American scientists who received Nobel Prizes up to 1965—that is, 27 percent—were Jewish.[19] On a world scale Jews accounted for 16 percent of the 225 Prize winners in the sciences between 1901 and 1962.[20]

The two anti-Semitic totalitarian powers of the 1930's, Germany and Italy, had both been heavily dependent on their small minorities of Jews for scholarly leaders:

> Put the matter numerically and in the roughest way, in pre-Nazi Germany Jews formed about three quarters of 1 percent of the population. Of distinguished German mathematicians, physicists, and medical researchers, they provided something like 30 times their due proportion, for at least 25 percent of these were Jewish. In Italy, where the Jewish population was only one per thousand, Jewish intellectual supremacy was even higher in certain departments. Well over 50 percent of the distinguished mathematicians were Jews.[21]

If this latter figure seems astonishing given the small size of the Jewish population, it should be noted that in the 1920's, when a minute fraction of the Italian population attended university, about 25 percent of the Jewish men did. . . .[22]

[17]Nathaniel Weyl and Stefan Possony, *The Geography of Intellect* (Chicago: Henry Regnery, 1963), pp. 123–128.

[18]Lewis Feuer, *The Scientific Intellectual* (New York: Basic Books, 1963), pp. 301–302.

[19]Van den Haag, *op. cit.*, pp. 22–23.

[20]Weyl and Possony, *op. cit.*, p. 143.

[21]Charles Singer, "Science and Judaism," in Louis Finkelstein, ed., *The Jews*, Vol. II (New York: Harper and Brothers, 1960), pp. 1414–1415. See also, Ernst Heppner, *Juden als Erfinder und Entdecker* (Berlin: Henriette Beckerstiftung Welt Verlag, 1913); and Abraham Myerson and Isaac Goldberg, *The German Jew* (New York: Alfred Knopf, 1913).

[22]Salo Baron, "European Jewry Before and After Hitler," *American Jewish Year Book*, Vol. 63 (1962), p. 10; Carlo Tagliacozzo, "Presenza degli ebrei nelle scienze moderna," *Rassegna mensile di Israel* (Milan), especially pp. 212–216.

There is probably no country in which Jews have been able to do as well intellectually as in the United States, given the extraordinary spread of higher education in this country in the post-World War II years. Studies of undergraduate enrollment indicate that about 80 percent of college-age Jews are enrolled in higher education, as compared to 40 percent for the population as a whole.[23] And the Jewish students are heavily located in the more selective (higher academic standards) schools.[24] A 1969 American Council on Education survey of college freshmen found that, as a group, those of Jewish parentage had higher secondary-school averages than their Gentile counterparts; this in spite of the fact that a much larger proportion of Jews than non-Jews go on to college.[25] Moreover, Jews seemingly perform better as students, once admitted to college; for example, they have been represented in the membership of Phi Beta Kappa at about twice their proportion of the undergraduate population.[26]

The generalizations and findings concerning the propensity of Jews to achieve intellectually are reinforced by our data. By every criterion of academic accomplishment, Jewish faculty as a group have far surpassed their Gentile colleagues. . . . (There is, of course, a considerable range of variation among Jews and non-Jews). Thus, Jews are much more likely than Christian faculty to be located in universities rather than in four- or two-year colleges. They are heavily represented on the faculties of Ivy League schools, other elite private universities, the "Big Ten," and the various campuses of the University of California; they are considerably underrepresented in the other, generally less prestigious, state universities. When the schools in the sample are rank ordered according to an index of academic quality (Scholastic Aptitude Test scores required for admission, research dollars per student, and revenue per student) 32 percent of the Jews are at schools which are in the highest quality category, in contrast to 9 percent of the Christian professors. Conversely, over 40 percent of the latter are at the lowest quality category schools, as compared to 13.5 percent of the Jews (Table 4).

[23] "The American Jew Today," *Newsweek*, 1 March 1971, p. 63.

[24] David E. Drew, *A Profile of the Jewish Freshman* (Washington, D.C.: American Council on Education, 1970), pp. 11–12.

[25] *Ibid.*, p. 35.

[26] Nathaniel Weyl, *The Creative Elite in America* (Washington, D.C.: The Public Affairs Press, 1966), p. 94.

The same pattern of accomplishment is reflected in the data on publications. The Jewish faculty have published many more books and articles than their Gentile compeers. . . . To some degree, these variations in research accomplishments are linked to the fact that the Jews in the sample, on the average, spend more time "on professional reading, writing, or research" than do their non-Jewish colleagues. They also are much more likely than other professors to report themselves as primarily interested in research. . . .

These accomplishments of Jews in academe are in part only a special variant of the propensity of Jews for hard work—and resultant success—generally. In a detailed summary of the evidence concerning Jewish achievements from the 1930's through the 1950's, Nathan Glazer pointed out that the gains made by Jews surpassed those of all other immigrant groups, and indeed those of "old stock" Americans. In this period, Jews moved rapidly into the ranks of professionals and the self-employed generally, although relatively few of their parents had been in these occupations. And uniformly by the 1940's within specific occupations, "Jews earned more than non-Jews."[27] In seeking to account for Jewish success in business, the professions, and intellectual life, Glazer concluded that the explanation lay in the group's adherence to a particular syndrome of values and habits, which led members to emphasize hard work and learning, to be careful, and to postpone present pleasures for future security and satisfaction. These orientations, which characterized the behavior of poor, often unlearned and unskilled Jews in the East European ghettos and in the crowded slums of American cities, are precisely the ones making for achievement, for mobility into the urban middle class. Max Weber stressed the emergence of such traits in Western Europe to form the capitalist ethic out of Calvinism. But, as Glazer noted, these were omnipresent among Jews as a result of historic experiences reinforced by the conditions of ghetto life:

> There is no question that Judaism . . . emphasizes the traits that businessmen and intellectuals require, and has done so since at least 1,500 years before Calvinism. . . . The strong emphasis on learning and study can be traced that far back, too. The Jewish habits of foresight, care, moderation, probably arose early during the 2,000

[27]Nathan Glazer, "Social Characteristics of American Jews," in *American Jewish Year Book*, Vol. 56 (1955), pp. 28–29. See also Ernest Havemann and Patricia Slater West, *They Went to College* (New York: Harcourt Brace, 1952), pp. 186–189.

TABLE 4
*Respondent's school as classified by an index of academic quality**

	Number	Percent					
		1 (highest quality)	2	3	4	5 (lowest quality)	Total
Jewish faculty	5,907	31.6	12.6	12.1	30.2	13.5	100
Catholic faculty	9,096	8.1	6.6	11.8	31.6	41.9	100
Protestant faculty	37,804	9.5	8.3	11.8	28.0	42.5	100
All faculty	60,028	11.7	8.5	11.8	28.7	39.3	100

*The index was composed by combining the Scholastic Aptitude Test score (selectivity), research dollars per student code (research), and the revenue per student code (affluence).

years that Jews have lived primarily as strangers among other peoples.[28]

The propensity of Jews for academic achievement would also seem to be linked to their greater commitment to intellectual activities. Jews form a highly disproportionate part of the market and audience for art and literature. Wealthy Jews are relatively more generous in their support for such endeavors than equivalent Gentiles. Alvin Toffler described the extensive contribution of Jews to American cultural life:

> . . . although there is no statistical data that even attempts to analyze the racial or religious background of the arts public, conversations with gallery directors, orchestra managers, and other art administrators in many cities lead one to conclude that the culture public

[28]Glazer, *op. cit.*, p. 31.

> contains a higher than proportionate number of Jewish people. Jews, of course, have always been prominent as artists. . . . The extension director of a university in California, in discussing the rising level of cultural activity in Los Angeles, cites the growth of the Jewish population as the causative agent. A museum director in San Antonio says: "The vast majority of collectors here are Jewish." In Dallas the arts attract considerable support from the Jewish community.[29]

Sam Welles, in an article in *Fortune,* stressed the contribution of the New York Jews to "the world of art, theater, and music . . . sometimes strident, generally exciting, and often original and profound." He wrote:

> An educated guess has it that perhaps a third of the city's art galleries are Jewish owned or managed. In the theater, Jews are prominent as owners, directors, playwrights and actors. They have been leaders in radio and television from the earliest days of these media. In music they have enriched the city with special abundance.[30]

Jews in academe reflect this group disposition in exhibiting a greater commitment to "intellectuality" than their non-Jewish fellow professionals. Previous studies of academe have indicated that Jewish professors are more likely to think of themselves as "intellectuals" than comparably located Gentiles.[31] And this difference in self-perception is associated with a greater involvement in serious culture, as reflected by reading habits and other cultural tastes.[32] The much more extensive Carnegie sample validated these earlier findings. Thus, twice as many Jews (36 percent) as Christians (17 percent) strongly agreed with the statement, "I consider myself an intellectual" (Table 5). This variation between the religious groups is linked to quite different tastes. More than half of the Jewish professors almost never attend an athletic event (53 percent), in contrast to but one third (32 percent) among Gentiles. . . . The Jews, on the other hand are more likely to attend concerts and plays regularly, and to go to "art" films. . . .

[29] Alvin Toffler, *The Culture Consumers* (New York: St. Martin's Press, 1964), p. 34.

[30] Sam Welles, "The Jewish Elan," *Fortune,* February 1960, p. 166.

[31] Charles H. Anderson, "Kitsch and the Academic," *Sociology and Social Research,* July 1967, p. 452.

[32] *Ibid.*, pp. 447–449.

TABLE 5
"I consider myself an intellectual"

		Percent				
	Number	Strongly agree	Agree with reservations	Disagree with reservations	Strongly disagree	Total
Jewish faculty	5,907	35.7	46.5	13.9	3.9	100
Catholic faculty	9,096	18.1	50.3	23.9	7.7	100
Protestant faculty	37,804	16.2	51.7	24.4	7.8	100
All faculty	60,028	19.1	50.6	22.9	7.3	100

The greater commitment of Jewish academics to the intellectual role and activities clearly has its roots in Jewish culture.[33] Many have sought to explain this trait as a secularization of the emphasis on religious study which characterized life in the ghetto for over a millennium. Presumably, the status given to the religious scholar and the activities of the mind remains within secularized Jewish culture, transferred in large part to the intellectual and his work. Some evidence that the intellectual orientation of the current crop of Jewish faculty members is not due to the greater educational and intellectual achievements of their parents may be seen in the fact that they come from less educated families, which were less represented in the teaching professions and in other occupations requiring high levels of education, than the families of the Gentile professors. A larger percentage of the Jews had fathers who had not graduated from high school than did the rest of academe. And more Gentiles, particularly the predominant Protestants among them,

[33]For a description of the historic commitment to education among Jews see Weyl, *The Creative Elite in America, op. cit.*, pp. 151–168, and Pierre Aubery, *Milieux juifs de la France contemporaine* (Paris: Plon, 1962), pp. 248–257, 265–275.

had fathers who had attended college (41 percent) than did the Jews (35 percent). . . . A similar pattern is reflected in family occupational background. Almost half the Jews had fathers who were in business, 45 percent, as contrasted with 16 percent among the others. Although 8 percent of the Protestants had fathers who had been employed in education at some level, only 3 percent of the Jews gave similar reports (Table 6). Thus, though the Jewish professors must have absorbed their drive for intellectual accomplishment in their home environment, more of them than of their non-Jewish colleagues were the "first-generation" of their families to attend college.

TABLE 6

"What is (was) your father's principal occupation?"

	Percent			
Occupation	*Jewish faculty n=5,907*	*Catholic faculty n=9,096*	*Protestant faculty n=37,804*	*All faculty n=60,028*
College/ university teaching	1.0	1.5	4.2	3.6
Elementary/ secondary teaching	2.2	1.8	4.0	3.4
Other professional	16.4	10.7	15.3	14.7
Managerial	9.9	18.1	16.2	15.8
Owner large business	4.3	2.0	1.2	1.7
Owner small business	40.8	16.2	14.8	17.6
Farm owner	.6	5.5	12.9	10.3
Clerical & sales	9.3	9.1	7.7	7.9
Skilled worker	10.8	23.0	16.1	16.7
Semi & unskilled worker	4.8	12.2	7.5	8.1
TOTAL	100.0	100.0	100.0	100.0

Religious Involvement

All surveys of religious commitment, belief, and practice in the United States indicated that Jews are much less involved in religious activities than Protestants, who in turn are less active than Catholics (Table 7). To an increasing degree, identification as Jewish has become ethnocultural rather than religious. Our data on faculty beliefs and practices show essentially the same pattern. Somewhat

TABLE 7
"What is your present religion?"
Faculty of Jewish, Catholic, and Protestant parentage, by age

		Percent				
	Number	*Protestant*	*Catholic*	*Jewish*	*Other and none*	*Total*
Jewish						
60 years and over	165	1.9	0.1	68.1	29.9	100
50–59	825	1.9	0.1	67.7	30.3	100
40–49	1,745	1.5	0.6	69.7	28.2	100
30–39	2,124	0.7	0.1	69.8	29.4	100
Under 30 years	1,048	0.3	0.5	67.8	31.5	100
All ages	5,907	1.1	0.3	69.4	29.2	100
Catholic						
60 years and over	306	11.3	78.6	0.0	10.1	100
50–59	1,532	5.2	80.1	0.0	14.7	100
40–49	2,365	6.4	76.1	0.0	17.5	100
30–39	3,256	6.1	67.4	1.1	25.4	100
Under 30 years	1,637	0.4	73.4	0.0	26.2	100
All ages	9,096	5.2	73.1	0.4	21.3	100
Protestant						
60 years and over	3,314	79.8	5.4	0.2	14.6	100
50–59	6,628	81.9	2.4	0.0	15.7	100
40–49	10,283	72.5	3.2	0.1	24.2	100
30–39	12,060	70.1	2.2	0.0	27.7	100
Under 30 years	5,519	57.8	6.0	1.0	35.2	100
All ages	37,804	72.0	3.3	0.2	24.5	100

fewer Jews than Christians report their present religion as that in which they were brought up.[34] More of Jewish background (26 percent) now consider their religion to be "none," than do those of Christian stock (20 percent). Jews are very much less likely to

TABLE 8
"How often, on average, do you attend a religious service?"
Faculty of Jewish, Catholic, and Protestant parentage, by age

		Percent					
	Number	*Once a week or more*	*2 or 3 times a month*	*About once a month*	*A few times a year*	*Once a year or less*	*Total*
Jewish							
60 years & over	165	8.2	6.5	6.5	26.5	52.3	100
50–59	825	4.3	5.9	6.6	28.5	54.6	100
40–49	1,745	7.5	7.4	8.3	26.9	49.9	100
30–39	2,124	3.4	3.7	6.0	25.1	61.7	100
Under 30 years	1,048	4.7	2.4	3.7	25.1	64.0	100
All ages	5,907	5.1	5.0	6.4	26.1	57.4	100
Catholic							
60 years & over	306	60.0	2.4	3.6	5.5	28.5	100
50–59	1,532	71.6	2.1	1.8	3.8	20.7	100
40–49	2,365	64.9	6.0	6.9	6.5	15.6	100
30–39	3,256	55.6	10.0	2.9	7.8	23.7	100
Under 30 years	1,637	61.2	4.9	1.2	8.2	24.5	100
All ages	9,096	61.6	6.6	3.5	6.9	21.4	100
Protestant							
60 years & over	3,314	39.4	14.1	10.0	14.6	21.9	100
50–59	6,628	32.3	17.9	11.0	13.4	25.5	100
40–49	10,283	34.7	16.7	4.8	15.9	27.9	100
30–39	12,060	29.4	14.5	8.1	14.4	33.6	100
Under 30 years	5,519	26.4	11.5	6.1	15.3	40.6	100
All ages	37,804	31.7	15.3	7.6	14.8	30.7	100

[34]See the annual studies of church attendance for different denominations, which have consistently shown Jews in the synagogue during the preceding week ranging around 20 percent, far less than Protestants (40) and these in turn far less than

attend religious services than Gentiles. Of course, Catholics, who have a religious obligation to go to church each week, attend much more frequently than Protestants (Table 8).

Given an assumption of growing secularization, it might be expected that younger Jews would be more irreligious than their elders. There is a clear tendency in this direction, but the proportion of younger Jewish academics who regard themselves as not having any religious identification, who do not attend services, or are hostile to religion, does not differ greatly from that of the

TABLE 9
Respondent's assessment of his religious orientation
Faculty of Jewish, Catholic, and Protestant parentage, by age

		Percent			
	Number	*Deeply religious*	*Moderately religious*	*Largely indifferent to religion*	*Basically opposed to religion*
Jewish					
60 years and over	165	5.7	31.2	52.8	10.3
50–59	825	4.8	29.6	51.0	14.6
40–49	1,745	5.0	31.3	47.8	15.8
30–39	2,124	5.0	24.9	51.4	18.6
Under 30 years	1,048	5.5	22.8	51.1	20.6
All ages	5,907	5.1	27.3	50.3	17.3
Catholic					
60 years and over	306	45.2	44.6	8.3	1.8
50–59	1,532	30.5	51.2	9.8	8.5
40–49	2,365	17.6	61.9	16.0	4.5
30–39	3,256	18.0	54.6	20.3	7.2
Under 30 years	1,637	21.8	47.6	21.8	8.8
All ages	9,096	21.2	54.5	17.5	6.8
Protestant					
60 years and over	3,314	25.4	57.2	16.6	0.9
50–59	6,628	17.1	59.6	19.2	4.1
40–49	10,283	15.3	55.1	24.2	5.4
30–39	12,060	12.8	49.6	31.1	6.6
Under 30 years	5,519	10.5	43.2	34.8	11.6
All ages	37,804	15.0	52.6	26.4	6.1

Catholic (60). The most recent comprehensive report is George Gallup, Jr. and John O. Davies, III, "Religion in America," *The Gallup Opinion Index*, Report No. 70, April 1971.

older (Tables 7, 8, and 9). This finding is especially surprising since other data in the survey, particularly on political opinions, indicate very large differences associated with age. Increased age is consistently accompanied by greater political conservatism on a variety of measures. Among Protestants and Catholics, the differences in religiousness among the age strata are generally much larger than among Jews. This is not, as Tables 7, 8, and 9 make clear, because young Gentiles are more irreligious than young Jews—they are in fact less so—but because a posture of irreligion came to Gentile academics in the United States much later.

Politics

Jewish academics belong to two groups which have been more liberal or leftist politically than other strata or ethnic-religious collectivities. Intellectuals and Jews generally have been more disposed to back liberal, Democratic, and left-wing third-party candidates than other segments of the population have been.[35] The propensity of Jews to be located on the left has been discussed in a number of writings; we will not detail them here.[36] Some link this orientation to aspects of Jewish religious teaching. Most, however, relate it to the historic pattern of discrimination which forced or disposed Jews to oppose conservative parties, so often aligned against the claim of Jews for equal rights. While discrimination was greater in much of Europe than in the United States at any time, American Jews did face barriers in employment, in admission to professions, and in access to leading private universities, as well as

[35]For a detailed survey of the extant empirical literature on the politics of college faculty, published before the Carnegie study, see Lipset, "The Politics of Academia," in David C. Nichols, ed., *Perspectives on Campus Tensions* (Washington, D.C.: American Council on Education, 1970), pp. 85–118. An earlier survey of the literature pertaining to the politics of American intellectuals generally may be found in Lipset, *Political Man* (Garden City: Doubleday-Anchor Books, 1963), pp. 332–371.

[36]These include the following works: L. H. Fuchs, *The Political Behavior of American Jews* (New York: The Free Press, 1956); Werner Cohn, "The Politics of American Jews," in M. Sklare, ed., *The Jews* (New York: The Free Press, 1958), pp. 614–626; Nathaniel Weyl, *The Jew in American Politics* (New Rochelle: Arlington House, 1968); Nathan Glazer, "The Jewish Role in Student Activism," *Fortune*, January 1969, pp. 112–113, 126–129; Louis Ruchames, "Jewish Radicalism in the United States," in Peter I. Rose, ed., *The Ghetto and Beyond* (New York: Random House, 1969), pp. 228–252; Charles S. Liebman, "Toward a Theory of Jewish Liberalism," in Donald R. Cutler, ed., *The Religious Situation: 1969* (Boston: Beacon Press, 1969), pp. 1034–1059; Glazer and Moynihan, *op. cit.*, pp. 166–171; Lipset, *Revolution and Counterrevolution* (Garden City: Doubleday-Anchor Books, 1970), pp. 376–400.

sanctions against their participation, even when well-to-do and highly educated, in the social activities of the predominantly Protestant affluent strata.

The propensity of intellectuals, including academics, to back the left has been related to a number of other factors, especially the emphasis on innovation and the rejection of tradition inherent in the very concept of the intellectual as a *creator* of knowledge, art, or literature. Some have argued that inherent in the obligation to create is the tendency to reject the status quo, to oppose the existing or the old as philistine. Intellectuals are also more likely than persons in other occupations to be partisans of the ideal, and thus to criticize reality from the standpoint of the ideal. The need to express the inner logic of their discipline or art form also presses intellectuals to oppose the established leadership that prefers continuity to change.

In his analysis of Jewish intellectual traits, Veblen linked the inherently critical orientation of the creative intellectual to the status of the secularized Jew as an "outsider" in Gentile societies. The Jew was disproportionately successful as an intellectual precisely because his social position made him a discontented skeptic, an orientation basic to intellectual achievement and, of course, to antiestablishment politics:

> The first requisite for constructive work in modern science, and indeed for any work of inquiry that shall bring enduring results, is a skeptical frame of mind. The enterprising skeptic alone can be counted on to further the increase of knowledge in any substantial fashion. This will be found true both in the modern sciences and in the field of scholarship at large. . . . For [the intellectually gifted Jews] as for other men in the like case, the skepticism that goes to make him an effectual factor in the increase and diffusion of knowledge among men involves a loss of that peace of mind that is the birthright of the safe and sane quietist. He becomes a disturber of the intellectual peace. . . .[37]

As Veblen noted, all intellectuals should possess this skepticism. While it and other factors linked to intellectual activity will press them to be critical politically, rejection of the status quo is, of course, compatible with a strongly conservative or right-wing position, as well as with a liberal or radical one. With rare

[37]Veblen, *op. cit.*, pp. 226–227.

exceptions, however, the situation experienced by Jews has located Jewish intellectual criticism on the left. This has meant that in countries with significant Jewish populations and important collections of right-wing intellectuals, such as Weimar Germany, the intellectual battle between rightist and leftist forces has often appeared as a fight between Gentile and Jewish intellectuals.[38]

The extent to which the political background of Jewish academics differs from that of others may be seen in the responses to the Carnegie survey question: "What were your father's politics while you were growing up?" Forty-six percent of the Jews, as contrasted to 19 percent of the Catholics and but 14 percent of the Protestant majority, reported fathers who were "left" or "liberal" in their views. Conversely, less than 20 percent of the Jewish professors had "conservative" fathers, while 63 percent of the Protestant academics indicated such a background. . . .

Family political-intellectual tradition affects the behavior of the children of academics. Among those faculty with children of college age, a majority (56 percent) of the Jews report that their children have "been active in civil rights, anti-Vietnam, or other demonstrations," as contrasted with little more than one-fifth (22 percent) of the Gentile professors. The reason, of course, is that the children of liberal academics participate much, much more in demonstrations than children of conservative academics, and Jewish faculty are disproportionately liberal. That the correlation is between parental politics and participation is made clear by Table 10, which shows that 68 percent of the *left* faculty having children of the right age—regardless of religion—said their children had been active in demonstrations, compared to just 4 percent of the *strongly conservative* professors.

The contribution of faculty of Jewish background to liberal and left political groups has been stressed in a number of surveys preceding our own. Almost all earlier studies found that close to 90 percent of Jewish academics regularly voted Democratic in presidential elections.[39] Jewish faculty also were found to contribute heavily to the backing of leftist third parties. Thus, according to a

[38]See George L. Mosse, *Germans and Jews* (New York: Howard Fertig, 1970); Peter Gay, *Weimar Culture* (New York: Harper and Row, 1968); Istvan Deak, *Weimar Germany's Left-Wing Intellectuals* (Berkeley: University of California Press, 1968); Harold L. Poor, *Kurt Tucholsky and the Ordeal of Germany, 1914–1935* (New York: Scribner's, 1968).

[39]Lipset, "The Politics of Academia," *op. cit.*, pp. 97–100.

TABLE 10

"Have any of your children been active in civil rights, anti-Vietnam, or other demonstrations?"

*Faculty with children of appropriate age, by ideological position**

		Percent		
	Number	*Yes*	*No*	*Total*
Left	3,062	68.0	32.0	100
Liberal	3,356	40.6	59.4	100
Middle-of-the-road	3,261	24.1	75.9	100
Moderately conservative	3,562	10.6	89.4	100
Strongly conservative	3,321	3.7	96.3	100

*Opinions on five questions were combined to construct a general liberalism-conservatism scale for national issues. Four of these were equally weighted: position on the Vietnam war, the legalization of marijuana, the causes of Negro riots, and on busing as a means for school integration. One question was double weighted, the faculty member's self-characterization of his political views. The five categories in the table above are positions defined by scores on this liberalism-conservatism scale.

1948 study, fully 30 percent of the Jewish professors voted for Henry Wallace[40]. . . . Recent studies of American college professors conclude that Jews have been much more heavily opposed to the Vietnam war, and stronger supporters of student activism, than their Gentile colleagues.[41]

The Carnegie Commission's national survey yielded the same strong relationships. The Jewish faculty were much more inclined to identify their politics as "left" or "liberal" than Protestants and Catholics (Table 11).[42] Jews contributed disproportionately to the small group who backed left-wing third-party presidential candidates in 1968; they were much more likely to have been for the

[40]Lawrence C. Howard, "The Academic and the Ballot," *School and Society*, 22 November 1958, p. 418.

[41]David Armor, *et al.*, "Professors' Attitudes Toward the Vietnam War," *Public Opinion Quarterly*, Summer 1967, p. 170.

[42]The 1969 American Council on Education study of college freshmen reported a comparable pattern: 55 percent of the Jewish freshmen described their politics as "left" or "liberal," compared to 38 percent of those of other religions. Only 14 percent of the Jews, but 33 percent of the others, considered themselves conservatives. Drew, *op. cit.*, p. 41.

TABLE 11
"How would you characterize yourself politically at the present time?"

		Percent				
	Number	*Left*	*Liberal*	*Middle-of-the-road*	*Moderately conservative*	*Strongly conservative*
Jewish faculty	5,907	12.4	62.1	18.2	6.6	.7
Catholic faculty	9,096	4.4	40.3	30.0	23.2	2.1
Protestant faculty	37,804	3.8	36.9	28.0	28.4	3.0
All faculty	60,028	4.9	40.2	27.2	25.0	2.6

*The categories in this table are based on the replies to one question. Those in the preceding one are, as explained in the note, a product of position on an attitude scale.

nomination of Eugene McCarthy than of Hubert Humphrey at the Democratic convention, and gave Richard Nixon an exceptionally low vote in the election. In 1964 only 2 percent of the Jewish faculty voted for Barry Goldwater, compared to 24 percent of those of Protestant parentage. . . .

The Jews, as a group, took much more liberal positions on such issues as the use of force at the Chicago Democratic convention in 1968, the Vietnam war, student activism, the treatment of blacks in both the university and the larger society, and the legalization of marijuana. . . . The gap between Jews and Christians on these issues is very large, while among Christians, Protestants are usually slightly more conservative than Catholics. For example, 59 percent of the Jews gave general approval to "the emergence of radical student activism in recent years," compared to 44 percent of the Catholics and 40 percent of the Protestants. The proportion of Jews favoring immediate United States withdrawal from Vietnam was twice that of non-Jews. Three-fifths of the Jews favored the legalization of marijuana (59 percent), compared to 33 percent of the Catholics and 29 percent of the Protestants.

Although Jews were invariably more liberal and change-oriented than Gentiles in their reponses to all politically relevant queries in the Carnegie questionnaire, it is striking that the gap between Jewish and non-Jewish faculty is smallest for items pertaining to changes in academic standards. Jews are only somewhat more willing than others to waive academic standards in appointing members of minority groups to the faculty, or in admitting them to the student body (Tables 12 and 13). . . . The same pattern of response occurs with respect to questions dealing with "student power." Though relatively sympathetic to campus activism, the Jewish scholars are not much more disposed to give students a major voice in important decisions within the university than are their Gentile colleagues. . . .

This weakening of Jewish "liberalism" when academic standards are involved is reflective of a general phenomenon: successful, creative, and research-oriented faculty are more liberal or left on general political questions, but they are also heavily committed to the university and scholarship. This latter involvement reduces, though it does not eliminate, the impact of their general political ideology on matters internal to academe.

The faculty differ considerably in their political views not only by religion, but also by discipline and by scholarly quality. Academics in the "pure" or "basic" liberal arts fields are

TABLE 12
"The normal academic requirements should be relaxed in appointing members of minority groups to faculty here."

		Percent				
	Number	*Strongly agree*	*Agree with reservations*	*Disagree with reservations*	*Strongly disagree*	*Total*
Jewish faculty	5,907	6.4	24.7	28.8	40.2	100
Catholic faculty	9,096	4.3	17.4	27.8	50.5	100
Protestant faculty	37,804	3.7	16.6	27.8	51.9	100
All faculty	60,028	4.2	17.6	27.9	50.3	100

TABLE 13

"More minority group undergraduates should be admitted here even if it means relaxing normal academic standards of admission."

		Percent				
	Number	*Strongly agree*	*Agree with reservations*	*Disagree with reservations*	*Strongly disagree*	*Total*
Jewish faculty	5,907	19.2	34.0	24.4	22.4	100
Catholic faculty	9,096	12.7	27.2	28.7	31.3	100
Protestant faculty	37,804	11.2	26.5	28.7	33.6	100
All faculty	60,028	12.4	27.3	28.3	32.0	100

considerably to the left of those in the more applied professional schools. Within the liberal arts, social scientists are the most liberal, the natural scientists the most conservative, with the humanists falling in the middle. And, as noted earlier, those who are heavily involved in research activity, who are more successful, and who are at the more prestigious institutions are more liberal than other academics. An examination of the differences in political veiws among the different religious groups in these varying academic contexts reveals that each factor—religion, discipline, and academic prestige—continues to have an impact. That is, Jews and Christians in the social sciences or in high quality schools are more liberal than their fellow-religionists in other fields and lower-tier colleges. The difference is smaller among Jews than among Gentiles when the additional factor of discipline or school quality is introduced. Catholics and Protestants in the applied fields are *much more* conservative than their coreligionists in the liberal arts. Jews are only *somewhat more* conservative. Similarly, Jews at the better schools are slightly more liberal than those at less distinguished and research-oriented institutions. But the differences between Christian professors in schools of varying caliber is quite considerable. Seemingly, the elements of a Jewish environment which dispose its products to leftist views are much stronger than the factors within academe which affect political beliefs. . . . In this respect, the behavior of Jews within academe resembles their behavior outside. For all studies of Jewish political opinion agree that the social-class factors which strongly divide non-Jews on political lines in the larger community have little effect on the view or party choices of Jews.

Religious and Irreligious Jews Differences in Politics and Scholarship

We assumed that a faculty member's commitment to religious practice or his irreligion is 1) part of a much larger mind set which also includes his political perceptions, and 2) related to the niche he has found in academe. Political and religious conservatism are strongly associated.[43] And it seemed likely that professors who move in the highly secularized academic world of the major universities and who have committed themselves to the questioning and critical pursuit of scholarship would be much less likely than their less scholarly colleagues at lower-tier "teaching" colleges to find congenial the intellectual life of traditional religious pursuits.

The Carnegie data strongly support the first of these assumptions. The correlations between religiousness and political opinions are consistently among the highest encountered in the survey for the various biographic and personal characteristics of faculty, on the one hand, and their politics, on the other. The pattern for the Jewish faculty here is essentially the same as for Protestants and Catholics; those more deeply committed to, and involved in, religious practice are politically much more conservative. For example, only 4 percent of those who attend synagogue a few times a month or more often identify their politics as "left," compared to 24 percent of the birthright Jews who describe their present religion as "none". . . . Half of the latter would withdraw immediately from Vietnam, a position taken by only 22 percent of those who attend religious services regularly. . . . Over half (52

[43]It is true, as Lenski has pointed out, that one cannot find in the general public a liberal-conservative dimension that encompasses both political and religious commitments, but that is, in significant measure, testimony to the fact that most people do not impose any ideological dimension on social and political events. College professors are a very special group whose "business" is ideas and whose social and political views are highly organized or ideological in the sense Converse uses the latter term. See Gerhard Lenski, *The Religious Factor* (Garden City, N.Y.: Doubleday-Anchor Books, 1963), pp. 208–211; and Philip E. Converse, "The Nature of Belief Systems in Mass Publics," in David Apter, ed., *Ideology and Discontent* (New York: The Free Press, 1964), pp. 206–261.

percent) who often go to synagogue strongly agree that disruptive students should be expelled from college; only 26 percent of the "none" category take that position. . . . Just 40 percent of the most religious, but 68 percent of irreligious Jews, give general approval to "radical student activism". . . . And fifty-eight percent of the Jewish faculty who consider themselves "deeply religious" preferred Humphrey to McCarthy for the Democratic presidential nomination in 1968, while only 21 percent of the "basically opposed to religion" favored Humphrey.

If the interrelation of religiousness and political opinion is close, as had been expected, the association of religous commitment and scholarly achievement has proved to be weaker than we had anticipated. We had looked for a powerful link going both ways, that is, as both cause and effect. It seemed likely that faculty members of a skeptical and questioning bent would be the most successful—for a restless and probing intellect is essential to any significant scholarly work—and that such academics would by this very same quality question all manner of regular religious beliefs and practices. Conversely, an intellectual approach that would leave an academic comfortable with organized religion should militate against his chances for scholarly achievement. At the same time, the major research universities are the most secular and irreligious; so that whatever his previous orientation to religion, the faculty member experiencing such an environment should be influenced by it in the direction of irreligion.

While the relationships which we discovered are uniformly in the direction posited by the above, they appear to us surprisingly weak. About 18 percent of the Jewish faculty who attend synagogue two or three times a month or more often are among the more productive (5 or more publications in the last two years), compared to 23 percent of the irreligious Jews (attendance of religious services a few times a year or less). . . . About 8 percent of the most productive Jewish professors (more than 10 publications) attend services regularly, as do 10 percent of those not publishing at all. Among the Jewish faculty, 7 percent at elite colleges and 12 percent at the lower-tier schools frequently go to synagogue, while 88 percent at the former and 81 percent at the latter attend only a few times a year, or not at all. . . . A higher percentage of the irreligious than of the religious Jews is teaching at the better schools, but again the difference is modest. . . . the relationship between religiousness and academic achievement is somewhat stronger for Christian faculty. This is as expected, because support for intellectual activity has been stronger in Judaism than in the Christian denominations generally. Still, the most striking aspect of our findings is the relative weakness of the association between religious orientation and scholarship, for Christians and Jews alike. The strength of the relationship is not altered by recourse to other measures of religiousness.

Conclusion

We have seen that the most irreligious Jewish academics are much more liberal-left politically and somewhat more successful academically than their fellow Jews who are very religious. It is fitting, perhaps, that we end this report on the characteristics of the Jewish professoriate in the United States with this seeming paradox: while Jews differ significantly from Gentiles, particularly with respect to their academic achievements and political orientations, the least Jewish Jews differ the most.

Thorstein Veblen pointed to this phenomenon a half century ago. He suggested that more important than the ancient intellectual heritage of the Jews, in regard to their modern capacity for scholarly achievement, was the impact of their "hyphenate" status, of having left the traditional Jewish world, but not becoming fully part of Gentile society. Thus Veblen assumed, "only when the gifted Jew escapes from the [Jewish] cultural environment . . . [does] he come into his own as a creative leader in the world's intellectual enterprise. It is by loss of allegiance, or at the best by force of a divided allegiance to the people of his origin, that he finds himself in the vanguard of modern inquiry."[44]

In the United States today, of course, almost all Jews, even the most Orthodox and practicing among them, have become hyphenate in Veblen's sense; and it is likely that the group's capacity for intellectual achievement has been thereby enhanced. It may be worthwhile to note that earlier outbursts of Jewish scientific creativity—that of the Marranos (the overtly converted Iberian Jews who remained secretly Jewish) during the sixteenth century, of the Jews of Central Europe in the century preceding Hitler, and of the Soviet Jews before World War II—all have in common a breakdown in the controls exercised by the Jewish community and, with this, a fostering of hyphenate status among assimilating Jews. The relationship between marginality and achievement has been well described by Charles Singer:

[44]Veblen, *op. cit.*, pp. 225–226.

> The Marranos, like their later counterparts, carried some residue of the old Jewish culture and, like them, they had not completely absorbed the culture of their environment. The double maladjustment, not so great as to constitute a spiritual conflict of the gravest kind, was yet enough to give an independence of approach, a philosophic detachment to the entrant into the newly accessible scientific field. This was certainly an advantage. An impartial outlook is a significant part of the equipment of the man of science. . . . [In the nineteenth century] there arose in the German-speaking countries a movement closely resembling Marranism. Among nineteenth-century Jews . . . only a small proportion were "believers" in any profound sense. . . . Naturally, they carried with them some elements of their traditional habits of thought. . . . Jewish emancipation coincided with an era of enormous scientific advance, the result of extreme fragmentation in the scientific field resulting from the natural product of increasingly complex techniques. . . . The frustrated and culture-starved German Marranos eagerly occupied this new field. They gave to it a certain spiritual significance that they drew from their half-forgotten religious heritage. . . . But when all is said there remains an essential something that is a real source of wonder. A people scattered, disunited, numerically less than one of the smallest nations of Europe, has for a century provided from an effective German-speaking population of some two millions an ever-increasing proportion of the best scientific exponents in central Europe.[45]

Many of the same factors have affected the propensity of Jews to contribute to the intellectual and scholarly life of nations as disparate as the United States, the Soviet Union, Britain, and Argentina for the past half century. Seemingly, these same factors have also put them in the forefront of political criticism, of those rejecting the status quo. Whether the latter propensity will continue to place them heavily on the left, however, would seem to be somewhat questionable. The Left now holds power in many countries, and has become a repressor of both free intellectual inquiry and Judaism. And even in the non-Communist world, left-wing extremists are increasingly anti-intellectual and emotive. Hence, the opposition to Israel apart, there is reason to anticipate a decline in the commitment of intellectual Jews to the new brands of ritualistic leftism.

[45]Charles Singer, "Science and Judaism," in Louis Finkelstein, ed., *The Jews,* Vol. II (New York: Harper and Brothers, 1960), pp. 1412–1414.

JEWISH LIFE AND THOUGHT IN AN ACADEMIC COMMUNITY

by HENRY COHEN

INTRODUCTION

HENRY COHEN'S article is essentially a community study of a city where the impact of a university is strong. Focusing on the problem of Jewish identity, his material provides a case study of some of the perspectives which emerge from the Lipset and Ladd essay.

At the time of Cohen's study there were roughly 250 Jewish households in the Champaign-Urbana community. The population was almost equally divided between "town" families and "gown" families. Most of the males in the town families were businessmen or professionals, while men in the gown families were members of the faculty of the University of Illinois. As the rabbi of the single temple in the city, Cohen was naturally concerned with the problem of Jewish identity in Champaign-Urbana. Soon after his arrival in the community it became apparent to him that the problem of the maintenance of Jewish identity in gown families was different from that in town families. However superficial the Jewishness of town families, they were much more closely tied to the Jewish community than were gown families.

In order to clarify the problem Cohen proceeded to study the community intensively. He administered questionnaires and interviewed strategically placed individuals. He discovered that the pressures which operated to keep town Jews attached to the Jewish community were not present in the case of gown Jews. The gown Jews had an option which town Jews did not have—what Cohen terms "Academic Commitment": both an alternative ideology and an alternative community. Cohen suggests that ". . . the university itself has become, in a certain sense, the religion of the faculty."

Cohen found that there was a small group of faculty who retained ties to the Jewish community. Despite his obvious interest in magnifying religious values Cohen stresses that the small group of academicians who displayed a strong religious tie also had a strong ethnic tie. He infers that the former derived from the latter.

Although Cohen gathered his data over a decade ago—that is, before the full impact of the Jew on the academy had been felt and before the academy had its full impact upon the Jew—his analysis of the contrast between the Jewishness of University of Illinois faculty and of Champaign-Urbana business and professional men, and of their families, is still valid. It can be supplemented by pointing to the recent emergence of a small group of academicians whose Jewish identity exceeds that of the committed academicians whom Cohen discovered at the University of Illinois. This is partly a function of the fact that since academia is attracting larger numbers of Jews it now draws upon a wider cross-section of the American Jewish community. Thus it is not unusual for present-day faculties to include individuals who possess an intensive religious commitment. In some instances such individuals are Orthodox Jews. Furthermore, there are now also faculty members with a very high level of ethnic involvement, particularly with Israel. In both instances these academicians resist full integration into the ideological consensus of the academy as well as into its communitarian aspects. Furthermore, in recent years latent ethnic loyalties of less committed faculty members have surfaced more frequently than before. Israel's struggle for survival and the perilous condition of Soviet Jewry have evoked a response among a segment of the academic community that had not been involved in the Jewish community either on the religious or on the ethnic level.

M. S.

THE PURPOSE of this study is to examine Jewish life and thought among the faculty members of a particular university community and to delineate those characteristics that are distinctive when compared with the life and thought of the local "town" Jews. After observing the more striking contrasts between "town and gown," we shall view the academic community more closely, attempt to discover the marked differences *within* that world, and speculate as to why they obtain. The bisected community which we shall be discussing is not large—approximately 250 families, almost equally divided between town and gown and circling the campus of the University of Illinois in Champaign-Urbana. . . .

Any study of "town and gown" should carefully consider the particular town that is the basis for comparison. In the twin cities of Champaign-Urbana live approximately 77,000 people; about 1 percent of them are Jews. The community's chief "industry" is the university, and the academic families, coming from all over the United States and indeed from all over the world, contrast dramatically with the native midwestern businessman. The Jewish "town" of 122 families is exceedingly well integrated into the larger community. There is, for instance, no discrimination in the country club, which includes many Jewish members. There are no Jewish neighborhoods, and—while parents socialize largely with Jewish friends—their children do not form a "Jewish crowd" and do socialize quite freely within their schools and neighborhoods. While there is no significant anti-Semitism, a few bigots are "known," and there is considerable sensitivity to Gentile opinion. Half of the Jewish husbands are independent businessmen, and over half of them deal in clothing, food, or liquor. Thirty-two percent are professional men, of whom two-thirds are in the medical field. There are townspeople in real estate, scrap iron, manufacturing, and wholesaling; and there are a few salesmen and skilled workers. . . .

Most characteristic of the town are the deep divisions that make for proud denominationalism in larger cities, but that dramatically inhibit Jewish life in a smaller community. There are the "old families" of German background. In 1904, 22 of these families founded a Reform congregation. Their children are still quite active in Sinai Temple and look back on "the old days" when the temple was closely connected with the Hillel Foundation, which—as a national movement—began at the University of Illinois and which shared its rabbi with the community. In 1950, the temple elected its own rabbi, and the Hillel director served the needs of more than 2,000 students.

There are the "old families" of East European background who look back to 1912, when their community began to take shape, and to a *shul* that is no longer active. Some are now members of Sinai Temple, especially if they have young children. Almost all are quite active in B'nai B'rith and Hadassah.

Finally, there are the families who have moved to Champaign-Urbana during the past twenty years from urban Jewish areas. They represent a cross-section of Jewish life and are most notable for having a high proportion of professional (especially medical) men. Most of these couples are quite happy to live in this small Jewish community that is highly integrated into the larger community and that has little of the intense Jewish cultural life of metropolitan areas. Some do reminisce about the old *shul* or Jewish center in Chicago, and a few enterprising and understanding students satisfy this nostalgic hunger by importing delicatessen products and selling them to the exiles.

To speak of the Jewish faculty families as a "community" is misleading, as Jewishness is—for many—an insignificant aspect of their lives. Nevertheless, it *is* a common, if not a uniting, factor, and we are concerned with how the "Jewish professor" reacts to his ethnic and religious background. We shall rather arbitrarily consider as "Jewish" all faculty members who were raised by parents who considered themselves Jewish *or* who converted to Judaism *and* who have not converted to another faith. There is no "religious" listing of the academic staff, and so the precise number of Jewish families is a matter of some conjecture. The United Jewish Appeal "list" includes all those known to the identifying members of the community and totals 117. Estimates run as high as 150, but for the purposes of this study we shall consider the "known" community. Those who have not been detected by the UJA perhaps deserve to be considered "assimilated."

There are no reliable figures on the growth of this community. According to one of the older families, in 1912 there were 4 Jewish members of the faculty. The majority seems to have come to the university during the past ten years, and at the present time approximately 6 percent of the total faculty is Jewish. Of these, 33 percent are in the social sciences; 30 percent in mathematics and the physical or biological sciences; 16 percent in engineering and related "applied" sciences; 15 percent in the humanities; and 6 percent in miscellaneous fields—including a football coach and a fencing master. The largest concentration is found in the department of mathematics: sixteen in all. Other areas with prominent Jewish representation are psychology, sociology, and physics.

This is a young community, and the father's average age is close to forty. Approximately two-thirds of the academic community are first generation—that is, born in America of at least one foreign-born parent. About one-sixth are foreign-born, and the remaining sixth, from second-, third-, and fourth-generation homes. Thirty-seven percent were reared in homes which they considered Orthodox; 31 percent Conservative; 12 percent Reform; 20 percent culturally Jewish but nonreligious. Forming the larger proportion, then, are the children of the later Eastern European immigrants, children who were raised in the stormy days of the Depression and New Deal. . . .

Having sketched the two communities in broad outline, we turn now to our central area of concern: How do town and gown differ regarding their Jewish life and thought? The most obvious difference is that of institutional affiliation. The percentages of families affiliated with either the temple or the local B'nai B'rith are: 96 percent of the town and 34 percent of the gown.[1] The effect of children on affiliation is clearly seen when we observe that approximately 55 percent of the faculty parents who have children of Sunday school age are members of the congregation, membership being a prerequisite for sending the children to the school. Virtually all town children attend the school.

The impulsive explanation for the smaller proportion of faculty

[1]Eighty-four percent of the town are affiliated with the temple. The additional 12 percent are generally more traditional families who have no children of Sunday school age and for whom B'nai B'rith membership is the preferred form of Jewish affiliation. Thirty-two percent of the gown are temple-affiliated. An additional 2 percent are members of B'nai B'rith.

"affiliated" is that the academic community is "not religious." If by "religious" are meant traditional observance and worship, then the townspeople are hardly more distinguished by a personal need for faith. To cite but one statistic, while only 15 percent of the faculty members attend worship services on at least six Sabbaths during the year, the proportion of temple-going townspeople is but 25 percent—not so dramatic a contrast as to account for the very much higher percentage of town affiliation. There must be more significant factors.

In the town, church or synagogue affiliation is an almost universal custom among business and professional people. A "good citizen" supports his church—this is almost a *sine qua non* for civic respectability. Furthermore, the Jewish citizens, with an eye on non-Jewish opinion, have the additional incentive of wanting their community to be well-respected by the larger society. One Friday evening, shortly after the stores began Friday night opening, some twenty-two Methodists visited the synagogue service unannounced and outnumbered the Jews in attendance. The congregation was informed of this exposure of Jewish religiosity. On the next Sabbath there was a near-capacity congregation—but no Methodists. In the town, religious affiliation is "the thing to do," and the Jewish community is not going to be the exception.

In striking contrast, there is no comparable custom within the academic community. In fact, middle-class organizational life in general and religious institutions in particular are considered rather low-brow by large numbers of the faculty. A typical comment was that of a professor who admitted that Judaism has stood for important values, namely, love of learning and concern for human rights; however, he continued, these values *he* could find more easily in the academic world than in the local Jewish community. The implication of this and of numerous other attitudes indicates that the university itself has become, in a certain sense, the religion of the faculty.

How many aspects of religious faith and fellowship we find in the Academic Commitment! There is the dominant philosophy of naturalism. Its method is scientific; its faith, that all being can be explained in terms of a single order of efficient causation in which a supernatural Deity has no place; its morality, the ideals of humanism rooted in finite human experience; its messianic hope, that man—through understanding the consequences of his actions—can build a better world. There are, of course, denominations. The "high church" of Art and Humanities expresses in the aesthetic mode man's striving for fulfillment. There are the monks who seem remote from human life, but who commune with Nature in search of deeper Knowledge. Certainly there are those who consider the Social Gospel to be the justification of all learning and who work for the improvement of human relations in the larger community. There is even the skeptic who analyzes the world, but can find no naturalistic reason to care about humanity. Finally, as in many religions, there is a fellowship that is so exclusive as to be in conflict with the universal ideals of the faith. Thus, the Academic Commitment generally espouses democracy and the maximum interaction between groups, while the faculty families voluntarily segregate themselves into a kind of intellectual country club with its departmental clans. Frequently condescending toward the provincialism of the Midwesterner, the academic club is virtually closed to even the more intelligent members of the larger community.[2]

With such a faith and fellowship, can we be surprised that conventional religious affiliation does not have a powerful appeal? There *are* those who are not entirely satisfied with the academic creed, who want "something more." Still, the primary force behind the affiliation of most academic families is: "So the children should know something." Following a common urban pattern, once the children are of Sunday school age (rarely before), the parents "join." They want their children to understand the history, the literature, and (in some cases this is a concession) the religion of their cultural heritage. Some feel quite strongly about the survival of Jewish life; others simply wish the child to feel secure as part of the group with which he will be identified by society.

A condition that does *not* exist in the town is the real possibility of raising a child without any formal religious education. The case is otherwise in the gown. Almost half of the academic families are able to dispense with religious education for their children, because church affiliation is far from universal among the faculty. Especially if the family lives in a university neighborhood, friends can come over on Sunday morning to play spaceman instead of trundling off to church school. When, however, there was a room-shortage in the temple and the suggestion was made to suspend the kindergarten

[2]This degree of closeness—it has been suggested—is particularly pronounced in academic communities which are cut off from large centers of culture.

temporarily, it was [a] *town* mother who objected: "But the neighbor's child goes to church!"

So the absence of a compulsory social custom and the presence of a community that seems to provide a way of life—these factors, together with the more commonly cited condescension toward religion, are decisive in explaining the difference between town and gown in the quantity and quality of affiliation. Nevertheless, affiliation itself barely indicates the attitudes toward faith and people. In comparing first the religious attitudes, we will not insist on one definition of "religious." Rather shall we examine separately certain aspects of life and thought that have historically been considered elements of the Jewish faith: a belief in God, an ethical way of life, the use of traditional symbols for worship and home observance, and the study of Torah.

The most significant difference may well be the contrast between the naturalistic orientation of the faculty and the supernaturalism of the town. The belief that

> . . . there is a God who is all-powerful, all-wise, and all-righteous . . . [who] guides and controls our destinies . . . who somehow "hears" the prayers of man . . .

was held with or without qualifications by 74 percent of the townspeople polled.[3] Of the faculty, however, only about 8 percent of the men and 15 percent of the women expressed agreement with this traditional theistic view. Included in this handful are those who, while not comfortable with a faith in a righteous, all-powerful Being, do believe in a God not reducible to aspects of nature or man's aspirations. Some may hold to a pantheistic mysticism somewhat parallel to the Emersonian tradition in the Unitarian Church. There is also a trace of interest in the ideas of Milton Steinberg and Martin Buber. Nevertheless, the existence of a God who is considered a Being with awareness is not taken seriously by over 90 percent of the academic community.

This is not to say that our professor is without a kind of faith. Eighty percent of the responding faculty members expressed agreement with the statement:

> If a man learns to care for the well-being of the oppressed and the stranger and to strive for a world of righteousness, he will find more

[3]Seventy-two percent of the men; seventy-six percent of the women.

> satisfaction in life than will a person whose concern is limited to himself and his immediate friends and family.

This proposition is the basis of Mordecai M. Kaplan's value theory: "When we defeat love by yielding to an impulse which we share with the sub-human, we cannot be happy."[4] Awareness of God is, for Kaplan, the "feeling that man's ethical aspirations are part of a cosmic urge, by obeying which man makes himself at home in the universe."[5] Our professor generally would agree that the universe is so constituted that man will feel "at home" when he follows the basic values of his Jewish heritage. He feels, however, no need to label this quality of reality "God" or to speak of Godhood as whatever helps man toward this "salvation" or to use such vitalistic phrases as "cosmic urge." It frequently appears that our professor accepts the essence of Kaplan's theology but refuses to speak his language.

Finally—and typically—the academic Jew does not care to participate in worship services for the purpose of assuring himself that his ideals will help him feel at home in the universe or experiencing fellowship with other Jews or affirming the worthwhileness of life. That is, he finds great difficulty in "reconstructing" the meaning of worship so that he may pray to a Power, Process, or Quality which is without awareness of man. There are exceptions: 10 percent of the faculty members are *non*-supernaturalists who *do* attend services with some regularity. . . .

While there is a marked contrast in theological belief between town and gown, the contrast in synagogue attendance is surprisingly mild. While three-fourths of the town expresses a belief in a supernatural Deity, only one-fourth attends services with any regularity—as compared with 15 percent of the gown. Among the townspeople, furthermore, there is no correlation between the "attenders" and the "believers." Perhaps the belief is superficial—what one is supposed to believe about God. More likely, there is here a latent faith in God that becomes activated in extreme situations when one's personal powers cannot meet an overwhelming crisis.

An interesting sidelight is the discovery that while the faculty

[4]Mordecai M. Kaplan, *Basic Values in Jewish Religion* (New York: Reconstructionist Press, 1957), p. 89.

[5]Kaplan, *The Meaning of God in Modern Jewish Religion* (New York: Behrman House, 1937), pp. 244–45.

wives are almost as naturalistically inclined as their husbands and attend services with the same infrequency, when they *do* attend, they seem to have a more meaningful experience. They are particularly more prone to be introspective, to attempt self-understanding and to find a feeling of serenity in the service.[6] No such discrepancy between the experience of the town husbands and wives was evident.

Turning briefly to our approximation of religious observance in the home, we can observe an interesting phenomenon among the faculty families: While 6 percent do not eat pork, 17 percent light Sabbath candles, 30 percent hold a Passover *seder* regularly—and 50 percent light Chanukah candles. The most marginal of families visit the sisterhood gift shop and the children's library before Chanukah. The Christ in Christmas makes it most difficult for Jews to leave Judaism altogether.

The ethical aspect of religion does not lend itself to statistical comparisons. Both town and gown are "for brotherhood." Their contrasting views regarding specific social issues reflect the general difference between academic values and middle-class standards. It might be more fruitful to ask to what degree, if any, our two Jewish communities differ in their social concerns from the larger communities of which they are a part.

The popular image of the academic world is that of a nest of long-haired radicals. Actually, there is wide variety of social viewpoints—varying from predominantly Republican faculty neighborhoods to a department known for extreme conservatism to the social scientists who generally take "liberal stands" on national and community issues. The Jewish faculty members are active, out of proportion to their numbers, in the local organizations concerned with assuring equal opportunities for members of minority groups. While Jews represent about 6 percent of the faculty, they provided 18 percent of the signatures on a controversial petition in behalf of academic freedom. . . .

The townspeople are part of a Midwestern middle-class community. Such a large proportion of the Jewish families are, however, from urban immigrant backgrounds that there is no

[6]Various kinds of worship experience were tallied, and—based on the same scale—the wives scored 76 to the husbands' 42. For example, 33 percent of the wives stated, that during services, they frequently "try by self-understanding to resolve [personal] problems." Only 4 percent of the husbands admitted to self-examination during worship.

clearly dominant view on any social issue. A significant proportion of Jewish families do participate in the League of Women Voters, braille programs, and other civic endeavors; but—and this is pure impression—the Jewish community does not appear to be any more active in these areas than are the liberal Protestant fellowships. As would be expected, the town merchant does not share the professor's enthusiasm for such measures as a state Fair Employment Practices Commission.

Turning finally to the study of Judaism, we find that in neither community is there anything approaching the traditional concern with Torah as a guide for living. Among the faculty members there is some concern with the problems of being Jewish today. A group of professors meets triweekly to discuss such themes as the constants of Judaism, and there is interest when the temple's adult education program deals with the theologies of Kaplan, Steinberg, or Buber.[7] The mood, however, varies from mild curiosity to a search for meaning that never seems to be answered . . . again, the desire "for something."

Within the town, there is no such searching. The townspeople, by and large, have few conscious doubts about their Jewishness and Judaism. Their views are more settled, and they are less inclined to question them. A small Men's Club holds a monthly Bible class, and the preferred sermon topic is Jewish history and literature. What is sought from these studies is more knowledge about the Jewish heritage and, perhaps, some general principles for living. Excursions into such questions as how the values of Torah can be applied to social and economic realities are often considered "not Jewish" and an unnecessary duplication of news commentary. . . .

When Jewish life is considered in its nonreligious aspect, the faculty community appears considerably more involved than has been indicated thus far. For example, about 60 percent of the faculty have contributed to the UJA at least twice in the last three years, and this is easily as high a proportion as the town can claim. Approximately 20 percent of the Jewish faculty members have stated that at least 75 percent of their close friends are Jewish. Even among those who make no contribution to any Jewish institution or philanthropy (one of the better signs of marginality in our gown community), approximately half of the respondents observed that *half of their close friends are Jews.* Almost everyone enjoys "Jewish"

[7]About 20 percent of the faculty show at least some interest in these discussions.

food and jokes, and the best-known Jewish author is Sholom Aleichem. All this is a reflection of the largely first-generation urban background. Consequently, a much more significant proportion of the faculty could be considered "ethnically," as opposed to religiously, oriented.

Most characteristic of the nature of this ethnic identification is its *wide variation*—from the ardent Reconstructionist to the avowed assimilationist. While among the townspeople there is a rather *even* degree of ethnic involvement, within the university community there is dramatic contrast between the strongly identified who are trying to preserve Jewish culture in a midwestern cornfield and the cosmopolites who feel that there are enough barriers between people in this world without the clannishness of Jews. Between the two extremes we find the larger proportion of the faculty, culturally affirming their Jewishness by discussing Jewish problems, giving to the UJA, and sending their children to Sunday school.

Should one wish to compare the general ethnic involvement of town and gown, the two extremes within the academic community would cancel each other, and the town would be found to be more deeply conscious of its connection with the Jewish people. At least 60 percent of the townspeople would say that three-fourths of their close friends are Jewish—compared with 20 percent of the gown. Mixed marriages represent 6.5 percent of the town community and approximately 20 percent of the gown.[8] The 4 Jewish-born couples who joined the Unitarian Church are all academic families. A special kind of involvement with the Jewish people, though most notable among Jews who do not consider themselves ethnically involved, is the tendency to be "very much concerned" when Jews behave publicly in an unethical manner. Sixty-eight percent of the responding town men, as compared with 30 percent of the gown men, expressed such concern.[9] Among the most concerned in the town are a few families who are members of the American Council for Judaism.

Why does the academic community present the unusual configuration of ardent ethnic feeling, a mild affirmation of Jewishness, and an outright assimilationist view—all expressed by

[8]In both communities, in about one out of three instances, the children are being raised as Jews.

[9]An interesting "sex difference": neither town nor gown wives were nearly so concerned with non-Jewish opinion as were their husbands. The figures for the ladies: Town—32 percent (cf. 68 percent); Gown—10 percent (cf. 30 percent).

families from largely first-generation urban backgrounds? . . . let us suggest that once the memories of Jewish culture become vague, the *town* Jew can still find reasons to remain within the fold: He retains a latent supernatural faith, and the larger community expects him to be Jewish. By contrast, once the *gown* Jew no longer finds meaning in the ethnic fellowship or the folkways, he has neither traditional belief nor strong social pressure to encourage his identity. While some still feel closely attached to Jewish cultural life, most express a mild nostalgia, and a sizable portion drift away altogether. . . .

We turn now to an area of crucial importance for all those concerned with the Jewish faith and its future. What meaning do the more religiously oriented professors find in their Judaism? We shall be concerned with the small number—15 percent—who attend worship services at least six Sabbaths during the year, for this attendance indicates at least a willingness to use religious symbols to express certain aspirations. Of these, two-thirds would consider themselves naturalists who could never believe in a supernatural Deity. What do they find in religious traditon that eludes their equally naturalistic colleagues?

The most dramatic fact is that seven-eighths of the religiously oriented have a strong ethnic identification. These are the families who come from Conservative or Orthodox homes, in which Jewish culture was warmly present—families who have deep attachments not only to religious traditions, but also to that cluster of nostalgia called *yiddishkeit.* With two individual exceptions, the religiously oriented have extremely close ties to the Jewish people as people. In most cases, then, a deep feeling for Jewish culture in all its forms seems a precondition for a willingness to worship within the tradition. One is led to conclude that the ethnic tie is primary. . . .

There are no sons of Reform homes among the religiously oriented, for the Reform home in the thirties did not provide the ethnic tie that seems to be needed to hold the Jew who has lost his theistic belief. If the religious service is primarily a way of expressing an identity with the Jewish community, why should he bother. . .

INTERMARRIAGE IN THE UNITED STATES

by ARNOLD SCHWARTZ

INTRODUCTION

ARNOLD SCHWARTZ'S article, "Intermarriage in the United States," should be studied against the backdrop of the heightened concern of American Jews with the problem of intermarriage. In the editor's previous reader on the sociology of American Jewry an extended article on demography disposed of the subject of intermarriage in less than a paragraph. The author—the late Ben B. Seligman—reviewed the results of some thirteen Jewish community surveys conducted during the 1940's and early 1950's and centered his discussion on such standard topics of demographic analysis as age composition, sex ratio, marital status, family size and fertility, occupation, and education. The data allowed him no alternative—with the exception of the study conducted in New Orleans in 1950, none of the Jewish community surveys of the period gathered statistics on intermarriage.*

By way of contrast, today's Jewish demographer is centrally concerned with intermarriage. The questionnaires employed in recent Jewish community surveys invariably utilize one or more items on intermarriage and therefore provide a ready source of data.

*See Ben B. Seligman with the assistance of Aaron Antonovsky, "Some Aspects of Jewish Demography" in *The Jews: Social Patterns of an American Group*, ed. by Marshall Sklare (Glencoe, Ill.: The Free Press, 1958), pp. 45–93.

Sidney Goldstein's article in the present volume thus includes a detailed discussion of intermarriage (see pp. 93–162). And as the article which follows suggests, present-day interest in intermarriage is not confined to professional demographers.

The contrast between the earlier Jewish community surveys and those of today reflects in part the fact that the rate of intermarriage has been rising. But the contrast also reflects a shift in mood. In earlier decades the Jewish community was confident that intermarriage represented a minor problem—one which could hardly threaten group continuity. While there is presently a difference of opinion about exactly how serious a problem intermarriage is, even the optimists are ready to concede that it is a prime threat to Jewish continuity.

It is also possible to explain the failure to deal with the topic of intermarriage at an earlier period as having its source in a kind of avoidance behavior. Consideration of the intermarriage question may have been repressed because it confronted the Jewish community with the bitter possibility that the simultaneous goals of Jewish survival and of integration into the body politic were in conflict. In any case, during the 1960's the rising incidence of intermarriage forced the subject into public consciousness. Intermarriage came to be treated in popular magazines as well as in scholarly works. It became a favorite topic of discussion among Jews—to the point, some felt, of fixation.

There has been no definitive empirical study of intermarriage. The Jewish community surveys offer incomplete data for calculating accurate intermarriage rates since they are frequently conducted in smaller communities rather than in larger ones, and since they are not geared to sampling either marginal or assimilated Jews. A definitive study of intermarriage would in any event have to go beyond the framework of the community survey; the ethnic and religious identity of both the Jewish and the Gentile spouse would have to be painstakingly analyzed, as would that of the children of intermarried couples; the frequency as well as the impact of conversion by Gentile spouses to Judaism would have to be studied; and in order to discover the actual results of a Jewish-Gentile union, intermarried couples would have to be matched with endogamous couples.

Since Schwartz's article is based on existing research it cannot offer a definitive answer to such difficult questions as the rate of intermarriage or the impact of intermarriage on Jewish identity and *continuity. Nevertheless Schwartz offers a wealth of helpful perspectives and useful data. Some of his most suggestive data come from projects initiated outside the Jewish community. The most notable exmple is a NORC sample survey of the career plans of seniors who were members of the 1961 graduating class at 135 American colleges and universities. In 1964 NORC conducted a follow-up study of their sample. In the three-year interval some 57 percent of the Jewish students had married.*

The investigators discovered an intermarriage rate of 12 percent—a rate considerably higher than that uncovered in most community studies. Since in some 21 percent of the unions one of the partners was born a Gentile, the intermarriage rate of only 12 percent resulted, in part, from the frequency of conversions to Judaism. Thus the analyst is confronted with the difficult problem of estimating what the long-term effect of such conversion will be, as well as the intricate question of the impact of intermarriage on the Jewish identity of the Jewish partner.

Schwartz correctly points out that the rate of 12 percent errs on the conservative side. Since intermarried couples tend to marry at a more advanced age than endogamous couples, the future intermarriage rate of the unmarried group should exceed that of the already married group. Furthermore, the rate of 12 percent may not reflect current realities—today's graduates appear to have been socialized in a more pervasive youth culture than obtained as recently as the 1950's and early 1960's.

M. S.

INTERMARRIAGE, said Robert Gordis, is "part of the price that modern Jewry must pay for freedom and equality in an open society."[1] Rabbi Gordis is not alone in urging a reluctant acceptance of an inevitable but tolerable level of intermarriage. In 1965 Rabbi Judah Cahn wrote:

> I believe that such marriages and such losses are part of the price that we must pay for the freedom we have gained. Social equality, intellectual equality, economic equality have made inevitable a greater number of social contacts between people of different faiths. We must, therefore, recognize and accept that this greater freedom will result in a greater number of mixed marriages.[2]

More recently, at the 1970 convention of the Rabbinical Assembly of America, outgoing president Rabbi Ralph Simon declared, "The inevitable price we pay for living in an open society is the possibility that our children may desire to marry persons of another faith."[3]

However, from time to time, anxious observers, raising demographic-survivalist concerns, proclaim that the price being paid may be too dear. A rising incidence of intermarriage, they fear, may steadily diminish the size of the American Jewish community, ultimately to the point of its disappearance. As Rabbi Richard L. Rubenstein observed, "Few problems concern the Jewish community more directly than that of intermarriage. On it hinges the community's continuing ability to maintain itself."[4] Rabbi Leo Jung characterized intermarriage as "one of the fastest ways toward the

[1]Robert Gordis, *Judaism in a Christian World* (New York: McGraw-Hill, Inc., 1966), p. 186.

[2]Judah Cahn, "The Rabbi, Mixed Marriages and Jewish Education," *Reconstructionist,* 19 February 1965, p. 13.

[3]*Jewish Chronicle* (London), 10 April 1970.

[4]Richard L. Rubenstein, "Intermarriage and Conversion on the American College Campus," in Werner J. Cahnman, ed., *Intermarriage and Jewish Life* (New York: Herzl Press, Jewish Reconstructionist Foundation, 1963), p. 122.

destruction of our religion."[5] Others, both within and outside the rabbinate, share these anxieties over the demographic losses intermarriage exacts from the Jewish community.[6] Recent studies bearing on intermarriage rates and their demographic consequences are reviewed here in an attempt to evaluate the grounds for these concerns.

INTERMARRIAGE AND JEWISH DEMOGRAPHY

In its simplest sense, Jewish intermarriage refers to the marriage between Jew and non-Jew. But the definition is no simple matter. Jewish intermarriage may refer to those Jewish by birth alone, who may be only nominally Jewish or to those now actively identifying as Jews. Rates of intermarriage will vary depending on which definition is chosen. Ultimately, choosing among them reflects a position on the question of "who is a Jew," though in practice the choice is often dictated by the urgencies of gathering data.

A recent dictionary of sociology adds to the concept the element of communal disapproval:

> Marriage between persons belonging to two social groups or categories, the members of one or both of which normally disapprove, at least to some extent, of marriage with members of the other, thereby creating possible difficulties between the husband and wife and/or between them and their respective groups or families of origin. Usually intermarriage is described as involving persons from different religious, social, or ethnic backgrounds."[7]

[5]Rabbi Leo Jung, at American Jewish Congress, Commission on Jewish Affairs symposium, "Intermarriage: The Challenge to Jewish Survival," 1 December 1963, n.p. (mimeo.).

[6]See for example Marshall Sklare, "Intermarriage and the Jewish Future," *Commentary,* April 1964, and "Intermarriage and Jewish Survival," *ibid.*, March 1970; also Milton Himmelfarb, "The Vanishing Jews," *ibid.*, September 1963.

[7]George A. Theodorson and Achilles G. Theodorson, *A Modern Dictionary of Sociology* (New York: Crowell-Collier Publishing Co., 1969), p. 212.

It is useful to distinguish between marriages in which the partners retain their original religious identification and marriages in which one partner assumes, usually by conversion, the religious identification of the spouse. This distinction is sometimes noted terminologically, "mixed marriage" referring to the former situation and "intermarriage" to the latter. When involving a conversion to Judaism, intermarriage has also been called "*mitzvah* marriage," the *mitzvah* being that "the faith and identity of the Jew was strong enough to bring the Gentile partner into the household of Israel."[8]

For evaluating Jewish demographic losses it may be useful to refine the concept further. The sociologist J. Milton Yinger, for example, suggests conceiving of intermarriage as a variable. Individuals, then, would be considered not either intermarried or intramarried, but intermarried to a greater or lesser degree:

> If we begin to take account of the several dimensions of religion, we may discover that those who are intermarried when viewed in terms of one dimension may be *intramarried* when viewed in terms of another. . . .
> Once we think of intermarriage as a variable, not an attribute, we can turn to the task of designing scales to measure it. Two scales, I think are needed. The first will measure the degree to which the couple is intramarried, considering similarity on the many possible religious factors. . . .
> The second scale will measure the extent to which a married couple is bound into an "integrating" or "separating" network of other persons and groups. If all the persons with whom they interact and all of their significant others are of the same faith, then they are strongly intramarried on this group dimension. If they interact with many other persons of a different faith, if some of their relatives are intermarried, then they are partially intermarried, even if they are members of the same church and hold the same beliefs.[9]

It may be useful to devise ways of tracing significant events in the careers of intermarried couples and individuals, such as changes in the religious or ethnic self-identification of the partners, formal

[8]Allen S. Maller, "Mixed or Mitzvah Marriages," *Jewish Spectator*, March 1966, p. 8.

[9]J. Milton Yinger, "On the Definition of Interfaith Marriage," *Journal for the Scientific Study of Religion*, Spring 1968, p. 105.

conversions, the times at which Jewish identifications submerge, and when they surface. These suggestions, useful as they may be, have not yet been taken up in intermarriage studies. Furthermore, there has yet to be developed a calculus of the demographic consequences of Jewish intermarriage that would include all the relevant factors—the intermarriage rate, the conversion rate, the divorce rate, the comparative fertility of intermarriages, the proportion of children reared as Jews, the eventual self-identifications of the children of intermarried couples, and their marital choices. Nevertheless, in an attempt to assess the current intermarriage situation the available data for each of these characteristics, at best sparse and fragmentary, will be reviewed in turn.

INTERMARRIAGE RATES

U.S. Census Sample Survey

Estimates of the rate of Jewish intermarriage derive primarily from government records, Jewish community studies, and sample surveys. Among the data collected by government, the potentially most important are census materials. However, because of American sensitivity to governmental inquiry into matters of religion, questions on religious identification were excluded from most censuses, including that of 1970. The last to include questions pertaining to religion was the sample census of 1957.[10]

Though already dated, the 1957 U.S. Census National Sample Survey yielded valuable benchmark figures on Jewish intermarriage, which could be compared with those of local community studies. Presumably, it had the advantage of including Jews on the periphery of Jewish community life, who are generally excluded or underrepresented in community surveys.

Intermarriage was defined in the 1957 census in terms of the

[10]U.S. Bureau of the Census, "Religion Reported by the Civilian Population of the United States: March 1957," *Current Population Reports,* Series P-20, No. 29, 2 February 1958. See Usiel O. Schmelz, "Evaluation of Jewish Population Estimates," *American Jewish Year Book,* Vol. 70 (1969), pp. 279–284.

current self-identification of respondents and their spouses. The sample therefore did not include marriages in which the non-Jewish partner had converted to Judaism, nor those in which the Jewish partner no longer identified as a Jew. Of all married couples with at least one Jewish partner, 7.2 percent included a non-Jewish partner.

Surveys of Marriage Records

Marriage records maintained by government are another source of intermarriage data. Only in two states, Iowa and Indiana—neither of which has a large Jewish population—do these records include the religious identification of registrants.

Iowa marriage records were analyzed by Erich Rosenthal.[11] Intermarriage was defined in terms of the religious identification of bride and groom at the time of marriage, as confirmed by two witnesses and the officiant. A total of 676 marriages involving Jews and contracted between 1953 and 1959 were examined. Of all marriages involving a Jewish spouse, 42.2 percent were intermarriages.

The Iowa figure should not be generalized. It includes only marriages contracted within the state, and therefore excludes marriages of Iowa residents contracted outside the state, where presumably more Jewish partners could be found. Also, the small, relatively isolated Jewish population of Iowa is not typical of the national Jewish population as a whole, of which 80 percent are concentrated in urban areas of 500,000 or more.

Rabbi David Eichhorn, conducting his own investigation of the intermarriage situation in Iowa, has come up with considerably different results. He made inquiry of all Iowa rabbis who had been with their congregations for two or more years. The total membership of their congregations equaled half of the state's estimated Jewish population. During their incumbencies they had officiated at 551 marriages, of which 51, or 9.3 percent, had been intermarriages.[12] Eichhorn's figures, of course, are restricted to marriages conducted under religious auspices, whereas many of the intermarried couples in Rosenthal's data were probably married in civil ceremonies.

[11]Erich Rosenthal, "Studies of Jewish Intermarriage in the United States," *American Jewish Year Book*, Vol. 64 (1963) pp. 3–53.

[12]David M. Eichhorn, "Comments on 'Who is a Jew,'" *Reconstructionist*, 6 December 1968.

Rosenthal has also examined records of all marriages in Indiana involving Jews over a four-year period, from 1960 through 1963.[13] Intermarriage was defined in terms of the religious self-identification of groom and bride at the time of marriage. Of the 785 marriages involving a Jew, 48.8 percent were intermarriages.

Indiana marriage records were also studied by Christensen and Barber whose findings closely resemble those of Rosenthal.[14] Of 762 marriages involving Jews, solemnized from 1960 to 1963, 47.3 percent were intermarriages. Of all Jews marrying, 31 percent married a non-Jew.[15]

As in the case of Iowa, the Indiana figures represent the intermarriage rate of an atypical Jewish community. Similarly, they exclude the marriages of Indiana residents which took place out of state. As Rosenthal has indicated, they also include a significant proportion of couples from out of the state, who presumably eloped and were married in Indiana. The eloped couple is more likely to be an intermarried couple escaping parental and family sanctions.

Community Population Studies

Population studies conducted by the Jewish community are another source of intermarriage data. Usually undertaken by local Jewish community councils or federations, primarily for planning purposes, these studies frequently include questions relating to intermarriage. But their samples, usually cast from master membership lists of Jewish organizations, tend to exclude intermarried Jews who are only marginally involved with the Jewish community. They also cannot include Jewish intermarriages in which the Jewish partner no longer identifies as a Jew. Community studies therefore report *minimal* intermarriage rates. Their findings are remarkably similar; taken together they report the relatively narrow range of 4 to 9 percent. Of course, the main drawback of the studies is the diversity of the samples. They are not representative of

[13]Erich Rosenthal, "Jewish Intermarriage in Indiana," *American Jewish Year Book* Vol. 68, (1967), pp. 243–264.

[14]Harold Taylor Christensen and K.E. Barber, "Interfaith versus Intrafaith Marriage in Indiana," *Journal of Marriage and the Family*, August 1967, pp. 461–469.

[15]Intermarriage rates based on individuals and those based on couples are often conflated. The distinction, however, is significant. Couple rates are always higher: If for example, of 100 Jews, 80 are intramarried (forming 40 couples) and 20 are married to non-Jews, the intermarriage rate by individuals would be 20 percent (20/100); by couples it would be 33 percent (20/60 couples).

the country's Jewish population, if for no other reason then that there has been no study of the Greater New York area, with fully 40 percent of the country's Jewish population. It is to be hoped that the national sample population survey now being conducted by the Council of Jewish Federations and Welfare Funds will overcome some of these shortcomings.

Since 1960 the following Jewish communities have gathered data on intermarriage: Rochester, New York; Long Beach, California; Providence, Rhode Island; Camden, New Jersey; Boston and Springfield, Massachusetts; Baltimore, Maryland; Los Angeles, California.

a) *Rochester.* A survey of this Jewish community of 20,000 was conducted in 1961 under the auspices of the city's Jewish Community Council. The sample was drawn largely from a master membership list of Jewish organizations. Intermarriage rates were reported in terms of both religion at birth and religious self-identification after marriage. Of all married couples 8.0 percent included a non-Jew. In 2.7 percent of all couples the non-Jewish partner had converted to Judaism.[16]

b) *Long Beach.* The Jewish community of Long Beach, Lakewood, and Los Alamitos, California (some 14,000 to 15,000 individuals), was studied in 1961–62 under the auspices of the Jewish Community Federation. Of all married couples 9.0 percent included a non-Jew. In 1.9 percent the non-Jewish partner had converted.[17]

c) *Providence.* A study of the Greater Providence Jewish community of some 20,000 was conducted in 1963 under the sponsorship of the General Jewish Committee of Greater Providence. In terms of the stated religion at birth of respondent and spouse, 4.5 percent of all married couples were intermarried. Rates were also reported by individuals, reflecting whether or not the non-Jewish spouse had converted to Judaism. Of all Jewish married men, 4.4 percent were married to non-Jews: 1.8 percent to a spouse who had converted, and 2.6 percent to one who had not.[18]

[16]Jewish Community Council of Rochester, *The Jewish Population of Rochester* (Rochester, N.Y.: 1961).

[17]Fred Massarik, *A Study of the Jewish Population of Long Beach, Lakewood and Los Alamitos, 1962* (Long Beach, Cal.: Jewish Community Federation, 1962).

[18]Sidney Goldstein, *The Greater Providence Jewish Community: A Population Survey* (Providence, R.I.: General Jewish Committee of Providence, 1964). Also, Sidney Goldstein and Calvin Goldscheider, *Jewish Americans: Three Generations in a Jewish Community* (Englewood Cliffs, N.J.: Prentice-Hall, Inc., 1968).

d) *Camden.* The Jewish community of Camden (some 15,000 individuals) was studied in 1964. A sample was drawn from a master list of Jewish residents supplemented from other sources. Intermarriage rates were reported in terms both of religion at birth and current religious identification, as reported by those interviewed. Of all married couples between 5 and 6 percent included a non-Jew. In 2 percent the non-Jewish partner had converted to Judaism.[19]

e) *Boston.* The Greater Boston Jewish population of approximately 208,000 was surveyed in 1965 under the auspices of the Combined Jewish Philanthropies of Greater Boston. Advanced sampling techniques assured the inclusion of even those Jews who usually slip through uncounted in Jewish community surveys. An individual was considered to be a Jew if he so considered himself, or if his parents identified as Jews. Of all married couples involving a Jew, 7 percent were intermarried couples.[20]

f) *Springfield.* This small Jewish community was studied in 1966–67, under the auspices of the Springfield Jewish Community Council. Of all married couples 4.4 percent included a non-Jew. In 2.6 percent the non-Jewish partner had converted.[21]

g) *Baltimore.* The Greater Baltimore Jewish community was studied in 1967–68 under the auspices of Baltimore's Associated Jewish Charities. The sample for the study was drawn primarily from Associated Jewish Charities and Welfare Fund master lists with some attempt to add names from other sources. Religion of spouses was determined by self-identification. Presumably, these referred to current religious identification and therefore included both individuals born into and converted to Judaism. Of all married couples 4.9 percent included a non-Jew.[22]

h) *Los Angeles.* A 1968 study found that 5.4 percent of all married couples involving a Jew constituted intermarriages.[23]

[19]Charles F. Westoff, *Population and Social Characteristics of the Jewish Community of the Camden Area, 1964* (Camden, N.J.: Jewish Federation of Camden County, 1965).

[20]Morris Axelrod, Floyd J. Fowler, Jr., and Arnold Gurin, *A Community Survey for Long Range Planning: A Study of the Jewish Population of Greater Boston* (Boston: Combined Jewish Philanthropies of Greater Boston, 1967).

[21]Sidney Goldstein, *A Population Survey of the Greater Springfield Jewish Community* (Springfield, Mass.: Jewish Community Council, 1968).

[22]*The Jewish Community of Greater Baltimore: A Population Study* (Baltimore, Md.: Associated Jewish Charities of Baltimore, 1969).

[23]*A Report on the Jewish Population of Los Angeles* (Los Angeles: Jewish Federation Council, 1968).

Analysis by Age and Generation

From the perspective of demographic concern, the intermarriage situation reflected in these studies would seem small cause for alarm. A rate of 4 to 9 percent, one would imagine, is a price the Jewish community can afford to pay—but only if it reflects current trends. These studies report overall ratios of intermarried couples to all marriages involving Jews and, as such include marriages contracted forty, fifty, or more years ago. But how many young Jews, the perpetuators of the Jewish community, are currently marrying non-Jews? Some of the community studies touch upon this question.

A cross-sectional analysis by age of the Providence data did not reveal a marked pattern of intermarriage increasing among the young. While the youngest husbands, those between 20 and 29, had the highest intermarriage rate—7.7 percent, compared to 1.7 percent for those between 30 and 39—intermarriage was nearly as frequent (7 percent), among those between 40 and 49. Rate differentials according to generational status showed much the same weak pattern. Slightly more than 5 percent of third-generation men were intermarried, compared to slightly more than 1 percent of first-generation men; but, again, slightly more than 5 percent of second-generation men had intermarried.

One might expect to find the highest intermarriage rate among young third-generation Jews. Actually, the highest rate, over 12 percent, was found among third-generation men between the ages of 40 and 59. Third-generation men between the ages of 20 and 39 intermarried at a rate of less than 4 percent.[24]

The Springfield study also included cross-sectional analysis by age and generation, and again a clear trend was not apparent. The rate for men between 20 and 29 was about 4 percent; it was about the same for those between 30 and 39, and was *higher*, nearly 6 percent, for those between 40 and 49. By generational status, the rate was *lowest* among third-generation men, below 2 percent.[25]

The figures from Boston tell a different story, one of increasing incidence of intermarriage among younger couples. Seven percent of the marriages in which the husband was between 31 and 50 were intermarriages, but of marriages in which the husband was under 30, 20 percent were intermarriages.[26]

[24]Goldstein and Goldscheider, *op. cit.*, p. 159. ff.

[25]Goldstein, *op cit.*, pp. 145–148.

[26]Axelrod *et al.*, *op. cit.*, p. 169.

Marshall Sklare has extrapolated from the Boston figures to a serious nationwide situation. "If by 1965 one in five young Jewish couples in Boston constituted a case of intermarriage, we can safely assume that the figure is now approaching one in four. And if this is true in so conservative a city as Boston, it must mean that intermarriage has reached large-scale proportions throughout the country as a whole."[27]

Boston, however, includes a large student and graduate-student population, as well as individuals employed by universities and the super-modern technical industries that surround Boston. It is a highly mobile population, fully 31 percent having lived at their current address for less than five years. It is difficult to determine the extent to which these factors affect the results, but they do put in question the "conservative" character of the Boston Jewish community. That Boston's 20 percent is a good indicator of the national situation cannot so readily be assumed.

NORC Study

A better source than the Boston study for information on current intermarriage rates is a large-scale national sample survey undertaken in 1961 by the National Opinion Research Center (NORC), which collected data for a study of career plans from members of the 1961 graduating class at 135 American colleges and universities. Of the 34,000 respondents in the initial survey in 1961, some 3,650 were Jews. In 1964 a follow-up questionnaire was returned by 23,000 respondents, about 10 percent of them Jews. In the interval between the first survey and the 1964 follow-up, 60 percent of the respondents had married; the percentage among Jewish students was 57. Since the survey instrument included questions on the religious identification and marital status of the students, the data collected are a valuable source of information on the current intermarriage situation. They reach beyond the local scope of community studies. They have drawn into their net Jews who might not be included in samples drawn from Jewish community master lists—i.e., any student who declared that he was a Jew or was willing to acknowledge that his parents were Jews—at a time when the large majority of young Jews are in college: a rich catch, indeed. The data

[27]Marshall Sklare, "Intermarriage and Jewish Survival," *Commentary*, March 1970, p. 52.

are currently being analyzed for a study of intermarriage by Fred Sherrow of Columbia University.[28]

However valuable and inclusive, the findings of the NORC survey, too, must be regarded as underestimating the extent of current intermarriage. The data refer to a young population of whom only a portion had married; available evidence suggests that those who intermarry tend to marry at a later age than those who remain endogamous.[29] It is therefore likely that the intermarriage rate of the 43 percent not yet married in 1964 will be somewhat higher than that reported for the already married population.

Sherrow derives various Jewish intermarriage rates from the NORC data, ranging from 5 to 21 percent. Twenty-one percent of all married couples with at least one partner a Jew by birth are intermarried couples, one spouse being a non-Jew *by birth*. This figure is comparable to the 20 percent found in Boston. But when current religion, rather than religion of origin, is examined, the rate falls sharply, to 12 percent. A considerable portion of the drop is to be attributed to conversion of non-Jewish spouses to Judaism. Another part is to be attributed to an opposite cause, the abandonment of Jewish identification by the Jewish partner.

These rates are for couples. The intermarriage rates of individuals are considerably lower. The NORC data reveal that between 10 and 12 percent of individuals who were Jews by birth married a spouse of non-Jewish origin. With *current* religious identification the individual rate drops to 7 percent.

It is frequently stated that more Jewish men than women intermarry. Israel Ellman reports that "An outstanding feature in all surveys of Jewish intermarriage, not only in America, is the fact that a far larger number of Jewish males marry out than do Jewish

[28]Fred Sherrow, *Patterns of Intermarriage Among Recent College Graduates*, Ph.D. dissertation (in process), Columbia University. We thank Mr. Sherrow for having shared his preliminary findings with us.

[29]The reasons for this phenomenon usually refer to the limited availability of marriage partners of one's own religion, and the loosening of ties with parents, who are a force against intermarriage, as one gets older. "After a certain number of marriageable years have passed and a Jew has been unable to find a Jewish mate, the intermarriage taboo apparently loses some of its force": Louis A. Berman, *Jews and Intermarriage: A Study in Personality and Culture* (South Brunswick, N.J.: Thomas Yoseloff, Inc., 1968), pp. 94–95. See also Jerrold S. Heiss, "Premarital Characteristics of Religiously Intermarried," *American Sociological Review*, 1960, pp. 47–55, and Erich Rosenthal, "Jewish Intermarriage in Iowa," *American Jewish Year Book*, Vol. 64 (1963), pp. 46–49.

females. . . .The evidence is overwhelming."[30] Berman, who agrees with the finding, speculates about why this is so:

> In a society in which exogamy is strong discouraged, the taboo is more likely to be violated by males, whose sex role designates a greater degree of independence and aggressiveness. The Jewish daughter, on the other hand, would seem to be more vulnerable to threats of ostracism.[31]

Rabbi Eichhorn, on the other hand, suggests that this is no longer the case:

> This was true until perhaps about ten years ago, but it is no longer. Time was when a Jewish daughter was subjected to much stronger family and communal pressure in an intermarriage situation than was a Jewish son, and many a fearful Jewish girl chose to die an old maid rather than marry a dearly beloved non-Jewish boy. This particular species of Jewish female is getting rarer.[32]

Sherrow's analysis of the NORC data contributes significantly to resolving the question of differential intermarriage rates for Jewish men and women. A difference was found, though not nearly as great as some community studies indicate. (In Providence, for example, only 0.1 of the 4.5 percent of intermarriages involved a woman.) By religious origin, the rates for men and women are 14 and 10 percent, respectively; by current religious preference, they are 8 and 5 percent, respectively. The narrowing gap between male and female intermarriage rates may have resulted from the inclusion of that portion of the Jewish population most frequently underrepresented in intermarriage studies—the Jewish girl who marries out and is lost to the Jewish community—as well as from real changes in intermarriage patterns.

[30]Israel Ellman, "Jewish Intermarriage in the United States of America" *Dispersion and Unity* (Jerusalem: World Zionist Organization, 1969), p. 125.

[31]Berman, *op. cit.*, p. 94.

[32]Eichhorn, *loc. cit.*, p. 19.

EFFECT ON JEWISH COMMUNITY

Summing up the various studies of intermarriage rates and recognizing the limitations of the available data, one can hazard a guess that in the United States somewhere between 10 and 15 percent of all married persons who are Jews by birth have spouses who are non-Jews by birth. This estimate is higher than the figures given in most of the studies reviewed here, which, for the most part and for various reasons, report minimal estimates. About the same percentage probably is currently intermarrying. These figures are higher than in earlier decades, when the Jewish commitment to endogamy was stronger (or when the welcome from Gentile quarters was less warm). But the rates are not yet high enough to warrant fear of an imminent dissolution of the American Jewish community by intermarriage.

Intermarriage results in losses to the Jewish community, but the net loss is less than the gross intermarriage.

Conversion

First of all, there are the non-Jewish spouses who convert to Judaism. The various community studies indicate that their number is sizable: in Rochester almost 30 percent; about 20 percent in Long Beach; more than 40 percent in Providence; about 30 percent in Camden; more than 50 percent in Springfield.

And there is some evidence suggesting an increasing rate of conversion to Judaism. In Providence, Goldstein and Goldscheider found that there had been no conversion of spouses in intermarriages where the husband was over 60; that where the husband was between 40 and 59, 4 out of every 10 spouses had converted; in the youngest group, with the husband under 40, there were 7 conversions for every 10 intermarriages.[33] The same trend was noted when generational comparisons were made. In intermarriages involving the foreign born one-third of the non-Jewish spouses had converted, but in those involving the third generation

[33]Goldstein and Goldscheider, *op. cit.*, p. 157.

more than half. Similar results were found in Springfield. In intermarriages involving Jewish men over 50 about a quarter of the non-Jewish wives had converted, but in those involving men under 30 two-thirds of the non-Jewish wives.

Speculation about the reasons for the apparent increase in conversions has focused on the improved status and successful acculturation of the Jew in America. As Jews have risen in status and adopted American ways, they have became more acceptable to Gentiles, and thus conversion to Judaism has become a more viable option for the non-Jewish spouse. As Berman put it, "Today a Jewish father-in-law is more likely to be a well-educated professional and member of a Reform temple, than an immigrant peddler who *davens* in the Anotevsker *shul*."[34]

Data from the NORC study do not corroborate a trend toward increasing conversion among the young. They show a conversion rate in intermarriages of less than 20 percent, far lower than that of the younger population of the community studies. Eighteen percent of the Protestant wives of Jewish husbands, and 15 percent of Protestant husbands of Jewish wives, converted to Judaism. Eighteen percent of Catholic women married to Jews converted, and 13 percent of Catholic men. Fourteen percent of women with no religious identification who married Jews converted to Judaism, and 9 percent of no-religion men.

The substantially lower conversion rate among the NORC respondents can be variously explained. The conversion rates found in Providence and Springfield may not be representative of the national situation. It also may be that the NORC data suggest a newly emerging conversion pattern reflecting a weakening of proscription against intermarriage. The process leading to such a change may be this:

While the proscription still retains effectiveness, it is breached, even as it is acknowledged. The intermarrying couple's attempt to make their act acceptable by formal conversion is an expression of that acknowledgment. As the proscription is breached with increased frequency, conversions, too, increase, but grow ever more formal, until they come to be regarded as only a formality. Eventually conversion is seen by the marrying couple, their peers, their parents, and, in some instances, by their rabbi, as dispensable and unnecessary. At that point in the weakening of the

[34]Berman, *op. cit.*, p. 44.

intermarriage proscription, conversions can be expected to decline. The NORC data may suggest that we are now at that point.

Jewish Identification of Intermarried Individuals

Many intermarried Jews continue to identify as Jews, even where spouses do not convert. Indeed, intermarriage may spur an individual's discovery of his Jewish identity. Thinking himself indifferent toward his Jewish background, of which he is largely ignorant; tempted by the Gentile world; lured by an ideal of romantic love and a democratic universalism, both of which disregard group distinctions and allegiances, he may enter into an intermarriage innocently and in good faith, and only later discover significance. He may discover basic values or orientations, or small phrases rich with familial meaning, or an occasional and surprising emotional stirring at small or great events in the Jewish world that cannot be shared or appreciated by the non-Jewish spouse. From the demographic perspective, the new recognition is of significance only if it culminates in a reaffirmation of Jewish identity. Of course, no data are available on the frequency of such recognitions resulting in reaffirmation of Jewish identity.

The NORC study does provide data on the retention of Jewish identification among those who intermarry. Sixty-six percent of Jewish men married to Protestants remained Jews, and 58 percent of Jewish girls married to Protestants. Of Jews married to Catholics, 62 percent of the men and 53 percent of the women remained Jews. Of Jewish men married to spouses having no religious identification, 38 percent continued to identify as Jews; of Jewish women, 50 percent. In sum, more than 55 percent of all intermarried individuals retained their Jewish identification.

By considering the retention of Jewish identification and conversion to Judaism, on the one hand, and the abandonment of Jewish identification through indifference or active conversion, on the other, Sherrow has calculated from the NORC data the demographic loss to the Jewish population caused by various types of intermarriage. In intermarriages involving Protestants, the net loss for Jews was 20 percent; in marriages involving Catholics, 26 percent, and in marriages between Jews and those of no religious identification, 47 percent. The net demographic loss from all Jewish intermarriages was 30 percent of the population involved in intermarriages.

Elsewhere, and especially in a study of the small town, it was found that many of those who intermarry remain actively involved in the structures and forms of Jewish life. Nearly all the intermarried individuals attended services and observed some Jewish rituals. The exogamous person remained "part of the Jewish community, maintaining his position in the temple and other Jewish organizations. Even . . . [as] teachers of religion and community leaders, exogamous Jews are accepted."[35]

The retention of Jewish identity and the continued involvement in Jewish activity by those who intermarry diminish Jewish losses. But the situation has another aspect. The example of the intermarried Jew who retains a position in the Jewish community, often of influence and leadership, may weaken the effectiveness of the intermarriage proscription. As Rabbi Henry Kagan has asserted, "To our youth it appears that as long as a high status as a Jew is achieved it is all right to marry a Christian."[36] Schoenfield has in fact described an ideological shift in the small towns from compulsory to "preferred" endogamy.

Divorce

Divorce has for long been the workhorse argument of those who would discourage intermarriage. Under the best circumstances, the argument runs, marriage requires a difficult adjustment and accommodation between two very different individuals. The introduction of religious differences only complicates the marital adjustment, causing additional conflict and unhappiness. Intermarriage, the argument continues, is most likely to end in divorce. Among its recent proponents are Rabbis Allen S. Maller, Ira Eisenstein, and William Berkowitz.[37]

This argument is today losing ground. The individual to whom it is addressed, who is challenged, in effect, to weigh the strength of his love or his will against the odds for marital happiness, need find

[35]Eugene Schoenfield, "Intermarriage and the Small Town: The Jewish Case," *Journal of Marriage and the Family*, February 1969, p. 63.

[36]Henry E. Kagan, "Summation of Intermarriage Conference—17 November 1968. Sponsored by Synagogue Commission of New York Federation of Jewish Philanthropies," *News and Views*, February-March 1969, p. 10.

[37]Allen S. Maller, "New Facts About Mixed Marriage," *Catholic Digest*, September 1969, pp. 115–117; Ira Eisenstein, "Intermarriage," *Jewish Information*, No. 2, 1969, pp. 49–59; William Berkowitz, *Ten Vital Jewish Issues* (South Brunswick, N.J.: Thomas Yoseloff, Inc., 1964), pp. 89–108.

only one successful intermarriage to be encouraged in his plans. Finding such a marriage has become increasingly less difficult. Also, the individual may claim, and today often with some justification, that between him and his prospective spouse there are no religious differences, only differences in religious labels. Still, what little recent statistical evidence there is—and it hardly is compelling—suggests that divorce *is* more frequent among intermarried than among intramarried Jews.

In an examination of marriages in Indiana which were contracted in 1960 and ended in divorce or annulment within five years, Christensen and Barber found divorce more frequent in mixed marriages involving Jews than among Jewish intramarriages. Using a standard whereby one (1) equaled the average Indiana divorce rate of 8.4 percent, they found the divorce rate among intramarried Jews to be .31 and among intermarried Jews 1.83. However, the findings are based on only 52 marriages and are limited to a five-year period after marriage, and therefore are not conclusive.[38]

In Providence, Goldstein and Goldscheider found a higher intermarriage rate for remarriages than for first marriages. Among men between 40 and 59, married twice or more often, 25 percent intermarried; for those married once, the intermarriage rate was only 4 percent.[39] Rosenthal found a similar situation in Iowa and Indiana.[40]

These findings do not deal directly with marital instability as a consequence of intermarriage, for we do not know whether the first marriages were inter- or intramarriages. Indeed, those who remarried non-Jews may have first been married unsuccessfully to Jewish partners. But the findings are suggestive, and lend some indirect support to the contention that intermarriage and marital instability are related. Berman suggested that those who intermarry are prone to divorce: "Attitudes which predispose a person to flout society's opposition to intermarriage should also help him flout society's opposition to divorce. . . . In each case the individual is guided by the dictum that his marital state is a private affair."[41] In

[38]Christensen and Barber, *op cit.*

[39]Goldstein and Goldscheider, *op. cit.*, p. 164.

[40]Rosenthal, "Jewish Intermarriage in Indiana," *loc. cit.*, pp. 259–260; "Jewish Intermarriage in Iowa," *loc. cit.*, pp. 41–42.

[41]Berman, *op. cit.*, p. 178 ff.

some instances, intermarriages ending in divorce may be followed by endogamous remarriages, thus further diminishing demographic losses.

Children

It is sometimes suggested that intermarried couples have fewer children than intramarried couples. However, data are sparse, the only recent findings being those of Goldstein and Goldscheider in Providence. There a significantly higher proportion of intermarried than of intramarried couples were childless, 26.1 percent compared to 9.7 percent among those couples where the wife was over 45, and 14.3 percent compared to 8 percent where the wife was under 45. Similarly, the mean number of children ever born to intermarried couples was lower than of those born to intramarried couples: 1.6, compared to 2.2, in the older group. Goldstein and Goldscheider speculate that the narrowing of the fertility gap among the younger intermarried couples may reflect an increase in the social acceptability of interfaith marriages.[42] Others, speculating on the reasons for inconclusively demonstrated lower fertility among the intermarried, have suggested that it reflects a poor marital adjustment, or an awareness by intermarried couples of the problems their children would have to face. Berman sees the lower fertility, together with the willingness to intermarry and the proneness to divorce, as manifestations of weak commitment to the norms of marriage and parenthood. The intermarried individual may have instead a greater commitment to a professional career, to leisure interests, or personal comfort.[43]

The children of intermarried couples whose non-Jewish partner has converted tend to be raised as Jews. In Camden,[44] Providence,[45] and Springfield,[46] all such children were being raised as Jews. A significant proportion of the children in homes where the non-Jewish spouse has not converted were also being raised as Jews: a third in Camden, about two-fifths in Providence, and more than two-thirds in Springfield. Additional data concerning the children of

[42]Goldstein and Goldscheider, *op. cit.*, p. 167 ff.

[43]Berman, *op. cit.*, p. 179.

[44]Westoff, *op. cit.*, p. 88.

[45]Goldstein and Goldscheider, *op. cit.*, p. 168.

[46]Goldstein, *op. cit.*, p. 147.

intermarried couples—the religious identifications they eventually adopt and their marriage choices—are not available.

THE FUTURE

Sociological factors bringing young marriageable Jews and Gentiles into contact (or, conversely, keeping them apart), or separating young marriageable Jews from one another, will play a major part in determing the future of Jewish intermarriage in the United States. A consideration of these factors suggests that the stage is set, at least sociologically, for a rising incidence of intermarriage.

First, the cultural differences between Jew and non-Jew have diminished, allowing for extensive and deep personal contact. For the most part, American Jews have improved their status and entered the mainstream of American life. Their levels of education, income, and occupation are as high as those of virtually any other religious group in the country. Besides, according to some observers, differences have further narrowed, as "the tastes, ideas, cultural performance, and life styles professed by many Jews are more and more becoming to be shared by non-Jews."[47]

Second, there are forces bringing Jew and Gentile into more immediate contact, the most important of them related to education and occupation. About 85 percent of Jewish youth attend colleges and universities, which are also attended by non-Jewish youth. The college campus and the college years, a place and time of personal growth in which religious and ethnic boundaries are often viewed as confining parochialisms, provide favorable opportunities for deep and intimate contact between people from various religious and ethnic backgrounds.

The challenge of the campus to Jewish endogamy has for some time been the focus of acute and concerned attention. In partial response to the challenge, B'nai B'rith Hillel Foundations have sought to improve the understanding and counseling skills of Hillel directors. Parents have sometimes responded by sending their sons and daughters to schools with large Jewish student populations.

[47]Ellman, *op. cit.*, p. 134.

Choosing such a school is facilitated by the B'nai B'rith Hillel Foundations and B'nai B'rith Vocational Service *College Guide for Jewish Youth,* which gives information on the Jewish populations and facilities of American colleges. It is, of course, impossible to say how far such measures reach, or how effective they are in stemming the extremely powerful forces encouraging the kinds of contact that may lead to intermarriages.

Changes in the occupations of Jews also have brought Jew and Gentile into contact. As Ellman notes "The general tendency of the young generation to leave the traditional Jewish occupations, with their strong Jewish family and social associations, and the shift to the salaried professions combine to make the changing Jewish occupational structure one of the most potent causes of Jewish intermarriage. Jews are now working with Gentiles as colleagues instead of serving them as merchants and professionals."[48]

A recent study of Jewish college freshmen undertaken by the American Council of Education for the American Jewish Committee shows that their career plans would continue to place them in occupations fostering contacts with Gentiles.

Intermarriage would be further encouraged within the context of cultural convergence and personal contact if a special complementary or mutual affinity existed between Jew and Gentile. It has been suggested that at times this is the case. Berman hypothesizes that the Jewish ethos fosters traits fitting exceedingly well the masculine role in Western society. The Jewish male tends to be serious-minded, hard-working, ambitious, and intellectual, all of which make him an attractive potential mate for the Gentile girl. Berman further suggests that the traits fostered in Jewish girls may, by comparison, make Gentile girls more attractive to the Jewish male. He approvingly cites Werner Cahnman:[49] "Jewish mothers sensitize their daughters more to their rights than to their obligations, so that they insist that their future husbands be conveniently docile in the home, moderately 'ambitious' in the marketplace, and capable of satisfying the highest material expectations of 'happiness.'" Berman continues: "Jewish men 'feel oppressed by the expectations of the relentless pressure of the obligations to which they will be subjected in the families of

[48]Ellman, *op. cit.*, p. 134.

[49]Werner J. Cahnman, "Intermarriage Against the Background of American Democracy," in Werner J. Cahnman, ed., *Intermarriage and Jewish Life: A Symposium* (New York: Herzl Press, 1963), p. 190.

prosperous Jewish spouses,' a burden which he need not shoulder if he married 'a simple Gentile girl.'"[50]

Hacker, perhaps more facilely, offers a suggestion along similar lines: "Both Jews and women are outsiders; neither feel entirely comfortable in a world dominated by Gentile males."[51]

The proscriptions against intermarriage, if powerful, could effectively neutralize the sociological factors encouraging intermarriage. The relatively low incidence of intermarriage indicates that the proscription does retain force. Intermarriage still is disapproved in large measure. But the signs are that the intermarriage ban is being weakened. Studies of parental attitudes indicate that disapproval is often balanced by a significant incidence of only mild disapprobation, or indifference, or even approval.

In Kansas City 54 percent of Jewish parents strongly disapproved of intermarriage, 20 percent indicated mild disapproval, 13 percent were indifferent, while 8 percent indicated mild or strong approval.[52] In Baltimore 67 percent disapproved outright, while 20 percent expressed reserved opposition, and another 8 percent expressed either indifference or approval.[53] In Fargo, North Dakota, 46 percent disapproved and 47.2 approved.[54] In Boston 26 percent strongly approved, 44 percent would discourage it, while an additional 25 percent were neutral or accepted it.[55] In Lakeville 29 percent would be very unhappy, 43 percent somewhat unhappy, and 24 percent indifferent.[56]

Disapproval itself is generally tempered by the American ethos, shared by most American Jews, which places primary emphasis on the individual—his will, his choices, his personal well-being. Young people about to marry participate in this ethos when they conceive of marriage as a path to *personal* happiness, as *personal* fulfillment.

[50]Berman, *op. cit.*, p. 341.

[51]Andrew Hacker, "How You Got Your Jewish Son-in-Law," *New York* (World Journal Tribune), 26 March 1967, p. 3.

[52]Manheim Shapiro, *The Kansas City Survey* (American Jewish Committee, 1961), p. 97.

[53]*As We See Ourselves* (American Jewish Committee, 1964), p. 7.

[54]Robert Lazar, *From Ethnic Minority to Socio-Economic Elite: A Study of the Jewish Community of Fargo, North Dakota* (Ph.D. dissertation, University of Minnesota, 1968), p. 196.

[55]Axelrod *et. al.*, *op. cit.*

[56]Marshall Sklare and Joseph Greenblum, *Jewish Identity on the Suburban Frontier* (New York: Basic Books, 1967).

The individual weighing a marriage decision expresses the ethos when, in considering a potential spouse, he brings to bear the egalitarian, universalist principles upon which he had been nurtured: that people should be judged by their personal merits, not by race or religion. Parents acknowledge it when they argue against intermarriage as allegedly leading to marital discord and unhappiness, instead of invoking the religious prohibitions. (In Lakeville, for one, the most frequent objections to intermarriage have to do with just such issues of personal happiness.) Similarly, parents acknowledge the primacy of individual choice when, however heavyhearted, they accept their children's intermarriages, rather than go into mourning, as was traditionally done. . . .

Potentially and in fact, this ethos is in conflict with the proscription against intermarriage. In purpose and consequence the proscription is trans-individual, expressing the will of the group and its law. Where Jewish consciousness is not particularly strong, the ethos of individual well-being and of individual will can lead effortlessly to intermarriage. Where a commitment to Jewish existence retains any force at all, conflict between the ethos of the individual and the intermarriage ban is felt on all levels: by the young couple, by their parents, at times even by their rabbis. It is frequently the intermarriage ban that gives ground. The dilemma described by Rabbi Richard J. Israel, Hillel director at Yale University, is a case in point.

When confronted by a student considering intermarriage, he finds his goals as campus rabbi and as counselor incompatible. As counselor, his role is to help the counselee understand as clearly as possible his situation, to help him "come to the best possible decision he can." As counselor, therefore, his commitment is to the individual, who, in his freedom and in the best understanding of his situation, may very well choose to go ahead with his intermarriage plans. But as rabbi, Israel's goals refer to his Jewish commitment, and he wants "very much to break up the impending marriage." Caught in this crosscurrent, he resolves to "go about doing the best possible counseling job he can, permitting the students to come to their own decisions in the presence of one who accepts them as people, while not sharing their value systems."[57] To do otherwise, to admonish, Rabbi Israel declares, simply does not work. . . .

[57]Richard J. Israel, "A Note on Counseling Young People Contemplating Intermarriage," in *Campus 1966: Change and Challenge* (Washington, D.C.: B'nai B'rith Hillel Foundation, 1966), p. 54.

Rabbi Israel accepts the individual's decision as a consequence of his assumption of the counselor role. Other members of the rabbinate have acknowledged the primacy of individual choice in their role as rabbis, even when the choice leads to intermarriage. Whether as a strategy for Jewish survival or as religious conviction, the position of these rabbis tends to weaken the effectiveness of the intermarriage proscription within the larger community.

At the extreme are those whose acceptance of individual decision is so radical that they are prepared to accept as its consequence the dissolution of Judaism. They are few in number. Rabbi Sherwin T. Wine, the "ignostic" rabbi of Detroit, expresses that viewpoint. . . .[58] Similarly, Rabbi Everett Gendler sees the possibility of a new religion in the making, and would encourage its development by having established Judaism support interfaith marriages. . . .[59]

More typical is the position, based in part on religious persuasion, that inwardness and sincere conviction are the only grounds for establishing what is religiously valid—a position which justifies itself as one way of assuring Jewish survival. Its proponents accede to an individual's desire to intermarry, but with the ostensible purpose of demonstrating the reasonableness of Judaism, and hoping thereby to gain adherents. It is, one would suspect, the position taken by the majority of Reform rabbis willing to officiate at mixed marriages without requiring conversion of the non-Jewish partner. According to Rabbi David Max Eichhorn, today they number well over 100.[60]

The argument in support of this position was advanced by Rabbi Charles E. Shulman:

> If the end sought by the rabbi is adequate Jewish living and closer affiliation with the lot of the Jewish people, the personal conversation which he holds with the mixed couple may do more to portray to them the character and beauty of the Jewish religious experience than all the impersonal instruction in a class for converts can possibly do. *Per contra*, a rabbi's negative attitude . . . may create an impression of

[58]See B.Z. Sobel and Norman Mirsky, "Ignosticism in Detroit: An Experiment in Jewish Religious Radicalism," *Midstream*, December 1966, pp. 35–45, for a discussion of Wine's unique position within Reform Judaism.

[59]Everett Gendler, "Identity, Invisible Religion, and Intermarriage," *Response*, Winter 1969–70, p. 31.

[60]Norman Mirsky, "Mixed Marriage and the Reform Rabbinate," *Midstream*, January 1970, pp. 40–46.

> Judaism that will not evoke much appreciation of its merits in the minds of the mixed couple. . . . The rabbi's refusal to officiate will have no bearing on their intentions, but may serve only to create an image in their eyes of a harsh and unyielding religion.[61]

Almost total accession to individual choice may be based on an unabashed universalism unqualified by a belief in the necessity and the mystery of Jewish continuity. Or, it may be based on a belief that the only important Jewish allegiance is one freely chosen by the individual, without the compulsion of objective law. In either case, it seriously undercuts the intermarriage proscription. As has been argued, to officiate at mixed marriages is to encourage them by bestowing upon them a legitimacy, making them acceptable to the Jewish community. Rabbi Eichhorn, himself, has expressed only a lukewarm disapproval of intermarriage. . . .[62]

The legitimation of intermarriage by sectors of the rabbinate creates structural problems for the Jewish community, establishing or emphasizing divisions that may become unbridgeable. Rabbi Jakob Petuchowski has pointed to these: Whereas the ostensible goal of officiation at mixed marriages is to keep individuals within the Jewish fold (by not antagonizing them), its effect is to bring down the fences defining that fold. Within the realm of marriage, the ultimate consequence of polydoxy—the view that Reform Judaism "has only one dogma, the absolute freedom of the individual to think and do what he likes"—is to isolate Reform Judaism from other forms of historical Judaism by creating "a state of affairs where the offspring of the marriage at which we 'officiate' is unable to intermarry with the offspring of the other heirs of historical Judaism."[63]

The violation of a group's prohibition focuses consciousness on the transgression, and, by doing so, often provides occasion for recommitment to the group's traditional values. The violation of the intermarriage proscription in some sectors of the American Jewish community may serve to encourage its reaffirmation in other sectors. Certainly, the Orthodox and Conservative branches have remained unwavering in their assertion of the ban on intermarriage.

[61]Charles E. Shulman, "Mixed Marriage, Conversion and Reality," *CCAR Journal*, January 1964, p. 31.

[62]David Max Eichhorn, "Comments on 'Who is a Jew'," *loc. cit.*, p. 20.

[63]Jakob J. Petuchowski, "Realism About Mixed Marriages," *CCAR Journal*, October 1966, p. 38.

The Orthodox position has recently been restated by Rabbi Chaim Rozwaski:

> The Torah prohibits marriage between a Jew and a non-Jew and violation of this injunction is to be punished. Such a marriage is banned and not legally binding or effective. Consequently, an intermarried Jew does not live in a state of marriage at all, but rather in that of promiscuity. . . . A Jew living with a non-Jewess lives in a state of harlotry and is responsible for violating all the moral laws concerning such behavior. . . .[Judaism] leaves no room for intermarriage within the Jewish way of life and grants it no quarter within its faith.[64]

The Conservative position, while less severe in tone, also reaffirms "unqualified opposition to the marriage of a Jew to a non-Jew."[65]

Even within the Reform rabbinate, the willingness to make concessions to individual will, at the expense of the intermarriage law, has not spread deep, far, or wide. As Mirsky notes, "Reform rabbis are still not happy with those of their colleagues who perform [mixed marriages]. . . ."[66]

The future of Jewish intermarriage in America cannot be forecast. On the one hand, powerful influences from within the Jewish community, and from without, encourage its increase. On the other hand, currents in American and Jewish life, at this moment only dimly noted, may tend to curb it. Major shifts in the sociological position of the Jews in America could have unforeseen consequences for the future of intermarriage, as could radical alterations in the level and intensity of Jewish religious or group consciousness.

[64]Chaim Z. Rozwaski, "Jewish Law and Intermarriage," *Jewish Life*, July–August 1969, pp. 18–23.

[65]Max J. Routtenberg, "The Jew Who Has Intermarried," *Proceedings of the Rabbinical Assembly of America*, 1964, p. 245: majority opinion of Committee on Jewish Law and Standards, Rabbinical Assembly, 15 January 1963.

[66]Mirsky, *loc. cit.*, p. 42.

THE AMERICAN JEW AND ISRAEL

AMERICAN ALIYA
SOCIOLOGICAL AND DEMOGRAPHIC PERSPECTIVES

by CALVIN GOLDSCHEIDER

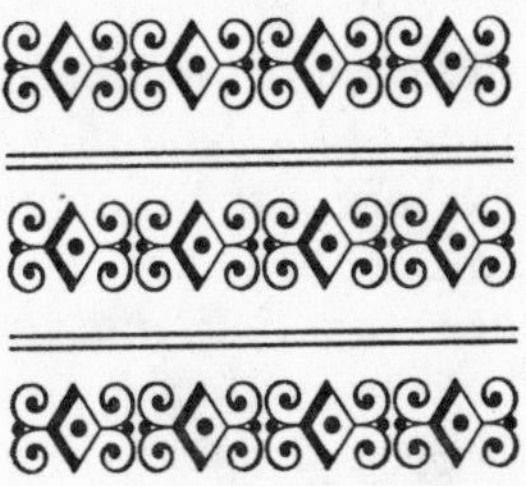

INTRODUCTION

THE RELATIONSHIP of American Jews to Israel is both one of the oldest and one of the newest topics in the sociology of the American Jew. As Calvin Goldscheider points out, the link of American Jews to Palestine is over a century old. However, most American Jews, and even many American Zionists, conceived of this link exclusively in philanthropic, political, or cultural terms. American Jews would give financial assistance to the Jews of Palestine and later of Israel, and might also be helpful by influencing American foreign policy in a pro-Israel direction. Such assistance would be reciprocated in two ways: 1) Israel would serve as a symbol of Jewish affirmation and achievement, and 2) Israel would constitute a center where Jewish culture would develop free of the limitations inherent in the Diaspora. While Israeli culture could never be transferred in toto to America it would nonetheless provide American Jews with a significant source of cultural enrichment that would in turn constitute a valuable resource in the fight against assimilation.

While a small group of ultra-Reform Jews resisted any link with Israel the dominant tendency of American Jews from the beginning was to nourish and strengthen their connection to the Jewish state. Minimalists saw the relationship of the American Jew to Israel as centered in philanthropic aid, while maximalists emphasized cultural interchange as well as political action. To be sure, a segment of Zionist youth maintained that the relationship of the American Jew to Israel went beyond philanthropy, political action, and cultural exchange—that there was a responsibility for American Jews to participate personally in the upbuilding of the land through aliya [migration]. This view, however, was hardly the dominant one. America was considered exceptional: it had no "Jewish problem," it was a land of immigration, not emigration, and there were no grounds for expecting a significant American aliya.

A number of Israeli spokesmen have suggested that sooner or later a Jewish problem will emerge in the United States, and will disprove this doctrine of American exceptionalism. Others have maintained that while anti-Semitism is not in fact a problem, assimilationism will become so rampant as to undermine completely the Jewish identity of the American Jew. It must be said that neither position has been argued with real conviction, and that no one has ever really seemed to harbor great expectations for a large-scale emigration of American Jews to Israel.

The fact is, however, that there has been an American aliya for many decades. Carefully analyzing the available statistics Goldscheider provides us with the most reliable data yet available on the ebb and flow of this emigration. He does not treat all American olim [migrants] as a single type, but indicates rather their different motivations and personal characteristics as well as those factors which they have in common.

At the present moment aliya has assumed an importance in the relationship between American Jews and Israel which rivals the traditional avenues of philanthropy, political support, and cultural exchange.

Given the new significance of aliya it is essential that we improve our knowledge about the demographic characteristics of American olim. Goldscheider not only provides such information but, on the basis of previously unpublished data concerning the attitudinal, behavioral, and personal characteristics of olim, analyzes their level of Jewish education, the frequency of their synagogue attendance, the level of their ritual observance, and their affiliation with Zionist organizations. His conclusions provide the starting point for future research on what he terms "the intricate web of interdependence between the American Jewish community and Israeli society."

M. S.

ALIYA from the United States[1] is but one small segment of the complex, symbiotic, and dynamic relationships between the State of Israel and the American Jewish community. Since the Six Day War of 1967, dramatic and revolutionary changes have occurred in these interdependencies and have been reflected in the changing nature of American Jewish immigration to Israel. In addition to the increase in the volume of American aliya, American *olim* have become more conspicuous within Israeli society and, of equal importance, aliya from the United States has become acceptable, normative, and institutionalized within the American Jewish community.

No contemporary sociological analysis of American Jews can be considered complete without a discussion of the role of Israel, and in particular the place of American aliya, in American Jewish life. This had not always been the case, despite the long-standing ties and connections between American Jews and Israel. Social scientists in the 1950's and 1960's had in fact dismissed the importance of the establishment of the State of Israel for the inner life of American Jews and had argued that the idea of a serious impact of Israel on Judaism in America was largely illusory. Large-scale aliya from the United States was thought to represent "wishful thinking" and except for sporadic emigration, no mass movement appeared likely. Indeed, the prognosis was made that in order to have "a wholesale immigration to Israel from the United States, there would have to be a revolution in the situation and mentality of American Jews, the vast majority of whom belong to the middle classes and, in the absence of religious motivation, can

[1]*Aliya*, literally "ascent," is used to mean immigration to Israel; persons who go on aliya are called *olim*—or in the singular, *oleh*.

Note: The research reported in this paper was started 1969–70 while I was on leave from the University of California, Berkeley. Initial support from the National Foundation for Jewish Culture and from the Institute of International Studies, University of California, Berkeley is gratefully acknowledged. Cooperation from the Israel Central Bureau of Statistics, its former director, Professor Roberto Bachi, and its current director, Dr. Moshe Sicron, is most appreciated. I am grateful to Etan Sabatello, Zion Rabi, and Zvi Eisenbach, all of the Central Bureau of Statistics, for providing access to unpublished data and assisting me in numerous ways.

feel no temptation to uproot themselves and settle in Israel."[2]

In the pre-1967 era, American Jews and among them American Zionists, assumed that aliya would come from other countries, where Jews faced persecutions and hostility. The role of American Jews was at most to provide adequate economic support and effective political aid to Israel. Paradoxically, the American Zionist expressed great opposition to the idea of American aliya; the thought of his own immigration to Israel never seriously entered his mind while the idea of aliya on the part of his children "struck him as fundamentally absurd in theory and entirely to be rejected in actual practice."[3] It is against the background of these assumptions that the radical change in the character of American aliya must be viewed.

There is a variety of sociological and demographic contexts within which American aliya may be analyzed, each requiring a somewhat different set of orientation questions. American aliya may be viewed, for example, as part of the migration interchanges between countries; hence, the study of American immigration to Israel would include an analysis of alternative migratory flows—the movement of Israelis to the United States and return migration of Americans and Israelis to their respective countries of origin. A somewhat different orientation treats the aliya of Americans as part of all immigration to Israel, focusing on the place of American aliya within the variety of migration streams to Israel and examining the differential absorption or integration of American and other olim within Israeli society. Often these approaches have been combined and American aliya has been placed in the broad context of world Jewish migrations.

A different starting point in the study of American aliya focuses on the role of American immigration to Israel as one aspect of the total social, cultural, economic, and political exchanges between

[2]Georges Friedmann, *The End of the Jewish People?* New York: Doubleday-Anchor Books, 1967 (translated by Eric Mosbacher), p. 231. See also Nathan Glazer, *American Judaism,* Chicago: University of Chicago Press, 1957, pp. 114, 115. My own pre-1967 research on the American Jewish community reflected this general tendency as well. See, for example, Sidney Goldstein and Calvin Goldscheider, *Jewish Americans,* Englewood Cliffs, New Jersey: Prentice-Hall, Inc., 1968, pp. 9–10. In contrast, Marshall Sklare's book *America's Jews,* New York: Random House, 1971, devotes an entire chapter to "The Homeland: American Jewry and Israel," pp. 210–223.

[3]From an article by S. Halkin, "American Zionism and the State of Israel," *Forum* I, December 1953; cited in Edward Neufeld, "Zionism and Aliya on the American Jewish Scene," *The Jewish Journal of Sociology,* 5 (June 1963), p. 112.

Israel and the American Jewish community. In this context, American aliya is investigated as one facet of the influences of American Jews on Israel and of Israel on American Jews: Aliya from the United States may be considered, on the one hand, part of the general flow of money, tourists, students, economic investments, political aid, and psychological support from American Jewry to Israel and, on the other hand, as a response to the ideological, cultural, and educational influences of Israel on the American Jewish community.

These perspectives have been utilized in one form or another to study American aliya and olim and in a general way serve as guidelines for the ensuing analysis. However, particular emphasis will be placed on understanding American aliya from the perspective of the sociology of the American Jewish community. The point of view to be explored treats American aliya as one of the multiple responses of American Jews to the problems of Jewish identity in a modern, secular society that is guided by universalistic rather than particularistic ideologies.

Faced with the options to choose, American Jews have responded in multiple directions: Some have moved in the direction of assimilation, intermarriage, loss of Jewish identity, and indifference to interaction, association, and affiliation with other Jews and the Jewish community; others have chosen Jewish segregation and isolation as a vehicle to protect and preserve Jewish particularism; others have attempted to retain ties to the Jewish community through various organizational or communal activities focused on local or national Jewish issues, Jewish defense, and issues of world Jewry (including, of course, Israel); still others have expressed their Jewishness by their concern with general issues of social justice and morality within a Jewish organizational framework or through philanthropic activities in a general or Jewish context. Some Jews have attempted to find new meaning for American Judaism and have searched for creative Jewish ways to express their social-religious identities; others have found religious significance and ethnic identity in ritual observances that are neither overly conspicuous nor intrusive in their daily lives and that fit most comfortably into the American scene. For some, however, the response to the dilemma of universalism-particularism, to the "conflicts" of religious (Jewish) identity in a secular (Christian) society and to minority status in a pluralistic nation has been aliya. Hence, immigration to Israel may be viewed as one of a multiple set of responses to a complex of challenges facing the American Jew.

This orientation to American aliya requires two major directions of empirical inquiry: First it is important to measure the changing volume of aliya from the United States. Through an analysis of the numbers of American olim at different periods in American, Israeli, and Jewish history, a picture of the changing quantitative importance of the aliya response may be outlined. After describing the changing numbers of Americans who become olim, the selectivity of American aliya must be investigated. What are the social characteristics of American olim, e.g., what types of American Jews have responded to the challenges of being Jewish in American society by immigrating to Israel? The exploration of these general themes provide the essential background for understanding the determinants, consequences for the American Jewish community, and possible future course of American aliya.

The volume of American aliya and the social characteristics of American olim are among the all too many topics in the sociology of American Jews about which a great deal has been written and little is known. Much of the discussion of American aliya in the Jewish mass media is tainted by ideological biases and distortions. Systematic empirical evidence to analyze American aliya in more objective terms is not available in the depth or in the quality that is desirable and necessary. Despite reservations and qualifications, a preliminary analysis can be presented in broad outline using two major sources of data: 1) official immigration registration data in Israel, and 2) sample survey materials.

The Central Bureau of Statistics in Israel collects a series of registration data on immigrants extending back to the establishment of the State of Israel. They are derived from questionnaires collected by border police on declared immigrants and temporary residents; for tourists settling, i.e., persons entering the country as tourists but changing their status to immigrants or temporary residents, data are obtained from the Ministry of Interior. Together these data show the number of immigrants arriving or tourists settling in Israel along with selected data on age, sex, marital status, occupation, country of birth, place of last residence. Special publications on immigration to Israel are issued[4] but these do not contain detailed information on immigrants from the United States. Unpublished data were made available to me by the Central Bureau of Statistics on American olim (defined by place of last residence) 1948–71, along with more detailed information on the characteris-

[4]See, for example, Israel Central Bureau of Statistics, *Immigration to Israel,* Special Series No. 349, Jerusalem, 1971.

tics of American olim arriving in 1970. Unfortunately, adequate data to measure return migration are not available; hence, the analysis is limited to American olim who arrive in Israel and not to those who remain.

An additional source of information about American olim is the "Survey on Absorption of Immigrants" conducted by the Israel Central Bureau of Statistics in conjunction with the Ministry of Immigrant Absorption and the Israel Institute of Applied Social Research. The purpose of the survey is to follow various aspects of the absorption process of new immigrants during their first three years in Israel. The survey population includes a representative sample of all immigrants and potential immigrants aged 18 and over, who immigrated to Israel between September 1969 and August 1970.[5]

As part of the survey on absorption, background questions on the characteristics of olim before aliya were obtained. Unpublished data on the social characteristics of immigrants and potential immigrants whose last place of residence was in the United States were made available by the Central Bureau of Statistics for this analysis.[6] The number of olim from the United States included in the sample was 167 and represents a random sample of all registered American immigrants and potential immigrants arriving in Israel, September 1969 to August 1970. Since the number of cases is small, sampling variation and error are large. Hence, the findings based on the data from the immigrant absorption survey should be viewed as preliminary and tentative, allowing for a margin of statistical error.

The data on American olim derived from these two sources will be compared to other olim (derived from published and unpulished data in the files of the Central Bureau of Statistics), the Jewish population of Israel (derived from official registration and census data), and the American Jewish population (derived from several sources).[7] Sources for historical materials on American aliya prior to the establishment of the State of Israel are cited *ad locum*.

[5]The details of the sample design and first results are presented in Israel Central Bureau of Statistics, *Survey on Absorption of Immigrants*, Special Series No. 381, Jerusalem, 1972. See below for discussion of "potential immigrants" and *ibid.* for definition and general description of olim in these two statuses.

[6]Part of the original material was recoded for the specific needs of this project and, hence, I remain responsible for the data and interpretations to be presented.

[7]I have relied heavily on the tabular material presented and analyzed in Sidney Goldstein, "American Jewry, 1970: A Demographic Profile," *American Jewish Year Book*, Vol. 72 (1971), pp. 3–88. These data summarize and organize a variety of Jewish community studies in addition to special tabulations of the Current Population Survey of 1957. For specific sources see Goldstein's bibliography and footnotes.

THE CHANGING VOLUME OF AMERICAN ALIYA

The most elementary starting point in the analysis of American aliya focuses on the quantitative issue: How many American olim settled in Israel at different points in time? The question is deceptively simple. It assumes that the definitions of "American" and "olim" are clear and uniform over time, that reliable, complete, and comparable statistics were collected under various political administrations (Turkish, British, Jewish), and that adequate measures are available to differentiate olim that arrive from olim that settled in Israel. It should be clear to anyone with even a casual acquaintance with social science data that these assumptions are not very realistic. From a strictly quantitative demographic point of view, there is no possibility to reconstruct in a statistically accurate form exactly how many Americans arrived and settled in Israel over the last several decades.

The objective of this section is more modest: Estimates of the approximate volume of American aliya from the middle of the nineteenth century to the 1970's will be presented, with an emphasis on patterns and processes. An overall quantitative picture of the patterns and processes of American aliya can be pieced together despite contradictory statistical reports, inadequate data coverage, and definitional changes in official records. Crude estimates of the number of American olim for various historical periods provide the necessary background to gauge 1) the changing patterns of American aliya over a period of 125 years; 2) changing proportions of American olim relative to all immigrants to Israel; 3) changing proportions of American olim relative to the estimated Jewish population of the United States. Since the data to be presented are estimates, a margin of error of 10 to 20 percent should be allowed, particularly for the earlier period. The discussion of the changing volume of American aliya will be related to three broad periods: 1) the early American aliya, from the mid-nineteenth century to World War I; 2) aliya during the British Mandatory Period, 1919–1948; 3) contemporary aliya, 1948–1971, to the State of Israel, with a special emphasis on the pre- and post-Six Day War (1967) periods.

THE EARLY AMERICAN OLIM

It is diffcult to identify a definitive migration stream from the United States to the land of Israel prior to World War I. Largely this is because the number of American olim was small, the reasons for aliya were idiosyncratic and diverse, and detailed statistics, records, or documents on early American immigration to the land of Israel are nonexistent. The absence of an identifiable, pre-twentieth-century American aliya does not imply that there were no American olim. On the contrary, scattered historical records reveal the settlement of individual American Jews in the land of Israel dating from the middle of the nineteenth century.

One of the earliest references to an "American oleh" is the case of the first American consul for the Middle East region, a Protestant, who moved to Jerusalem in 1845. After less than two years in this position, he converted to Judaism and founded an agricultural colony on the outskirts of Jerusalem. In time, at least 50 Americans joined this pioneer colony including some Protestants, converts to Judaism, and the ex-consul's bride—a Jewish woman from New York.[8]

This pattern was, in all probability, quite atypical for this period. Although the evidence is fragmentary and inadequate, selected documents suggest that most American immigrants to the land of Israel in the nineteenth century were neither Jewish converts nor agricultural pioneers. The majority were motivated by more "parochial" religious reasons—to live or die in the Holy Land. Like the majority of the Jewish settlers before 1880, American Jews in the land of Israel were concentrated in the four "holy" cities of Jerusalem, Hebron, Tiberias, and Safed. Settling in these cities was viewed by the majority of Jews as a religious duty or act of piety. These settlements were, however, not consolidated; rather, they were subdivided into communities and *landsmanschaften* according to place of origin. Moreover most of the early American olim failed to establish economic roots in the land of Israel; they were sustained

[8] P. E. Lapide, *A Century of U.S. Aliya*, Israel: The Association of Americans and Canadians in Israel, 1961, pp. 37–39.

by monies collected from European and American Jews. The American settlements were small, poor, and consisted mainly of unemployed older men and women dependent on the generosity of others for survival.[9]

American Jews had a long history of supporting "religious" settlements in Israel and "Palestinean messengers" made regular trips to collect money from the "rich Jews of America."[10] In the 1860's, however, the Jews of America witnessed a significant development in requests from Palestine: A small group of American olim complained that the money received from America was not being distributed among them and that American Jews did not realize that there was an American Jewish settlement in Israel. In a letter, dated November 1867, addressed to leaders of American Jewry, the U.S. consul in Jerusalem wrote:

> The number of American Jews residing in Jerusalem is very limited, a dozen altogether; but these unfortunates are the most miserable of all and do not receive pecuniary succor from any one, the German committees never having given them a cent, and those of America perhaps do not know them at all.[11]

Ten years later, the situation had not improved and another letter to leaders of American Jewry was sent by the American consul. In part, it stated:

> I think it proper that the Hebrew people in America should know the conditions of their brethren at Jerusalem, who are in distress, and need assistance. They are citizens of the United States, with naturalization papers and passports . . . one of them a soldier in the United States army four years, a dragoman, says he has had no food for two days, except the garbage picked up from the street. . . . There are 13 families or perhaps 15 representing 45 to 50 persons who need help and who, without help, must suffer. . . . They beg me to let their brethren in America know their situation.[12]

[9]This description follows that of Ben-Zion Dinur, "The Historical Foundations of the Rebirth of Israel," in L. Finkelstein (ed.) *The Jews*, Vol. I, 3rd edition, Philadelphia: The Jewish Publication Society of America, 1960, pp. 588–589.

[10]See the important article by Salo Baron and Jeannette Baron, "Palestinian Messengers in America, 1849–79: A Record of Four Journeys," in Salo Baron, *Steeled By Adversity: Essays and Addresses on American Jewish Life*, Philadelphia: The Jewish Publication Society, 1971, pp. 158–266. (This essay originally appeared in *Jewish Social Studies*, Vol. V. (1943), pp. 115–62, 225–92.)

[11]Cited *ibid.*, p. 219.

[12]*Ibid.*, p. 239.

By the turn of the century, funds were being distributed among over 200 members of the American settlement in Jerusalem.[13]

American Jews in the land of Israel were organized like Jews from other countries partly because monies were divided in terms of communities and partly for protection. In 1879, over one hundred American Jews in Jerusalem demanded that the U.S. consulate recognize them as an independent American community. A decade later, 800 U.S. citizens were under the protection of the Jerusalem consulate and in the early 1900's the number increased to more than 1,000.[14]

Not all Americans requesting protection or seeking formal recognition in order to obtain funds lived in Jerusalem. In the 1870's, for example, the U.S. consulate in Jerusalem received a request from a rabbi from New Jersey who resided in Tiberias. He sought permission to establish an American congregation. In his letter, the rabbi revealed that there were over 20 Americans living in the Galilee.[15]

In general, so little is known about American aliya prior to World War I that the entire period may be treated as a whole. As a rough estimate, it seems reasonable to accept the guess that no more than 2,000 Americans (defined by place of last residence and/or citizenship but not by country of birth) arrived to settle in Israel prior to 1914, representing less than 3 percent of the estimated 55,000 to 70,000 immigrants to the land of Israel, 1880 to 1914.[16]

There is precious little evidence to cite nor are data available to document changes in the volume or character of American aliya during this period. However, assuming that early American aliya did not differ radically from the patterns of general aliya, two additional observations may be made. First, the volume of American aliya probably increased slightly after the 1880's and certainly after 1900. It has been estimated that between 1903 and 1914 over 1,000 American *chalutzim* (pioneers) and pious Jews immigrated to the land of Israel; if accurate, this figure is as large as the total number

[13]*Ibid.*, p. 619, footnote 74. On this general topic, see Moshe Davis, *From Dependence to Mutuality: The American Jewish Community and World Jewry*, Jerusalem: The Magnes Press, The Hebrew University of Jerusalem, 1970, pp. 343–433 (Hebrew).

[14]Lapide, *A Century of U.S. Aliya*, p. 45.

[15]*Ibid.*, p. 45.

[16]American olim are estimated by Lapide, p. 132. On the estimated number of all olim, see *Statistical Yearbook of Israel*, 1971, p. 125, Table E/1.

of registered American citizens under the protection of the American consulate in Jerusalem in 1902.[17].

A second related point concerns the shift in the motivations for aliya and in the characteristics of olim. Toward the end of the nineteenth century, American aliya was increasingly characterized by a stream of young, American pioneers, agriculturists and secularists, joining or establishing Jewish settlements outside of the "holy" cities.[18] Unlike prior American olim, these Americans were part of the growing *Yishuv* (Jewish settlement) who were inspired by secular nationalism, emphasized the need and value for Jewish agricultural labor, and formed part of what is referred to as the First and Second aliya.

It is clear, nevertheless, that American immigration to the land of Israel prior to World War I did not constitute an independent stream or wave of migration. Initially, the movement was motivated by traditional religious commitments and subsequently secular-nationalists from America (these "Americans" were largely recent immigrants from Eastern Europe to America) joined other Jews in settling agricultural lands. To understand the nature of this early aliya and to prepare the way for the analysis of subsequent immigration waves an additional question must be raised: Why did so few American Jews immigrate to the land of Israel?

The small number of American olim is not surprising or unexpected given what is known of the American Jewish community and the Jewish settlement in the land of Israel during this period. In general, there was little "pull" to the land of Israel and almost no "push" from the United States. Indeed, the pull was in the opposite direction—to America, not away from it.

Except for the few who were strongly motivated by religious or secular ideologies, the small number of Americans who became olim is consistent with the difficulties of travel, of pioneering, of foreign domination and the barrier of distance. In general, few Jews from anywhere came to settle in the land of Israel—there were about 25,000 Jews in the land of Israel in the 1880's and by 1914 the Jewish settlement numbered less than 85,000.[19] But in addition to

[17] Lapide does not document his source for this and all other figures cited so it is impossible to determine its accuracy. See pp. 45–50.

[18] On the general pattern, *cf.* Dinur, "The Historical Foundations of the Rebirth of Israel," pp. 589–593.

[19] *Ibid.*, pp. 588–589.

the general lack of "pull" factors to encourage aliya, there were opposite pulls to America. Indeed the attraction of Jews from around the world, but in particular from Eastern Europe where there were religious and economic persecutions, was to the "new Zion," the promised land of America.

Beginning with a small population of about 15,000 Jews in 1840, the Jewish community of the United States increased fifteenfold by 1880 to almost a quarter of a million, doubled two more times to one-million by 1900, and further tripled by 1917. This Jewish "population explosion" came in large part from waves of Eastern European migrants who made their choice of a promised land when they came to America; the land of Israel was simply not the land of "opportunity" and did not loom very large in their consciousness.[20]

Up to the 1880's the size of the American Jewish population was too small to contribute much to aliya; subsequently, the social composition of the American Jewish population precluded mass out-migration. Most American Jews, during this early period, were newly acculturating Central or Eastern Europeans who either wanted or had begun to share some of the economic rewards of industrializing America. The country whose history was being shaped and defined by immigration could hardly serve as a major source of aliya; the nation that attempted to be a beacon to all was particularly attractive to politically and religiously oppressed Jews. In a sense America and Israel "competed" for the refugees of world Jewry. Given the choice, few Jewish refugees immigrated to the land of Israel. Once in America, most Jews no longer thought of themselves as refugees. The land of Israel was distant both psychologically as well as geographically.

AMERICAN ALIYA IN THE MANDATORY PERIOD

American aliya continued on a small scale after World War I. In contrast to the absence of immigration records for the early American aliya, official statistics are available for the British

[20]See Oscar and Mary Handlin, "A Century of Jewish Immigration to the United States," *The American Jewish Year Book*, Vol. 50 (1948–49), pp. 78–80.

Mandatory Period showing the number of registered legal immigrants to Palestine by country of origin, 1919–1948. From these data, a first approximation of the volume of American aliya during these three decades may be obtained.

Data in Table 1 show one set of official registration statistics on the number of immigrants to Palestine from the United States, 1919–1948. According to these data, 6,613 American olim were registered as immigrants, an average of 220 per year for 30 years, representing 1.5 percent of all registered olim. Fluctuation in the volume of aliya should be noted, specifically the increase in annual numbers during the late 1920's and 1930's and the sharp reduction

TABLE 1

Registered olim from the United States, Mandatory Period, 1919–1948: Numbers and rate per 1,000 total olim

Period	*Number*		
	*Total**	*Average per year*	*Per 1,000 total registered olim*
Total Mandatory (1919–48)	6,613	220	15
Third Aliya (1919–23)	601	122	17
Fourth Aliya (1924–31)	1,985	248	24
Fifth Aliya (1932–38)	3,854	551	20
During and after World War II (1939–48)	173	17	2

*Includes only legal immigrants from the United States registered by place of origin.

Source: Data on American and total registered olim were adapted from Moshe Sicron, *Immigration to Israel, 1948–1953, Statistical Supplement,* Falk Project for Economic Research in Israel and Central Bureau of Statistics, Special Series No. 60, Jerusalem, December 1957, p. 6, Table A8.

during the war years. In particular, American aliya during the "fifth aliya," 1932–1938, averaged over 500 per year; owing to the general increase in immigration to Palestine during this period, the proportion of American olim relative to total olim declined slightly.

The increase in the number of American olim during the 1930's coincided with the economic depression in the United States and perhaps reflected the general trend toward emigration from America. (During the early 1930's net immigration from the United States was negative for the only time in American history.) Unlike other immigrant groups in America, few Jews wanted to return to their countries of origin (i.e., Eastern Europe) and, if motivated to emigrate, were somewhat more inclined toward Palestine as their "national homeland." Subsequent to the increases in American aliya during the 1930's, a significant decline in aliya resulted from conditions associated with World War II. These fluctuations in American aliya parallel the changing rates of all immigration to Palestine.

There is general agreement in most discussions of American aliya during the Mandatory Period that: a) aliya from the United States was low, relative to the total aliya and to the size of the Jewish population in America, and continuous from the pre-Mandatory period; b) fluctuations in the flow of American olim to Palestine were tied to the U.S. economic situation in the 1930's and the general slowdown of aliya during World War II. There is wide disagreement, however, about the absolute numbers of American olim who arrived in Palestine.

It is almost impossible and in large part unnecessary to review all the various guesses and estimates that have been made about American aliya during the Mandatory Period. Few authors provide specific references for their estimates and, hence, the source or sources of all the numerical confusion cannot be traced. Moreover, since Jewish immigration was a sensitive political and ideological issue during these decades, it is not unexpected that variations in the reporting of immigration figures were a function of considerations other than technical, statistical, or demographic. Yet arguments over the "exact" number must be placed in some perspective. Without plunging into a detailed debate about contradictory data that are irreconcilable, we may note several major points:

1. The figures presented in Table 1 were prepared by Sicron[21]

[21]See source cited bottom of Table 1.

from official data of registered olim by "country of origin." Data available from the *Statistical Yearbook of Palestine* are consistent with these data, except for the 1932–38 period. According to the data reported by the British government, the number of persons registered as immigrants 1932–38, whose previous place of residence was the United States, was 5,933.[22] This averages to 848 per year (but ranges from a high of 1,892 American olim in 1935 to a low of 121 American olim in 1938), representing 28 per 1,000 total registered immigrants of the fifth aliya. If we accept the higher figure for 1932–38, American aliya totals 8,692 for the three decades in place of 6,613.

2. Some confirmation of the higher figure is provided by Lestschinsky.[23] Detailed data he collected from a variety of sources place the number of American olim, defined by country of origin, at over 8,000 for this period; the number of American olim defined by country of birth is closer to Sicron's figure of around 6,600. Apparently, much confusion surrounded the distinction between Americans defined by country of birth, by national citizenship, by country of last residence, or by origin. Because of the large proportion of immigrants among the American Jewish population, distinctions between country of birth and country of last residence among American olim are critical. For example, the annual report of the Palestine Department of Migration listed the number of immigrants to Palestine from the United States in 1936 by country of birth (109), country of citizenship (325), and "country of past abode" (387).[24] While these numbers are small by any criterion, cumulative differences over several years are of sufficient magnitude as to yield discrepant estimates using one or the other definition.

3. The highest estimate of American olim during the Mandatory Period is 11,195 (with 3,585 returning to America—leaving less than 8,000 American settlers).[25] It is not at all clear how these data were obtained, how the number of return migrants was

[22]See data in *Statistical Abstract of Palestine,* 1937–38, Jerusalem, 1938, p. 36, Table 40 and the 1943 volume, p. 19.

[23]Jacob Lestschinsky, "Jewish Migrations, 1840–1956," in L. Finkelstein (ed.), *The Jews,* Vol. II, 3rd edition, Philadelphia: Jewish Publication Society, 1960, p. 1572, Table 8 and p. 1584, Table 14.

[24]Palestine, Department of Migration, *Annual Report,* 1936, Jerusalem, 1937, Tables IV, V, VI, VIII.

[25]Lapide, *A Century of U.S. Aliya,* p. 132; similar figures are presented in the *Encyclopedia of Zionism and Israel,* ed. Raphael Patai, New York: Herzl Press/McGraw-Hill, 1971, Vol. I, pp. 26–27.

determined, and whether the data relate to North Americans or Americans. Without further support, this estimate must be treated as an exaggeration. Nevertheless, this level of American aliya represents only 3 percent of all aliya 1919–48 and in no way distorts the notion that the volume was small.

4. If we assume that the level of American aliya 1919–48 is somewhere between the lowest and highest estimate, we may conclude with only a small margin of error that no more than 9,000 Americans (by the most generous definition) immigrated to Palestine during the British Mandatory Period, averaging less than 300 per year, and less than 3 percent of all olim.

5. Finally we know very little either of the social characteristics of American olim during this period or their staying power, i.e., rates of return migration. We may suspect that many more young *chalutzim* were among the American olim of the Mandatory Period than in the earlier aliya, more were imbued with secular nationalism, and were more conspicuously American either because they were born in the United States or had spent a longer time living there. Given what is known of general rates of return migration from Palestine, it is not unreasonable to suggest that 30 percent (plus or minus 10 percent) of the American olim returned to America.

AMERICAN ALIYA TO THE STATE OF ISRAEL

The numerically small flow of American olim, beginning in the mid-nineteenth century and gathering some momentum in the 1930's, continued after the establishment of the State of Israel in 1948. The period 1948 to 1971 may be subdivided into three periods: 1) 1948–60; 2) 1961–66; 3) 1967–71. The data in Table 2 show the number of American immigrants, 1948–1971, defined by place of last residence, and include tourists settling in Israel. These are official data, gathered from the files of the Israel Central Bureau of Statistics, and have hitherto been unpublished. (Others have relied on data from Jewish Agency records both in Israel and abroad, newspaper reports, estimates from Zionist organizations, or from the Association of Americans and Canadians in Israel. These data are often biased for political or ideological purposes and in no case can they be used without important qualifications and reservations. As far as can be determined, data in the files of the Central Bureau of Statistics are the most complete and accurate in Israel.)

The total number of American olim arriving in Israel between 1948–60 was 5,528, ranging from a low of 187 in 1956 (part of the period when Israel was facing severe economic problems) to a high of close to 1,000 in 1949. These data relate only to declared immigrants and do not count temporary residents. Other estimates, based on alternative statistical sources and using other estimation procedures to include the non-declared immigrants, range to a high of 7,595 American olim and "pseudo-olim" for this period.[26]

On the average, about 425 American olim arrived yearly in Israel (using official data), close to double the average yearly number of American olim during the three decades to 1948. Nevertheless the rate of American aliya per 1,000 total olim never exceeded 18 and appears to have been significantly lower than during the overall Mandatory Period and considerably below the periods covering the Fourth and Fifth aliya. In large part, the increase in annual numbers of American olim along with the increase in annual rates per 100,000 estimated American Jewish population was counterbalanced by the even larger increase in total aliya. Therefore, for the first decade or so following the establishment of the State of Israel the number of American and total olim increased—the latter substantially more than former. As a consequence American olim represented far less than one percent of all olim during the period 1948–60.

The period 1961–1966 (and the first six months of 1967) witnessed several significant developments in the history of American aliya. These changes have often been ignored or overlooked because of the more conspicuous and dramatic changes in American aliya and in Israeli society following the Six Day War of 1967. A careful examination of American aliya during the six years preceding that war, however, is essential in placing contemporary American aliya in perspective.

First, the number of American immigrants increased noticeably. During the six years 1961–66, 4,763 declared immigrants from the United States arrived in Israel, about 800 annually. To these, however, must be added another category, "temporary residents."

[26]Lapide, *A Century of American Aliya*, p. 129; *cf.* Neufeld, *op. cit.*, pp. 128–133.

TABLE 2

Number of American olim[a] and rate per 1,000 total olim, 1948–1971

	Immigrants[b]	*Temporary residents[c]*	*Total*	*Per 1,000 total olim[d]*
1948	510[e]	N.A.	510	5
1949	990[e]	N.A.	990	4
1950	761	N.A.	761	4
1951	579	N.A.	579	3
1952	292	N.A.	292	12
1953	202	N.A.	202	18
1954	294	N.A.	294	16
1955	321	N.A.	321	9
1956	187	N.A.	187	3
1957	271	N.A.	271	4
1958	378	N.A.	378	14
1959	330	N.A.	330	14
1960	413	N.A.	413	17
1961	592	1,279	1,871	35
1962	619	1,733	2,352	35
1963	868	1,982	2,850	39
1964	1,006	2,276	3,282	53
1965	924	2,598	3,522	91
1966	754	2,473	3,227	136
1967	665	3,383	4,048	162
1968	932	5,284	6,216	192
1969	671	5,068	5,739	152
1970	1,093	5,789	6,882	187
1971	1,049	6,315	7,364	176

[a]American by place of last residence.

[b]Includes tourists settling.

[c]After 1969 these are defined officially as "potential immigrants."

[d]Total olim, 1948–60, do not include temporary residents; total olim 1961–68 includes temporary residence; total olim, 1969–71 includes "potential immigrants."

[e]Data on country of residence (U.S.) are not available officially for 1948 and 1949. Estimates were prepared based on country of birth (U.S.) data. The average ratio of country of birth (U.S.) to country of last residence (U.S.) 1950–53 was applied to country of birth (U.S.) data 1948–49.

Source: Data on American olim are from unpublished official data in the files of the Central Bureau of Statistics, Israel. Data on total olim were derived from Central Bureau of Statistics, *Statistical Yearbook of Israel*, No. 22 (1971), Tables D/1, E/1 and from unpublished data in the files of the Central Bureau of Statistics, Israel.

Defined formally, temporary residents were "foreign citizens entering Israel for a stay of over six months for purposes of temporary work, study, etc."[27] This ambiguous status was selected by many Americans not eager to risk the possible loss of their American citizenship by declaring formal "immigrant" status. (Before a May 1967 American Supreme Court decision, it was not clear that Americans could hold dual citizenship. Since immigrant status in Israel confirms citizenship automatically, many American olim opted for "temporary resident" status.[28]) To be sure, a large number, perhaps a majority, of Americans who were "temporary residents" stayed only for the purpose of temporary work or study. Clearly, however, these Americans were not tourists and a significant, if only a minority, proportion settled. Between 1961 and 1966 over 12,000 Americans were registered as temporary residents, averaging more than 2,000 annually.

As part of the increase in the numbers of American olim (including temporary residents), and some slowdown in the aliya of other Jews, the relative proportion of American olim of the total aliya increased noticeably in these six years. In 1961, 35 out of every 1,000 olim to Israel were American; by 1966, 13.6 percent of all olim were Americans. In no period prior to 1961 was the rate of American aliya as high.

One central conclusion to be derived from these data is that the increase in American aliya, in absolute volume and in the rate per 1,000 total olim, had its roots *before* the events of June, 1967; the Six Day War accelerated the tempo of a phenomenon that had already started.

This is not to minimize the importance of the Six Day War, through its impact on American Jewish life and on the shape and character of Israeli society, in stimulating American aliya. Indeed between 1967 and 1971, the number of Americans who were "immigrants" averaged 882 per year, totaling 4,410 for the five year period; the number of "temporary residents" (referred to formally after June 1969 as "potential immigrants") averaged over 5,000 per year and totaled more than 25,000, 1967–71. Adding these two categories together, a total of over 30,000 American olim arrived in Israel in a five-year period. How many of these olim have or will

[27]For definitions of "temporary residents," "potential immigrants," and other migration categories see *Statistical Abstract of Israel,* 1971, No. 22, pp. xxxviii–xxxix.

[28]This is one of the central themes in Harold R. Isaacs, *American Jews in Israel,* New York: The John Day Co., 1966.

return, in what ways those who stay become part of Israeli society, are some of the issues that will be studied over the next several years. What is clear at this stage is that the increased volume of American olim after 1967 is unprecedented; it is also clear that not all the increase can be attributed simply to the Six Day War and its aftermath since these patterns were emerging well before June, 1967.

Another feature of the post-1967 American aliya is the increase in the proportion of total olim who are from the United States. Although a clear pattern of increase in the rate of American aliya per 1,000 total olim may be discerned in the late 1950's, the levels reached in the post-1967 period are unprecedented. Some fluctuation in these rates reflects external events affecting total aliya, in particular the unexpected increase in the immigration to Israel of Soviet Jewry in the last several years.

Data in Table 3 summarize the changes in American aliya 1919–71. The data are official estimates and are grouped into

TABLE 3

American[a] olim, 1919–71, summary of official data

	1919–48[b]	*1948–60[c]*	*1961–68[d]*	*1969–71[e]*
Number	6,613	5,528	27,368	19,985
Average per year	220	425	3,421	6,662
Per 1,000 Total olim	15	6	73	172
Per 100,000 estimated U.S. Jewish population per year	4.9	8.1	59.5	113.3

[a]American by place of last residence.
[b]These are Sicron's estimates; see discussion in text for other estimates.
[c]Includes immigrants and tourists settling.
[d]Includes immigrants, tourists settling, and temporary residents.
[e]Includes immigrants, potential immigrants, tourists settling.
Source: Data on American olim and total olim derived from sources listed in Tables 1 and 2; estimates of the U.S. Jewish population were derived from data appearing in the *American Jewish Year Book.*

somewhat different periods, reflecting changes in the definitions of olim, particularly the shift from "temporary resident" status to "potential olim" in 1969. The dramatic increases over more than a half-century in the absolute number and yearly average number of American olim, and changes in the rate of American aliya per 1,000 olim and per 100,000 estimated U.S. Jewish population, per year, are clearly evident.

SOCIAL CHARACTERISTICS OF AMERICAN OLIM

Up to this point the analysis has focused on the changing volume of American aliya and technical issues related to the various definitions of American olim. Another set of questions revolve around the types of Americans who have immigrated to Israel. Who are American olim? What are their social characteristics? How do they differ from other olim? Do American olim represent a cross-section of the American Jewish population? In what ways do American olim fit the stereotyped versions of the "American in Israel"? These are some of the elementary but essential questions that demand empirical comparisons between the social characteristics of American olim and those of selected populations: other olim, American Jews, and Israelis. Despite important defects in the quality and detail of existing data-sources on American olim and the American Jewish population, a more or less consistent picture of the types of Americans immigrating to Israel in the contemporary period emerges.

Undoubtedly, there have been changes in the social characteristics of American olim over the last several decades, if only because the social characteristics of American Jews have changed radically. However, no source of data is available that provides a dynamic portrait of the changing characteristics of American olim or that permits their retrospective reconstruction. Hence, the analysis to be presented only sketches a cross-sectional picture of the types of contemporary American Jews immigrating to Israel.[29]

[29]For some impressionistic but methodologically problematic analyses of pre-1967 social characteristics of American olim, see Isaacs, *op. cit.*, and Gerald Engel, "North American Jewish Settlers in Israel," *American Jewish Year Book*, Vol. 71 (1970), pp. 161–187.

Several major objectives guide the analyses that follow. First, insight into the general determinants of American aliya may be obtained from an investigation of the social characteristics of American olim. The fact, for example, that American olim are concentrated in particular age categories or are more likely to define themselves as "religious" becomes an important first clue in the identification and isolation of the complex matrix of factors determining the social composition of immigration streams from the United States. From the types of American olim, we may infer the determinants of American aliya.

A related theme in the analysis of the characteristics of American olim is the extent to which the selectivity of American olim constitutes a "drain" of American Jewish human resources. To be sure, the small number of American olim relative to the population size of American Jewry reduces the quantitative impact of American aliya on the social composition of the American Jewish community. Nevertheless, certain implications about the Jewish organizational and religious structure of the American Jewish community may be inferred from the Jewish organizational and religious characteristics of American olim. This may be particularly dramatic and conspicuous in middle-sized and smaller American Jewish communities where the aliya of even a small number of key Jewish leaders may indeed reflect a Jewish "brain drain."

A third perspective in the analysis of the social characteristics of American olim is the degree to which American olim are conspicuous within Israeli society because of their exceptional social and economic characteristics. Whether or not American olim are representative of the American Jewish population, they may be exceptional when compared to the Israeli population. Clearly any investigation of American aliya must deal with the similarities and differences between the social characteristics of American olim and the Israeli population not only for the purpose of studying the integration and absorption of American olim into Israeli society but for the equally important objective of understanding the basic processes of American aliya. Analogously, the social characteristics of American olim need to be compared to olim from other countries.

These themes in the analysis of the social characteristics of American olim—providing clues to the determinants of American aliya, examining the extent of the selectivity of American olim from the point of view of the American Jewish community, Israeli society, and other olim—constitute the framework for interpreting the empirical findings derived from registration and survey data in Israel.

A convenient starting point in the analysis of the social characteristics of American olim is to examine two variables that have been linked to important areas of American Jewish heterogeneity and are reflective of the particular historical development of the American Jewish community—region and generation status.

REGION

It is clear even to the casual observer of the American Jewish scene that region of residence is a powerful differentiator of American Jewry. Region of residence is important precisely because it is inextricably interrelated with almost every social, economic, ethnic-religious variable subdividing American Jews. In part this is true of states and certainly true of city-suburban variation. However the sample of American olim drawn from the absorption survey is too small to permit a detailed classification of American cities and states where olim resided before aliya.

As a preliminary step, the last place of residence in the United States of olim was classified according to broad geographic regions comparable to those used to classify the estimated distribution of the American Jewish population. Remarkably little difference appears in the distributions of American olim (1969–70) and of the U.S. Jewish population (1968) according to regions: About 65 percent of both populations are from the Northeast, 10 percent are from the South, 13 percent are from the North Central region and the remainder are from the West (Table 4). An examination of the two states with the largest American Jewish populations (New York and California) reveal that 46 percent of the American olim resided in New York before aliya and 9 percent immigrated to Israel from California. Compared to the estimated distribution of the American Jewish population, these data show a slight overrepresentation among olim of New Yorkers (46 percent compared to 43 percent) and an underrepresentation of olim from California (9 percent compared to 12 percent). Whether these comparisons permit the inference of regional or state selectivity in aliya or are an artifact of sampling error (of American olim in the survey) or estimation error (of the American Jewish population) must await more detailed study. At this point it appears reasonable to conclude that no conspicuous selectivity by state or region characterizes recent American aliya.

TABLE 4
Distribution of American olim and U.S. Jewish population by region

Region	*American olim, 1969–70*	*U.S. Jewish population, 1968*
Northeast	66.2	64.0
North Central	12.8	12.5
South	9.7	10.3
West	11.3	13.2
Total	100.0	100.0

Source: Data on American olim refer to region of last residence and are from special tabulations of the sample survey on immigrant absorption in the files of the Central Bureau of Statistics, Israel; the distribution of the U.S. Jewish population is based on estimates presented in Alvin Chenkin, "Jewish Population in the United States," *American Jewish Year Book*, Vol. 70 (1969), pp. 260–72.

GENERATION STATUS

In dealing with the question, who is an American oleh, it was concluded that "American" did not necessarily imply American born. In terms of the social characteristics of American olim, we may now inquire, how "American" are American olim? More specifically, how does the distribution of American olim by generation status compare to the distribution of the American Jewish population by generation status? (Generation status refers to whether American- or foreign-born and, if American born, whether parents were American- or foreign-born.)

Indeed, most sociological research, implicitly or explicitly, has concentrated on the importance of generation status as the critical analytic dimension in understanding American Jewish life.[30] Any attempt to clarify the transformation of the American Jewish community during the last century, to analyze the dynamics of variation within and between Jewish communities in the United States, or to project the direction of change toward which American Jews are moving must take as its elementary starting point an analysis of the trends and variations in generation status. A wide range of behavioral, attitudinal, and structural variables have been linked theoretically and empirically to the generation status of American Jews. Hence, it is important to discover the extent to which American aliya is selective of Jews in one generation status or another.

In the early American aliya, before World War I, perhaps 80–90 percent of American olim were not born in the United States. Some were American by citizenship; all were American by place of last residence. This reflected in large part the fact that most Jews in the United States at that time were not American-born. The American Jewish population was transformed during the course of the twentieth century to a predominantly native-born population; hence, it is not unexpected that American aliya has increasingly become a movement of native-born Americans.

Results of the immigration survey point to the fact that about 70 percent of the American olim 1969-70 were born in the United States and 30 percent were foreign-born residents of the United States before aliya (i.e., first-generation Americans). Among the American-born olim 60 percent were of parents born in the United States (i.e., at least third-generation Americans) and 40 percent were of foreign-born parents (i.e., second-generation Americans).

Comparisons between the generation-status distributions of American olim and the American Jewish population are hampered by the absence of national American data on the generation status of Jews. Most Jewish community studies taken during the 1960's reveal that foreign-born Jews represent between 20 and 25 percent of the total Jewish population, while an estimated 37 percent of the New York Jewish population are foreign born.[31] However, the survey data on American olim relate to the adult population only (18 years of age and older) and thus Jewish community studies covering

[30]See Goldstein and Goldscheider, *Jewish Americans.*

[31]Data reported in Sidney Goldstein, "American Jewry, 1970," pp. 53–56.

the total population, including children, are more weighted toward native-born Americans.

In general it does not appear that contemporary American aliya is conspicuously selective of foreign- or native-born Americans. However, some selectivity seems to be related to the difference between the second generation (Americans born of foreign-born parents) and the third generation (Americans born of American-born parents). Contemporary American olim tend to be more concentrated among American born of American-born parents (40 percent) than might be predicted from the estimated distribution of the adult American Jewish population. Some insight into this question emerges from an analysis of age differentiation between American olim and the American Jewish population.

Clearly, there is a strong correlation between generation status and age (see Table 5). Almost all (91 percent) of American-born

TABLE 5

Generation status[a] of American olim, 1969–70, by age

	GENERATION STATUS			
Age group	*First generation*	*Second generation*	*Third generation*	*Total[b]*
18–24	15.2	16.2	51.0	31.8
25–34	4.4	27.0	45.3	27.1
35–44	8.7	16.2	1.9	7.3
45–54	19.6	27.0	0.0	13.2
55–64	15.2	10.8	1.9	8.6
65+	37.0	2.7	0.0	11.9
TOTAL	100.0	100.0	100.0	100.0
Percent in each generation	30.4	29.4	40.1	100.0

[a]Generation status refers to place of birth and related to status in the United States. For definition, see text.

[b]Total includes small number of unknown Generation Status.

Source: Special tabulations of the sample survey on immigrant absorption in the files of the Central Bureau of Statistics, Israel.

olim of American-born parents are less than 30 years of age and over half are age 18–24. In contrast, 72 percent of American olim not born in the United States are over age 45 and half are 55 years of age and older. Put in another way, of all American olim age 65 and over, 95 percent were not American born; of all American olim 18–29 years of age, over 70 percent were born in the United States of American-born parents. Given this strong relationship between age and generation status, the question of selectivity of American aliya by generation status can be investigated indirectly by examining selectivity by age. The analysis of the age distribution of American olim has the added advantage of being comparable to data available on the American Jewish population. We shall, however, return to the direct examination of generation status in conjunction with other social characteristics of American olim.

AGE, SEX, MARITAL STATUS

In addition to the importance of age selectivity in American aliya as an indirect reflection of generation status, age (and sex) distributions are fundamental to understanding the demographic and social structure of populations.[32] Furthermore one of the few universal empirical generalizations about internal and international migration relates to the tendency of young adults to migrate more often than others. Hence we now turn to the question of whether American olim are characterized by particular patterns of age and sex when compared to the American Jewish community, the Israeli population, and other olim

No systematic pattern of difference emerges when the age distributions of American olim and all olim in 1970 are compared (Table 6). In general olim tend to be young, approximately half are below age 25. Whereas the average ages of American and total olim are almost the same, American olim tend to be relatively more concentrated in the 20–34 age group (39 percent compared to 30 percent of all olim) and less concentrated in the "middle ages," 35–64 years of age.

[32]See the discussion in Calvin Goldscheider, *Population, Modernization, and Social Structure*, Boston: Little, Brown & Co., 1971, Chapters 1 and 8.

TABLE 6
Age and sex distribution of American olim, total olim, and U.S. Jewish population

	American olim, 1970		*Total olim, 1970*		*U.S. Jewish pop., 1957*	
Age group	*Percent*	*Percent male*	*Percent*	*Percent male*	*Percent*	*Percent male*
Total	100.0	47.3	100.0	47.6	100.0	N.A.
Under 15*	22.4	53.0	22.1	51.2	23.2	N.A.
15–19*	7.1	46.9	11.6	48.2	6.9	45.7
20–24	18.1	36.1	15.8	40.2	4.6	54.5
25–34	20.6	44.3	14.2	47.1	13.1	46.8
35–44	8.9	54.2	10.6	48.8	14.5	44.7
35–64	12.0	49.0	17.2	49.1	27.7	50.1
65+	10.8	53.0	8.4	46.9	10.0	45.7
Median Age	25.9	––	25.3	––	36.7	––

*For U.S. Jewish population the lowest age categories are "under 14" and "14–24."
Source: Data on American olim were tabulated from unpublished immigration registration records in the files of the Central Bureau of Statistics, Israel; data on total olim were adapted from Central Bureau of Statistics, *Immigration to Israel, 1970,* Special Series No. 349, Jerusalem, 1971, Tables 5 and 8; data on the U.S. Jewish population, 1957 were calculated from U.S. Bureau of the Census, "Religion Reported by the Civilian Population of the United States: March 1957," *Current Population Reports,* Series P-20, No. 79, February, 1958, Tables 5 and 7.

The contrast between the age distributions of American olim and the American Jewish population is more distinct and significant. The population of American olim is, on average, ten years younger than the U.S. Jewish population and is overrepresentative of the 20–34 age group and underrepresentative of the 35–64 age group. Whereas 18 percent of American olim are age 20–24 and 21 percent are 25–34 years of age, only 5 percent and 13 percent, respectively, of the American Jewish population are in these age groups. At the other end of the age scale, over one out of every four American Jews are 45–64 years of age compared to less than one out of every eight American olim. In short, out of every ten American olim approximately four are age 20–34 and two are age 35–64; out of every ten American Jews the reverse is the case—about two are age 20–34 and four are 35–64. This finding about the age selectivity of American olim is most consistent with our guess that American olim tend to overconcentrate among American born of American-born parents and are underrepresentative of the American born of foreign-born parents. Third-generation American Jews are most typified by the 20–34 age group and second-generation American Jews by the 35–64 age group. Interestingly the proportions of American olim and the American Jewish population in the 65-and-over age category are about the same, adding weight to the argument that the selectivity of American olim by generation status is not to be located in the distribution between those born in the United States and the foreign born.

It should be emphasized that the age distribution of the American Jewish population refers to 1957. The question naturally arises whether the American Jewish population has become younger in the dozen or so years since 1957 to account for the younger age distribution among American olim. While no definitive answer can be given, there are no signs that such is the case. There are, for example, no indications that fertility among American Jews has increased after 1957 to influence the age structure. Indeed, if the past is any guide, we should expect that American Jewish fertility followed the prevailing pattern and trend of the general American population, which since 1957 has been downward.[33] Moreover comparing data on American olim to information obtained from 13 Jewish communities studied since 1957 supports the finding that American aliya is selective of the young. From these community studies we know that between 10 and 17 percent of the Jewish population are concentrated in the 15–24 age group and between 23–28 percent are in the 45–64 age group.[34] This contrasts to 25 percent and 12 percent of American olim in these respective age categories.

In addition to the selectivity of American olim by age there is selectivity by sex (Table 6). American olim tend to be more concentrated among women, particularly in the early adult ages, 20–34. The sharp undersupply of American male olim 20–24 should be contrasted with the high proportion of males age 35–44 (54 percent) and age 65 and over (53 percent). Although all young olim are somewhat more concentrated among women, Americans accentuate the pattern: Approximately 60 percent of the American olim in the age groups 20–24 and 25–29 are women. Among the

[33]For a discussion of Jewish fertility, see *ibid.*, Chapter 10; general American fertility is discussed briefly in Chapter 6.

[34]Data derived from Goldstein, "American Jewry, 1970," p. 58, Table 14.

middle and older ages, males are more likely to undertake aliya. Detailed data not shown indicate that fully 55 percent of the over-70 age group are males. This is surprising given the higher male mortality rates in the middle and older ages but perhaps understandable given the tendency for greater economic and family dependence among widows and their general low rates of migration.

One clue to these patterns of age and sex selectivity lies in the comparative analysis of marital status for American olim, all olim, and the U.S. Jewish population (Table 7). Comparing the marital status of American and total olim, only relatively small differences emerge, with a tendency among American olim toward a lower proportion married. The comparison between American olim and the U.S. Jewish population, however, reveals strikingly sharp differentiation. About twice as many American olim are single when compared to the U.S. Jewish population and the contrast is stronger among women. In support of our earlier hypothesis, widowed men

TABLE 7

Marital status distribution of American olim, total olim, and U.S. Jewish population

	American olim, 1970[a]		*Total olim 1970*[a]		*U.S. Jewish population 1957*[b]	
Marital status	*Male*	*Female*	*Male*	*Female*	*Male*	*Female*
Single	44.2	45.2	42.4	38.8	23.5	17.7
Married	49.3	43.5	52.9	46.7	73.0	67.4
Widowed	3.4	7.4	2.7	11.1	2.5	13.4
Divorced	3.2	4.0	2.0	3.4	1.0	1.4
TOTAL	100.0	100.0	100.0	100.0	100.0	100.0

[a]15 years of age and over
[b]14 years of age and over
Source: Data on American olim were tabulated from unpublished immigration registration records in the files of the Central Bureau of Statistics, Israel; data on total olim were adapted from Central Bureau of Statistics, *Immigration to Israel,* 1970, Special Series No. 349, Jerusalem, 1971, Table 10; data on U.S. Jewish population, adapted from U.S. Census Bureau, Current Population Survey of 1957, as cited in Goldstein, "American Jewry, 1970," Table 4.

tend to come to Israel in slightly larger proportions than their representation in the American Jewish population while considerably fewer widows go on aliya than their proportion in the American Jewish population.

Some of the differences in the marital status distributions of American olim and the American Jewish population are the results of the different age distributions of these two populations: American olim are younger and, hence, are more likely to be nonmarried than Jews in the United States. Can the large differences in the proportion married among American olim and the American Jewish population be attributed solely to the differential distributions of these populations by age? It seems an unreasonable assumption. A crude empirical examination—crude because detailed data by sex and marital status for all ages are not available for the U.S. Jewish population—shows that, at least for the four age groups for which data are available, male and female olim are much more likely to be nonmarried than the Jewish population of the United States (Table 8). Most importantly, differences are pronounced in the 25–34 age group: 70 percent of U.S. Jewish males and 90 percent of U.S. Jewish females are married in this age category compared to only about half of the American olim.

In sum, American aliya is selective by three major demographic characteristics: age, sex, and marital status. Olim from the United States clearly do not represent a demographic cross-section of the American Jewish population. A description of the demographic selectivity of American aliya reveals: a) American olim tend to be young; b) young women are more likely to undertake aliya than young men; c) young, unmarried women are more likely to be olim than married women; d) widowers are more prone to aliya than widows.

Taken together these data suggest that one facilitating factor in the aliya of Americans relates to the extent of age-marital-family attachments. Young and single are two social characteristics providing for the greatest freedom of movement; widowhood, at least for men, operates in a similar way. Moreover, the unusually high proportion of young American women olim who are unmarried suggests that at least for some, Israel is perceived to represent a potential marriage market. It may also be expected that the highest rates of return migration (*yerida*) among American olim will characterize precisely those groups who have the greatest freedom to move, i.e., the young and unmarried. Those who come

TABLE 8
Proportion married of American olim and U.S. Jewish population by age and sex

	American olim, 1969–70		*U.S. Jewish population, 1957*	
Age	*Male*	*Female*	*Male*	*Female*
25–34	50.0	53.6	69.3	88.6
35–44	75.0	83.4	92.6	87.5
45–64	83.3	66.7	90.0	75.0
65+	66.7	40.0	80.0	42.5
TOTAL*	57.4	42.9	73.0	67.4

*For American olim total is for those 18 years of age and older; For U.S. Jewish population total is for those 14 years of age and older.
Source: Data on American olim were obtained from special tabulations of the sample survey on immigrant absorption in the files of the Central Bureau of Statistics, Israel; data on the U.S. Jewish population were adapted from U.S. Census Bureau, Current Population Survey of 1957, as cited in Goldstein, "American Jewry, 1970," Table 4.

to Israel in search of a mate either succeed and stay, succeed and leave with their mate, fail and stay, or fail and leave. We suspect that the largest majority return to the United States in the same marital status category they had upon arrival in Israel.

EDUCATION AND OCCUPATION

Educational attainment and occupational skills are social characteristics of American olim that are important from the point of view of the American Jewish community and Israeli society. The relatively small number of olim from the United States precludes any real quantitative impact of educational and occupational selectivity on the American Jewish community. This is not necessarily the case for Israeli society, particularly in specialized occupational categories. In any case, the education and occupation of American olim are significant indicators of the types of Americans undertaking aliya.

The extraordinary educational achievements of American Jews including the dramatic increases in college attendance among the younger generation are well documented trends.[35] It is therefore not unexpected that American olim are well educated (Table 9): Over 40 percent of the American olim in the survey had 16 or more years of education compared to 18 percent of all olim (1969–70) and 6 percent of the Jewish population of Israel (1970). Whereas 9 percent of the olim from the United States had less than some high school education about half of the Jewish population of Israel and over a third of all olim had less than 9 years of education.

As might be expected, these total data on American olim are distorted by complexities of age and generation status. Among American olim who were not born in the United States (first generation) 30 percent had less than a high school education and two-thirds did not attend college. In contrast, none of the American olim born in the United States of American-born parents had not graduated from high school and fully 84 percent had some college education. Bearing in mind that 21 percent of the third generation are 18-21 years of age and 38 percent are 22-24 years of age, we may safely assume that their extraordinary educational level already achieved does not represent a final stage. Indeed differences between American olim of the second and third generation who completed at least 16 years of schooling reflect this age factor.

The fact that 78 percent of the second generation and 84 percent of the third generation among American olim had some college education establishes American olim as an educational elite in Israeli society. To what extent, however, do American olim represent an educational cross-section of American Jews? Although we are dealing with small numbers of American olim, gross comparisons between the educational level of American olim and the U.S. Jewish population reveal sharp educational selectivity. The comparison is limited to 1957 data of the American Jewish population 25 years of age and over, and relates separately to males and females (Table 10).

Although the educational level of Jewish males in the United

[35]See the discussion in Goldstein and Goldscheider, *Jewish Americans*, Chapter 4; Goldstein, "American Jewry, 1970," pp. 60–68.

TABLE 9

Years of school completed, Jewish population of Israel, all olim, American olim (total and by generation status), aged 18 and over

		AMERICAN OLIM 1969–70[a]				
Years of school completed	*Jewish population of Israel 1970*	*All olim[a] 1969–70*	*Total[a]*	*First generation*	*Second generation*	*Third generation*
Less than 9 years	49.7	35.7	9.3	29.9	0.0	0.0
9–12	35.5	31.7	23.8	36.4	21.6	15.7
13–15	9.2	14.9	25.2	16.8	13.5	32.7
16+	5.6	17.7	41.7	16.8	64.9	51.5
TOTAL[b]	100.0	100.0	100.0	100.0	100.0	100.0

[a]Includes potential immigrants.
[b]Total includes small number of cases of unknown generation status.
Source: Data for all olim and Jewish population of Israel were adapted from Central Bureau of Statistics, *Survey on Absorption of Immigrants*, Special Series No. 381, Jerusalem, 1972, Table B, P. XI. Data on American olim are from special tabulations of the sample survey on immigrant absorption in the files of the Central Bureau of Statistics, Israel.

TABLE 10

Years of school completed by American olim and U.S. Jewish population 25 years of age and older, by sex

Years of school completed	*American olim, 1969–1970*			*U.S. Jewish population, 1957*		
	Total	*Male*	*Female*	*Total*	*Male*	*Female*
Elementary						
0–7	8.1	2.6	11.7	15.6	14.7	16.6
8	6.1	10.3	3.3	13.1	13.1	13.1
High school						
1–3	9.1	15.4	5.0	10.0	9.7	10.2
4	16.2	5.1	23.3	29.0	21.5	35.8
College						
1–3	18.2	10.3	23.3	12.7	12.6	12.8
4+	42.4	56.4	33.3	17.3	25.6	9.7
Not reported	0.0	0.0	0.0	2.3	2.8	1.8
TOTAL	100.0	100.0	100.0	100.0	100.0	100.0

Source: Data on American olim are from special tabulations of the sample survey on immigrant absorption in the files of the Central Bureau of Statistics, Israel; data on U.S. Jewish population derived from U.S. Census Bureau, Current Population Survey of March 1957 as cited in Goldstein, "American Jewry, 1970," Table 16.

States is high by total U.S. population standards,[36] it is clearly lower than that attained by American olim. About one out of four male Jews in the United States had completed college or attended graduate school and 38 percent had at least some college education. Among male olim, fully two-thirds attended college and over half had at least four years of college education. The difference in college attendance is even sharper among women: Among American women olim, 57 percent had some college education and one-third had at least four years of college education; among

[36]See Goldstein, "American Jewry, 1970," Table 16, p. 63.

American Jewish women the proportions are 23 and 10 percent, respectively.

Part of the differences between the educational attainment of American Jews and olim from the United States reflect age differences (and, in turn, generational differentiation) between these populations. As noted earlier, olim tend to be younger and more concentrated among the American born of American-born parents, categories associated with higher educational attainment. Some additional part of the educational differences between American olim and U.S. Jews is a function of the changing level of education among American Jews between 1957 and 1969–70. Indeed more recent data from nine Jewish communities in the United States suggest such an increase: Studies between 1958 and 1966 show that about 25 percent of the adult Jewish population in these communities had four or more years of college education.[37] This level equals the U.S. national Jewish male educational level in 1957 but is higher than the educational level attained by the total 1957 U.S. Jewish population. Nevertheless, this level remains considerably below the proportion of American olim completing at least four years of college (42 percent). Hence, the evidence available points to a clear education selectivity in American aliya.

Consistent with these data on educational selectivity, the available information from immigration records in Israel points to an unmistakable and accentuated occupational selectivity among American olim in 1970 (Table 11). Over 60 percent of the male American olim and two-thirds of the female American olim were classified on arrival in Israel as professionals; over 80 percent of the male American olim and almost all the American women olim who were in the labor force had white-collar occupations. The occupational distribution of American olim is clearly extreme even by the distortedly high white-collar concentration—particularly professional and managerial—of the American Jewish population.[38]

Comparisons between the occupational patterns of American olim on arrival in Israel and the only available national occupational data for American Jews (1957) reveal the relative over-concentration of professionals among male and female olim. Moreover the comparison points to the relative absence of managers and proprietors among American olim—whereas over a third of the U.S.

[37]*Ibid.*, Table 15, p. 62.

[38]*Ibid.*, pp. 68–79.

TABLE 11

Occupational distribution of American olim, total olim, and U.S. Jewish population by sex

	American olim 1970		*Total olim 1970*		*U.S. Jewish population 1957*	
	Male	*Female*	*Male*	*Female*	*Male*	*Female*
Professional	62.5	66.9	39.0	47.3	20.3	15.5
Managers and proprietors	4.1	0.7	1.8	4.7	35.2	9.1
Clerical workers	5.1	27.2	11.1	29.0	8.0	43.9
Sales workers	10.3	1.1	16.0	2.9	14.1	14.4
Blue-collar	17.9	4.1	32.1	16.1	22.2	17.0
TOTAL	100.0	100.0	100.0	100.0	100.0	100.0

Source: Data on American olim were tabulated from unpublished immigration records in the files of the Central Bureau of Statistics, Israel; data on total olim were adapted from Central Bureau of Statistics, *Immigration to Israel, 1970,* special series No. 349, Jerusalem, 1971, tables 18 and 19; data on total and American olim refer to occupation declared on arrival in Israel; data on the U.S. Jewish population were derived from the U.S. Census Bureau, Current Population Survey of 1957 as cited in Goldstein, "American Jewry, 1970," Table 21.

Jewish labor force was concentrated in the managerial group, only 4 percent of American olim were in this category. Similarly clerical and sales work characterized twice as many of the Jewish women working in the United States when compared to American women olim.

To be sure, the occupational distribution of the American Jewish population in 1957 is but a rough approximation of the patterns in 1970. Nevertheless information for over a dozen Jewish communities in the United States between 1958 and 1969 shows a range of 27 percent to 57 percent of the Jewish population in managerial positions and a range of 18 percent to 36 percent in professional positions.[39] Comparisons between the extremes of

[39] *Ibid.*, Table 18, p. 70.

these ranges and the occupational distribution of American olim on arrival in Israel adds confirmation to the view that American aliya is overselective of professionals and underselective of managers. Moreover, selectivity extends to specific occupations within general categories. For example, detailed data not shown point to the fact that over half of the American olim classified as "professionals" were either teachers or engineers.

It should be noted that compared to the Jewish population in Israel (1970), olim from all countries tend to be more concentrated in white-collar, particularly professional, occupations. In Israel about 16 percent of the labor force is in the professional category, 19 percent are managers and clerks and a total of 43 percent are in white-collar occupations.[40] In contrast, data in Table 11 show that among all olim in 1970, 39 percent of the males and 47 percent of the females were in the professional category and two-thirds of the males and five-sixths of the females were in white-collar occupations. Hence what distinguishes American olim from the Israeli Jewish population and other olim is not the direction of occupational concentration, but its extreme form.

American olim therefore represent an occupational and educational elite in Israel. Whether they continue in these jobs in Israel and whether there is differential integration within Israeli society by occupational background are open questions that data to be gathered in the next several years will help answer. Nevertheless, what is clear from the current stage of analysis is that aliya from America is highly selective of professionals and underselective of managers. This reflects, in part, the greater ease in transferring professional skills from one labor market to another. On the other hand, managerial positions are much more localized and difficult to transfer between cultures. This is particularly true for those types of managerial positions that are dependent on personal contact and/or represent proprietorship—positions that are prevalent among a significant segment of the American Jewish population.

A final point relates to the types of professionals emigrating from the United States to Israel. These, we noted earlier, are very much concentrated in two categories—teachers and engineers. Although it would require more intensive analysis with more detailed data than now available, it seems reasonable to postulate

[40]Israel Central Bureau of Statistics, *Survey on Absorption of Immigrants*, Table D, p. xiv.

that some Jewish teachers have responded to the personal, social, and professional problems of urban-racial conflict in the school system by deciding on aliya. Similarly, it is not unlikely that the over-concentration of engineers among American olim reflects the tight, over-supplied market for engineers in the United States. Hence, "push" factors may be playing an important role in the selective movement of American teachers and engineers to Israel. If this speculation is correct, it follows that the occupational composition of future American aliya will reflect variations in occupational opportunities for Jews within the United States. Perhaps, changes in the economic situation of the United States and in particular changing demands for certain skills will affect the level of Jewish immigration to Israel. At the same time, we should not lose sight of the fact that most Jewish teachers and engineers have not responded, and most likely will not respond in the future, to occupational difficulties by deciding on aliya. Rather the analysis of the occupational selectivity of American olim suggests that for some small segment of the American Jewish community, job factors are part of the total complex of issues that result in differential decisions for aliya.

THE RELIGIOUS-IDEOLOGICAL DIMENSIONS OF AMERICAN ALIYA

The fact that a significant proportion of American olim may have come to Israel searching for youthful adventure, quiet retirement, a job, or a mate does not necessarily reduce the significance of the "ideological" component of aliya. For every oleh who is a frustrated teacher, an unemployed engineer, an unmarried woman, or a retired widower, hundreds—more likely thousands—of American Jews in similar positions have sought alternative solutions to these situations *within* the American community. Nor should we lose sight of the fact that many American olim have voluntarily given up excellent jobs, homes, and incomes to settle as a family in Israel. Hence, the ideological components of aliya must be analyzed for all olim so that the motivational structure may be isolated and identified. On the other hand, whatever role ideological factors play in aliya, they cannot be understood independently, or to the exclusion, of other migration pushes and pulls. Nor is it justifiable analytically to conceptualize ideology as a singular, uniform dimension or treat it in a narrowly defined context. The intricate ways in which ideological factors blend with other determinants of American aliya have not been identified fully; nor have the multifarious meanings of ideology been satisfactorily unraveled. Despite the preliminary stage of our analysis, one conclusion seems fully justified by the evidence: Ideology, at least those components that are more conspicuous and measurable, plays an important, if not critical, role in shaping the amount and type of American aliya. This ideology seems much less "Zionist" in the narrow, formal sense and much more "religious" in its broadest, sociological meaning.

It seems clear from the above that one central dimension in the sociological analysis of American aliya revolves around the religio-ethnic-ideological complex. To what extent, for example, do American olim conform to the prevalent pattern of religious identification, affiliation, ritual observances that have emerged in the American Jewish community? Does aliya constitute a qualitative drain of American Jewish (religious and secular) leadership? Are formal membership and active participation in Zionist organizations prerequisites for aliya? How is Jewish education related to aliya? The analysis of these and related issues is indispensable in any attempt to understand American aliya, to gauge its most likely future course, and to appraise the impact of aliya on the American Jewish community.

A full and complete picture of religio-ideological selectivity in American aliya cannot be drawn, simply because the requisite information on Jews in the United States is not available. Although general information and insightful journalistic evidence might be of some help, as are several community studies, there is no way to overcome the basic limitation that we do not know in simple quantitative terms the most elementary facts about the distribution of religio-ideological variables among American Jews.

The data on the religio-ideological characteristics of American olim are preliminary results of the absorption survey described earlier (derived from unpublished materials in the files of the Central Bureau of Statistics) and are limited by the small number of cases (about 150) for detailed analysis. Yet, consistent patterns emerge from the data that are at variance with what is generally held to characterize American Jewry and, hence, allow for tentative conclusions to be reached with respect to the religio-ideological selectivity of contemporary American aliya.

We shall focus on five interrelated components of the religio-ideological syndrome: 1) membership and activity in Zionist organizations; 2) Jewish education; 3) religious identification; 4) synagogue attendance; 5) ritual observances. For each component, data on American olim will be presented by generation status.

ZIONIST ORGANIZATIONAL MEMBERSHIP

We do not have a measure of the extent to which specific Zionist ideological factors played a role in the recent aliya from the United States. Aliya itself is clearly the fulfillment of a central tenet of Zionist ideology, whether or not the oleh feels that way. Nevertheless, it should be noted that formal membership in Zionist organizations or active participation therein is not a necessary prerequisite for aliya. On the other hand, the lack of membership or activity in Zionist organizations does not necessarily imply the lack of Zionist ideology as a powerful motivating force in aliya.

The data from the survey of American olim show that about half of the American olim were not members of any Zionist organization before aliya and only about one out of every five American olim defined themselves as very active members (Table 12). Of equal importance, particularly for gauging the future, are generational patterns. Among American olim who were not born in America about 60 percent were members of American Zionist organizations; among American olim born in the United States of American-born parents 60 percent were not members of American Zionist organizations. Whether this generational pattern reflects the disenchantment of young American Jews with Zionist organizational affiliation, or simply reflects life-cycle factors, or general (rather than specifically Zionist) organizational non-affiliation among the young are open questions. What is clear is the noncorrelation between Zionist organizational affiliation and American aliya.[41]

[41]For similar conclusions, see Engel, "North American Jewish Settlers in Israel," pp. 163–164. See also Fred Sherrow and Paul Ritterband, "An Analysis of Migration to Israel," *Jewish Social Studies*, 32 (July 1970), pp. 214–223.

TABLE 12

Zionist organizational affiliation by generation status, American olim, 1969–70

Zionist organizational affiliation	*GENERATION STATUS* First	*Second*	*Third*	*Total**
Very active member	19.6	27.0	18.9	20.9
Active member	26.1	21.6	9.4	18.4
Not very active member	15.2	5.4	11.3	11.4
Non-member	39.1	45.9	60.4	49.4
TOTAL	100.0	100.0	100.0	100.0

*Total includes small number of cases where generational status is unknown.

Zionist organizational membership is neither a necessary precondition to aliya (i.e., half of those on aliya have not been members) nor is it a sufficient precondition to aliya (i.e., not all members of Zionist organizations go on aliya). The absence of comparative data on membership rates in Zionist organizations among American Jews prevents us from analyzing the extent to which American olim are more likely to be Zionist organization members than American non-olim. It is reasonable to assume that American olim are more likely to be affiliated with Zionist organizations but that such affiliation is a consequence rather than a causal factor in the chain of aliya determinants.

JEWISH EDUCATION

American olim are characterized by a fairly intensive background of Jewish education (Table 13). Fully 85 percent had some Jewish education and of those 63 percent attended for six or more years. Fully one-third of all American olim attended a Hebrew day school

TABLE 13
Jewish education by generation status, American olim, 1969–70

	GENERATION STATUS			
	First	*Second*	*Third*	*Total**
Jewish education: Type				
Sunday school only	0	3	21	10
Afternoon Hebrew school	33	38	25	32
Hebrew day school	33	38	31	33
Other	16	8	8	10
No Jewish education	19	14	15	15
Total percent	100	100	100	100
Jewish education: Years				
Proportion with 6 or more years	62.9	65.6	63.6	63.2

*Total includes small number of cases of unknown generation status.

or yeshiva and of these 70 percent attended ten or more years. Although there is no way of comparing these data with evidence for the American Jewish population, there is no doubt that American olim have a more intensive Jewish education background than a cross-section of the American Jewish community.[42]

Reflecting changes in the American Jewish community, a larger proportion of American born olim of American-born parents received only a Sunday school Jewish education than American olim who were not born in the United States. However, what appears most conspicuous in the distribution of Jewish education by the generation status of American olim are two facts: 1) the proportion attending Hebrew day schools varies little between generations—about one-third of the American olim of each generation attended Hebrew day school; 2) very little generation change may be noted in the proportion with at least six years of exposure to some form of Jewish education.

[42] *Cf.* Engel, "North American Jewish Settlers in Israel," p. 165.

These data suggest that exposure to intensive Jewish education is an important factor determining American aliya—either because intensive Jewish education is an indicator of heightened Jewish-Zionist consciousness and/or because Jewish education imparts the religio-Zionist ideology of aliya.

RELIGIOUS IDENTIFICATION

Data in Table 14 show that over one-third of the American olim defined themselves as Orthodox and the remainder were about equally divided among Conservative, Reform, and other. Fully 46 percent of American olim defined themselves either as religious or very religious and about one-fourth defined themselves as not at all religious or secular. Not unexpectedly, a larger proportion defined their parental home as religious or very religious than so defined themselves. Over 60 percent of the American olim came from homes that were in their view religious or very religious and only 14 percent came from homes that were not at all religious.

These overall patterns of religious identification among American olim reveal a clear tendency toward the more Orthodox religious segment; a tendency not at all expected on the basis of the religious patterns in the American Jewish community. Data by generation status point in the same direction that would be expected from generational differentials in the United States, i.e., trends toward less religious identity among the third generation. However, what appears exceptional in the patterns of religious identification among American olim are not the trends but the concentration—over one-fourth of the American olim born in the United States of American-born parents define themselves as Orthodox and fully 43 percent of third-generation Americans on aliya define themselves as religious or very religious. Similarly no shift in the concentration of the Orthodox or of the "religious-very-religious" may be noted between the foreign born and the American born of foreign-born parents among American olim—a shift that would be unquestionably expected on the basis of evidence available on American Jews.

In sum, what emerge from these data on the religious

TABLE 14

Selected measures of religious identification by generation status, American olim 1969–70

	GENERATION STATUS			
	First	*Second*	*Third*	*Total**
Institutional identification				
Orthodox	42	41	28	37
Conservative	24	19	18	20
Reform	14	27	28	22
Other	20	14	26	21
TOTAL	100	100	100	100
Self-identification				
Very religious	23	8	9	13
Religious	26	43	34	33
Not very religious	28	24	37	30
Not at all religious	23	24	20	24
TOTAL	100	100	100	100
Religious identification of parental home				
Very religious	39	24	10	23
Religious	33	38	45	40
Not very religious	17	19	29	23
Not at all religious	11	19	16	14
TOTAL	100	100	100	100

*Total includes small number of cases where Generation Status is not known.

identification of American olim are patterns of over-concentration and selectivity among religious and Orthodox Jews relative to the American Jewish population.

SYNAGOGUE ATTENDANCE AND RITUAL OBSERVANCES

Synagogue attendance among American olim before aliya seems well out of proportion to that generally estimated for the American Jewish population but quite consistent with the data on Jewish education and religious self-identification (Table 15). Almost 40 percent of the American olim attended synagogue at least once a week and less than a third never attended or attended only for the High Holidays (three times a year). Even among the third

TABLE 15
Synagogue attendance and selected rituals by generation status, American olim, 1969–70

	GENERATION STATUS			
	First	*Second*	*Third*	*Total*[a]
Synagogue attendance				
Once a week or more	44	46	32	38
Often[b]	15	22	25	21
Occasionally[c]	22	3	6	10
High holidays only	9	14	17	14
Never	11	16	21	17
TOTAL	100	100	100	100
Proportion fasting on Yom Kippur	77	81	69	75
Proportion observing dietary regulations	64	60	39	53

[a]Total includes small number of cases where generation status is not known.
[b]Often = "often and on holidays."
[c]Occasionally = "only on holidays and high holidays."

generation over 55 percent attended synagogue services at least several times a month. Among the American born of American-born parents there is a tendency toward less regular attendance at synagogue services and a trend toward non-attendance. These are not unexpected patterns given our impressions and studies of American Jewish communities. Again what is different among American olim is the unusually high level of regular attendance at synagogue services for each generation status category and not the trends between generation-status categories.

The data on two crude measures of ritual observances—fasting on Yom Kippur and observing dietary regulations—present a similar unexpected pattern (Table 15). Fully three-fourths of American olim fasted on Yom Kippur (before aliya) and over half observed dietary regulations. These levels appear quite high relative to impressionistic and scattered evidence on the American Jewish community. Again, the patterns generationally follow the expected trend, i.e., less observance among the American born of American-born parents. However, of more importance is the fact that 70 percent of third-generation Jews in America who are olim fasted on Yom Kippur and 40 percent observe religious dietary regulations.

THE FUTURE OF AMERICAN ALIYA

What can be pieced together from the analysis of data on the changing volume of American aliya and the social characteristics of contemporary American olim that may shed light on possible future patterns? We can do no more than project patterns of the past and present into the future. Assuming all other things are equal (they never are), some guesses about the future character and volume of aliya from the United States seem more reasonable than others.

To take a look first at the question of future mass aliya from the United States, several facts are clear. Since the middle of the nineteenth century, a small steady trickle of Americans has immigrated to Israel. Although the rate of aliya and the absolute number of olim from America have increased, particularly since the early 1960's, the level of aliya relative to the population size of the

American Jewish community is still minuscule. The events surrounding the Six Day War clearly accelerated the tempo of American aliya. Yet it seems that the forces operating to encourage aliya from the United States were rooted in pre-1967 conditions. Whereas some American aliya must have been precipitated by the "crises of 1967," it seems reasonable to argue that two more lasting factors were at work: 1) the radical political, economic, and psychological changes that followed in the wake of the Six Day War in Israeli society and 2) the changing relationship of Jews, particularly among the young third generation, to America and the American Jewish community that had in fact begun before 1967. These two sets of factors, in combination, were powerful elements in reinforcing the interdependence between American Jews and Israel and in channeling some of this new interdependence into aliya. Moreover, as in other migratory streams, aliya tends to feed on itself—through chain migration and through the recognition, acceptance, and institutionalization of aliya among American Jews.

The question of the future volume of aliya, therefore, revolves around 1) the continuance of social changes within Israeli society; 2) the degree to which aliya from the United States has reached its climax, having already drawn those American Jews who have not found American society conducive to their Jewish identity; and 3) the continuance of selected disenchantment among Jewish youth of America and American Jewish society. In the fall of 1972, there were early signs, statistical and impressionistic, that American aliya was declining. Whether this will be confirmed by future evidence and whether this can be attributed to changes in the political-social-psychological-economic situation in Israel and in the United States, or is a function of the shift in aliya encouragements and priorities to Russian Jewry, or is a consequence of disenchantment and dissillusionment among American olim and *yordim* (returnees), or is some combination of these factors, are open questions. One conclusion, nevertheless, appears certain: Barring unforeseen and unpredictable circumstances, no mass aliya of Jewish Americans (mass in the sense of a significant proportion of American Jews) can be expected to occur in the near future. In large part, this is because alongside the nearly universal American Jewish concern for Israel lies the almost unanimous Jewish commitment to America and the genuine indifference (although no longer major hostility) to aliya. Hence large-scale aliya from the United States remains in the realm of fantasy.

A social profile of contemporary American olim includes several different components, reflecting some historical continuity but mostly revealing the heterogeneity of aliya determinants and differential probabilities of integration and absorption. Clearly, aliya from the United States does not represent a cross-section of the American Jewish population. American olim are on average more likely than Jews in the United States to be young, American born of American-born parents, female, and unmarried. Olim also tend to be selective by education and occupation and are much more likely to identify themselves religiously in a variety of ways.

Given a basic ideological thrust behind all aliya, several overlapping types of olim may be identified: 1) young men and women searching for adventure, education, religious and ethnic identity, or marriage; 2) older men and women settling in Israel after retirement; 3) educated and technically trained Jews who are in greater demand in Israel than in America; 4) Jews in search of Jewishness and Judaism who see Israeli society as a rich, natural environment for the expression of their own Jewish identity and that of their children.

While these types of American olim undoubtedly appeared in the past, one critical change lies in the broad area of religious identity. In the past, aliya was viewed by a select handful as a religious duty in the narrowest sense; contemporary aliya appears to be more a reflection of Jewish consciousness in the broadest sense. Aliya, for some, represents a response to the particular dilemmas of Jewish identity in an American pluralistic context.

The preliminary evidence available suggests quite clearly that it is unacceptable analytically to treat American olim as a homogeneous group with respect to background social characteristics, reasons for aliya, or requirements for social integration and absorption. A more intensive examination of the degrees of integration and the levels of return migration among American olim must await the collection of additional empirical materials. We may conclude, however, that aliya from the United States in the post-1967 era does not imply the severance of ties to America. American aliya must be viewed as an extension of the unique American Jewish dilemma. It has also become the master symbol of the intricate web of interdependence between the American Jewish community and Israeli society.

SUGGESTIONS FOR FURTHER READING

The following information will be helpful in utilizing this bibliography:

1. A current annotated bibliography on the subject matter of this volume is not available. We are in no position to remedy this defect; because of limitations of space the bibliography which follows is selective rather than exhaustive. However, while this bibliography is selective the items in it are of differing value and are drawn from a variety of sources; in areas where the level of scholarship is not high, for example, items have been included which would otherwise have remained unlisted.

2. As a corollary to the above, we have included some items by individuals active in American Jewish life as leaders or organizational executives, rather than primarily as scholars. We believe the student can often profit as much from analyzing such documents as from studying the results of scholarly investigations.

3. Books and articles reproduced or excerpted in this volume are not listed in the bibliography. In some cases the user will want to consult the original source, which may contain more information on the topic than we utilize, or may contain material on topics other than the one we focus upon.

4. A number of items in the bibliography—particularly those cited in the sections entitled "Background Reading" and "General Treatments"—are readers or collections of articles. Such volumes generally deal with a wide variety of topics. In some cases, in addition to citing the book itself, we cite individual items from it as well; but we have attempted to restrict this practice as much as possible. The user is therefore advised to check individual tables of contents for articles on the particular topic of his interest.

5. In most cases we cite only a single edition of a book, generally the latest hardcover edition. The availability of a paperback edition can be readily ascertained by referring to *Paperbound Books in Print* published by the R. R. Bowker Company.

6. Even a selective bibliography needs to be supplemented by newly published items. Two good sources exist for this purpose, both issued at regular intervals by the Blaustein Library of the American Jewish Committee, 165 East 56 Street, New York, N.Y. 10022: "Articles of Interest in Current Periodicals" and "Recent Additions to the Library." The Committee's bulletins are particularly exhaustive in the field of intergroup relations, but they also include most of the topics dealt with in our bibliography.

ENCYCLOPEDIAS, YEARBOOKS, AND BIBLIOGRAPHIES

American Jewish Year Book, prepared by the staff of the American Jewish Committee and published annually by The American Jewish Committee and The Jewish Publication Society of America. An index to Volumes 1–50 of the *American Jewish Year Book* was prepared by Elfrida C. Solis-Cohen and published by Ktav Publishing House, Inc., (New York: 1967). (Hereafter the *American Jewish Year Book* is abbreviated *AJYB*.)

Elazar, Daniel J., "The Pursuit of Community: Selections from the Literature of Jewish Public Affairs, 1965–1966," *AJYB* 1967 (Vol. 68), pp. 178–229.

———, "The Rediscovered Polity: Selections from the Literature of Jewish Public Affairs, 1967–1968," *AJYB* 1969 (Vol. 70), pp. 172–237.

———, "Selections from the Literature of Jewish Public Affairs, 1969–1971," *AJYB* 1972 (Vol. 73), pp. 301–383.

Encyclopedia Judaica (Jerusalem: Keter Publishing House Ltd., 1972), 16 vols.

Gartner, Lloyd, "The Contemporary Jewish Community" in *The Study of Judaism: Bibliographical Essays* (New York: Ktav Publishing House, Inc., for The Anti-Defamation League of B'nai B'rith, 1972), pp. 185–206.

Linzer, Norman, ed., *Jewish Communal Services in the United States: 1960–1970, A Selected Bibliography* (New York: Federation of Jewish Philanthropies, 1972).

Universal Jewish Encyclopedia (New York: Universal Jewish Encyclopedia, Inc., 1939), 10 vols.

BACKGROUND READING

Medieval and Modern Jewish History and Culture

Baron, Salo W., "The Modern Age" in Leo W. Schwarz, ed., *Great Ages and Ideas of the Jewish People* (New York: Random House, 1956), pp. 315–484.

Dawidowicz, Lucy, *The Golden Tradition* (New York: Holt, Rinehart, and Winston, 1967).

Elbogen, Ismar, *A Century of Jewish Life* (Philadelphia: The Jewish Publication Society of America, 1944).

Katz, Jacob, *Out of the Ghetto: The Social Background of Jewish Emancipation, 1770–1870* (Cambridge, Mass.: Harvard University Press, 1973).

———, *Tradition and Crisis: Jewish Society at the End of the Middle Ages* (New York: The Free Press, 1961).

Sachar, Howard M., *The Course of Modern Jewish History* (Cleveland: World Publishing Co., 1958).

Wischnitzer, Mark, *To Dwell in Safety: The Story of Jewish Migration Since 1800* (Philadelphia: The Jewish Publication Society of America, 1949).

Zborowski, Mark and Herzog, Elizabeth, *Life Is With People* (New York: International Universities Press, 1952).

American Jewish History

Baron, Salo W. and Blau, Joseph L., eds., *The Jews of the United States, 1790–1840: A Documentary History* (New York and Philadelphia: Columbia University Press and The Jewish Publication Society of America, 1963).

Critical Studies in American Jewish History: Selected Articles from American Jewish Archives, 3 vols. (Cincinnati and New York: American Jewish Archives and Ktav Publishing House, Inc., 1971).

Glanz, Rudolf, *Studies in Judaica Americana* (New York: Ktav Publishing House, Inc., 1970).

Karp, Abraham J., ed., *The Jewish Experience in America: Selected Studies from Publications of The American Jewish Historical Society,* 5 vols. (Waltham and New York: American Jewish Historical Society and Ktav Publishing House, Inc., 1969).

Learsi, Rufus, *The Jews in America: A History,* with epilogue by Abraham J. Karp (New York: Ktav Publishing House, Inc., 1972).

Teller, Judd L., *Strangers and Natives* (New York: Delacorte Press, 1968).

GENERAL TREATMENTS

Glazer, Nathan and Moynihan, Daniel P., *Beyond the Melting Pot: The Negroes, Puerto Ricans, Jews, Italians, and Irish of New York City* (second edition, Cambridge, Mass.: MIT Press, 1970).

Goldstein, Sidney and Goldscheider, Calvin, *Jewish Americans: Three Generations in a Jewish Community* (Englewood Cliffs, N.J.: Prentice-Hall, Inc., 1968).

Janowsky, Oscar I., ed., *The American Jew: A Reappraisal* (Philadelphia: The Jewish Publication Society of America, 1964).

Kramer, Judith R. and Leventman, Seymour, *Children of the Gilded Ghetto: Conflict Resolutions of Three Generations of American Jews* (New Haven: Yale University Press, 1961).

Liebman, Charles S., *The Ambivalent American Jew* (Philadelphia: The Jewish Publication Society of America, 1973).

Manners, Ande, *Poor Cousins* (New York: Coward, McCann and Geoghegan, 1972).

Neusner, Jacob, *American Judaism: Adventure in Modernity* (Englewood Cliffs, N.J.: Prentice-Hall, Inc., 1972).

Patai, Raphael, *Tents of Jacob: The Diaspora—Yesterday and Today* (Englewood Cliffs, N.J.: Prentice-Hall, Inc., 1971).

Rose, Peter I., ed., *The Ghetto and Beyond* (New York: Random House, 1969).

Rosenberg, Stuart E., *America Is Different* (New York: Thomas Nelson and Sons, 1964).

Sherman, Charles Bezalel, *The Jew Within American Society* (Detroit: Wayne State University Press, 1961).

Sidorsky, David, ed., *The Future of the Jewish Community in America* (New York: Basic Books, 1973).

Sklare, Marshall, *America's Jews* (New York: Random House, 1971).

———, ed., *The Jews: Social Patterns of an American Group* (New York: The Free Press, 1958).

——— and Greenblum, Joseph, *Jewish Identity on the Suburban Frontier: A Study of Group Survival in the Open Society* (New York: Basic Books, 1967).

Van den Haag, Ernest, *The Jewish Mystique* (New York: Stein and Day, 1969).

AMERICAN JEWRY: SOCIAL HISTORY

Angel, Marc D., "The Sephardim of the United States: An Exploratory Study," *AJYB 1973* (Vol. 74), pp. 77–138.

Baron, Salo W., "The Emancipation Movement and American Jewry" in Jeannette M. Baron, ed., *Steeled by Adversity: Essays and Addresses on American Jewish Life by Salo W. Baron* (Philadelphia: The Jewish Publication Society of America, 1971), pp. 80–105.

Birmingham, Stephen, *The Grandees: America's Sephardic Elite* (New York: Harper & Row, 1971).

———, *Our Crowd: The Great Jewish Families of New York* (New York: Harper & Row, 1967).

Brandes, Joseph, *Immigrants to Freedom: Jewish Communities in Rural New Jersey Since 1882* (Philadelphia: University of Pennsylvania Press, 1971).

Brotz, Howard, *The Black Jews of Harlem* (New York: The Free Press of Glencoe, 1964).

Halpern, Ben, *The American Jew: A Zionist Analysis* (New York: Herzl Press, 1956).

Handlin, Oscar and Handlin, Mary, "The Acquisition of Political and Social Rights by Jews in the United States," *AJYB 1955* (Vol. 56), pp. 43–98.

———, "A Century of Jewish Immigration to the United States," *AJYB 1948/1949* (Vol. 50), pp. 1–84.

Rischin, Moses, *The Promised City: New York's Jews, 1870–1914* (Cambridge, Mass.: Harvard University Press, 1962).

Sanua, Victor D., "A Study of the Adjustment of Sephardi Jews in the New York Metropolitan Area," *The Jewish Journal of Sociology,* Vol. 9, No. 1 (June 1967), pp. 25–33.

Supple, Barry E., "A Business Elite: German Jewish Financiers in Nineteenth-Century New York," *Business History Review,* Vol. 31, No. 2 (Summer 1957), pp. 143–178.

Weinryb, Bernard D., "Jewish Immigration and Accommodation to America" in Marshall Sklare, ed., *The Jews: Social Patterns of an American Group* (New York: The Free Press, 1958), pp. 4–22.

SOCIAL CHARACTERISTICS OF AMERICAN JEWS

Baltzell, E. Digby, "The Development of a Jewish Upper Class in Philadelphia: 1782–1940" in Marshall Sklare, ed., *The Jews: Social Patterns of an American Group* (New York: The Free Press, 1958), pp. 271–287.

Datta, Lois-Ellin, "Family Religious Background and Early Scientific Creativity," *American Sociological Review,* Vol. 32, No. 4 (August 1967), pp. 626–635.

Davis, James A., *Great Aspirations: The Graduate School Plans of America's College Seniors* (Chicago: Aldine, 1964).

Glazer, Nathan, "Social Characteristics of American Jews, 1654–1954," *AJYB 1955* (Vol. 56), pp. 3–41.

Glenn, Norval D., and Hyland, Ruth, "Religious Preference and Worldly Success: Some Evidence from National Surveys," *American Sociological Review,* Vol. 32, No. 1 (February 1967), pp. 73–85.

Goldberg, Albert I., "Jews in the Legal Profession: A Case of Adjustment to Discrimination," *Jewish Social Studies,* Vol. 32, No. 2 (April 1970), pp. 148–161.

Goldberg, Nathan, *Occupational Patterns of American Jewry* (New York: Jewish Teachers Seminary and People's University Press, 1947).

Goldstein, Ronald M., "American Jewish Population Studies Since WW II," *American Jewish Archives,* Vol. 22, No. 1 (April 1970), pp. 15–48.

Goldstein, Sidney, "Socioeconomic Differentials Among Religious Groups in the United States," *American Journal of Sociology,* Vol. 74, No. 6 (May 1969), pp. 612–631.

Horowitz, C. Morris and Kaplan, Lawrence J., *The Jewish Population of the New York Area 1900–1975* (New York: Federation of Jewish Philanthropies of New York, 1959).

Hurvitz, Nathan, "Sources of Motivation and Achievement of American Jews," *Jewish Social Studies,* Vol. 23, No. 4 (October 1961), pp. 217–234.

Lieberson, Stanley, "Ethnic Groups and the Practice of Medicine," *American Sociological Review,* Vol. 23, No. 5 (October 1958), pp. 542–549.

Massarik, Fred and Chenkin, Alvin, "United States National Jewish Population Study," *AJYB 1973* (Vol. 74), pp. 264–306.

Rhodes, A. Lewis and Nam, Charles B., "The Religious Context of Educational Expectations," *American Sociological Review,* Vol. 35, No. 2 (April 1970), pp. 253–267.

Rosenthal, Erich, "Five Million American Jews," *Commentary,* Vol. 26, No. 6 (December 1958), pp. 499–507.

Stodolsky, Susan S., and Lesser, Gerald, "Learning Patterns in the Disadvantaged," *Harvard Educational Review,* Vol. 37, No. 4 (Fall 1967), pp. 546–593.

Strodbeck, Fred I., "Family Interaction, Values and Achievement" in Marshall Sklare, ed., *The Jews: Social Patterns of an American Group* (New York: The Free Press, 1958).

Weyl, Nathaniel, *The Creative Elite in America* (Washington, D.C.: Public Affairs Press, 1966).

THE JEWISH FAMILY

Balswick, Jack, "Are American Jewish Families Closely Knit?," *Jewish Social Studies,* Vol. 28, No. 3 (July 1966), pp. 159–167.

Freid, Jacob, ed., *Jews and Divorce* (New York: Ktav Publishing House, Inc., 1968).

Goldscheider, Calvin, "Fertility of the Jews," *Demography,* Vol. 4, No. 1 (1967), pp. 196–209.

———, "Ideological Factors in Jewish Fertility Differentials," *The Jewish Journal of Sociology,* Vol. 7, No. 1 (June 1965), pp. 92–105.

———, "Socio-Economic Status and Jewish Fertility," *The Jewish Journal of Sociology,* Vol. 7, No. 2 (December 1965), pp. 221–237.

———, "Trends in Jewish Fertility," *Sociology and Social Research,* Vol. 50, No. 2 (January 1966), pp. 173–186.

Kaplan, Benjamin, *The Jew and His Family* (Baton Rouge: Louisiana State University Press, 1967).

Leichter, Hope J. and Mitchell, William E., *Kinship and Casework* (New York: Russell Sage Foundation, 1967). A summary of one section of this book can be found in Robert F. Winch and Louis W. Goodman, eds., *Selected Studies in Marriage and the Family* (third edition, New York: Holt, Rinehart and Winston, 1968), pp. 139–148.

Rosenthal, Erich, "Jewish Fertility in the United States," *AJYB 1961* (Vol. 62), pp. 3–27.

Rosenthal, Gilbert S., ed., *The Jewish Family in a Changing World* (New York: Thomas Yoseloff, 1970).

Schlesinger, Benjamin, *The Jewish Family: A Survey and Annotated Bibliography* (Toronto: University of Toronto Press, 1971).

Westoff, Charles F., et al., *Family Growth in Metropolitan America* (Princeton: Princeton University Press, 1961).

Winch, Robert; Greer, Scott; and Blumberg, Rae Lesser, "Ethnicity and Extended Familism in an Upper-Middle-Class Suburb," *American Sociological Review*, Vol. 32, No. 2 (April 1967), pp. 265–272.

Wolfenstein, Martha, "Two Types of Jewish Mothers" in Marshall Sklare, ed., *The Jews: Social Patterns of an American Group* (New York: The Free Press, 1958), pp. 520–534.

JEWISH RELIGION AND THE AMERICAN JEW

Borowitz, Eugene B., *A New Jewish Theology in the Making* (Philadelphia: Westminster Press, 1968).

Dawidowicz, Lucy S., "Middle-Class Judaism: A Case Study," *Commentary*, Vol. 29, No. 6 (June 1960), pp. 492–503.

Eichhorn, David Max, ed., *Conversion to Judaism* (New York: Ktav Publishing House, Inc., 1966).

Glazer, Nathan, *American Judaism* (Chicago: University of Chicago Press, 1972).

Gordon, Albert I., *The Nature of Conversion* (Boston: Beacon Press, 1967).

Herberg, Will, *Protestant, Catholic, Jew* (Garden City, N.Y.: Doubleday, 1955).

Kaplan, Mordecai M., *Judaism As a Civilization* (New York: The Macmillan Company, 1934). (Also enlarged edition [New York: Reconstructionist Press, 1957].)

Lasker, Arnold A., "Motivations for Attending High Holy Day Services," *Journal for the Scientific Study of Religion*, Vol. 10, No. 3 (Fall 1971), pp. 241–248.

Lenski, Gerhard, *The Religious Factor* (Garden City, N.Y.: Doubleday, 1961).

Liebman, Charles, "Religion, Class, and Culture in American Jewish History," *The Jewish Journal of Sociology*, Vol. 9, No. 2 (December 1967), pp. 227–241.

Rosen, Bernard C., *Adolescence and Religion: The Jewish Teenager in American Society* (Cambridge, Mass.: Schenkman, 1965).

Schachter, Melech, "The Problems of Conversion Today," *Jewish Life*, Vol. 32, No. 4 (May–June 1965), pp. 7–18.

Schmidt, Nancy J., "An Orthodox Jewish Community in the United States: A Minority within a Minority," *The Jewish Journal of Sociology*, Vol. 7, No. 2 (December 1965), pp. 176–206.

Siegel, Richard; Strassfeld, Michael; and Strassfeld, Sharon, eds., *The Jewish Catalog* (Philadelphia: The Jewish Publication Society of America, 1973).

Sleeper, James A. and Mintz, Alan L., eds., *The New Jews* (New York: Vintage Books, 1971).

Warner, W. Lloyd and Srole, Leo, "Assimilation or Survival: A Crisis in the Jewish Community of Yankee City" in Marshall Sklare, ed., *The Jews: Social Patterns of an American Group* (New York: The Free Press, 1958), pp. 347–356.

Waskow, Arthur I., *The Bush is Burning: Radical Judaism Faces the Pharaohs of the Modern Superstate* (New York: The Macmillan Company, 1971).

JEWISH IDENTITY: SELF-SEGREGATION, ACCULTURATION, ASSIMILATION

Self-Segregation, Acculturation, Assimilation

Alter, Robert, *After the Tradition: Essays on Modern Jewish Writing* (New York: E. P. Dutton, 1969).

Anderson, Charles H., "The Intellectual Subsociety Hypothesis: An Empirical Test" in Charles H. Anderson and John D. Murray, eds., *The Professors: Work and Life Styles Among Academicians* (Cambridge, Mass.: Schenkman, 1971), pp. 227–245.

Anisfeld, Moshe; Munoz, Stanley; and Lambert, Wallace, "The Structure and Dynamics of the Ethnic Attitudes of Jewish Adolescents," *Journal of Abnormal and Social Psychology*, Vol. 66, No. 1 (1963), pp. 31–36.

Antonovsky, Aaron, "Like Everyone Else, Only More So: Identity, Anxiety and the Jew" in Maurice R. Stein, Arthur J. Vidich, and David M. White, eds., *Identity and Anxiety* (Glencoe: The Free Press, 1960), pp. 415–434.

Barron, Milton L., "Ethnic Anomie" in Milton L. Barron, ed., *Minorities in a Changing World* (New York: Alfred A. Knopf, 1967), pp. 15–44.

Bell, Daniel, "Reflections on a Jewish Identity," *Commentary*, Vol. 31, No. 6 (June 1961), pp. 471–478.

Bernards, Solomon S., ed., *Who is a Jew?* (New York: Anti-Defamation League of B'nai B'rith, 1966).

Bernheimer, Charles S., ed., *The Russian Jew in the United States* (Philadelphia: The John C. Winston Co., 1905). (Reprinted by Jerome S. Ozer, Publisher Inc., New York, 1971.)

Canter, Irving, *Christmas in the Life of a Jewish Teenager* (Washington, D.C.: B'nai B'rith Youth Organization, 1961).

Eichhorn, David M., "Conversions to Judaism by Reform and Conservative Rabbis," *Jewish Social Studies,* Vol. 16, No. 4 (October 1954), pp. 299–318.

Fishman, Joshua A., "Childhood Indoctrination for Minority-Group Membership," *Daedalus* (Spring 1961), pp. 329–349.

Friedman, Norman, "Jewish or Professional Identity? The Priorization Process in Academic Situations," *Sociological Analysis,* Vol. 32, No. 3 (Fall 1971), pp. 149–157.

———, "The Problem of the 'Runaway Jewish Intellectuals': Social Definition and Sociological Perspective," *Jewish Social Studies,* Vol. 31, No. 1 (January 1969), pp. 3–19.

Galanter, Marc, "A Dissent on Brother Daniel," *Commentary,* Vol. 36, No. 1 (July 1963), pp. 10–17.

Gans, Herbert J., "American Jewry: Present and Future," *Commentary,* Vol. 21, No. 5 (May 1956), pp. 422–430; Vol. 21, No. 6 (June 1956), pp. 555–563.

Gerson, Walter M., "Jews at Christmas Time: Role-Strain and Strain-Reducing Mechanisms" in Walter M. Gerson, ed., *Social Problems in a Changing World: A Comparative Reader* (New York: Crowell, 1969), pp. 65–76.

Glick, Ira O., "The Hebrew Christians: A Marginal Religious Group" in Marshall Sklare, ed., *The Jews: Social Patterns of an American Group* (New York: The Free Press, 1958), pp. 415–431.

Gordon, Albert I., *Jews in Suburbia* (Boston: Beacon Press, 1959).

Gordon, Milton M., *Assimilation in American Life* (New York: Oxford University Press, 1964).

———, "Marginality and the Jewish Intellectual" in Peter I. Rose, ed., *The Ghetto and Beyond* (New York: Random House, 1969), pp. 477–491.

Greenberg, Irving, "Adventure in Freedom—or Escape from Freeedom?," *American Jewish Historical Quarterly,* Vol. 55, No. 1 (September 1965), pp. 5–21.

Guttman, Allen, *The Jewish Writer in America: Assimilation and the Crisis of Identity* (New York: Oxford University Press, 1971).

Himmelfarb, Milton, *The Jews of Modernity* (New York: Basic Books, 1973).

Kallen, Horace M., *Cultural Pluralism and the American Idea: An Essay in Social Philosophy* (Philadelphia: University of Pennsylvania Press, 1956).

Kazin, Alfred, "The Jew as Modern Writer," in Norman Podhoretz, ed., *The Commentary Reader* (New York: Atheneum, 1966), pp. xv–xxv.

Lazerwitz, Bernard, "Contrasting the Effects of Generation, Class, Sex, and Age on Group Identification in the Jewish and Protestant Communities," *Social Forces,* Vol. 49, No. 1 (September 1970), pp. 50–59.

———, "Some Factors in Jewish Identification," *Jewish Social Studies,* Vol. 15, No. 1 (January 1953), pp. 3–24.

———, and Rowitz, Louis, "The Three-Generations Hypothesis," *American Journal of Sociology,* Vol. 69, No. 5 (March 1964), pp. 529–538.

Lewin, Kurt, "Self Hatred Among the Jews" in Gertrud W. Lewin, ed., *Resolving Social Conflicts* (New York: Harper and Brothers, 1948).

Lichtenstein, Aharon, "Brother Daniel and the Jewish Fraternity," *Judaism,* Vol. 12, No. 3 (Summer 1963), pp. 260–280.

Lowi, Theodore, "Southern Jews: The Two Communities," *The Jewish Journal of Sociology,* Vol. 6, No. 1 (July 1964), pp. 103–117.

Matz, Milton, "The Meaning of the Christmas Tree to the American Jew," *The Jewish Journal of Sociology,* Vol. 3, No. 1 (June 1961), pp. 129–137.

Mazur, Allan, "The Socialization of Jews into the Academic Subculture" in Charles H. Anderson and John D. Murray, eds., *The Professors: Work and Life Styles Among Academicians* (Cambridge, Mass.: Schenkman, 1971), pp. 265–287.

Nahirny, Vladimir C. and Fishman, Joshua A., "American Immigrant Groups: Ethnic Identification and the Problem of Generations," *The Sociological Review,* Vol. 13, No. 3 (November 1965) pp. 311–326.

Porter, Jack Nusan and Dreier, Peter, eds., *Jewish Radicalism* (New York: Grove Press, Inc., 1973).

Sanua, Victor D., "Patterns of Identification with the Jewish Community in the U.S.A.," *The Jewish Journal of Sociology,* Vol. 6, No. 2 (December 1964), pp. 190–212.

Segalman, Ralph, "Jewish Identity Scales: A Report," *Jewish Social Studies,* Vol. 29, No. 2 (April 1967), pp. 92–111.

Sklare, Marshall, "Assimilation and the Sociologists," *Commentary,* Vol. 39, No. 5 (May 1965), pp. 63–67.

———, "The Conversion of the Jews," *Commentary,* Vol. 56, No. 3 (September 1973), pp. 44–53.

———, "The Values of East European Jewry and of American Society," *Jewish Frontier,* Vol. 28, No. 7 (July 1961), pp. 7–11.

Snyder, Charles R., *Alcohol and the Jews* (Glencoe: The Free Press, 1958).

Steiner, George, "A Kind of Survivor," *Commentary*, Vol. 39, No. 2 (February 1965), pp. 32–38. (Reprinted in: *Idem, Language and Silence: Essays on Language, Literature and The Inhuman* [New York: Atheneum, 1967].)

Weinreich, Beatrice S., "The Americanization of Passover" in Raphael Patai, ed., *Studies in Biblical and Jewish Folklore* (Bloomington: Indiana University Press, 1960), pp. 329–366.

Wilensky, Harold and Ladinsky, Jack, "From Religious Community to Occupational Group: Structural Assimilation Among Professors, Lawyers, and Engineers," *American Sociological Review*, Vol. 32, No. 4 (August 1967), pp. 541–561.

Yinger, J. Milton, "Social Forces Involved in Group Identification or Withdrawal," *Daedalus* (Spring 1961), pp. 247–262.

Intermarriage and Conversion

Appel, John J., "Christian Science and the Jews," *Jewish Social Studies*, Vol. 31, No. 2 (April 1969), pp. 100–121.

Berman, Louis, *Jews and Intermarriage: A Study in Personality and Culture* (New York: Thomas Yoseloff, 1968).

Cahnman, Werner J., ed., *Intermarriage and Jewish Life* (New York: Herzl Press, 1963).

Caplovitz, David and Levy, Harry, *Interreligious Dating Among College Students* (Processed, New York: Bureau of Applied Social Research of Columbia University, 1965).

Davis, Moshe, "Mixed Marriage in Western Jewry: Historical Background to the Jewish Response," *The Jewish Journal of Sociology*, Vol. 10, No. 2 (December 1968), pp. 177–220.

Drachsler, Julius, *Democracy and Assimilation* (New York: The Macmillan Company, 1920).

Federation of Jewish Philanthropies of New York, Commission on Synagogue Relations, *Intermarriage and the Future of the American Jew* (New York: Federation of Jewish Philanthropies, 1965).

Federation of Jewish Philanthropies of New York, Commission on Synagogue Relations, *The Psychological Implications of Intermarriage: Proceedings of a Conference* (New York: Federation of Jewish Philanthropies, 1966).

Feldman, Ephraim, "Intermarriage, Historically Considered," *Yearbook of the Central Conference of American Rabbis*, Vol. 19 (1909), pp. 271–307.

Gordon, Albert I., *Intermarriage: Interfaith, Interracial, Interethnic* (Boston: Beacon Press, 1964).

Heiss, Jerold S., "Interfaith Marriage and Marital Outcome," *Marriage and Family Living*, Vol. 23, No. 3 (August 1961), pp. 228–233.

Lazerwitz, Bernard, "Intermarriage and Conversion: A Guide for Future Research," *The Jewish Journal of Sociology*, Vol. 13, No. 1 (June 1971), pp. 41–63.

Levinson, Maria H., and Levinson, Daniel J., "Jews Who Intermarry: Socio-Psychological Bases of Ethnic Identity and Change," *YIVO Annual of Jewish Social Science*, Vol. 12 (1958–59), pp. 106–128.

Mayer, John E., *Jewish-Gentile Courtships* (New York: The Free Press, 1961).

Rosenthal, Erich, "Jewish Intermarriage in Indiana," *AJYB 1967* (Vol. 68), pp. 243–264.

———, "Studies of Jewish Intermarriage in the United States," *AJYB 1963* (Vol. 64), pp. 3–53.

Rubenstein, Richard L., "Intermarriage and Conversion," *The Reconstructionist*, Vol. 28, No. 5 (20 April 1962), pp. 11–21.

Schoenfield, Eugene, "Intermarriage and the Small Town: The Jewish Case," *Journal of Marriage and the Family*, Vol. 31, No. 1 (February 1969), pp. 61–64.

Sklare, Marshall, "Intermarriage and the Jewish Future," *Commentary*, Vol. 37, No. 4 (April 1964), pp. 46–52.

———, "Intermarriage and Jewish Survival," *Commentary*, Vol. 49, No. 3 (March 1970), pp. 51–58.

Stern, Malcolm H., "Jewish Marriage and Intermarriage in the Federal Period (1776–1840)," *American Jewish Archives*, Vol. 19, No. 2 (November 1967) pp. 142–143.

THE AMERICAN JEW AND ISRAEL

Alter, Robert, "Israel and the Intellectuals," *Commentary*, Vol. 44, No. 4 (October 1967), pp. 46–52.

Antonovsky, Aaron and Katz, David, "Factors in the Adjustment to Israeli Life of American and Canadian Immigrants," *The Jewish Journal of Sociology*, Vol. 12, No. 1 (June 1970), pp. 77–87.

Baron, Salo W., and Baron, Jeannette M., "Palestinian Messengers in America, 1849–79: A Record of Four Journeys" in Jeannette M. Baron, ed., *Steeled by Adversity: Essays and Addresses on American Jewish Life* by Salo W. Baron (Philadelphia: The Jewish Publication Society of America, 1971), pp. 158–266.

Bronsen, David, "A Talk with Henry Roth," *Partisan Review*, Vol. 36, No. 2 (Winter 1969), pp. 265–280.

Engel, Gerald, "Comparison Between Americans Living in Israel and Those Who Returned to America," *Journal of Psychology*, Vol. 74 (January 1970), pp. 195–204; Vol. 75 (July 1970), pp. 243–251.

———, "North American Settlers in Israel," *AJYB* 1970 (Vol. 71), pp. 161–187.

Halkin, Hillel, "Americans in Israel," *Commentary*, Vol. 53, No. 5 (May 1972), pp. 54–63.

Halpern, Ben, "Zion in the Mind of American Jews" in David Sidorsky, ed., *The Future of the Jewish Community in America* (New York: Basic Books, 1973), pp. 22–45.

Herman, Simon N., *American Students in Israel* (Ithaca: Cornell University Press, 1971).

Hertzberg, Arthur, "Israel and American Jewry," *Commentary*, Vol. 44, No. 2 (August 1967), pp. 69–73.

Himmelfarb, Milton, "In the Light of Israel's Victory," *Commentary*, Vol. 44, No. 4 (October 1967), pp. 53–61.

Isaacs, Harold R., *American Jews in Israel* (New York: John Day Co., 1967).

Lapide, Pinchas E., *A Century of U.S. Aliyah* (Jerusalem: The Association of Americans and Canadians in Israel, 1961).

Levy, David L., "Why Some American Jews Are Moving to Israel," *The Jewish Digest*, Vol. 17, No. 8 (May 1972), pp. 31–42.

"Papers and Proceedings of the Joint Conference on the Impact of Israel on the American Jewish Community," *Jewish Social Studies*, Vol. 21, No. 1 (January 1959), pp. 1–88.

Peretz, Martin, "The American Left and Israel," *Commentary*, Vol. 44, No. 5 (November 1967), pp. 27–34.

Sherrow, Fred S., and Ritterband, Paul, "An Analysis of Migration to Israel," *Jewish Social Studies*, Vol. 32, No. 3 (July 1970), pp. 214–223.

Sklare, Marshall, "Lakeville and Israel: The Six-Day War and its Aftermath," *Midstream*, Vol. 14, No. 8 (October 1968), pp. 3–21.

SOURCES

Lloyd P. Gartner, "Immigration and the Formation of American Jewry, 1840–1925," in *Jewish Society through the Ages,* edited by H. H. Ben-Sasson and S. Ettinger (New York: Schocken Books, 1971), pp. 297–312.

C. Bezalel Sherman, "Immigration and Emigration: The Jewish Case," from *The Jew Within American Society* by C. Bezalel Sherman (Detroit: Wayne State University Press, 1960), pp. 59–61.

Lucy S. Dawidowicz, "From Past to Past: Jewish East Europe to Jewish East Side," *Conservative Judaism,* Winter 1968, pp. 19–27.

Ben Halpern, "America is Different," from *The American Jew* by Ben Halpern (New York: Theodor Herzl Foundation, 1956), pp. 12–33.

Sidney Goldstein, "American Jewry, 1970: A Demographic Profile," in *American Jewish Year Book 1971,* Vol. 72 (New York and Philadelphia: The American Jewish Committee and the Jewish Publication Society of America, 1971), pp. 3–88.

Zena Smith Blau, "The Strategy of the Jewish Mother," a revised version of "In Defense of the Jewish Mother" by Zena Smith Blau, *Midstream,* February 1967, pp. 42–49.

William E. Mitchell, "Descent Groups Among New York City Jews," *Jewish Journal of Sociology,* Vol. III, No. 1, June 1961, pp. 121–128.

Sidney Goldstein and Calvin Goldscheider, "Jewish Religiosity: Ideological and Ritualistic Dimensions," from *Jewish Americans: Three Generations in a Jewish Community* by Sidney Goldstein and Calvin Goldscheider (Englewood Cliffs, New Jersey: Prentice-Hall, Inc., 1968), Chapter 9.

Charles S. Liebman, "The Religion of American Jews," from *The Ambivalent American Jew* by Charles S. Liebman (Philadelphia: The Jewish Publication Society of America, 1973), pp. 46–87.

Seymour Martin Lipset and Everett Carll Ladd, Jr., "Jewish Academics in the United States," in *American Jewish Year Book 1971,* Vol. 72 (New York and Philadelphia: The American Jewish Committee and the Jewish Publication Society of America, 1971) pp. 89–128.

Henry Cohen, "Jewish Life and Thought in an Academic Community," *American Jewish Archives,* November 1962, pp. 107–128.

Arnold Schwartz, "Intermarriage in the United States," in *American Jewish Year Book 1970,* Vol. 71 (New York and Philadelphia: The American Jewish Committee and the Jewish Publication Society of America, 1970), pp. 101–121.

INDEX